GREEK SERIES FOR COLLEGES AND SCHOOLS

EDITED

UNDER THE SUPERVISION OF

HERBERT WEIR SMYTH, Ph.D.

ELIOT PROFESSOR OF GREEK LITERATURE IN HARVARD UNIVERSITY

THE ACROPOLIS OF ATHENS.

(The "Theseum" in the foreground.)

BEGINNER'S GREEK BOOK

ALLEN ROGERS BENNER

PROFESSOR OF GREEK IN PHILLIPS ACADEMY, ANDOVER

AND

HERBERT WEIR SMYTH, Ph.D.

ELIOT PROFESSOR OF GREEK LITERATURE IN HARVARD UNIVERSITY

———∘⦂∘———

NEW YORK · CINCINNATI · CHICAGO
AMERICAN BOOK COMPANY

PREFATORY SUGGESTIONS

THIS book contains all the grammar that is needed by beginners in the first year of Greek. It is not at all designed, however, to restrict or to replace the use of a larger Greek Grammar in connection with the study of the *Anabasis* and of Homer. Experience has shown that the systematic (but not merely mechanical) study of grammar is indispensable throughout the preparatory course if the student is to deal successfully with the authors commonly read at a more advanced stage of his education. With the view, therefore, that the larger grammar will be used by the student after his first year, the makers of this book have felt free to limit its contents to the strict essentials of the language. The result has been to eliminate some matters that are usually found in books intended for beginners.

It has been found possible, and in fact advisable, to omit altogether the paradigms of certain infrequent words. Such are nouns and adjectives of the " Attic second declension," rare contract nouns like ὀστοῦν, and, in particular, the adjectives χαρίεις and μέλας. While adjectives in -εις, -εσσα, -εν are usual in Homer, χαρίεις alone is relatively common in standard Attic prose, but even there the form χαρίεσσα (and *not* χαρίεττα) shows that the word was poetic in character. Of χαρίεις there is but one occurrence in the *Anabasis* (iii. 5. 12). A similar case is presented by μέλας, which occurs twice in the same work (iv. 5 13, iv. 5. 15). The only other adjective which is declined like

5

μέλας, namely the poetic τάλας, does not occur in the *Anabasis* at all. It is obviously inadvisable to impede the beginner's progress by requiring him to memorize paradigms of these and similar words.

In the case of some words which are generally required of beginners, opinions may justly differ. Such words, if omitted from the Lessons of this book, are printed in the Summary of Forms (after the Lessons), out of deference to the opinion of teachers who may wish to use them. The list includes ναῦς, omitted from the Lessons with some hesitation; also κέρας, Ἡρακλῆς, Ζεύς, the verb κάθημαι, and one word not found in the *Anabasis*, νεανίας (for which Ξενίας is substituted in the paradigms of Lesson XII).

The retention of the dual number in the paradigms may be thought inconsistent with the design of a simple book, particularly as first-rate books, like Kaegi's *Kurzgefasste griechische Schulgrammatik*, regularly omit the dual from the paradigms proper. In this book the dual has been retained out of respect to a widespread opinion among American teachers, that since the dual is needed for the study of Homer, it is most economically memorized at the outset. Those teachers, however, who prefer to omit the forms of the dual may readily do so, inasmuch as no instances of its use have been introduced into the exercises.

Regarding the development of the forms of the verb, special attention is called to the fact that the most frequent tenses as well as the tenses adapted to initial study are the present (and imperfect), future, and aorist. Only after these have been in some degree mastered are the perfect tenses introduced in the Lessons.[1] And the per-

---

[1] Regard to the symmetrical development of the subject has caused the introduction of the comparatively uncommon future passive before the perfect is taken up.

fect itself is much simplified by the omission of some forms which are commonly given in the Grammars (*e.g.* λελύκω, λελύκοιμι), but which rarely occur in the reading of most students. Attention is also called to the early introduction of infinitives and participles and of compound verbs. In the first fifty Lessons the prefix of a compound verb is regularly separated from the verb proper by a hyphen.

In matters of syntax the rule of the Editors has been to give early preference to the most common idioms as far as is possible in a book where precedence must obviously be given to the development of forms. In determining questions of the relative frequency of syntactical usages, the exhaustive work of Joost (*Sprachgebrauch Xenophons in der Anabasis*) has been of great assistance, and the placing of several usages has been settled by it. The Editors wish also to make mention of Bennett and Bristol's manual on *The Teaching of Latin and Greek in the Secondary School*, which they have found suggestive as to the presentation of both forms and syntax.

Certain constructions that are shown by Joost to be comparatively rare in the *Anabasis* are omitted from the Lessons. φθάνω with the participle will serve as an example, a construction regularly set before beginners and invariably difficult to them. Yet this construction occurs but four times in the seven books of the *Anabasis*, and in the first four books only twice (i. 3. 14, iii. 4. 49). Further, these instances are regularly explained, where they occur, in the notes of our best American editions.

A glance at the Table of Contents will show the early prominence given to certain important constructions.

It is suggested that the teacher should not assign the whole Introduction at the outset, but only such parts of it as are immediately necessary, particularly the alphabet and the subjects of pronunciation and accent. The arrangement in Lessons or Chapters is solely for convenience, to mark divisions of the subject where exercises may properly be introduced. One class may do a whole Chapter, another class may do no more than half a Chapter, for a day's lesson. The ability of the class will therefore determine the length of the lessons, which should be assigned by the numbered sections.

The vocabularies contain only such words as are used by Xenophon, with preference given to the commoner words of the *Anabasis*.

The exercises for translation from English into Greek have been made short designedly. For it is desirable that the teacher should have the class turn the English rendering of the Greek sentences themselves back into Greek without the aid of the book, — an unexcelled method of teaching this part of the subject. Teachers who so desire may omit some sentences if time fails for all. Lessons L to LX have been specially arranged so that the second division of each exercise may be omitted altogether, or may be taken up in connection with review work.

On the completion of the sixty Lessons, the student should be able to translate, without much difficulty, simple Attic prose. Many students will be found competent to begin at once the first Book of Xenophon's *Anabasis*. But if, in the judgment of the teacher, the class is not ripe for this work, a simplified text of the *Anabasis* will make the transition from the Beginner's Book easier.

For the use of such teachers and classes there have been provided the simplified Selections from the *Anabasis* which follow the Greek Lessons in this book. It is hoped that they are so remote from the introductory chapters of

the *Anabasis* as not utterly to spoil the freshness of Xenophon's narrative when the student takes up the original
work. On the other hand, they are passages that will
well stand re-reading when the student meets them again.
All the new words that occur in the Selections will be
found in the Vocabulary.

The directions about Greek pronunciation in §§ 1 and
22 are for practical use. As a matter of fact, they are not
designed to reproduce, in every particular, the pronunciation of Greek current in the fifth and fourth centuries B.C.,
— partly because we do not know how every letter was
then sounded, and partly because some of the known
sounds are too difficult for beginners. Pedantry in pronunciation is an abomination; but every teacher should be
at least familiar with the fact that, while most of the pro-
nunciations recommended in this book are approximately
those of the period from Pericles to Demosthenes, certain
others are distinctly later and concessions to established
usage.

Thus a divergence between the ancient and the modern
practice of pronunciation is illustrated by the sounds ϕ, χ,
and θ. These letters were anciently pronounced respectively as *ph* in 'up*h*eaval,' *kh* in 'bac*kh*and,' and *th* in
'ho*th*ouse'; in Greek, however, both sounds occur in the
same syllable. When two aspirates (ϕ, χ, θ) came together,
probably only one *h* (the second) was heard; thus, δίφθογ-
γος was pronounced δίπθογγος (διπτόγγος). Probably not
until after 300 A.D. were ϕ, χ, and θ pronounced as in
'*Ph*ilip,' German 'a*ch*,' and '*th*eater.' The latter are the
sounds in modern Greek. ζ was probably sounded *zd*.
though there is some evidence that it was sounded as *dz*;
in Hellenistic times it certainly was equivalent to *z* in
'*z*eal,' and is so sounded in modern Greek.

Short *a*, *ι*, *υ* differed in sound from the long *a*, *ι*, *υ* only in being less prolonged. The vowel *ε* was evidently sounded like French *é*, as in *bonté*. *ω* was not diphthongal like English *ō* (i.e. *o* with a vanishing *u* sound), but rather like *o* in the French *encore*. Greek *o* was sounded like *o* in French *mot*.

The teacher is urged to make every effort to preserve the proper quantity, which is often disregarded in American pronunciation of Greek; special care is required to prevent an *accented* vowel from being sounded as long when it is short; *e.g.* φίλος may easily be mispronounced *félos*, instead of *fĭlos*.

These Lessons are the result of considerable experience in teaching Greek to beginners; and each section has been tested in the class room before it was incorporated in this book.

The Editors gratefully acknowledge the criticisms which they have received from Mr. Horace M. Poynter of Phillips Academy and Mr. Louis E. Lord of Oberlin College, who have read the proof sheets of the Lessons.

CONTENTS

INTRODUCTION

THE ALPHABET OF ATTIC GREEK

NAME	FORM Capitals	FORM Small Letters	SOUND AS IN	LATIN EQUIVALENT
1. *alpha*	A	a	(ă) f*a*ther / (ă) h*a*ha'	a
beta	B	β	*b*oy	b
gamma	Γ	γ	*g*irl	g
delta	Δ	δ	*d*ay	d
epsilon	E	ε	m*e*t	ĕ
zeta	Z	ζ	*z*eal, da*z*e	z
eta	H	η	f*ê*te	ē
theta	Θ	θ	*th*eater	th
iota	I	ι	(ī) mach*i*ne / (ĭ) the first *e* in *e*ternal	i
kappa	K	κ	*k*eep	c
lambda	Λ	λ	*l*ed	l
mü	M	μ	*m*an	m
nü	N	ν	*n*ow	n
xi	Ξ	ξ	a*x*	x
omicron	O	ο	*o*mit	ŏ
pi	Π	π	*p*in	p
rho	P	ρ	*r*un	r
sigma	Σ	σ ς	*s*it	s
tau	T	τ	*t*in	t
üpsilon	Υ	υ	Ger. T*ü*r, Fr. t*u*[1]	y
phi	Φ	φ	*Ph*ilip	ph
chi	X	χ	Ger. a*ch*, Scotch lo*ch*	ch
psi	Ψ	ψ	to*ps*y	ps
omega	Ω	ω	v*o*te	ō

---

[1] The short vowel (υ) is less prolonged in sound than the long vowel (ῡ).

2. The form ς is used at the end of a word; in other places σ is used.

The capital letters are used as initials of proper names. In current practice they are not used at the beginning of a sentence unless the sentence begins a paragraph or a quotation.

3. There is no separate letter to represent English *h*. But many Greek words begin with this sound, which is indicated by writing a sign called the **rough breathing** over the initial vowel of a word; as ὁρίζων *horizon*. If an initial vowel is not pronounced with *h*, a **smooth breathing** is written over it; as ἀντίθεσις *antithesis*. These breathings are not written over capital letters, but in front of them; as Ὁρίζων, Ἀντίθεσις.

4. Initial ρ regularly has the rough breathing (ῥ = *rh*); as ῥήτωρ *rhetor*.

5. The letter γ is pronounced *ng* when it comes before κ, γ, χ, or ξ. It is then called **gamma nasal**. Thus ἄγκυρα *anchor*, σφίγξ *sphinx*.

6. **Double consonants**, so called because they unite two sounds in one character, are ζ, which equals *zd* or *dz*; ξ, which equals *ks* (i.e. *x*); and ψ, which equals *ps*.

7. The **vowels** are Α Ε Η Ι Ο Υ Ω; in small letters, α ε η ι ο υ ω. Η (or η) is the long form of Ε (or ε); Ω (or ω) is the long form of Ο (or ο). So this list corresponds to the English: *a e i o u*. The long and short forms of *a*, *ι*, and *υ* are not distinguished by separate characters; but it is usual in grammars to mark these vowels when *long*, thus: ᾱ, ῑ, ῡ. This is the practice in this book.

8. Each Greek word has as many **syllables** as it has separate vowels or diphthongs (§ 22). This rule is the same in Latin also.

9. In dividing a word into syllables a consonant is regularly written after the hyphen; and if there are two or three consonants, they too are written after the hyphen, *provided* they represent a combination which may begin a Greek word. For illustrations see § 11.

a. A group formed of a mute (§ 27) and μ or ν, or μν, belongs after the hyphen; as πρᾶ-γμα *thing*.

10. Greek words may end only in a vowel or in one of these consonants: ν, ρ, ς with ξ and ψ.

EXERCISE IN PRONUNCIATION

11. Pronounce *aloud* the following words, referring to the table under § 1 for the equivalent English sounds. The English transliterations in the second column may be pronounced like Latin words (except in respect to accent) after the Roman method; *ü* is the Latin *y*.

	To be accented thus	Meaning
νέ-κταρ	ne'-ktar	nectar
δε-σπό-της	de-spo'-tēs	despot
πο-τα-μός	po-ta-mos'	river
λο-χᾱ-γός	lo-chā-gos'	captain
χω-ρί-ον	chō-ri'-on	stronghold
φί-λος	phi'-los	friend
θε-ός	the-os'	god
κώ-μη	kō'-mē	village
θά-λατ-τα	tha'-lat-ta	sea
ὁ ἀ-νήρ	ho a-nēr'	the man
ἡ γυ-νή	hē gü-nē'	the woman

	To be accented thus	Meaning
ἠ-μέ-ρᾱ	hē-me'-rā	day
ὑ-ψη-λός	hü-psē-los'	lofty
φά-λαγξ	pha'-langks	phalanx
ὀ-πι-σθο-φύ-λαξ	o-pi-stho-phü'-laks	rear-guard
πε-ζός	pe-zos'	afoot
τύ-πτω	tü'-ptō	I strike
ἄ-στρον	a'-stron	star
Βα-βυ-λών	Ba-bü-lōn'	Babylon

ACCENT

12. Most Greek words are written with accents. **The acute accent** is illustrated by the words in the preceding exercise (§ 11). On inspection it will be seen that this accent stands sometimes on the last syllable of a word, sometimes on the last but one, and again on the last but two.

13. When a word having the acute accent on its final syllable is immediately followed by another word, without any intervening mark of punctuation, the accent of the first word is written thus, `; this is called the **grave accent**. Thus ὑψηλὸν χωρίον *a lofty stronghold*. The grave accent is written on the last syllable only, and only under the conditions just stated.

14. There is a third common mark of accentuation, called the **circumflex** (ˆ). It may stand on the last syllable of a word, or on the last but one. It may not stand on the last but two, as the acute may. And, what is very important, it may stand only on a *long* vowel or a diphthong (§ 22). Hence, if a vowel has the circumflex accent, no other mark to indicate its quantity is needed or used. Thus σῖ-τος *food*.

15. The last syllable of a word is called the **ultima**; the last but one, the **penult**; and the one before the penult, the **antepenult**.

16. The acute accent may stand on the ultima or the penult or the antepenult. The circumflex accent may stand on the ultima or the penult. The grave accent stands on the ultima only.

17. There are three important rules of accent that must be mastered at the outset, in addition to the principles already stated.

1. The acute accent cannot stand on the antepenult when the ultima is long.

2. The circumflex accent cannot stand on the penult when the ultima is long.

3. When the ultima is short, an accented penult has the circumflex if it contains a long vowel or a diphthong (§ 14).

Illustrations of these rules are provided in §§ 11 and 24.

a. What accent a word has and *where* it stands must be learned with the letters that spell the word itself.

18. Accent means to us a *stress* of the voice, *i.e.* force of utterance. This is also what an accent mark means to the native Greeks of to-day. So far as pronunciation goes, we make no distinction between the acute, the grave, and the circumflex accent. When originally invented and introduced, however, the accent marks interpreted to foreigners the *tone* or *pitch* of the voice in pronouncing syllables. The acute indicated a *higher* pitch; the grave, a *lower* pitch; and the circumflex, a higher followed by a lower pitch of the voice on the same syllable. The spoken language was therefore melodious.

19. When marks of both accent and breathing (§ 3) belong to the same vowel, the accent mark, if acute, follows the breathing; if circumflex, is written directly over the breathing. The accent, like the breathing, is written in front of a capital letter, but over a small one. Thus ἔξω *outside;* ἦσαν *they were;* Ἶρις *Iris.* In the case of a diphthong, both the accent and the breathing must be written over the second vowel. Thus οἶνος *wine.*

a. The mark of diaeresis (¨) indicates a separate pronunciation of two successive vowels. Thus ἰχθύϊ *to* or *for a fish.*

20. Not all Greek words have accents. There is one small class of monosyllables, called **proclitics**, that are pronounced with the words that follow them and so lack accents of their own. Thus ὁ and ἡ of § 11.

21. There is another class of words, called **enclitics**, that are pronounced with the words that precede them. These, too, usually have no accents of their own. This subject is taken up in §§ 103, 104, 105, 305.

DIPHTHONGS

22. The diphthongs are:

	ENGLISH VALUE			ENGLISH VALUE
αι	*ai*sle		ηυ	ê (f*ê*te) + oo (m*oo*n), pronounced in close succession
ει	v*ei*l			
οι	*oi*l			
αυ	h*ou*se		ου	m*oo*n
ευ	e (m*e*t) + oo (m*oo*n), pronounced in close succession		υι	French h*ui*t, English *we*

ᾳ	like simple	ᾱ	⎫	This *iota*, which is written beneath the
ῃ	" "	η	⎬	other vowel and not pronounced, is
ῳ	" "	ω	⎭	called *iota subscript.*

With capitals *iota subscript* is written in the same line, but not pronounced. Thus Ἅιδης (*i.e.* ᾅδης) *Hades*.

23. In quantity all diphthongs are long. But final -οι and -αι are reckoned short in influencing the accent of a penult or antepenult, — thus ἄνθρωποι *men*, and οἶνοι *wines*, — except the adverb οἴκοι *at home* and certain verb forms (§ 253).

EXERCISE IN PRONUNCIATION

24. Pronounce aloud the following words, referring to the tables under §§ 1 and 22 for the equivalent English sounds :

βα-σι-λεύς	king	ἡ-μεῖς	we
Ζεύς	Zeus	ἑ-αυ-τοῦ	of himself
στρά-τευ-μα	army	παί-ω	I strike
πλοῖ-ον	boat	δι-καί-ως	justly
πο-ρεί-ᾱ	journey	λε-λυ-κυῖ-α	having loosed
χείρ	hand	πο-τα-μῷ	to *or* for a river
οἶ-νος	wine	κώ-μῃ	to *or* for a village
οὗ-τος	this	ἡ-μέ-ρᾳ	to *or* for a day
αὐ-τός	self, same	λύ-ου-σιν	they loose

GREEK WORDS IN ENGLISH

25. 1. Some scholars prefer to transliterate Greek proper names directly into English. Thus Αἰσχύλος *Aischylos;* Θουκυδίδης *Thoukydides;* Κλέαρχος *Klearchos;* Ἀλκαῖος *Alkaios;* ὁ Βοιώτιος *the Boiotian.*

2. Others prefer to follow the fashion of the Romans of the Augustan age, and to interpret the Greek names through the Latin equivalents. This has been a long prevailing custom. The table of Latin equivalents for the Greek letters has already been given (§ 1). It must

be supplemented, however, by calling attention to the following letters or combinations:

γ nasal (§ 5) = *n*   but final -οι = *ī*   final -ος = *us*
αι = *ae*   ου = *ū*   " -ον = *um*
οι = *oe*   ει = *ī* or *ē*   " -ρος = *er*

a. At the present time ει is often transliterated *ei*, pronounced like *i* in *mine*. Words in -ειον are best transliterated -*ēum;* as Θησεῖον *Thesēum.*

26. ILLUSTRATIONS OF TRANSLITERATION THROUGH LATIN INTO ENGLISH

Κῦρος   = *Cyrus*   Αἰσχύλος   = *Aeschylus*
Κλέαρχος   = *Clearchus*   Θουκυδίδης = *Thucydides*
Αἰνείᾱς   = *Aenēas* (an-   ᾿Αλκαῖος   = *Alcaeus*
                  glicized)   Τεῦκρος   = *Teucer*
Δᾱρεῖος   = *Darīus* (an-   ᾿Αλέξανδρος = *Alexander*
                  glicized)   Σπερχειός   = *Spercheius* (or
᾿Αρταξέρξης = *Artaxerxes*   *Sperchēus*)
Παρύσατις   = *Parysatis*   ῾Ρῆσος   = *Rhesus*
᾿Ικόνιον   = *Iconium*   Δελφοί   = *Delphi*
ὁ Βοιώτιος = *the Boeotian*   Σαγγάριος   = *Sangarius*

LIQUIDS AND MUTES (OR STOPS)

27. The following classification of consonants is important, and should be committed to memory:

LIQUIDS, so called from their smoothly
        "flowing" sounds, are   λ   μ   ν   ρ

Mutes (or stops) are so called because they are formed by a position of the organs of the mouth which stops the passage of the breath, no sound being heard while the closure of these organs continues.

CLASSES OF MUTES	Labial mutes, *i.e.* stops made with the lips (*labium*)	π β ϕ
	Palatal mutes, *i.e.* stops made with the soft palate (*palātum*)	κ γ χ
	Lingual or dental mutes, *i.e.* stops made with the tongue (*lingua*) or teeth (*dēns*)	τ δ θ

28. Another important classification of these mutes is the following:

ORDERS OF MUTES	Smooth mutes (not aspirated)	π	κ	τ
	Middle mutes	β	γ	δ
	Rough mutes (aspirated)	ϕ	χ	θ

It will be observed that this table is only another arrangement of the preceding one, the first column of which (§ 27) represents the "smooth" mutes, the second the "middle," and the third the "rough."

ELISION

29. The loss of a final short vowel is called *elision*; it occurs only before a word beginning with a vowel, and is marked by the apostrophe. Thus ἀλλ' ὁ ἀνήρ *but the man* (for ἀλλά), ἡ δ' ἡμέρᾱ *but the day* (for δέ).

a. Elision is often omitted.

b. When a preposition or conjunction suffers elision of the accented vowel, the accent is also lost.

CRASIS

30. Crasis (κρᾶσις *mingling*) is the contraction of a vowel or diphthong at the end of a word with a vowel or diphthong beginning the following word. Over the syllable resulting from crasis is placed a ', as κἄν for καὶ ἄν *and if;* τἀπιτήδεια for τὰ ἐπιτήδεια *the provisions.*

ASPIRATION

31. A smooth mute (§ 28) is roughened before the rough breathing (§ 3). Thus ἐφ' ἵππου *on horseback* for ἐπ(ὶ) ἵππου; καθήκω *come down* for κατά + ἥκω.

–N MOVABLE

32. The letter ν may be annexed to all words ending in σι, to the third person singular of verbs when this ends in ε, and to ἐστί *is.* In modern practice this -ν (called -ν movable) is used only when the next word begins with a vowel, or at the end of a sentence.

PUNCTUATION MARKS

33. The Greek uses the comma and the period like the English. But the Greek question mark is like the English semicolon (;). For the colon (or semicolon) the Greek uses a point set at the top of the line, thus: Κῦρος ·

The English question mark (?) is not used in Greek.

Marks of quotation (" ") are commonly introduced into modern Greek texts. But editors often prefer not to use this modern device; and instead, they begin the first word of the Greek quotation with a capital letter. This is the practice of the translators of the English Bible.

NUMBER

34. The Greek has three numbers: singular and plural, as in Latin and English; and dual, to indicate *two.* In the oldest Greek (Homer) the dual was common; but it was comparatively little used in the Greek of the fifth and fourth centuries B.C. It will not be used at all in the exercises of this book.

GENDER

35. The Greek has three genders: masculine, feminine, and neuter. Like Latin, Greek makes a formal distinction of gender among objects without life; thus ποταμός *river* is masculine (ὁ), and ἡμέρᾱ *day* is feminine (ἡ).

CASE

36. The Greek has five cases: nominative, genitive, dative, accusative, and vocative. These cases are used like the corresponding cases in Latin. The Greek has no ablative; and the functions of the Latin ablative are performed in Greek partly by the genitive (of separation) and partly by the dative (locative and instrumental).

VOICE

37. The Greek verb has three voices: active, middle, and passive. The active and passive voices are used as in Latin and English. The uses of the middle voice are explained in §§ 315, 316.

MOOD

38. The Greek verb has four moods, — indicative, subjunctive, optative, imperative, — besides the infinitive and participle. The uses of these moods are explained and illustrated as they are introduced in the lessons.

TENSE

39. The Greek verb has the following tenses:

PRIMARY

Present:	*I loose* or *I am loosing*
Perfect:	*I have loosed*
Future:	*I shall loose*
Future Perfect:	*I shall have loosed*

SECONDARY

Imperfect:	*I loosed* or *I was loosing*
Aorist:	*I loosed*
Pluperfect:	*I had loosed*

FIG. 1.—Winged Victory inscribing a trophy of armor.

I

PRESENT INDICATIVE AND INFINITIVE OF Ω–VERBS IN THE ACTIVE VOICE.   RECESSIVE ACCENT

40. The **stem** or **theme** of a Greek verb is the part which carries the permanent meaning; to this stem are joined various suffixes and prefixes to express person, number, tense, mood, and voice.

41. The stem of λύω *I loose* is λῡ- (in some tenses λῠ-). The endings that express different persons, as *I, you, he,* are joined to this stem in some tenses by means of a **thematic vowel**.   In the indicative mood this vowel is **o** before endings that begin with μ or ν, and ε before other letters.   It is distinctly seen in the following paradigm (§ 45) in the dual, and first and second persons plural.   In other forms of the present indicative the thematic vowel has suffered modification or has coalesced with the personal ending.

42.   The theme λῡ̄ + % forms the present tense-stem.

43.   The original personal endings (cp. § 639) in the singular of the present indicative are no longer apparent in the forms of the ω-verb.   But they will be seen later in the inflection of the μι-verb.   In the third person plural λύ-ουσι is for an original λύ-ο-ντι (λύ-ο-νσι).

44.   Verbs are regularly accented as far from the end as the laws of accent permit (§§ 12–17).   Such accent is known as **recessive accent**.

45. PRESENT INDICATIVE ACTIVE OF λύω

	SING.	DUAL	PLUR.
1.	λύ-ω *I loose* [1]		λύ-ο-μεν *we loose*
2.	λύ-εις *you loose*	λύ-ε-τον	λύ-ε-τε *you loose*
3.	λύ-ει *he looses*	λύ-ε-τον	λύ-ουσι(ν) [2] *they loose*

Present infinitive λύ-ειν *to loose*

46. VOCABULARY I

ἄγω : *lead.*
ἁρπάζω : *seize, make booty of, plunder.* Harpy.
ἔχω : *have, hold.*

λείπω : *leave.*
λύω : *loose, break, destroy.*
πείθω : *persuade.*
πέμπω : *send.*

EXERCISES FOR PRONUNCIATION AND TRANSLATION

47. I. πείθει. λείπω. ἁρπάζομεν. ἄγειν. λείπει. ἔχεις. ἄγουσιν. ἔχομεν. πείθουσι. ἔχω. ἁρπάζετε. πείθειν. λείπουσι. ἄγει. πείθομεν. ἁρπάζω. πέμπουσιν. πέμπετε. ἄγεις. λείπειν. πείθω. ἄγετε. ἁρπάζεις. πέμπει. ἔχετε. λείπομεν. πέμπεις.

II. You [3] leave. I send. He has. We send. I lead. To send. You [3] persuade. You [4] persuade. They seize. He seizes. They have. You [4] leave. We lead. To seize. To have.

---

[1] Or *I am loosing, you are loosing*, etc.
[2] Cp. § 32.

[3] Pl.
[4] Sing.

FIG. 2. — Spearhead (of iron) from Dodona.

II

DECLENSION OF O-STEMS. COMMON CONSTRUCTIONS. ARTICLE AS POSSESSIVE PRONOUN

48. Sing. N. ὁ φίλος *the friend*   ὁ ἵππος *the horse*
         G. τοῦ φίλου *of the friend*   ἵππου
         D. τῷ φίλῳ *to* or *for the friend*   ἵππῳ
         A. τὸν φίλον *the friend*   ἵππον
         V. — φίλε *friend*   ἵππε

Dual N. A.[1] τὼ φίλω   ἵππω
         G. D. τοῖν φίλοιν   ἵπποιν

Plur. N. οἱ φίλοι *the friends*   ἵπποι
         G. τῶν φίλων *of the friends*   ἵππων
         D. τοῖς φίλοις *to* or *for the friends*   ἵπποις
         A. τοὺς φίλους *the friends*   ἵππους
         V. — φίλοι *friends*   ἵπποι

49. Sing. N. τὸ πεδίον *the plain*   τὸ ἔργον *the work*
         G. τοῦ πεδίου *of the plain*   ἔργου
         D. τῷ πεδίῳ *to* or *for the plain*   ἔργῳ
         A. τὸ πεδίον *the plain*   ἔργον
         V. — πεδίον *plain*   ἔργον

Dual N. A.[1] τὼ πεδίω   ἔργω
         G. D. τοῖν πεδίοιν   ἔργοιν

Plur. N. τὰ πεδία *the plains*   ἔργα
         G. τῶν πεδίων *of the plains*   ἔργων
         D. τοῖς πεδίοις *to* or *for the plains*   ἔργοις
         A. τὰ πεδία *the plains*   ἔργα
         V. — πεδία *plains*   ἔργα

---

[1] There is no vocative case of the definite article ὁ *the;* but nouns have the nominative, accusative, and vocative dual alike. Thus φίλω is nominative, accusative, and vocative dual.

50. φίλος and ἵππος are masculine in gender, and are accordingly accompanied by the masculine form of the article ὁ *the*; πεδίον and ἔργον are neuter, and therefore the neuter article τό *the* is used with them.

51. All neuter nouns have the nominative, accusative, and vocative cases alike, in the three numbers.

52. For the grave accent seen in τὸν φίλον, etc., see § 13.

COMMON CONSTRUCTIONS

These fundamental rules, most of which the student will have already learned in Latin, are sufficiently illustrated, without special examples, in the exercises of this book.

53. *a.* The subject of a finite verb is in the nominative case.

　　b. The direct object of a transitive verb is in the accusative case.

　　c. The indirect object of a verb is regularly in the dative case (*to* or *for* dative).

　　d. The dative is often used to indicate the person interested (*to* or *for* dative, sometimes denoting advantage or disadvantage).

　　e. But after a verb of motion, *to* is generally expressed by a preposition with the accusative (not by the dative), as πρός *to* with the accusative. See § 55. 6. Cp. Latin *ad*.

　　f. The genitive case denotes *of* relations. It may be "subjective" (*fuga hostium* the flight of the enemy) or "objective" (*amor patriae* love of fatherland) in Greek as in Latin. It often denotes possession.

　　g. The subject of the infinitive is in the accusative case.

h. A finite verb agrees with its subject in person and number.

i. Adjectives and participles agree in gender, number, and case with the nouns that they modify.

j. A noun in apposition to another noun agrees with it in case.

k. A noun or adjective in the predicate, denoting the same person or thing as the subject, agrees with the subject in case. Adjectives agree also in gender and number.

54. ## VOCABULARY II

ἐν, prep. with dat. only : *in ;* as to accent, proclitic (§ 20).

ἔργον, ου, τό : *work.*

ἵππος, ου, ὁ : *horse.*

λόχος, ου, ὁ : *company* of soldiers.

ὅπλον, ου, τό : *implement ;* com-monly pl. ὅπλα, τά : *arms* of war. See p. 28, Fig. 1.

πεδίον, ου, τό : *plain.*

πρός, prep. with acc. : *to, toward, against.*

φίλος, ου, ὁ : *friend.*

ὁ, gen. τοῦ, masc. art. : *the ;* τό, gen. τοῦ, neut. art. : *the.* The forms ὁ (nom. sing.) and οἱ (nom. pl. masc.) are proclitic (§ 20). — The forms of the definite article are often used for **possessive pronouns** of the first, second, or third person, either singular or plural, as suggested by the context, *i.e.* for *my, your* (sing. or pl.), *his, her, our, their.* — In the VOCABULARY ὁ, τό (and the fem. ἡ), placed after a noun, indicate its gender.

EXERCISES FOR TRANSLATION

55. I. 1. τοὺς ἵππους λύουσιν. 2. ἄγει τὸν λόχον. 3. πείθομεν τοὺς[1] φίλους. 4. λείπετε[2] τὸ ἔργον ;

---

[1] *our.*   [2] *are you leaving.*

5. ἁρπάζει τοὺς ἵππους.   6. πέμπω τὰ ὅπλα πρὸς τοὺς φίλους.   7. ἐν τοῖς πεδίοις ἔχουσι τοὺς ἵππους. 8. πρὸς τὸ ἔργον ἄγουσι τοὺς λόχους.   9. πέμπει τοὺς φίλους πρὸς τὸ ἔργον.   10. λύει ἵππους τῶν φίλων.   11. οἱ φίλοι ἄγουσι τοὺς ἵππους πρὸς τὰ πεδία.   12. ἔχεις φίλους;

II. In turning English into Greek, *first* compose each sentence aloud in Greek; *next* write it down, taking care to observe the accent and, where necessary, the breathing of each word.   Always write the accent of a word before passing to the next word.

Vocabulary for oral practice: friends[1]; we have; horses[1]; the horses[1]; he looses; we leave; to[2] the plain[3]; in the plain[4]; to[5] the friends; he leads; we lead; of the friends; he persuades; the company.[1]

1. We have friends.   2. He-is-loosing[6] the horses.   3. We leave our[7] horses in the plain.   4. He leads horses to[5] his[7] friends.   5. We lead horses of our[7] friends.   6. He persuades his friends.   7. He leads his company.

III

DECLENSION OF O–STEMS (*Continued*)

56.	Sing.	N.	ποταμός, ὁ, *river*	ἄνθρωπος, ὁ, *man*
		G.	ποταμοῦ	ἀνθρώπου
		D.	ποταμῷ	ἀνθρώπῳ
		A.	ποταμόν	ἄνθρωπον
		V.	ποταμέ	ἄνθρωπε

---

[1] Acc.
[2] *Or* for.
[3] Two words only.
[4] ἐν with dat.
[5] πρός.
[6] = looses.
[7] = the.

Dual N. A. V.	ποταμώ	ἀνθρώπω
G. D.	ποταμοῖν	ἀνθρώποιν
Plur. N. V.	ποταμοί	ἄνθρωποι
G.	ποταμῶν	ἀνθρώπων
D.	ποταμοῖς	ἀνθρώποις
A.	ποταμούς	ἀνθρώπους

57. The accent of the nominative case must be learned by observation (§ 17. *a*).

58. A long ultima (§ 15) in the genitive or dative case, if accented, receives the circumflex accent. Thus ποταμοῦ.

59. In the declension of a noun the accent is kept, if possible, on the syllable on which it rests in the nominative case; but if in the nominative the acute accent rests on the antepenult, as in ἄνθρωπος, a long ultima in other cases draws the accent forward (§ 17. 1) one syllable. Thus ἀνθρώπου.

For the short ultima of ἄνθρωποι see § 23.

60.

Sing. N.	οἶνος, ὁ, *wine*	πλοῖον, τό, *boat*
G.	οἴνου	πλοίου
D.	οἴνῳ	πλοίῳ
A.	οἶνον	πλοῖον
V.	οἶνε	πλοῖον
Dual N. A. V.	οἴνω	πλοίω
G. D.	οἴνοιν	πλοίοιν
Plur. N. V.	οἶνοι	πλοῖα
G.	οἴνων	πλοίων
D.	οἴνοις	πλοίοις
A.	οἴνους	πλοῖα

61. While the tendency of the accent is to remain the same as in the nominative case, a circumflex accent on the penult of the nominative must be changed to the acute on the penult of those cases that have the ultima long (§ 17. 2). Thus οἶνος, οἴνου.

62.   VOCABULARY III

ἀγαθός (declined like ποταμός),
masc. adj., neut. ἀγαθόν (declined like πλοῖον, except the
accent): *good, brave.*

ἄνθρωπος, ου, ὁ: *man.* Philanthropy (φίλος).

ἄπορος (declined like ἄνθρωπος),
masc. and fem. adj., neut.
ἄπορον: *impassable.*

ἦν, 3 sing. impt.: *he (she or it) was.*

ἦσαν, 3 pl. impf.: *they were.*

καί, conj.: *and, also.* καί . . . καί:
both . . . and.

οἶνος, ου, ὁ: *wine.*

πλοῖον, ου, τό: *boat.*

ποταμός, οῦ, ὁ: *river.* Hippo-
potamus (ἵππος).

στρατηγός, οῦ, ὁ: *general.*

σύν, prep. with dat. only: *with,
with the aid of.*

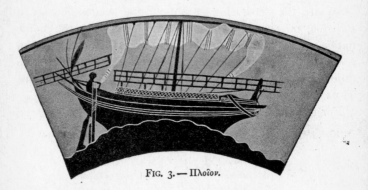

Fig. 3. — Πλοῖον.

EXERCISES FOR TRANSLATION

63. I. 1. ἄγει τὸν ἵππον πρὸς τὸν ποταμόν. 2. ὁ ποταμὸς ἁρπάζει τὰ ὅπλα. 3. ἔχει καὶ πλοῖα καὶ οἶνον.
4. πέμπει οἶνον τῷ φίλῳ.[1] 5. πείθομεν τοὺς ἀνθρώπους. 6. λύει ἵππους τῶν ἀνθρώπων. 7. σὺν τοῖς
φίλοις ἁρπάζει τοὺς ἵππους καὶ τὰ ὅπλα. 8. ὁ φίλος
ἦν ἀγαθός. 9. ὁ ποταμὸς ἦν ἄπορος. 10. λείπετε

---

[1] The dative is sometimes used with πέμπω instead of πρός with the accusative, when there is the further idea of advantage — *for* his friend, § 53. *d.*

τὰ πλοῖα ;   11. ἐν τοῖς πλοίοις ἦσαν οἱ στρατηγοί.
12. ἔχεις οἶνον τοῖς ἀνθρώποις ;

II. 1. The men have boats and horses.   2. He has
wine in his[1] boat.   3. Are you unhitching[2] the horses
for your friends?   4. They have good horses.   5. The men
were brave.   6. The company[3] was brave.   7. They lead
the men to the river.

IV

DECLENSION OF O–STEMS (*Continued and Reviewed*)
NOUNS AND ADJECTIVES DECLINED TOGETHER.
ATTRIBUTIVE POSITION.   PREDICATE POSITION.
ATTRIBUTIVE PHRASES.   AGREEMENT OF VERB
WITH NEUTER PLURAL SUBJECT.   POSITION OF
POSSESSIVE GENITIVE

64.   Sing. N.   ὁ ἀγαθὸς λοχᾱγός *the brave captain*
          G.   τοῦ ἀγαθοῦ λοχᾱγοῦ *of the brave captain*
          D.   τῷ ἀγαθῷ λοχᾱγῷ *to* or *for the brave captain*
          A.   τὸν ἀγαθὸν λοχᾱγόν *the brave captain*
          V.   ὦ ἀγαθὲ λοχᾱγέ *O 'brave captain*

       Plur. N.   οἱ ἀγαθοὶ λοχᾱγοί *the brave captains*
          G.   τῶν ἀγαθῶν λοχᾱγῶν *of the brave captains*
          D.   τοῖς ἀγαθοῖς λοχᾱγοῖς *to* or *for the brave captains*
          A.   τοὺς ἀγαθοὺς λοχᾱγούς *the brave captains*
          V.   ὦ ἀγαθοὶ λοχᾱγοί *O brave captains*

The dual need not be included in these paradigms for
practice.

---

[1] = the.   [2] *i.e.* loosing.   [3] of soldiers.

65.　Sing. N.　ποταμὸς ἄπορος *an impassable river*
　　　　　　G.　.ποταμοῦ ἀπόρου
　　　　　　D.　ποταμῷ ἀπόρῳ
　　　　　　A.　ποταμὸν ἄπορον
　　　　　　V.　ποταμὲ ἄπορε

　　　　Pl. N. V.　ποταμοὶ ἄποροι
　　　　　　G.　ποταμῶν ἀπόρων
　　　　　　D.　ποταμοῖς ἀπόροις
　　　　　　A.　ποταμοὺς ἀπόρους

66.　Sing. N. A. V.　χωρίον ἀφύλακτον *an unguarded stronghold*
　　　　　　　G.　χωρίου ἀφυλάκτου
　　　　　　　D.　χωρίῳ ἀφυλάκτῳ

　　　Plur. N. A. V.　χωρία ἀφύλακτα
　　　　　　　G.　χωρίων ἀφυλάκτων
　　　　　　　D.　χωρίοις ἀφυλάκτοις

Decline also τὸ ἀφύλακτον χωρίον *the unguarded strong-hold*.

67. Attributive position of adjectives. — When an adjective is used with the definite article and a noun, as in the expression *the brave captain*, the adjective commonly stands between the article and the noun in Greek as in English (cp. the paradigm, § 64). But it may follow the noun, in which case the article must be repeated before it : ὁ λοχᾱγὸς ὁ ἀγαθός *the brave captain*.

　a. Least frequently of all, the first article is omitted : λοχᾱγὸς ὁ ἀγαθός *the brave captain*.

68. Predicate position of adjectives. — If the adjective precedes the article, or follows the article and the noun *without* repetition of the article, it stands in a predicate relation to the noun which it modifies ; *i.e.* a verb is expressed or understood between the noun and the adjective.

69.   SUMMARY WITH EXAMPLES

Attributive position $\begin{cases} \text{ὁ ἀγαθὸς λοχᾱγός,} \\ \text{less frequently} \\ \text{ὁ λοχᾱγὸς ὁ ἀγαθός,} \\ \text{least frequently} \\ \text{λοχᾱγὸς ὁ ἀγαθός,} \end{cases}$ *the brave captain*

Predicate position $\begin{cases} \text{ἀγαθὸς ὁ λοχᾱγός } brave\ [is]\ the\ captain \\ \text{ὁ λοχᾱγὸς ἀγαθός } the\ captain\ [is]\ brave \end{cases}$

70. Attributive phrases. — A prepositional phrase or an adverb may be used like an adjective in the attributive position :

οἱ ἐν τῷ χωρίῳ ἄνθρωποι the men in the stronghold.

a. In this phrase the word for *men* may be omitted without affecting the sense :

οἱ ἐν τῷ χωρίῳ the men (*or* those) in the stronghold.

b. Similarly the noun is omitted in other phrases :

οἱ σὺν Κύρῳ the men with Cyrus ;
τὰ Κύρου the affairs of Cyrus.

71. Agreement of verb with neuter plural subject. — A subject in the neuter plural commonly takes a singular verb :

πλοῖα ἦν there were boats.

72. Position of possessive genitive. — The genitive denoting possession commonly stands in the attributive position :

οἱ Κύρου λοχᾱγοί the captains of Cyrus.

73.   VOCABULARY IV

ἀ-φύλακτος (declined like ἄνθρωπος and ἄπορος), masc. and fem. adj., neut. ἀφύλακτον : *unguarded.*

Κῦρος, ου, ὁ : *Cyrus.*

λοχᾱγός, οῦ, ὁ : *captain* (cp. λόχος and ἄγω).

σῖτος, ου, ὁ : *grain, food.* In the pl. the declension irregularly changes to neut. τὰ σῖτα.

χωρίον, ου, τό : *place, stronghold.*

ὤ, interj. : *O*, often preceding the vocative case.

EXERCISES FOR TRANSLATION

74. I. 1. τὸ χωρίον ἦν ἀφύλακτον. 2. οἱ σὺν Κύρῳ[1] ἄγουσι τὸν ἄνθρωπον πρὸς ποταμὸν ἄπορον. 3. τὰ ἐν τῷ χωρίῳ σῖτα ἦν[2] ἀγαθά. 4. πέμπομεν οἶνον ἀγαθὸν πρὸς Κῦρον. 5. οἱ ποταμοὶ ἦσαν ἄποροι. 6. καὶ τὰ πλοῖα ἦν ἀφύλακτα. 7. λείπουσι τὰ πλοῖα ἀφύλακτα.[3] 8. ὦ ἀγαθοὶ στρατηγοί, πέμπετε πλοῖα; 9. ἐν τῷ ἀφυλάκτῳ χωρίῳ ἦσαν ἄνθρωποι ἀγαθοί. 10. καὶ οἱ Κύρου λοχᾱγοὶ ἦσαν ἐν τῷ πεδίῳ. 11. ἁρπάζουσι τὸ ἀφύλακτον χωρίον. 12. ἔχομεν λόχους ἀγαθούς.

II. 1. The river was impassable. 2. The good men are-sending[4] food. 3. The men with Cyrus were brave. 4. And the boats were unguarded. 5. We leave the boats unguarded. 6. We have good wine.

V

IMPERFECT INDICATIVE OF Ω–VERBS IN THE ACTIVE VOICE. AUGMENT. SECOND AORIST INDICATIVE AND INFINITIVE. ARTICLE WITH NAME OF PERSON

75. The inflection of the imperfect tense of verbs whose themes end in a vowel (as λύ-ω) shows distinctly the theme or stem (*e.g.* λῡ̄), the thematic vowel (ο or ε), and the personal endings (-ν, -ς, etc.) throughout (see § 41). But there is no personal ending in the third singular; this applies to all secondary tenses (§ 39).

---

[1] See § 70. *b.* [3] Not *the unguarded boats*, but *the boats unguarded.*
[2] See § 71. [4] = send.

76. The imperfect tense stem of λύω, like the present, is λῡ%.

77. The imperfect, in common with the other secondary tenses of the indicative mood, has a prefix or increase at the beginning of the theme, known as the **augment**.

1. *Syllabic augment.* — If the theme begins with a consonant, the vowel *epsilon* (ἐ) is commonly prefixed to the secondary tenses.

2. *Temporal augment.* — But if the theme begins with a vowel, that vowel is lengthened in the secondary tenses thus:

a	becomes	η		αι	becomes	ῃ
ε	"	η		ᾳ	"	ῃ
ο	"	ω		αυ	"	ηυ
ι	"	ῑ		οι	"	ῳ
υ	"	ῡ				

78. ευ becomes ηυ or remains ευ; ει becomes ῃ or remains ει.
A verb beginning with a long vowel or with ου is not augmented.

79. A verb beginning with ῥ doubles this letter after the augment. Thus ῥίπτω *hurl,* impf. ἔρρῑπτον.

80. The imperfect indicative of ἔχω is εἶχον *I had,* with apparently irregular augment.

81.   IMPERFECT INDICATIVE ACTIVE OF λύω

Sing. 1. ἔ-λῡ-ο-ν *I was loosing* or *I loosed*
     2. ἔ-λῡ-ε-ς *you were loosing* or *you loosed*
     3. ἔ-λῡ-ε(ν)[1] *he was loosing* or *he loosed*

Dual 2. ἐ-λῡ́-ε-τον
     3. ἐ-λῡ-έ-την

Plur. 1. ἐ-λῡ́-ο-μεν *we were loosing* or *we loosed*
     2. ἐ-λῡ́-ε-τε *you were loosing* or *you loosed*
     3. ἔ-λῡ-ο-ν *they were loosing* or *they loosed*

---

[1] Cp. § 32.

82.   IMPERFECT INDICATIVE ACTIVE OF ἄγω

Sing. 1.   ἦγ-ο-ν *I was leading* or *I led*
      2.   ἦγ-ε-ς *you were leading* or *you led*
      3.   ἦγ-ε(ν)[1] *he was leading* or *he led*

Dual 2.   ἤγ-ε-τον
      3.   ἠγ-έ-την

Plur. 1.   ἤγ-ο-μεν *we were leading* or *we led*
      2.   ἤγ-ε-τε *you were leading* or *you led*
      3.   ἦγ-ο-ν *they were leading* or *they led*

SECOND AORIST INDICATIVE OF Ω-VERBS IN THE ACTIVE VOICE[2]

83. It has already been shown (§ 76) that the imper-fect is formed on the same stem as the present tense. There is another tense, belonging to *some* verbs, which is inflected exactly like the imperfect, and differs in the form of the *theme* only. This is called the **second aorist**. It usually exhibits the theme of the verb in its simplest form. Thus λείπω *leave*, imperfect ἔ-λειπ-ον, has a second aorist ἔ-λιπ-ον, inflected in § 85. λύω has no second aorist.

84. Meaning of the aorist indicative and infinitive. — The aorist indicative expresses a simple act (*i.e.* not continued or repeated) in past time.

a. The aorist infinitive, like the aorist indicative, denotes a simple act (*i.e.* not continued or repeated); but unlike the

---

[1] Cp. § 32.

[2] The second aorist is so called in distinction from the first aorist, which is to be learned in Lesson XIV. The second aorist is introduced here on account of its similarity in inflection to the imperfect, as well as on account of its frequent use.

aorist indicative, the aorist infinitive does not necessarily refer to past time.[1] It differs from the present infinitive in the *kind* of action only (cp. § 85).

85. SECOND AORIST INDICATIVE ACTIVE OF λείπω

SING.	DUAL	PLUR.
1. ἔ-λιπ-ο-ν *I left*		ἐ-λίπ-ο-μεν *we left*
2. ἔ-λιπ-ε-ς *you left*	ἐ-λίπ-ε-τον	ἐ-λίπ-ε-τε *you left*
3. ἔ-λιπ-ε(ν) *he left*	ἐ-λιπ-έ-την	ἔ-λιπ-ο-ν *they left*

Second aorist infinitive λιπ-εῖν *to leave*, the simple act; while the present infinitive λείπειν may mean *to be leaving* or *to keep leaving* as well as *to leave*.

a. The accent of the second aorist infinitive is not recessive (§ 44), but placed irregularly on the ultima.

b. The infinitive is not augmented (cp. § 77).

86. The verb ἄγω, which shows the theme in its simplest form in the present, has a peculiar reduplicated second aorist, with augment (§ 87).

87. SECOND AORIST INDICATIVE ACTIVE OF ἄγω

SING.	DUAL	PLUR.
1. ἤγ-αγ-ο-ν *I led*		ἠγ-άγ-ο-μεν
2. ἤγ-αγ-ε-ς	ἠγ-άγ-ε-τον	ἠγ-άγ-ε-τε
3. ἤγ-αγ-ε(ν)	ἠγ-αγ-έ-την	ἤγ-αγ-ο-ν

Second aorist infinitive ἀγ-αγ-εῖν *to lead*, the simple act

88. The second aorist indicative of ἔχω is ἔσχον *I got*, infinitive σχεῖν.

89. The name of a **person** may take the article if the person is well known or has been previously mentioned. It is usually not to be translated:

ὁ Κῦρος Cyrus.

---

[1] Except in the construction of indirect discourse, to be studied later (§ 110).

90. VOCABULARY V

ἀλλά, conj.: *but*; sometimes in an address, *well!* Final α may be elided before a vowel, thus ἀλλ'.

δέ, postpositive[1] conj.: *and, but*, weaker than ἀλλά. Final ε may be elided before a vowel, thus δ'.

εἰς, proclitic prep. with acc. only: *into, to.* Cp. πρός *to.*

ἐκ, proclitic prep. with gen. only: *out of, from*; before a vowel, ἐξ.

Κλέαρχος, ου, ὁ: *Clearchus.*

λαμβάνω (theme λαβ-, lengthened in pres. and impf.), impf. ἐλάμβανον, 2 aor. ἔλαβον, *take, receive, enlist.*

παλτόν, οῦ, τό: *javelin.*

φεύγω, impf. ἔφευγον, 2 aor. ἔφυγον: *flee, flee from, avoid, shun.* Cp. Lat. *fugiō.*

EXERCISES FOR TRANSLATION

91. I. ἥρπαζες, ἥρπαζον, ἐλείπετε, ἐλίπετε, ἐπέμπομεν, ἔπειθε, εἶχε,[2] ἔσχεν,[3] ἠγάγετε, ἦγεν, ἔλυον, ἐπείθομεν, ἔπεμπες, ἐλαμβάνομεν, φυγεῖν, ἔφευγε, ἐλάβετε.

II. He was leading. He led. We were plundering. You[4] left. He had. He was fleeing. He fled. You took.[5] They persuaded. They were sending. We loosed. To flee.[6]

92. I. 1. ἐπέμπομεν τοὺς ἀγαθοὺς ἀνθρώπους εἰς τὸ πεδίον. 2. ἐλείπομεν τοὺς ἀνθρώπους ἐν τῷ πεδίῳ. 3. ἤγομεν τοὺς σὺν Κύρῳ πρὸς τὸ πεδίον. 4. ἀλλ', ὦ Κῦρε, πέμπεις τὰ σῖτα; 5. ὁ Κῦρος ἔπειθε τοὺς φίλους. 6. ὁ δὲ Κῦρος ἤγαγε τοὺς ἵππους εἰς τὸ πεδίον. 7. Κλέαρχος ἔλιπε τὸν ἵππον καὶ ἔλαβε τὰ

---

[1] A postpositive word cannot begin a sentence, but must follow one or more words.

[2] § 80.   [4] Pl.   [5] Aor. or impf.

[3] § 88.   [6] Use both pres. and 2 aor.

παλτά. 8. οἱ σὺν Κλεάρχῳ ἔφυγον ἐκ τοῦ χωρίου.
9. οἱ δὲ λοχᾱγοὶ ἦσαν ἀγαθοί.

II. 1. But the captain was brave. 2. We took the
grain from the stronghold. 3. He fled into the plain.
4. Cyrus used-to-send[1] wine to his friends.[2] 5. They
kept-taking[1] the strongholds.

VI

DECLENSION OF Ā–STEMS. INFINITIVE USED AS OBJECT
OF VERBS MEANING *WISH*, *COMMAND*, ETC.

NOMINATIVES IN -η

93.

Sing. N.	ἡ μάχη *the battle*	ἡ ἀρχή *the beginning*[3]	
G.	τῆς μάχης *of the battle*	ἀρχῆς	
D.	τῇ μάχῃ *to* or *for the battle*	ἀρχῇ	
A.	τὴν μάχην *the battle*	ἀρχήν	
V.	— μάχη *battle*	ἀρχή	
Dual N. A. V.	—[4] μάχᾱ	ἀρχά	
G. D.	— μάχαιν	ἀρχαῖν	
Plur. N.	αἱ μάχαι *the battles*	ἀρχαί	
G.	τῶν μαχῶν *of the battles*	ἀρχῶν	
D.	ταῖς μάχαις *to* or *for the* *battles*	ἀρχαῖς	
A.	τὰς μάχᾱς *the battles*	ἀρχάς	
V.	— μάχαι *battles*	ἀρχαί	

94. See the rules for accent in §§ 57, 58.

---

[1] = impf.   [2] § 63. I. 4.   [3] Or *province, empire.*
[4] There are no separate feminine dual forms of the article; the masculine
forms (τώ, τοῖν) are used instead.

95. A special rule of accent that belongs to all words of the ā-declension is this: The genitive plural is always accented with the circumflex on the ultima.

96.

Sing. N. V.   κώμη καλή   *a beautiful village*
       G.   κώμης καλῆς
       D.   κώμῃ καλῇ
       A.   κώμην καλήν

Dual N. A. V.   κώμᾱ καλά
      G. D.   κώμαιν καλαῖν

Plur. N. V.   κῶμαι καλαί
       G.   κωμῶν καλῶν
       D.   κώμαις καλαῖς
       A.   κώμᾱς καλάς

97. For the short final -αι as in κῶμαι see § 23, and compare οἶνοι (§ 60).

98. The **infinitive**, with or without a subject accusative, is used as the object of verbs meaning *wish, command, hinder, persuade*, and the like. The negative with the infinitive is μή:

τοὺς λοχᾱγοὺς κελεύει μὴ φυγεῖν he commands the captains not to flee.

99.   **VOCABULARY VI**

ἀρχή, ῆς, ἡ: *beginning, rule, province, empire*.

ἐθέλω, impf. ἤθελον: *wish, desire*.

ἐνταῦθα, adv.: *there*.

ἡ, fem. art.: *the*; proclitic (§ 20) in nom. sing. and nom. pl. αἱ. Cp. ὁ and τό. ἡ δέ: *and she, but she*, indicating a change of subject from the preceding sentence. ἡ may mean *she*, but only with μέν and δέ.

κακός, masc. adj., fem. κακή, neut. κακόν: *bad, cowardly*.

καλός, masc. adj., fem. καλή, neut. καλόν: *beautiful, handsome, noble, honorable*.

κελεύω, impf. ἐκέλευον: *command, bid, order*.

κώμη, ης, ἡ: *village.*

μάχη, ης, ἡ: *battle, fight.*

μέν, postpositive particle, used with a word or clause that is contrasted with a following word (in another clause) or a second clause. The second word or clause often has δέ, which is sometimes replaced by another conjunction. μέν sometimes means *on the one hand;* but more often it is to be omitted in translation. ὁ μέν . . . ὁ δέ: *the one . . . the other;* οἱ μέν . . . οἱ δέ: *some . . . others.* See δέ (§ 90).

μεστός, masc. adj., fem. μεστή, neut. μεστόν: *full,* with gen.

μή, neg. adv.: *not,* with inf. and in other uses to be described later.

ὁ δέ: *and he, but he,* indicating a change of subject from the preceding sentence. ὁ may mean *he,* but only with μέν and δέ.

οὐ, proclitic neg. adv.: *not;* before a vowel with smooth breathing, written οὐκ; before a rough breathing, οὐχ. At the end of a sentence, οὔ.

σκηνή, ῆς, ἡ: *tent.*

φυλακή, ῆς, ἡ: *guard, garrison.*

EXERCISES FOR TRANSLATION

100. I. 1. πέμπει Κῦρον εἰς τὴν ἀρχήν. 2. ὁ δὲ Κλέαρχος οὐκ εἶχε φυλακήν. 3. οὐχ ἁρπάζει τὰς καλὰς κώμας. 4. πρὸς τὰς σκηνὰς ἔφυγον. 5. ὁ δὲ οὐκ ἤθελε λείπειν τὸν ἵππον. 6. αἱ δὲ κῶμαι ἔσχον σῖτα. 7. ἐνταῦθα ἦσαν κῶμαι μεσταὶ σίτου καὶ οἴνου. 8. καὶ τοὺς στρατηγοὺς ἐκέλευεν ἀγαγεῖν τοὺς λοχᾱγοὺς εἰς τὴν σκηνήν. 9. οἱ καλοὶ καὶ ἀγαθοὶ[1] ἦσαν ἐν τῇ μάχῃ. 10. ἡ δ᾽ ἔφυγεν εἰς τὴν καλὴν κώμην. 11. ἔπειθον τοὺς λοχᾱγοὺς μὴ λείπειν ἀφύλακτον τὸ χωρίον. 12. οἱ μὲν ἀγαθοὶ λοχᾱγοὶ ἦσαν ἐν τῇ μάχῃ, οἱ δὲ κακοὶ ἐν τῷ χωρίῳ.

II. 1. In the battle were noble and brave men. 2. Cyrus ordered his generals to enlist[2] brave men. 3. We do not

---

[1] Understand *men.*   [2] = to take.

wish our friends to flee out of the fight. 4. The generals[1] were brave, but the captains were cowardly. 5. He
orders the men with Cyrus[2] not to flee.

VII

PRESENT INDICATIVE AND INFINITIVE OF εἰμί *I am.*
ENCLITICS. SIMPLE CONDITIONS. PREDICATE SUB-
STANTIVE WITHOUT ARTICLE

101. PRESENT INDICATIVE AND INFINITIVE OF εἰμί *I am*

	SING.	DUAL	PLUR.
1.	εἰμί *I am*		ἐσμέν *we are*
2.	εἶ *you are*	ἐστόν	ἐστέ *you are*
3.	ἐστί(ν)[3] *he is*	ἐστόν	εἰσί(ν)[3] *they are*

Infinitive εἶναι *to be*

a. All these forms except εἶ and εἶναι are enclitic (§ 21).

102. ἔστι(ν) is thus accented when it means *is*, i.e. *exists*,
or *is possible;* at the beginning of a sentence; and after
καί, ἀλλά, οὐκ, μή, and εἰ (*if*).

HOW THE ENCLITIC AFFECTS THE ACCENT OF THE PRECEDING WORD

103. 1. If the preceding word naturally has an acute
on the ultima, that accent is retained, and any enclitic
loses its accent:

καλός τε καὶ ἀγαθός both handsome and good (for τε see the vocabu-
    lary of this lesson);
ἀγαθός ἐστιν he is good.

---

[1] οἱ μὲν στρατηγοί (cp. I. 12).   [2] § 70. *b.*   [3] Cp. § 32.

2. If the preceding word has an acute on the penult, its accent is not affected in any way. *Then* a monosyllabic enclitic, as usual, loses its accent; but *a dissyllabic enclitic retains its accent:*

πεδία τε καὶ ποταμοί both plains and rivers ;

τὰ πεδία ἐστὶ καλά the plains are beautiful (for the singular verb see § 71).

3. If the preceding word has an acute on the antepenult, it receives an additional acute on its ultima from the following enclitic, which loses its accent :

ἄπορός τε καὶ ἀδιάβατος both pathless and impassable ;

ὁ ἄνθρωπός ἐστι κακός the man is cowardly.

4. If the preceding word has a circumflex on the ultima, its accent is not affected in any way, and any enclitic loses its accent (cp. 1):

καλῶν τε καὶ ἀγαθῶν ἐστιν it is [the part] of noble and brave men.

5. If the preceding word has a circumflex on the penult, it receives an additional accent — the acute on its ultima — from the following enclitic, which loses its accent (cp. 3):

κῶμαί τε καὶ πεδία both villages and plains ;

κῶμαί εἰσιν ἐν τῷ πεδίῳ villages are in the plain.

104. Observe that the monosyllabic enclitic regularly loses its accent. The dissyllabic enclitic retains its accent only under condition 2 above.

105. A proclitic (§ 20) followed by an enclitic receives an acute accent :

οἵ τε στρατηγοὶ καὶ οἱ λοχᾱγοί both the generals and the captains.

106. **Simple conditions.** — A supposition that assumes a fact without in any way implying its truth or falsity is expressed by εἰ *if* and the appropriate tense of the indica-

tive mood. This is commonly called the *Simple Present Condition*, or, if in past time, the *Simple Past Condition*. The conclusion may be any verb form whatsoever that is required by the sense.

a. The *if* clause is called the *protasis;* the conclusion is called the *apodosis.*

b. The negative, if required with the protasis, is μή; with the apodosis, οὐ.

εἰ φεύγει, οὐκ ἔστιν ἀγαθός *if he is fleeing, he is not brave* is a simple present condition.

εἰ ἔφυγεν, οὐκ ἦν ἀγαθός *if he fled, he was not brave* is a simple past condition.

107. A **predicate substantive** (§ 53. *k*) usually lacks the article :

στρατηγὸς ἦν ὁ Κῦρος *Cyrus was general.*

108. VOCABULARY VII

ἀδιάβατος, masc. and fem., neut. ἀδιάβατον : *not to be crossed, impassable.*

εἰ, proclitic conj. : *if.*

εἰμί : *I am.* ἔστι(ν) : *it is possible.* ἦν : *it was possible.*

θεός, οῦ, ὁ : *god*; ἡ : *goddess.* Theology (λόγος *discourse*).

κωλύω, impf. ἐκώλυον : *hinder.*

οὐ (οὐκ, οὐχ), used in interrogative sentence : *not;* expects the answer *yes.* Cp. Lat. *nōnne.*

πεζός, fem. πεζή, neut. πεζόν : *afoot, on foot*; οἱ πεζοί : *the infantry.*

τε, enclitic conj. : *and.* τε . . . καί : *both . . . and.*

φόβος, ου, ὁ : *fear.*

EXERCISES FOR TRANSLATION

109. I. 1. αἱ κῶμαί εἰσι μεσταὶ σίτου καὶ οἴνου. 2. ἡ δ᾽ ἀρχή ἐστι μεστὴ καλῶν τε καὶ ἀγαθῶν ἀνθρώπων. 3. οἱ ποταμοί εἰσιν ἀδιάβατοι, εἴ τις[1] κωλύει. 4. ἤθελον[2] τοὺς ἀνθρώπους εἶναι καλούς τε καὶ ἀγα-

---

[1] *anybody,* enclitic.   [2] Either 1 sing. or 3 pl.

θούς.   5. ἐκελεύομεν τοὺς σὺν Κύρῳ μὴ λιπεῖν τοὺς
ἵππους.   6. εἰ μὴ ἤγαγε τοὺς ἵππους, οὐκ ἔστιν ἀγαθὸς
ἄνθρωπος.   7. οὐκ ἐπέμπετε τοὺς λοχαγοὺς πρὸς Κῦρον;
8. ἐκ τῶν κωμῶν ἁρπάζουσι τὰ σῖτά τε καὶ τὸν οἶνον.
9. καλοί τε καὶ ἀγαθοί ἐσμεν.   10. εἰ ἦγε τοὺς πεζοὺς
εἰς τὴν μάχην, ἀγαθὸς στρατηγὸς ἦν.   11. ἔχομεν φόβον
θεῶν τε καὶ ἀνθρώπων.

II. 1. The generals were both noble and brave.   2. The
general fled on foot [1] to a stronghold.   3. The plains were
both beautiful and full of wine.   4. He desired his men to
be brave in battle.   5. If anybody hindered,[2] it was not
possible to flee out of the village.

VIII

SIMPLE SENTENCES IN INDIRECT DISCOURSE AFTER VERBS OF *SAYING* AND *THINKING*. DATIVE WITH ADJECTIVES

110. *a*. When a statement is quoted after a verb of
saying (as φησί *he says*) or *thinking*, its main verb is
changed to the *same tense* of the infinitive.

b. Since there is no separate form for the imperfect
infinitive, an imperfect indicative of direct discourse necessarily becomes present infinitive in indirect discourse.

c. The subject of this "infinitive in indirect discourse"
is omitted when it is the same as that of the main verb of
saying (φησί) or *thinking*.   But it is regularly expressed
when it is different from that of the main verb.

---

[1] πεζός must agree with *the general*.   [2] Cp. I. 3.

d. The subject of an infinitive, when expressed, is in the accusative case. But a modifier of an omitted subject agrees with the subject of the main verb when it indicates the same person or thing.

e. The negative of the direct discourse is regularly retained in indirect. That is, the negative with the infinitive of indirect discourse is usually οὐ, not μή (cp. § 98).

EXAMPLES

Original statement: πέμπω ἐπιστολήν I send a letter.

Quoted statements: (1) Κῦρός φησι πέμπειν ἐπιστολήν Cyrus says he is sending a letter;

    (2) νομίζω Κῦρον πέμπειν ἐπιστολήν I think Cyrus is sending a letter.

Original statement: ὁ στρατηγὸς πιστὰ ἔλαβε the general took pledges.

Quoted statement: ἔφη τὸν στρατηγὸν πιστὰ λαβεῖν he said the general took [1] pledges.

Original statement: Κῦρος ἦρχε τῆς μάχης Cyrus began the battle.

Quoted statement: ἔφη Κῦρον ἄρχειν τῆς μάχης he said Cyrus began the battle. (ἄρχειν might also represent an ἄρχει of the original statement. The context of a narrative determines this matter.)

Original statement: Κῦρός εἰμι I am Cyrus.

Quoted statement: ἔφη Κῦρος εἶναι he said he was Cyrus. (Observe that in *English* a quoted tense is secondary if the leading verb is secondary. Such a change from present to past is *irregular* in Greek. Cp. the Latin *dīxit sē Cȳrum esse.*)

III. **Dative with adjectives.** — The *to* or *for* dative is used with many adjectives that express friendliness, hostility, association, fitness, and other ideas :

    φίλος Κύρῳ friendly to Cyrus ;

    ἦν πιστὸς τῷ ἀδελφῷ he was faithful to his brother.

---

[1] Lit. *to have taken* (cp. § 84. *a*).

112.   VOCABULARY VIII

ἀδελφός, οῦ, ὁ: *brother*. Phila-
delphia (φίλος).

ἄρχω, impf. ἦρχον: *begin, rule,
command*, with gen. Cp. ἀρχή.

βάρβαρος, ου, ὁ: *foreigner, barbarian*.

γάρ, postpositive conj.: *for*.

ἐπί (ἐπ' before a smooth breathing,
ἐφ' before a rough breathing,
§31), prep.: with GEN. *on, in the
time of* ; with DAT. *on, upon, at,
in the power of, for* ; with ACC.
against (often with idea of hostility), *to, upon*.

ἐπιστολή, ῆς, ἡ: *letter*. Epistle.

ἔφασαν, 3 pl. impf.: *they said.*

ἔφη, 3 sing. impf.: *he said.*

λόγος, ου, ὁ: *word, speech*.

νομίζω, impf. ἐνόμιζον: *think*.

οὐδέ (οὐ + δέ): *nor, not even* ; Lat.
nē . . . quidem.

οὔτε . . . οὔτε (οὐ + τε): *neither
.*. . nor*.

πιστός, fem. πιστή, neut. πιστόν:
trustworthy, faithful. πιστά,
ὦν, τά, neut. pl. subst.: *pledges*.

φᾱσί(ν), enclitic verb, 3 pl. pres.:
they say.

φησί(ν), enclitic verb, 3 sing.
pres.: *he says*.

φίλος, fem. φίλη, neut. φίλον:
friendly. The masc. φίλος has
been learned before in its substantive use (*friend*), § 48.

EXERCISES FOR TRANSLATION

113. I. 1. πείθω τὸν Κύρου ἀδελφόν.   2. ὁ δέ φησι
πείθειν τὸν Κύρου ἀδελφόν.   3. ἐθέλω λαβεῖν πλοῖα.
4. ἔφη ἐθέλειν λαβεῖν πλοῖα.   5. ἔφασαν ἐθέλειν πιστὰ
λαβεῖν.   6. οὔτε ὁ λοχᾱγὸς οὔτε ὁ στρατηγὸς ἔπεμπεν
ἐπιστολήν.   7. οὐδ' ἤθελε Κλέαρχος ἄρχειν τῆς μάχης.   8. οἱ δὲ βάρβαροι οὐ καλοί τε καὶ ἀγαθοί εἰσιν.
9. νομίζω τοὺς βαρβάρους οὐκ εἶναι καλούς τε καὶ
ἀγαθούς.   10. νομίζομεν τὸν Κῦρον οὐκ εἶναι ἐπὶ[1] τῷ
ἀδελφῷ.   11. Κῦρόν φᾱσι λιπεῖν τὰ πλοῖα.   12. τοὺς
Κύρου λόγους καλοὺς νομίζετε εἶναι;   13. Κύρῳ γὰρ
ἔφη πιστὸς εἶναι.   14. ἡ κώμη οὐκ ἦν Κύρῳ φίλη.

---

[1] *in the power of.*

II. 1. Cyrus is not in the power of his brother. 2. He thought Cyrus was[1] not in the power of his brother. 3. The generals fled[2] on[3] the boats. 4. He said that the generals [had] fled[2] on the boats.

IX.

DECLENSION OF Ā–STEMS (*Continued*). REVIEW OF ADJECTIVES OF THE O– AND Ā–DECLENSIONS. ADJECTIVES OF TWO ENDINGS IN -ος, -ον. DATIVE OF POSSESSION

NOMINATIVES IN -ᾱ

114. Nouns of the **ᾱ**-declension have *ă* and not *η* in the singular when this vowel is preceded by ε, ι, or ρ.

Sing. N. V.	στρατιά, ἡ, *army*		Plur. N. V.	στρατιαί
G.	στρατιᾶς		G.	στρατιῶν
D.	στρατιᾷ		D.	στρατιαῖς
A.	στρατιάν		A.	στρατιάς

Dual N. A. V. στρατιά
G. D. στρατιαῖν

For the accent see §§ 57, 58, 59, 95.

115.

Sing. N. V.	χώρᾱ πολεμίᾱ *a hostile country*	N.	ἡ ὀρθίᾱ ὁδός *the steep road*
G.	χώρᾱς πολεμίᾱς	G.	τῆς ὀρθίᾱς ὁδοῦ
D.	χώρᾳ πολεμίᾳ	D.	τῇ ὀρθίᾳ ὁδῷ
A.	χώρᾱν πολεμίᾱν	A.	τὴν ὀρθίᾱν ὁδόν
		V.	— ὀρθίᾱ ὁδέ
Plur. N. V.	χῶραι πολέμιαι	N.	αἱ ὄρθιαι ὁδοί
G.	χωρῶν πολεμίων	G.	τῶν ὀρθίων ὁδῶν
D.	χώραις πολεμίαις	D.	ταῖς ὀρθίαις ὁδοῖς
A.	χώρᾱς πολεμίᾱς	A.	τὰς ὀρθίᾱς ὁδούς
		V.	— ὄρθιαι ὁδοί

---

[1] Originally *is*.　　　[2] 2 aor.　　　[3] ἐπί with gen.

a. ὁδός belongs to the group of o-stems that are feminine, although most of the o-stems are masculine or neuter.

b. For the accent of πολέμιαι, πολεμίων and ὄρθιαι,
ὀρθίων see below, § 117. *a.*

REVIEW OF ADJECTIVES OF THE O– AND Ā–DECLENSIONS

ADJECTIVES IN -ος, -η, -ον

116. ἀγαθός *good, brave* is declined in the masculine like
ποταμός, in the feminine like ἀρχή, and in the neuter like
παλτόν.

		MASC.	FEM.	NEUT.
Sing.	N.	ἀγαθός	ἀγαθή	ἀγαθόν
	G.	ἀγαθοῦ	ἀγαθῆς	ἀγαθοῦ
	D.	ἀγαθῷ	ἀγαθῇ	ἀγαθῷ
	A.	ἀγαθόν	ἀγαθήν	ἀγαθόν
	V.	ἀγαθέ	ἀγαθή	ἀγαθόν
Dual N. A. V.		ἀγαθώ	ἀγαθά	ἀγαθώ
	G. D.	ἀγαθοῖν	ἀγαθαῖν	ἀγαθοῖν
Plur. N. V.		ἀγαθοί	ἀγαθαί	ἀγαθά
	G.	ἀγαθῶν	ἀγαθῶν	ἀγαθῶν
	D.	ἀγαθοῖς	ἀγαθαῖς	ἀγαθοῖς
	A.	ἀγαθούς	ἀγαθάς	ἀγαθά

ADJECTIVES IN -ος, -ā, -ον

		MASC.	FEM.	NEUT.
117. Sing.	N.	πολέμιος *hostile*	πολεμία	πολέμιον
	G.	πολεμίου	πολεμίας	πολεμίου
	D.	πολεμίῳ	πολεμίᾳ	πολεμίῳ
	A.	πολέμιον	πολεμίαν	πολέμιον
	V.	πολέμιε	πολεμία	πολέμιον
Dual N. A. V.		πολεμίω	πολεμία	πολεμίω
	G. D.	πολεμίοιν	πολεμίαιν	πολεμίοιν
Plur. N. V.		πολέμιοι	πολέμιαι	πολέμια
	G.	πολεμίων	πολεμίων	πολεμίων
	D.	πολεμίοις	πολεμίαις	πολεμίοις
	A.	πολεμίους	πολεμίας	πολέμια

a. While the preceding paradigm shows the regular
endings of the **o**- and **ā**-declensions, there are two forms
that depart from the rules of accent of the **ā**-declension
(§§ 59, 95). The nominative and genitive plural feminine
follow the masculine in accent: πολέμιαι and not πολεμίαι;
πολεμίων and not πολεμιῶν. This applies to all adjectives
and participles in -ος, -η (or -ā̆), -ον.

ADJECTIVES OF TWO ENDINGS IN -ος, -ον

118. There are many adjectives in -ος that have one
form for both masculine and feminine genders, and distinct
forms for the neuter in a few cases, as shown in the
following paradigm. They are declined like ἄνθρωπος and
πλοῖον in respect to case endings. Their accent is regularly recessive (§ 44).

	MASC. AND FEM.		NEUT.
Sing. N.	ἄπορος *impassable*		ἄπορον
G.		ἀπόρου	
D.		ἀπόρῳ	
A.		ἄπορον	
V.	ἄπορε		ἄπορον
Dual N. A. V.		ἀπόρω	
G. D.		ἀπόροιν	
Plur. N. V.	ἄποροι		ἄπορα
G.		ἀπόρων	
D.		ἀπόροις	
A.	ἀπόρους		ἄπορα

So, too, is declined ἀφύλακτος (§ 73).

119. Dative of possession (*to* or *for* dative). — The dative
case may be used with the verb *to be* to denote the possessor :

Κύρῳ ἀ χή ἐστιν Cyrus has a province (a province is to Cyrus).

120.   VOCABULARY IX

ἀγορά, ᾶς, ἡ : *market-place, market.*

δίκη, ης, ἡ : *justice, deserts.*

μεταξύ, adv. : *between*, with gen.

ὁδός, οῦ, ἡ : *way, road.* Hodo-
meter (μέτρον *measure*).

ὄρθιος, ᾱ, ον : *steep.*

ὅρκος, ου, ὁ : *oath.*

παρά (before a vowel παρ'), prep. :
with GEN. *from* the side of;
with DAT. *by* the side of, after
verbs of rest; with ACC. *to* the
side of, after verbs of motion;
contrary to.

πάροδος, ου, ἡ (παρά + ὁδός) : *road
by* or *past, passage, pass.*

πολέμιος, ᾱ, ον (πόλεμος *war*) : *of
war, hostile.* οἱ πολέμιοι, subst.
adj. : *the enemy.* Polemic.

σπονδή, ῆς, ἡ : *libation* ; pl. *truce.*
Spondee.

στενός, ή, όν : *narrow.* Steno-
graphy (γράφω *write*).

στόλος, ου, ὁ : *expedition.*

στρατιά, ᾶς, ἡ : *army.*

τάφρος, ου, ἡ : *ditch.*

χώρᾱ, ᾶς, ἡ : *country, land.*

EXERCISES FOR TRANSLATION

121. I. 1. τῷ δὲ Κύρῳ ἦν στρατιὰ ἀγαθή. 2. νομίζομεν δὲ τὸν στόλον ἐπὶ τοὺς πολεμίους εἶναι. 3. ἦν
γὰρ ἡ πάροδος στενή. 4. ἦν δὲ πάροδος στενὴ μεταξὺ
τοῦ ποταμοῦ καὶ τῆς τάφρου. 5. ἦγε δὲ τὴν στρατιὰν
παρὰ τὴν Κύρου σκηνήν. 6. Κλέαρχος δὲ ἐπὶ τοὺς
πολεμίους οὐκ ἦγεν. 7. εἰ Κλέαρχος παρὰ¹ τοὺς ὅρκους
ἔλυε² τὰς σπονδάς, τὴν δίκην ἔχει. 8. ἡ δ' ἀγορὰ ἦν
ἐν τῇ τῶν βαρβάρων χώρᾳ. 9. ἔφη τὴν ὁδὸν εἶναι
εἰς χώρᾱν καλήν. 10. ἡ δ' ὁδὸς ἦν ἄπορος, εἴ τις³
ἐκώλῦεν.

II. 1. He led the men from-the-side-of⁴ Cyrus to the
market-place.   2. The road to the market-place⁵ was
steep.   3. We think the country is beautiful.   4. Cyrus's
expedition is against his brother.

---

¹ *contrary to.*   ² *broke.*   ³ Enclitic, *anybody*, cp. § 105.

⁴ παρά.   ⁵ Put *to the market-place* in the attributive position.

X

SOME PRONOUNS: αὐτός, MEANINGS AND USES; ἄλλος, ὅς. POSSESSIVE ADJECTIVES. COMPOUND VERBS. RULES OF EUPHONY APPLYING TO σύν AND ἐν IN COMPOSITION. AGREEMENT OF RELATIVE. DATIVE WITH COMPOUNDS

DECLENSION OF αὐτός, *self, same*

		MASC.	FEM.	NEUT.
122.	Sing. N.	αὐτός	αὐτή	αὐτό
	G.	αὐτοῦ	αὐτῆς	αὐτοῦ
	D.	αὐτῷ	αὐτῇ	αὐτῷ
	A.	αὐτόν	αὐτήν	αὐτό
	Dual N. A.	αὐτώ	αὐτά	αὐτώ
	G. D.	αὐτοῖν	αὐταῖν	αὐτοῖν
	Plur. N.	αὐτοί	αὐταί	αὐτά
	G.	αὐτῶν	αὐτῶν	αὐτῶν
	D.	αὐτοῖς	αὐταῖς	αὐτοῖς
	A.	αὐτούς	αὐτάς	αὐτά

MEANING AND USES OF αὐτός

123. 1. As an intensive pronoun αὐτός means *self*,[1] *himself*, etc.:

ὁ Κῦρος αὐτός *or* Κῦρος αὐτός Cyrus himself.

2. When placed between the article and the noun, that is, when used in the attributive position, αὐτός means *same*:

ὁ αὐτὸς στρατηγός the same general.

3. In the genitive, dative, and accusative cases (the "oblique" cases), this word is the common personal pro-

---

[1] Cp. **auto-graph** (γράφω *write*).

noun of the third person. This use does *not* belong to
the nominative case, however :

ἦγον αὐτούς (or fem. αὐτάς) I *or* they led them.

See below, § 127.

ἄλλος, *other, another ; the other, the rest of* (if preceded by the article)

		MASC.	FEM.	NEUT.
124.	Sing. N.	ἄλλος	ἄλλη	ἄλλο
	G.	ἄλλου	ἄλλης	ἄλλου
	D.	ἄλλῳ	ἄλλῃ	ἄλλῳ
	A.	ἄλλον	ἄλλην	ἄλλο
	Dual N. A.	ἄλλω	ἄλλᾱ	ἄλλω
	G. D.	ἄλλοιν	ἄλλαιν	ἄλλοιν
	Plur. N.	ἄλλοι	ἄλλαι	ἄλλα
	G.	ἄλλων	ἄλλων	ἄλλων
	D.	ἄλλοις	ἄλλαις	ἄλλοις
	A.	ἄλλους	ἄλλᾱς	ἄλλα

THE RELATIVE ὅς, ἥ, ὅ, *who, which, that*

		MASC.	FEM.	NEUT.
125.	Sing. N.	ὅς	ἥ	ὅ
	G.	οὗ	ἧς	οὗ
	D.	ᾧ	ᾗ	ᾧ
	A.	ὅν	ἥν	ὅ
	Dual N. A.	ὥ	ὥ	ὥ
	G. D.	οἷν	οἷν	οἷν
	Plur. N.	οἵ	αἵ	ἅ
	G.	ὧν	ὧν	ὧν
	D.	οἷς	αἷς	οἷς
	A.	οὕς	ἅς	ἅ

POSSESSIVE ADJECTIVES

126 Possessive adjectives are ἐμός, ἐμή, ἐμόν, *my, mine ;*
σός, σή, σόν, *your* (sing.), *yours ;* ἡμέτερος, ἡμετέρᾱ, ἡμέτε-

ρον, *our, ours;* ὑμέτερος, ὑμετέρᾱ, ὑμέτερον, *your* (pl.), *yours*
They are declined regularly. These pronouns are regularly
accompanied by the article and stand in the attributive position when denoting a particular person or thing:

ὁ ἐμὸς ἀδελφός my brother.

ἀδελφὸς ἐμός means *a brother of mine.*

127. We have already learned (§ 54) that *his, her, their,*
etc., may be expressed by the article in agreement with its
noun. The possessive genitive of αὐτός may also be used,
and always in the predicate position (§§ 68, 69):

ἡ σκηνὴ αὐτοῦ his tent;
ἡ χώρᾱ αὐτῶν their country.

a. In this use αὐτοῦ is equivalent in meaning to the Latin
ēius, and is not reflexive.

COMPOUND VERBS

128. Prepositions, which originally were adverbs, are
very frequently prefixed to verbs, and modify the verbal
idea accordingly:

ἐξ-άγω lead out; εἰσ-άγω lead in; ἐκ-πέμπω send forth; συμ-πέμπω
(συμ- for συν- before π for the sake of euphony) send with;
ἐπι-βουλεύω plot against.

129. When a final vowel of the preposition comes before
an initial vowel of the verb, the final vowel of the preposition is regularly dropped:

ἀπ-άγω (ἀπό + ἄγω) lead off; ἀφ-αρπάζω (ἀπό + ἁρπάζω, π being
changed to φ before the rough breathing, § 31) snatch away,
seize.

130. Compound verbs are regularly augmented *after* the prefix. A final vowel of the prepositional prefix is likewise dropped before the augment:

ἐξ-ήγαγον they led out; ἐξ-έπεμπον they sent out; ἀπ-έφυγον they fled away; ἐπ-εβούλευε he plotted against.

131. The accent of a compound verb can never recede back of the augment:

ἐξ-ῆγον, *not* ἔξ-ηγον.

132. A compound verb is divided between the prefix and the verb proper, if a hyphen must be used, as at the end of a line:

ἀπ-έφυγον, *not* ἀ-πέφυγον (cp. § 9).

RULES OF EUPHONY: ν BEFORE OTHER CONSONANTS

133. If the prefix of a compound verb is σύν or ἐν, the nasal (ν) undergoes euphonic changes before certain consonants, conformably to the following laws:

1. Before a labial mute (§ 27) ν becomes μ:

   συμ-πέμπω send with.

2. Before a palatal mute (§ 27) ν becomes γ nasal (§ 5):

   ἐγ-γράφω inscribe (ἐν + γράφω write).

3. Before a liquid (§ 27) ν is assimilated to the liquid:

   συλ-λαμβάνω arrest.

4. Before σ, ν is dropped:

   συ-στρατεύω take the field with.

134. But the prefix always resumes its original form before the syllabic augment:

συν-έλαβον, συν-έπεμπον.

135. The **relative pronoun** agrees with its antecedent in person, gender, and number, but its case is determined by its construction in its own clause : [1]

πάρ-εστιν ὁ ἄνθρωπος ὃν ἔπεμπεν the man whom he sent is here.

136. Verbs compounded with ἐν, σύν, and ἐπί commonly take the **dative** case, if the object is dependent on the prepositional idea :

τοῖς δ' ἄλλοις ἐπι-βουλεύουσιν and they are plotting against the others.

137.   VOCABULARY X

For the meanings of αὐτός, ἄλλος, ὅς, ἐμός, ἡμέτερος, σός, ὑμέτερος, ee the preceding articles (§§ 123–127).

ἀπό (ἀπ' before smooth breathing, ἀφ' before rough breathing, § 31), prep. with gen. only : *off, from, away from.* Cp. Lat. *ab.*

ἀπο-θνήσκω, impf. ἀπ-έθνησκον, 2 aor. ἀπ-έθανον : *die off, die, perish, be slain.*

ἀπο-πέμπω, impf. ἀπ-έπεμπον : *send off* or *away, dismiss.*

εἶτα, adv. : *then, thereupon.*

ἐξ-άγω, impf. ἐξ-ῆγον, 2 aor. ἐξ-ήγαγον : *lead out.*

ἐπι-βουλεύω, impf. ἐπ-εβούλευον : *plot against,* with dat. (βουλεύω *plan.*)

ἥκω, impf. ἥκον : *come, have come;* pres. with pf. meaning.

πάλιν, adv. : *back, again.*

πάρ-ειμι, impf. (3 sing.) παρ-ῆν, (3 pl) παρ-ῆσαν : *be by, be at hand, be present, attend,* with dat.

συλ-λαμβάνω (σύν + λαμβάνω), impf. συν-ελάμβανον, 2 aor. συν-έλαβον : *take together, seize, arrest.* Cp. Lat. *comprehendō.*

συμ-πέμπω (σύν + πέμπω), impf. συν-έπεμπον : *send* a person (in acc.), *with* a person (in dat.).

EXERCISES FOR TRANSLATION

138. I. 1. ὁ δὲ ἀδελφὸς αὐτὸν ἔπειθεν.   2. εἶτα δ' ἐξ-ῆγον αὐτόν.   3. ὁ αὐτὸς στόλος ἐστὶ Κύρῳ καὶ τοῖς φίλοις αὐτοῦ.   4. Κῦρος δ' πάρ- στι σὺν τοῖς βαρβά-

---

[1] Except as is later explained in § 285.

ροις οἳ αὐτῷ εἰσι πιστοί.   5. ὁ αὐτὸς φόβος παρ-ῆν
τοῖς ἡμετέροις στρατηγοῖς.   6. Κῦρος δὲ ἧκει ἀπὸ τῆς
ἀρχῆς.   7. ἡ δὲ[1] ἀπο-πέμπει αὐτὸν πάλιν ἐπὶ τὴν ἀρχήν.
8. Κῦρος ἐπι-βουλεύει τῷ ἀδελφῷ.   9. ὁ δὲ ἀδελφὸς
σ⟩λ-λαμβάνει Κῦρον.   10. αὐτὸς δὲ συν-έλαβε τοὺς
ἄλλους στρατηγούς.   11. συμ-πέμπει δὲ λόχον αὐτοῖς.
12. Κῦρος δὲ αὐτὸς ἀπ-έθανεν.

II. 1. We do not plot against our friends.   2. They
have the same fear.   3. The other brothers of the general
were slain.   4. He himself was not present in the fight.

XI

DECLENSION OF Ā–STEMS (*Continued*).   INSTRUMENTAL
   DATIVE.   ACCUSATIVE OF EXTENT OF TIME OR
   SPACE.   ARTICLE WITH NAME OF COUNTRY

NOMINATIVES IN -ă

139. Hitherto there have been introduced only such
nouns of the ā-declension as have ă or η in the nominative
singular.   There are, however, some nouns of the ā-declension that have ă in the nominative singular.   They usually
have recessive accent (cp. § 44).   In the genitive and dative
endings ā appears if this vowel is preceded by ε, ι, or ρ
(cp. § 114), otherwise η is found.   The accusative and vocative singular have the vowel (ă) and accent of the nominative singular.   In the dual and plural all nouns of the ā-
declension are inflected alike.

---

[1] *and she.*

140.

		θάλαττα, ἡ, sea	γέφῡρα, ἡ, bridge	ἅμαξα, ἡ, wagon
Sing. N. V.		θάλαττα	γέφῡρα	ἅμαξα
	G.	θαλάττης	γεφῡρᾱς	ἁμάξης
	D.	θαλάττῃ	γεφῡρᾳ	ἁμάξῃ
	A.	θάλατταν	γέφῡραν	ἅμαξαν
Dual N. A. V.		θαλάττᾱ	γεφῡρᾱ	ἁμάξᾱ
	G. D.	θαλάτταιν	γεφῡραιν	ἁμάξαιν
Plur. N. V.		θάλατται	γέφῡραι	ἅμαξαι
	G.	θαλαττῶν	γεφῡρῶν	ἁμαξῶν
	D.	θαλάτταις	γεφῡραις	ἁμάξαις
	A.	θαλάττᾱς	γεφῡρᾱς	ἁμάξᾱς

141. The **instrumental dative** is used to denote means and manner:

γεφύρᾳ δια-βαίνει τὸν ποταμόν he crosses the river by a bridge.

142. The **accusative** may denote extent of time or space, answering the question *how long?* or *how far?*

ἐξ-ελαύνει δέκα σταθμούς he marches ten days' journey.

143. The name of a **country** may take the article, which is not to be translated (cp. § 89):

ἡ Κιλικίᾱ Cilicia.

144. VOCABULARY XI

ἅμαξα, ης, ἡ: *carriage, wagon.*

γέφῡρα, ᾱς, ἡ: *bridge.*

δέκα, indecl.: *ten.* Lat. *decem.* Deca-gon (γωνίᾱ *angle*).

διά (δι' before a vowel), prep.: with GEN. *through;* with ACC. *on account of, by means of.* Dia-meter (μέτρον *measure*).

δια-βαίνω, impf. δι-έβαινον: *go across, cross.* (βαίνω *go*.)

ἔδραμον, 2 aor.: *ran.* (Usually referred to τρέχω *run*.)

ἐντεῦθεν, adv.: *thence;* of time, *then.*

ἐξ-ελαύνω, impf. ἐξ-ήλαυνον: *drive out; march out* or *forth.* (ἐλαύνω *drive, ride, march.*)

θάλαττα, ης, ἡ: *sea.*

Κιλικίᾱ, ᾱς, ἡ: *Cilicia.*

Κίλισσα, ης, ἡ: *Cilician woman.*

λόφος, ου, ὁ : *hill.*

νίκη, ης, ἡ : *victory.*

παρ-ελαύνω, impf. παρ-ήλαυνον: *drive past* or *by* ; *march past, ride past.*

περί (never suffers elision of the final vowel), prep.: with GEN. *about, concerning, for,* as a prize ; with DAT. (not common in prose), *around, about* ; with ACC. *around, about, near.* Perimeter (μέτρον *measure*).

σταθμός, οῦ, ὁ : *day's journey, stage* ; *halting place* (first meaning, but less common).

EXERCISES FOR TRANSLATION

145. I. 1. ἡ δὲ Κίλισσα ἔφυγεν ἐπὶ τῆς ἀμάξης. 2. λύουσι τὰς γεφύρᾱς. 3. κῶμαι δὲ περὶ τὸν ποταμὸν ἦσαν. 4. καὶ ἔδραμον περὶ νίκης. 5. ἔστι[1] δὲ ἐν τῇ χώρᾳ λόφος ἐκ θαλάττης εἰς θάλατταν.[2] 6. λόφον δέ φᾱσιν εἶναι ἐν τῇ χώρᾳ ἐκ θαλάττης εἰς θάλατταν. 7. ἐντεῦθεν Κῦρος τὴν Κίλισσαν εἰς τὴν Κιλικίᾱν ἀποπέμπει. 8. καὶ συν-έπεμπεν αὐτῇ τοὺς λόχους οὓς Κλέαρχος εἶχε καὶ Κλέαρχον αὐτόν. 9. ἡ δὲ Κίλισσα παρ-ήλαυνεν ἐφ᾽ ἀμάξης.[3] 10. ἐντεῦθεν ἐξ-ελαύνει διὰ τῆς χώρᾱς τῆς Κιλίσσης σταθμοὺς δέκα. 11. δι-έβαινον τὴν γέφῡραν. 12. τὸν δὲ ποταμὸν δι-έβαινε γεφύρᾳ.

II. 1. He sent away the company (of soldiers)[4] to the sea. 2. Cyrus marched through Cilicia ten days' journey. 3. They cross the river by a bridge. 4. Cyrus sent to the Cilician woman a wagon which he had. 5. We destroyed the bridges which we crossed.

---

[1] § 102.   [2] *from sea to sea.*   [3] For ἐφ᾽ see § 31.   [4] Omit.

XII

DECLENSION OF Ā–STEMS (*Continued*). CLAUSES OF RESULT

MASCULINES IN -ης AND -ᾱς

146.

Sing.	N.	στρατιώτης, ὁ, *soldier*	πελταστής, ὁ, *peltast*
	G.	στρατιώτου	πελταστοῦ
	D.	στρατιώτῃ	πελταστῇ
	A.	στρατιώτην	πελταστήν
	V.	στρατιῶτα	πελταστά
Dual	N. A. V.	στρατιώτᾱ	πελταστά̄
	G. D.	στρατιώταιν	πελτασταῖν
Plur	N. V.	στρατιῶται	πελτασταί
	G.	στρατιωτῶν	πελταστῶν
	D.	στρατιώταις	πελτασταῖς
	A.	στρατιώτᾱς	πελταστά̄ς

Sing.	N.	τοξότης, ὁ, *bowman*	Ξενίᾱς, ὁ, *Xenias*
	G.	τοξότου	Ξενίου
	D.	τοξότῃ	Ξενίᾳ
	A.	τοξότην	Ξενίᾱν
	V.	τοξότα	Ξενίᾱ
Dual	N. A. V.	τοξότᾱ	
	G D.	τοξόταιν	
Plur.	N. V.	τοξόται	
	G.	τοξοτῶν	
	D.	τοξόταις	
	A.	τοξότᾱς	

a. Masculines in -της have vocatives singular in -ᾰ.

b. It is to be noted once more that all nouns of the ā̄-declension are inflected alike in the dual and plural.

147. Result is expressed by ὥστε *so that* with the indicative or infinitive. The indicative usually denotes the *actual* result; the infinitive, the *natural* result. With the indicative the negative is οὐ; with the infinitive, μή:

εἶχε πλοῖα ὥστε ἔλαβεν αὐτούς he had boats so that he captured them; εἶχε πλοῖα ὥστε λαβεῖν αὐτούς he had boats so as to capture them.

148.   VOCABULARY XII

ἀπο-φεύγω, impf. ἀπ-έφευγον, 2 aor. ἀπ-έφυγον: *flee away, escape.*

δρόμος, ου, ὁ: a *run.* δρόμῳ: *on the run.* Cp. ἔ-δραμ-ον. Hippodrome (ἵππος).

Ξενίας, ου, ὁ: *Xenias.*

ὁπλίτης, ου, ὁ: a heavy-armed soldier, *hoplite.* See p. 139, Fig. 18. Cp. ὅπλον.

παίω, impf. ἔπαιον: *strike, smite.*

πελταστής, οῦ, ὁ: a light-armed soldier, *peltast.*

Πῑσίδαι, ῶν, οἱ: *Pisidians,* natives of Pisidia.

στρατιώτης, ου, ὁ: *soldier.* Cp. στρατιά.

συν-άγω, impf. συν-ῆγον, 2 aor. συν-ήγαγον: *lead together, collect.*

τοξότης, ου, ὁ: *bowman.*

φυγή, ῆς, ἡ: *flight.* φυγῇ: *in flight.* Cp. φεύγω.

Χειρίσοφος, ου, ὁ: *Cheirisophus.*

ὥστε, conj.: *so that, so as, therefore* (§ 147).

Fɪɢ. 4. — Πελταστής (cp. p. 117, Fig. 14).

EXERCISES FOR TRANSLATION

149. I. 1. Ξενίᾱς δὲ εἶχεν ὁπλίτᾱς. 2. συν-ήγαγε δὲ τοὺς στρατιώτᾱς. 3. οἱ δ᾽ ἐκ τοῦ πεδίου πελτασταὶ δρόμῳ[1] ἔφυγον. 4. οἱ δ᾽ ἄλλοι στρατιῶται παίουσι τὸν ἄνθρωπον. 5. ἐκέλευε τοὺς πελταστὰς ἥκειν. 6. καὶ ὁ Χειρίσοφος συμ-πέμπει αὐτῷ τοὺς πελταστάς. 7. οἱ δὲ Ξενίου στρατιῶται ἥκουσιν. 8. οἱ δὲ τοξόται φυγῇ[1] λείπουσι τὸν λόφον. 9. οἱ δὲ πολέμιοι οὐκ ἀπο-φεύγουσιν· ἔχω γὰρ πλοῖα ὥστε λαβεῖν αὐτούς. 10. ἀλλ᾽ οὐκ ἦγες τοὺς πελταστάς; 11. ὥστε οὐκ ἐθέλω ἀπο-πέμπειν τοὺς στρατιώτᾱς αὐτῶν. 12. ἐνόμιζε δὲ τὸν στόλον εἶναι εἰς τοὺς Πῑσίδᾱς.

II. 1. He ordered the general to dismiss the soldiers. 2. He collected his soldiers and said that the expedition was[2] against Cilicia. 3. Therefore they did not wish to come with him.

---

[1] Dat. of manner; cp. § 141.   [2] Originally *is*.

FIG. 5. — Τοξότης.

XIII

FUTURE INDICATIVE AND INFINITIVE OF Ω–VERBS IN THE ACTIVE VOICE. RULES OF WRITING AND EUPHONY APPLYING TO MUTE THEMES: MUTES BEFORE *SIGMA*. GENITIVE OF TIME. FUTURE INFINITIVE IN INDIRECT DISCOURSE AND AFTER μέλλω

Review the statements about the formation of the present tense (§§ 41–43).

150. The future indicative active is formed from the verb theme, to which are added the future tense suffix and the personal endings. The future suffix is σο before μ and ν, σε before other letters. The personal endings are like the present.

151. FUTURE INDICATIVE ACTIVE OF λύω

Sing. 1. λύ-σω *I shall* or *will loose*
2. λύ-σεις *you shall* or *will loose*
3. λύ-σει *he shall* or *will loose*

Dual 2. λύ-σε-τον
3. λύ-σε-τον

Plur. 1. λύ-σο-μεν *we shall* or *will loose*
2. λύ-σε-τε *you shall* or *will loose*
3. λύ-σου-σι(ν) *they shall* or *will loose*

Future infinitive λύ-σειν

152. Verbs with themes ending in a vowel, *e.g.* κελεύω, regularly form the future like λύω. These are called **vowel themes**.

Verbs with themes ending in a mute (§ 27), *e.g.* πέμπω, are called **mute themes**.

RULES OF WRITING AND EUPHONY APPLYING TO MUTE THEMES: MUTES BEFORE *SIGMA*

153. 1. A labial mute (§ 27) unites with a following *sigma* and makes ψ ($= \pi s$).

2. A palatal mute (§ 27) unites with a following *sigma* and makes ξ ($= \kappa s$).

3. A lingual mute (§ 27) is dropped before a following *sigma*.

These rules are illustrated, for example, in the formation of the future of verbs with themes ending in a mute. Thus the future

of πέμπω is πέμψω (πεμπ-σω), of λείπω is λείψω (λειπ-σω);
of ἄγω is ἄξω (ἀγ-σω), of ἔχω is ἕξω (ἐχ-σω);
of ἁρπάζω[1] is ἁρπάσω (ἁρπαδ-σω).

154. The change of breathing in the future of ἔχω (ἕξω) is to be noted as unusual; there is also another future of ἔχω: σχήσω.

155. The **genitive** case may be used to denote *time within which*:

οὐχ ἥξει δέκα ἡμερῶν he will not come within ten days.

156. The **future infinitive** is used as follows:

1. In indirect discourse when it represents the future indicative of direct discourse (cp. § 110. *a*); this is its principal use:

οὐχ ἥξομεν we shall not come (*direct discourse*);
οὔ φᾶσιν ἥξειν they say they will not come (*indirect discourse*).

---

[1] The theme of ἁρπάζω is ἁρπαδ-, not ἁρπαζ-. This verb and similar verbs have for the present tense suffix $y\%$ instead of simple $\%$. So the ending -ζω is for -δyω.

a. Observe that the Greek prefers to place the negative before φᾱσί. Compare Latin *negō* for *dīcō nōn.*

2. After μέλλω *be about, intend;* but μέλλω also permits the present and the aorist infinitive:

μέλλουσιν ἥξειν they are about to come.

157. VOCABULARY XIII

ἅμα, adv. : *at the same time, together with,* with dat. ἅμα τῇ ἡμέρᾳ : *at the same time with the day, at daybreak.* Cp. Lat. *simul.* Hama-dryad (δρῦς *tree*).

ἐπιτήδειος, ᾱ, ον : *suitable, necessary.* τὰ ἐπιτήδεια (neut. pl. subst.) : *provisions, supplies.*

εὐθύς, adv. : *straightway, at once.*

ἡμέρᾱ, ᾱς, ἡ : *day.* Eph-emeral (ἐφ-).

μέλλω, impf. ἔμελλον, fut. μελλήσω (irreg.) : *be about, intend; delay.*

οἰκίᾱ, ᾱς, ἡ :ʼ *house.*

παρ-έχω, impf. παρ-εῖχον, fut. παρ-έξω (or παρα-σχήσω), 2 aor. παρ-έσχον : *hold beside, furnish, provide, supply.*

πέντε, indecl. : *five.* Penta-gon (γωνίᾱ *angle*).

EXERCISES FOR TRANSLATION

158. Give the meanings of λείψετε, σχήσουσι, ἄξομεν, ἁρπάσει, πέμψεις, πείσει, λείψουσι, κελεύσει, ἄρξομεν, κωλύσετε.

159. I. 1. ἕξομεν τὰ ἐπιτήδεια.[1] 2. νομίζουσιν ἕξειν τὰ ἐπιτήδεια. 3. ἥξουσιν εἰς κώμᾱς τῆς πολεμίᾱς χώρᾱς. 4. ἐνόμιζον δὲ ἥξειν εἰς κώμᾱς τῆς πολεμίᾱς χώρᾱς. 5. στρατηγοὺς δὲ ἔχουσιν οἳ αὐτοὺς ἄξουσιν. 6. ἀγορὰν δὲ παρ-έξομεν. 7. εὐθὺς ἀπο-πέμψει αὐτὸν εἰς τὴν οἰκίᾱν. 8. ἅμα δὲ τῇ ἡμέρᾳ οἱ πολέμιοι ἥξουσιν. 9. ἀλλὰ παίσομεν τοὺς πολεμίους. 10. ἄξει αὐτοὺς πέντε ἡμερῶν εἰς χωρίον. 11. ἀγορὰν δὲ οὔτε Κῦρος οὔτε Κλέαρχος παρ-έξειν ἔμελλεν.

---

[1] Sometimes τἀπιτήδεια by *crasis,* § 30.

II. 1. Within ten days they will come to the river.
2. At daybreak we shall supply provisions to the soldiers.[1]
3. We are about to destroy the bridges. 4. They say
they will not destroy the bridges. 5. He will send men
who will destroy the bridges.

XIV

FIRST AORIST INDICATIVE AND INFINITIVE OF Ω-VERBS IN THE ACTIVE VOICE. ἐπεί AND ἐπειδή *when* WITH IMPERFECT OR AORIST INDICATIVE

160. The first aorist indicative, as a secondary tense
(§ 39), has the augment (§ 77). To the augmented
theme are added the first aorist tense suffix σα and
the personal endings. The suffix σα becomes σε in
the third person singular. Reference should be made
to the personal endings already learned for the other
secondary tenses, imperfect and second aorist (§§ 81,
82, 85).

a. Personal endings are wanting in both the first and
the third persons singular of the first aorist indicative.

b. The *first aorist stem* is the theme of the verb plus σα,
as the future stem is the theme plus σ% (§ 150).

161. The first aorist indicative, like the second aorist
(cp. § 84), expresses a simple act in past time. The first and
the second aorist may often be translated with the auxiliary
had; this is regularly true when the aorist is introduced
by the conjunction ἐπεί or ἐπειδή *when.*

---

[1] Dat. of indir. obj.

162.   FIRST AORIST INDICATIVE ACTIVE OF λύω

SING.	DUAL	PLUR.
1. ἔ-λῦ-σα *I loosed*		ἐ-λύ-σα-μεν *we loosed*
2. ἔ-λῦ-σα-ς *you loosed*	ἐ-λύ-σα-τον	ἐ-λύ-σα-τε *you loosed*
3. ἔ-λῦ-σε(ν)[1] *he loosed*	ἐ-λῡ-σά-την	ἔ-λῡ-σα-ν *they loosed*

First aor. infin. λῦσαι *to loose*[2]; in indir. disc., *to have loosed*, etc. (§ 110)

163. Verbs with themes ending in a vowel regularly form the first aorist like λύω.

164. Verbs with themes ending in a mute (§ 27) form the first aorist in conformity to the euphonic laws mentioned in the last lesson (§ 153):

$$\pi έ μ π ω \quad (\pi ε μ π\text{-}), \quad \text{first aorist} \quad ἔ π ε μ ψ α$$
$$ἄ ρ χ ω \quad (ἀ ρ χ\text{-}), \qquad \text{"} \qquad \text{"} \qquad ἦ ρ ξ α$$
$$\pi ε ί θ ω \quad (\pi ε ι θ\text{-}), \qquad \text{"} \qquad \text{"} \qquad ἔ π ε ι σ α$$
$$ἁ ρ π ά ζ ω \;(ἁ ρ π α δ\text{-}), \quad \text{"} \qquad \text{"} \qquad ἥ ρ π α σ α$$

a. λείπω, ἄγω, ἔχω, and many other verbs have no first aorists; but their second aorists (§§ 85, 87, 88) do not differ in meaning from first aorists.

165. The first aorist of ἐλαύνω *drive, ride, march*, which has been seen in the compounds ἐξ-ελαύνω *march out* or *forth* and παρ-ελαύνω *drive* or *march past*, is ἤλασα.

166. The first aorist active infinitive is always accented on the penult. Thus συμ-βουλεῦσαι, not συμ-βούλευσαι.

167. ἐπεί and ἐπειδή meaning *when* and referring to a definite act in past time take the imperfect or aorist indicative:

ἐπεὶ τὴν κώμην δι-ήρπασαν, ἔφυγον when they had sacked the town, they fled.

---

[1] Cp. § 32.   [2] The simple act (cp. § 84. *a*).

168. VOCABULARY XIV

'Αρταξέρξης, ου, ὁ : *Artaxerxes*.

Βοιώτιος, ᾱ, ον : *Boeotian*.

δι αρπάζω (διά + ἁρπάζω), impf. δι-ήρπαζον, fut. δι-αρπάσω, aor. δι-ήρπασα : *tear in pieces, plunder utterly* or *thoroughly, sack*.

ἐπεί and ἐπει-δή, temporal conj. : *when, after*.

θαυμάζω (theme θαυμαδ-), impf. ἐθαύμαζον, fut. to be learned later, aor. ἐθαύμασα : *wonder, wonder at, admire*, with acc.

οὖν, postpositive particle : *therefore, accordingly, at any rate*.

Πρόξενος, ου, ὁ : *Proxenus*.

συλ-λέγω (σύν + λέγω *gather*), impf. συν-έλεγον, fut. συλ-λέξω, aor. συν-έλεξα : *gather together, collect*.

συμ-βουλεύω (σύν + βουλεύω), impf. συν-εβούλευον, fut. συμ-βουλεύσω, aor. συν-εβούλευσα : *plan with, advise*, with dat.

τρέπω, impf. ἔτρεπον, fut. τρέψω, aor. ἔτρεψα : *turn*. τρέπω εἰς φυγήν : *put to flight*.

χρῡσίον, ου, τό : *gold*. Chrys-anthemum (ἄνθεμον *flower*).

EXERCISES FOR TRANSLATION

169. Give the meanings of ἔσχον, ἐκώλῡσαν, ἦρξεν, ἐκελεύσατε, ἔλιπον, ἔπεισας, ἐπέμψαμεν, ἤγαγε, ἥρπασα.

170. I. 1. Πρόξενον δὲ τὸν Βοιώτιον ἐκέλευσεν ἥκειν. 2. ἡ δὲ Κίλισσα ἐθαύμασεν. 3. καὶ Κῦρος συν-έπεμψεν αὐτῇ τοὺς στρατιώτᾱς. 4. καὶ τοὺς στρατηγοὺς ἐκέλευσεν ὁπλίτᾱς ἀγαγεῖν.[1] 5. εἰς φυγὴν ἔτρεψε τοὺς στρατιώτᾱς. 6. ἐπεὶ δὲ Κλέαρχος ἔλαβε τὸ χρῡσίον, στρατιώτᾱς συν-έλεξεν. 7. καὶ τὰς ἁμάξᾱς οἱ σὺν Ἀρταξέρξῃ δι-ήρπασαν. 8. ἐπειδὴ δὲ Κῦρος τοὺς στρατιώτᾱς παρ-ήλασεν, ἔπεμψεν ἄνθρωπον πιστὸν παρὰ τοὺς στρατηγούς. 9. συν-εβούλευσεν οὖν αὐτοῖς μὴ λῦσαι τὴν γέφῡραν. 10. ἔφη δὲ Κῦρον ἐπιβουλεῦσαι τῷ ἀδελφῷ Ἀρταξέρξῃ. 11. Κλέαρχον δὲ κελεύουσι πέμψαι φυλακὴν παρὰ τὴν γέφῡραν.

[1] §§ 87, 98.

II. 1. The men with Cyrus had thoroughly plundered the land.   2. When the Cilician woman had ridden past the soldiers, she admired them.   3. We put[1] the enemy to flight.

XV

THE DEMONSTRATIVE PRONOUNS.   USES OF THE DE-
MONSTRATIVES.   PREDICATE POSITION OF THE
DEMONSTRATIVES.   NAME OF RIVER IN ATTRIBU-
TIVE POSITION.   PARTITIVE GENITIVE.   DATIVE
OF TIME.   COGNATE ACCUSATIVE

DECLENSION OF οὗτος *this*, ὅδε *this*, **AND** ἐκεῖνος *that*

		MASC.	FEM.	NEUT.
171.	Sing. N.	οὗτος *this*	αὕτη	τοῦτο
	G.	τούτου	ταύτης	τούτου
	D.	τούτῳ	ταύτῃ	τούτῳ
	A.	τοῦτον	ταύτην	τοῦτο
	Dual N. A.	τούτω	τούτω	τούτω
	G. D.	τούτοιν	τούτοιν	τούτοιν
	Plur. N.	οὗτοι	αὗται	ταῦτα
	G.	τούτων	τούτων	τούτων
	D.	τούτοις	ταύταις	τούτοις
	A.	τούτους	ταύτᾱς	ταῦτα

172. NOTE. — The declension of οὗτος, αὕτη, τοῦτο may be remembered thus : (1) forms with initial τ occur in all cases in which the article ὁ, ἡ, τό has initial τ, and not otherwise ; thus τούτου (τοῦ), οὗτοι (οἱ). (2) The penult has ου when the ultima contains the o sound (o or ω); otherwise the penult has αυ.

---

[1] 1 aor.

173. ὅδε is simply the definite article ὁ, ἡ, τό, + an enclitic -δε.

		MASC.	FEM.	NEUT.
Sing.	N.	ὅδε *this*	ἥδε	τόδε
	G.	τοῦδε	τῆσδε	τοῦδε
	D.	τῷδε	τῇδε	τῷδε
	A.	τόνδε	τήνδε	τόδε
Dual	N. A.	τώδε	τώδε	τώδε
	G. D.	τοῖνδε	τοῖνδε	τοῖνδε
Plur.	N.	οἵδε	αἵδε	τάδε
	G.	τῶνδε	τῶνδε	τῶνδε
	D.	τοῖσδε	ταῖσδε	τοῖσδε
	A.	τούσδε	τάσδε	τάδε

174. For the declension of ἐκεῖνος *that* (Lat. *ille*), cp. ἄλλος, § 124.

		MASC.	FEM.	NEUT.
Sing.	N.	ἐκεῖνος	ἐκείνη	ἐκεῖνο
	G.	ἐκείνου	ἐκείνης	ἐκείνου
	D.	ἐκείνῳ	ἐκείνῃ	ἐκείνῳ
	A.	ἐκεῖνον	ἐκείνην	ἐκεῖνο
Dual	N. A.	ἐκείνω	ἐκείνω	ἐκείνω
	G. D.	ἐκείνοιν	ἐκείνοιν	ἐκείνοιν
Plur.	N.	ἐκεῖνοι	ἐκεῖναι	ἐκεῖνα
	G.	ἐκείνων	ἐκείνων	ἐκείνων
	D.	ἐκείνοις	ἐκείναις	ἐκείνοις
	A.	ἐκείνους	ἐκείνᾱς	ἐκεῖνα

USES OF THE DEMONSTRATIVES

175. While οὗτος and ὅδε both mean *this, this man*, etc., οὗτος often refers to what has preceded, and ὅδε to what is to follow :

οὐδὲ τοῦτο ἔφη he admitted not even this (something that has been mentioned) ;

συν-εβούλευσεν αὐτοῖς τάδε he advised them as follows.

 a. ἐκεῖνος means *that, that man*, etc., much like the Latin *ille*.

 b. All three of the words may be used as pronouns, *he, she, it*, etc., just like the Latin *hīc, iste*, and *ille*.

176. When used as demonstrative adjectives meaning *this* and *that*, οὗτος, ὅδε, and ἐκεῖνος must have the *predicate* position (§ 68):

> οὗτος ὁ ἄνθρωπος this man.

177. The Greek often prefers the plural ταῦτα *these things*, when in English we properly use the singular *this* :

> ταῦτα συν-εβούλευσεν he advised this.

178. The name of a **river** regularly stands between the article and the noun :

ὁ Εὐφράτης ποταμός the Euphrates river (cp. the Hudson river).

179. The genitive is often used to denote the whole, of which a part is taken (**partitive genitive**):

> ἄλλος τῶν στρατιωτῶν another of the soldiers.

 a. The partitive genitive usually has the predicate position :

οἱ ἀγαθοὶ τῶν λοχᾱγῶν the good men among (*lit.* of) the captains.

180. The **dative** (locative) is used to denote *time when :*

> ἐκείνῃ τῇ ἡμέρᾳ ἧκεν on that day he came.

Compare the genitive of *time within which* (§ 155) and the accusative of *time how long* (§ 142).

a. Sometimes the preposition ἐν is used with the dative of time :

ἐν τῇδε τῇ ἡμέρᾳ on this day.

181. Cognate accusative or accusative of the inner object. — The direct object of a verb may repeat in the form of a noun (or adjective or pronoun) a meaning similar to that of the verb :

φυλακὰς φυλάττειν to do guard duty (*lit.* to guard guardings) ;
συν-εβούλευσε τάδε he advised as follows, *i.e.* he advised these [pieces of advice].

182. VOCABULARY XV

For the meanings and uses of ἐκεῖνος, ὅδε, and οὗτος, see §§ 175–177.

ἀγοράζω (theme ἀγοραδ-), impf. ἠγόραζον, fut. ἀγοράσω, aor. ἠγόρασα: *buy.* Cp. ἀγορά.

δῆλος, η, ον: *plain, clear, evident.*

δύο, generally used indeclinably: *two.* Cp. Lat. *duo.*

ἑκατόν, indecl. : *hundred.*

ἐλαύνω (for ἐλα-νυ-ω, theme ἐλα-), impf. ἤλαυνον, fut. to be learned later, aor. ἤλασα (cp. § 165): *drive, ride, march.* Much less common than its compounds.

Εὐφράτης, ου, ὁ : *Euphrātes.*

καὶ γάρ : *and in fact* ; or *for also, for even.* Sometimes may be rendered *yes, for*.

μέντοι, postpositive particle : *however, yet.*

μετά (before smooth breathing μετ᾽, before rough breathing μεθ᾽, § 31), prep.: with GEN. *with, in company with* ; with ACC. *into the midst of, after.*

παρασάγγης, ου, ὁ: *parasang,* a Persian measure of distance, about 3.3 English miles. Cp. our *league* (3 miles).

ὑστεραῖος, ᾱ, ον: *later, following.* τῇ ὑστεραίᾳ (supply ἡμέρᾳ) : *on the following day* (§ 180).

φυλάττω, impf. ἐφύλαττον, fut. φυλάξω, aor. ἐφύλαξα: *guard.* Cp. φυλακή.

NOTE. — The present of φυλάττω is formed from the theme φυλακ· plus the present suffix y%, κ + y by a euphonic law becoming ττ. Cp. § 153, footnote.

EXERCISES FOR TRANSLATION

183. I. 1. μετὰ ταῦτα Κῦρος ἐξ-ελαύνει ἐπὶ τὸν Εὐφράτην ποταμόν.   2. τοὺς δὲ στρατηγοὺς ἤγαγε διὰ
ταύτης τῆς χώρᾱς.   3. ἐκ ταύτης τῆς κώμης οἱ στρατιῶται ἠγόραζον τὰ ἐπιτήδεια.   4. ταύτην τὴν ἐπιστολὴν ὁ Κῦρος ἔλαβεν.   5. Ξενίᾱς μέντοι τούτων τῶν
στρατιωτῶν ἦρχεν.   6. οὐδ᾽ ἄλλος τῶν στρατιωτῶν ἐκ
ταύτης τῆς μάχης ἔφυγεν.   7. καὶ γὰρ στρατηγοὶ καὶ
λοχᾱγοὶ ἐφύλαττον ἐκεῖνον.   8. τοῦτον τὸν οἶνον τοῖς
φίλοις Κῦρος ἔπεμψεν.   9. τοὺς μέντοι ἀγαθοὺς τῶν
πελταστῶν συν-έλεξεν.   10. δῆλον δὲ τοῦτο τῇ ὑστεραίᾳ ἦν.   11. διὰ τούτου τοῦ πεδίου ἤλασε σταθμοὺς
δύο παρασάγγᾱς¹ δέκα.   12. ἦσαν δ᾽ οὖν οὗτοι ἑκατὸν
ὁπλῖται.   13. οἵ τε στρατηγοὶ καὶ οἱ λοχᾱγοὶ συν-
εβούλευσαν αὐτοῖς τάδε.

II. 1. Thence he marched five days' journey to the
Euphrates river.   2. These soldiers were not slain² on
that day.   3. The soldiers do guard duty.   4. He came
with³ his friends.   5. This wine he will send to his friends.

---

¹ § 142.   ² 2 aor. of ἀπο-θνῄσκω.   ³ Use μετά with the proper case.

Fig. 6. — Δρόμος.

XVI

GENERAL REVIEW

184. A thorough review of the past lessons is now most advisable. Of first importance is the vocabulary; and all the words hitherto given are here collected in alphabetical order (§ 186). They should be committed to memory from English into Greek as well as from Greek into English. The student should *make a list* of the English meanings and then write the Greek equivalents opposite. The same plan of review should be frequently followed later.

This list of words must be *thoroughly* mastered. It is a help to the memory to associate words that show the same stems and roots (*e.g.* χώρᾱ with χωρίον, λοχᾱγός with λόχος and ἄγω) and to recall similar stems in English (*e.g.* **philanthropy** from φίλος and ἄνθρωπος). See the special vocabularies for suggestions of this sort.

When verbs occur in the following list, the first persons singular of the imperfect, future, and aorist (first or second) are also given. In a few instances, however, certain verb forms have had to be postponed to a more advanced period of study. They may always be found in the general VOCABULARY.

Hereafter the imperfect will not be given, unless it shows an irregularity.

Typical words from the following list should be inflected both in written work and orally.

185. A common negative prefix is ἀ(ν)-; it is equivalent to Latin *in-* and English *un-*. It is known as *alpha priva-tive.* Cp. ἀ-διάβατος, ἀ-φύλακτος.

186.

ἀγαθός

ἀγορά

ἀγοράζω (cp. ἀγορά), ἠγόραζον, ἀγοράσω, ἠγόρασα

ἄγω, ἦγον, ἄξω, ἤγαγον

ἀδελφός

ἀδιάβατος (ἀ- priv. + δια-βαίνω)

ἀλλά (cp. ἄλλος)

ἄλλος

ἅμα, ἅμα τῇ ἡμέρᾳ

ἅμαξα

ἄνθρωπος

ἀπό

ἀπο-θνῄσκω, ἀπ-έθνῃσκον, fut. to be
learned later, ἀπ-έθανον

ἀπο-πέμπω, ἀπ-έπεμπον, ἀπο-πέμψω,
ἀπ-έπεμψα

ἄπορος

ἀπο-φεύγω, ἀπ-έφευγον, fut. to be
learned later, ἀπ-έφυγον

ἁρπάζω, ἥρπαζον, ἁρπάσω, ἥρπασα

Ἀρταξέρξης

ἀρχή (ἄρχω)

ἄρχω, ἦρχον, ἄρξω, ἦρξα

αὐτός

ἀφύλακτος (cp. φυλακή)

βάρβαρος

Βοιώτιος

γάρ

γέφῡρα

δέ

δέκα

δῆλος

διά

δια-βαίνω, δι-έβαινον, fut. and aor.
to be learned later

δι-αρπάζω, δι-ήρπαζον, δι-αρπάσω,
δι-ήρπασα

δίκη

δρόμος (ἔδραμον)

δύο

ἔδραμον

ἐθέλω, ἤθελον, ἐθελήσω, ἠθέλησα

εἰ

εἰμί, ἐστί(ν), ἔστι(ν), εἶναι

εἰς

εἶτα

ἐκ

ἑκατόν

ἐκεῖνος

ἐλαύνω, ἤλαυνον, fut. to be learned
later, ἤλασα

ἐμός

ἐν

ἐνταῦθα

ἐντεῦθεν

ἐξ-άγω, ἐξ-ῆγον, ἐξ-άξω, ἐξ-ήγαγον

ἐξ-ελαύνω, ἐξ-ήλαυνον, fut. to be
learned later, ἐξ-ήλασα

ἐπεί

ἐπειδή

ἐπί

ἐπι βουλεύω, ἐπ-εβούλευον, ἐπι-
βουλεύσω, ἐπ-εβούλευσα

ἐπιστολή

ἐπιτήδειος, τὰ ἐπιτήδεια

ἔργον

εὐθύς

Εὐφρᾱτης

ἔφασαν, ἔφη

ἔχω, εἶχον, ἕξω or σχήσω, ἔσχον

ἤ, ἡ δέ

ἥκω, ἧκον, ἥξω (these are all the
tenses)

ἡμέρᾱ

ἡμέτερος

ἦν

ἦσαν

θάλαττα

θαυμάζω, ἐθαύμαζον, fut. to be
   learned later, ἐθαύμασα

θεός

ἵππος

καί, καί . . . καί, καὶ γάρ

κακός

καλός

κελεύω, ἐκέλευον, κελεύσω, ἐκέλευσα

Κιλικίᾱ

Κίλισσα (cp. Κιλικίᾱ)

Κλέαρχος

Κῦρος

κωλύω, ἐκώλῡον, κωλύσω, ἐκώλῡσα

κώμη

λαμβάνω, ἐλάμβανον, fut. to be
   learned later, ἔλαβον

λείπω, ἔλειπον, λείψω, ἔλιπον

λόγος

λόφος

λοχᾱγός (λόχος, ἄγω)

λόχος

λύω, ἔλῡον, λύσω, ἔλῡσα

μάχη

μέλλω, ἔμελλον, μελλήσω, ἐμέλλησα

μέν

μέντοι

μεστός

μετά

μεταξύ (cp. μετά)

μή

νίκη

νομίζω, ἐνόμιζον, fut. to be learned
   later, ἐνόμισα

Ξενίᾱς

ὁ, ὁ δέ, ὁ μέν . . . ὁ δέ

ὅδε

ὁδός

οἰκίᾱ

οἱ μέν . . . οἱ δέ

οἶνος

ὁπλίτης (ὅπλα)

ὅπλον, ὅπλα

ὄρθιος

ὅρκος

ὅς

οὐ, οὐκ, οὐχ

οὐδέ

οὖν

οὔτε . . . οὔτε

οὗτος

παίω, ἔπαιον, παίσω, ἔπαισα

πάλιν

παλτόν

παρά

παρασάγγης

πάρ-ειμι, παρ-ῆν, fut. to be learned
   later, no aor.

παρ-ελαύνω, παρ-ήλαυνον, fut. to be
   learned later, παρ-ήλασα

παρ-έχω, παρ-εῖχον, παρ-έξω or παρα-
   σχήσω, παρ-έσχον

πάροδος (παρά + ὁδός)

πεδίον

πεζός (cp. πεδίον), οἱ πεζοί

πείθω, ἔπειθον, πείσω, ἔπεισα

πελταστής

πέμπω, ἔπεμπον, πέμψω, ἔπεμψα

πέντε

περί

Πῑσίδαι

πιστός (cp. πείθω), τὰ πιστά

πλοῖον

πολέμιος, οἱ πολέμιοι

ποταμός

Πρόξενος

πρός

σῖτος
σκηνή
σός
σπονδή, σπονδαί
σταθμός
στενός
στόλος (cp. ἐπι-στολή)
στρατηγός (cp. στρατιά and ἄγω)
στρατιά
στρατιώτης (cp. στρατιά)
συλ-λαμβάνω, συν-ελάμβανον, fut. to be learned later, συν-έλαβον
συλ-λέγω, συν-έλεγον, συλ-λέξω, συν-έλεξα
συμ-βουλεύω, συν-εβούλευον, συμ-βουλεύσω, συν-εβούλευσα
συμ-πέμπω, συν-έπεμπον, συμ-πέμψω, συν-έπεμψα
σύν
συν-άγω, συν-ῆγον, συν-άξω, συν-ήγαγον
τάφρος

τε, τε . . . καί
τό
τοξότης
τρέπω, ἔτρεπον, τρέψω, ἔτρεψα
ὑμέτερος
ὑστεραῖος, τῇ ὑστεραίᾳ
φᾱσί(ν)
φεύγω, ἔφευγον, fut. to be learned later, ἔφυγον
φησί(ν)
φίλος
φόβος
φυγή (cp. φεύγω)
φυλακή
φυλάττω, ἐφύλαττον, φυλάξω, ἐφύλαξα (cp. φυλακή)
Χειρίσοφος
χρῡσίον
χώρᾱ
χωρίον (cp. χώρᾱ)
ὦ
ὥστε

XVII

CONSONANT DECLENSION: STEMS ENDING IN A MUTE (PALATAL OR LABIAL). μέσος IN PREDICATE POSITION

STEMS ENDING IN A PALATAL OR LABIAL MUTE

187.

Sing. N. V.	κῆρυξ, ὁ, *herald*	φάλαγξ, ἡ, *phalanx*
G.	κήρῡκ-ος	φάλαγγ-ος
D.	κήρῡκ-ι	φάλαγγ-ι
A.	κήρῡκ-α	φάλαγγ-α
Dual N. A. V.	κήρῡκ-ε	φάλαγγ-ε
G. D.	κηρῡ́κ-οιν	φαλάγγ-οιν

Plur. N. V.	κήρῡκ-ες		φάλαγγ-ες
G.	κηρῡ́κ-ων		φαλάγγ-ων
D.	κήρῡξι(ν)[1]		φάλαγξι(ν)[2]
A.	κήρῡκ-ας		φάλαγγ-ᾰς
Sing. N. V.	διῶρυξ, ἡ, *trench*		κλώψ, ὁ, *thief*
G.	διώρυχ-ος		κλωπ-ός
D.	διώρυχ-ι		κλωπ-ί
A.	διώρυχ-α		κλῶπ-α
Dual N. A. V.	διώρυχ-ε		κλῶπ-ε
G. D.	διωρύχ-οιν		κλωπ-οῖν
Plur. N. V.	διώρυχ-ες		κλῶπ-ες
G.	διωρύχ-ων		κλωπ-ῶν
D.	διώρυξι(ν)[1]		κλωψί(ν)[1]
A.	διώρυχ-ας		κλῶπ-ας

188. The stem of a noun of the consonant declension is seen when the ending -ος is dropped from the genitive singular. Thus the stems of the preceding nouns are respectively κηρῡκ-, φαλαγγ-, διωρυχ-, κλωπ-.

189. The accent of the paradigms of κῆρυξ, φάλαγξ, and διῶρυξ comes under laws already learned (§§ 57, 59). But κλώψ, a word of *one* syllable, comes under a new law, peculiar to the consonant declension : Monosyllables of the consonant declension are accented on the ultima in the genitive and dative of all numbers, — with the circumflex, if the ultima has a long vowel or diphthong, otherwise with the acute.

190. The nominative singular of the preceding nouns ends in *sigma;* the dative plural in -σι. With κ, γ, or χ, *sigma* unites to form ξ, as has already been explained (§ 153. 2); with π, β, or φ, *sigma* unites to form ψ (§ 153. 1).

191. -ας of the accusative plural is short in the consonant declension, but long in the ā-declension (§ 93).

---

[1] Cp. § 32.

192. μέσος in the predicate position has a partitive sense, meaning *middle of :*

ἡ φάλαγξ μέση or μέση ἡ φάλαγξ the middle of the phalanx;

but ἡ μέση φάλαγξ means *the middle phalanx, i.e.* between two others.

193. VOCABULARY XVII

ἀκούω, fut. to be learned later, ἤκουσα: *hear, hear of, listen.* With object in gen. or acc. Acoustic.

ἀμφί (may be elided, ἀμφ', before a vowel), prep.: with GEN. *concerning, about* (but in prose περί is generally used in this sense); with ACC. *about.* οἱ ἀμφὶ Κῦρον: *Cyrus and his men* (lit. those [the men] about Cyrus). Amphi-bious (βίος *life*), amphi-theater (θέᾱτρον).

δι-έχω (for other forms, see ἔχω): *be apart, be separated.*

διώκω, διώξω, ἐδίωξα: *pursue.*

διῶρυξ, υχος, ἡ: *trench, canal.*

Θρᾷξ, Θρᾳκός, ὁ: *a Thracian, Thracian.*

θώρᾱξ, ᾱκος, ὁ: *breastplate.* See p. 86, Fig. 7. Thorax.

κῆρυξ, ῡκος, ὁ: *herald.*

κλώψ, κλωπός, ὁ: *thief.* Klepto-mania (μανίᾱ *madness*).

μέσος, η, ον: *middle, middle of.* ἐν μέσῳ: *in the midst, between* (with gen.). μέσος in predicate position means *middle of* (§ 192). Meso-potamia (ποταμός).

ὅλος, η, ον: *whole, entire, all.* Holo-caust (κάω *burn*).

οὐκ-έτι, adv.: *no longer, no more.*

πη, enclitic adv.: *anywhere.*

πρό (like περί, never suffers elision of the final vowel), prep. with gen. only: *before, in front of.* Lat. *prō.*

σάλπιγξ, ιγγος, ἡ: *trumpet.*

στάδιον, ου, τό: *stadium* (race course); then a measure of distance, *stade,* 600 Greek feet. Pl. both στάδιοι, οἱ, and στάδια, τά. See p. 95, Fig. 9.

φάλαγξ, αγγος, ἡ: *line of battle.* Phalanx.

φύλαξ, ακος, ὁ: *guard, sentinel.* Cp. φυλακή.

χίλιοι, αι, α: *thousand.* Kilo-meter (μέτρον *measure*).

EXERCISES FOR TRANSLATION

194. I. 1. κήρῡκας δὲ ἔπεμψε περὶ σπονδῶν. 2. πάρεστι δ' ὁ κῆρυξ. 3. τοὺς δὲ κλῶπας ἔλαβον. 4. καὶ

Κλέαρχος εἶχεν ὁπλίτᾱς χῑλίους καὶ πελταστὰς Θρᾶκας.
5. οἱ δὲ ἀμφὶ Ξενίᾱν ἤκουσαν τῆς σάλπιγγος. 6. Κῦρος
δὲ καὶ οἱ στρατιῶται αὐτοῦ εἶχον θώρᾱκας. 7. καὶ οὐκέτι δύο στάδια¹ δι-εῖχον αἱ φάλαγγες. 8. οἱ δὲ βάρβαροι ἦσαν ἐν μέσῳ τοῦ ποταμοῦ καὶ τῆς διώρυχος. 9. πρὸ
τῆς φάλαγγος μέσης ἦν Κῦρος. 10. οἱ δὲ πολέμιοι
αὐτοὶ ἔχουσι φύλακας. 11. εἰ δέ πῃ τοῦτο ἦν,² τῇ ὅλῃ
φάλαγγι κακὸν ἦν. 12. οἱ δὲ φύλακες ἐδίωξαν τοὺς
κλῶπας.

II. 1. We shall send heralds to Cyrus.   2. We think
we shall send heralds to Cyrus.   3. Between the canal and
the river are the guards of the enemy.   4. Our soldiers
no longer heard the trumpet.   5. Clearchus and his men
ran into the middle of the river.

---

¹ Cp. § 142.   ² = *happened.*

Fɪɢ. 7. — Θώρᾱξ.

XVIII

CONSONANT DECLENSION (*Continued*).   STEMS ENDING
IN A MUTE (LINGUAL).   GENITIVE OF SEPARATION

STEMS ENDING IN A LINGUAL MUTE

195.

Sing. N. V.	ἀσπίς, ἡ, *shield*	πούς, ὁ, *foot*	νύξ, ἡ, *night*
G.	ἀσπίδ-ος	ποδ-ός	νυκτ-ός
D.	ἀσπίδ-ι	ποδ-ί	νυκτ-ί
A.	ἀσπίδ-α	πόδ-α	νύκτ-α
Dual N. A. V.	ἀσπίδ-ε	πόδ-ε	νύκτ-ε
G. D.	ἀσπίδ-οιν	ποδ-οῖν	νυκτ-οῖν
Plur. N. V.	ἀσπίδ-ες	πόδ-ες	νύκτ-ες
G.	ἀσπίδ-ων	ποδ-ῶν	νυκτ-ῶν
D.	ἀσπί-σι(ν) [1]	πο-σί(ν) [1]	νυξί(ν) [1]
A.	ἀσπίδ-ας	πόδ-ας	νύκτ-ας

Sing. N. V.	ἄρχων, ὁ, *ruler*	χάρις, ἡ, *grace, gratitude*
G.	ἄρχοντ-ος	χάριτ-ος
D.	ἄρχοντ-ι	χάριτ-ι
A.	ἄρχοντ-α	χάρι-ν
Dual N. A. V.	ἄρχοντ-ε	χάριτ-ε
G. D.	ἀρχόντ-οιν	χαρίτ-οιν
Plur. N. V.	ἄρχοντ-ες	χάριτ-ες
G.	ἀρχόντ-ων	χαρίτ-ων
D.	ἄρχου-σι(ν) [1]	χάρι-σι(ν) [1]
A.	ἄρχοντ-ας	χάριτ-ας

Sing. N. A. V.	στράτευμα, τό, *army*
G.	στρατεύματ-ος
D.	στρατεύματ-ι
Dual N. A. V.	στρατεύματ-ε
G. D.	στρατευμάτ-οιν
Plur. N. A. V.	στρατεύματ-α
G.	στρατευμάτ-ων
D.	στρατεύμα-σι(ν) [1]

---

[1] Cp. § 32.

ἀσπίς, πούς, νύξ, χάρις

196. Four nouns of this group form the nominative singular by adding *sigma* to the stem. The stem of ἀσπίς is ἀσπιδ- (§ 188). In the nominative singular and in the dative plural, before *sigma*, the lingual mute is dropped (§ 153. 3). So with πούς (stem ποδ-), νύξ (νυκτ-), and χάρις (χαριτ-). A lengthening of o to ου occurs when ποδς becomes πούς; this is irregular. Since τ drops before σ, νύξ is for νυκ[τ]ς; χάρις, for χαρι[τ]ς; νυξί (dative plural) is for νυκ[τ]σι.

197. The accusative singular of χάρις is χάριν, not χάριτα. The ending -ιν or -υν, in the accusative singular, belongs to almost all nouns with stems in *unaccented* ι or υ followed by a lingual mute. It does not belong to ἀσπίς, for -ιδ- is accented.

198. For the accent of the monosyllables πούς and νύξ, see § 189.

ἄρχων, στράτευμα

199. The remaining two nouns of the group form nominatives singular from the mere stem, without any ending. The stem of ἄρχων is ἀρχοντ-; of στράτευμα, στρατευματ-. In both instances, final τ of the stem is dropped, for a Greek word cannot end in τ (§ 10). ἄρχων, having o lengthened to ω in the nominative singular, is typical of all present active masculine participles of ω-verbs, *e.g.* λύων *loosing* and ἔχων *having*; as well as of such second aorist participles as λιπών *having left* (observe that the latter differs in accent).

a. στράτευμα is typical of a very large number of neuters of this declension.

200. ἄρχουσι(ν), the dative plural of ἄρχων, is for ἀρχοντσι(ν). In compensation for the loss of both ν and τ (for ν

must also be dropped before *sigma*, § 133. 4), o is length
ened to *ov*.

201. Genitive of separation. — Besides the *of* genitive
(§ 53. *f*), there is also a *from* genitive, which is used with
verbs (and adjectives and adverbs) to express separation,
source, and similar ideas. It corresponds to the Latin
"ablative of separation":

ἀπ-έχειν τῆς Ἑλλάδος to be distant from Greece.

The measure of distance, if added, is in the accusative
(§ 142).

202. VOCABULARY XVIII

ἀπ-έχω: *be distant, be away*, with
gen. of person or place, and acc.
of extent of space.

ἄρχων, οντος, ὁ: *ruler, commander*.
Really the pres. masc. partic.
of ἄρχω. Archon.

ἀσπίς, ίδος, ἡ: *shield*. See p. 97.

Δᾱρεῖος, ου, ὁ: *Darīus*.

Ἑλλάς, άδος, ἡ: *Hellas*, the name
given by the Hellēnes to their
own country. From the Ro-
mans they received the appellation *Greeks* and their land was
called *Greece* (Lat. *Graecī,
Graecia*).

ἦλθον 2 aor.: *I* or *they came* or
went; inflected like ἔλιπον;
inf. ἐλθεῖν.

κλέπτω (theme κλεπ-), κλέψω,
ἔκλεψα: *steal*. Cp. κλώψ.

κνημίς, ίδος, ἡ: *greave*. See p. 101.

Λακεδαιμόνιος, ᾱ, ον: belonging
to Λακεδαίμων (*Lacedaemon*),
Lacedaemonian, Spartan.

νύξ, νυκτός, ἡ: *night*. μέσαι νύκτες: *midnight* (middle watches
of the night). Lat. *nox*.

ὄρνῑς, ῑθος, ὁ and ἡ: *bird*. Ornitho-
logy (λόγος *account*).

ὅτε, rel. adv.: *when, at the time when*,
commonly with impf. indic.

παῖς, παιδός, ὁ and ἡ: *child, boy, girl*.
The gen. and dat. dual is exceptionally accented παίδοιν, and
the gen. pl. παίδων. The voc.
sing. is παῖ. Ped-agogue (ἄγω).

πούς, ποδός, ὁ: *foot*. Also the
Greek unit of length. Lat.
pēs. Tri-pod (τρεῖς, τρία *three*).

στράτευμα, ατος, τό (cp. στρατιά):
army.

τόξευμα, ατος, τό (cp. τοξότης):
arrow.

φυγάς, άδος, ὁ (cp. φεύγω): *fugitive, exile*.

χάρις, ιτος, ἡ: *grace, favor, gratitude*. χάριν ἔχειν: *feel thankful*, with dat.

EXERCISES FOR TRANSLATION

263. I. 1. Κλέαρχος Λακεδαιμόνιος φυγὰς ἦν. 2. τοὺς δὲ φυγάδας ἐκέλευσε παρ-εῖναι. 3. ἐκέλευσε δὲ τὸν στρατηγὸν ἀπο-πέμψαι ὃ εἶχε στράτευμα.¹ 4. οἱ δὲ στρατιῶται εἶχον κνημῖδας καὶ ἀσπίδας. 5. ἐν δὲ ταῖς οἰκίαις ἦσαν ὄρνῖθες. 6. καὶ τοῖς τῶν πολεμίων ἄρχουσιν οὐκ ἐπ-εβούλευεν. 7. ἀπ-εῖχον δὲ τῆς Ἑλλάδος χίλια στάδια. 8. ἐπὶ δὲ τὰ ὅπλα οὐκ ἦλθον ταύτην τὴν νύκτα.² 9. ὅτε δὲ ταῦτα ἦν, μέσαι ἦσαν νύκτες. 10. ἀκούω τοὺς Λακεδαιμονίους εὐθὺς ἐκ παίδων³ κλέπτειν.⁴ 11. καὶ λαμβάνουσιν αὐτὸν καὶ τοὺς παῖδας καὶ τοὺς ἵππους. 12. τὰ δὲ τοξεύματα ἦλθε διὰ τῶν ἀσπίδων καὶ διὰ τῶν θωράκων. 13. Δαρείῳ δὲ ἦσαν παῖδες δύο, Ἀρταξέρξης καὶ Κῦρος. 14. τοῖς οὖν θεοῖς χάριν ἔχομεν. 15. ἐθαύμασαν δὲ τὰ πρὸ⁵ ποδῶν.

II. 1. The soldiers have beautiful shields. 2. They are distant from Greece a hundred parasangs. 3. I hear that the commanders are⁶ brave. 4. I hear the soldiers took the shields.

---

¹ *I.e.* τὸ στράτευμα ὃ εἶχε.
² *during this night*, § 142.
³ *from boyhood.*

⁴ § 110. *a.*
⁵ *the things before.*
⁶ Cp. sentence 10 above.

Fig. 8. — Σάλπιγξ.

XIX

DECLENSION OF PRESENT, FUTURE, AND AORIST AC-
TIVE PARTICIPLES OF THE Ω–VERB. DECLENSION
OF ὤν. ATTRIBUTIVE PARTICIPLES. SUBSTANTIVE
PARTICIPLES. CIRCUMSTANTIAL PARTICIPLES OF
TIME, CAUSE, ETC. SUPPLEMÉNTARY PARTICIPLES
WITH τυγχάνω

DECLENSION OF PARTICIPLES IN -ων, -ουσα, -ον

204. Participles in -ων (with stems in -οντ-) are declined,
in the masculine, like ἄρχων (§ 195). The neuter nominative and accusative singular consists of the mere stem,
which drops τ, since this letter cannot end a Greek word
(§ 10). The neuter nominative and accusative plural ends
in -α. Otherwise the neuter forms are like the masculine.
The feminine of these participles, ending in -ουσα, is
declined like θάλαττα (§ 140).

ὤν *being*, PRESENT PARTICIPLE OF εἰμί (§ 101)

		MASC.	FEM.	NEUT.
205.	Sing. N. V.	ὤν	οὖσα	ὄν
	G.	ὄντος	οὔσης	ὄντος
	D.	ὄντι	οὔσῃ	ὄντι
	A.	ὄντα	οὖσαν	ὄν
	Dual N. A. V.	ὄντε	οὔσᾱ	ὄντε
	G. D.	ὄντοιν	οὔσαιν	ὄντοιν
	Plur. N. V.	ὄντες	οὖσαι	ὄντα
	G.	ὄντων	οὐσῶν	ὄντων
	D.	οὖσι(ν)	οὔσαις	οὖσι(ν)
	A.	ὄντας	οὔσᾱς	ὄντα

a. The accent of ὤν in the genitive and dative, masculine and neuter, of all numbers is exceptional (§ 189).

κωλΰων *hindering*, PRESENT PARTICIPLE OF κωλΰω

		MASC.	FEM.	NEUT.
206.	Sing. N. V.	κωλΰων	κωλΰουσα	κωλῦον
	G.	κωλΰοντος	κωλυούσης	κωλΰοντος
	D.	κωλΰοντι	κωλυούσῃ	κωλΰοντι
	A.	κωλΰοντα	κωλΰουσαν	κωλῦον
	Dual N. A. V.	κωλΰοντε	κωλυούσᾱ	κωλΰοντε
	G. D.	κωλῡόντοιν	κωλυούσαιν	κωλῡόντοιν
	Plur. N. V.	κωλΰοντες	κωλΰουσαι	κωλΰοντα
	G.	κωλῡόντων	κωλυουσῶν	κωλῡόντων
	D.	κωλΰουσι(ν)	κωλυούσαις	κωλΰουσι(ν)
	A.	κωλΰοντας	κωλυούσᾱς	κωλΰοντα

a. κωλΰων is used in the paradigm, instead of λΰων, λΰουσα, λῦον, *loosing*, in order to show the accent in the neuter κωλῦον (not recessive). The two words are declined alike.

207. λΰσων, λΰσουσα, λῦσον, *about to loose*, future participle of λΰω, is declined like the present participle λΰων or κωλΰων.

SECOND AORIST PARTICIPLES IN -ών, -οῦσα, -όν

λιπών *having left*, SECOND AORIST ACTIVE PARTICIPLE OF λείπω

		MASC.	FEM.	NEUT.
208.	Sing. N. V.	λιπών	λιποῦσα	λιπόν
	G.	λιπόντος	λιπούσης	λιπόντος
	D.	λιπόντι	λιπούσῃ	λιπόντι
	A.	λιπόντα	λιποῦσαν	λιπόν
	Dual N. A. V.	λιπόντε	λιπούσᾱ	λιπόντε
	G. D.	λιπόντοιν	λιπούσαιν	λιπόντοιν
	Plur. N. V.	λιπόντες	λιποῦσαι	λιπόντα
	G.	λιπόντων	λιπουσῶν	λιπόντων
	D.	λιποῦσι(ν)	λιπούσαις	λιποῦσι(ν)
	A.	λιπόντας	λιπούσᾱς	λιπόντα

a. Observe that λιπών is accented like ὤν (§ 205).

FIRST AORIST ACTIVE PARTICIPLES IN -ᾱς, -ᾱσα, -αν

ἀκούσᾱς *having heard*, FIRST AORIST ACTIVE PARTICIPLE OF
ἀκούω (STEM ἀκουσαντ-)

		MASC.	FEM.	NEUT.
209.	Sing. N. V.	ἀκούσᾱς	ἀκούσᾱσα	ἀκοῦσαν
	G.	ἀκούσαντος	ἀκουσάσης	ἀκούσαντος
	D.	ἀκούσαντι	ἀκουσάσῃ	ἀκούσαντι
	A.	ἀκούσαντα	ἀκούσᾱσαν	ἀκοῦσαν
	Dual N. A. V.	ἀκούσαντε	ἀκουσάσᾱ	ἀκούσαντε
	G. D.	ἀκουσάντοιν	ἀκουσάσαιν	ἀκουσάντοιν
	Plur. N. V.	ἀκούσαντες	ἀκούσᾱσαι	ἀκούσαντα
	G.	ἀκουσάντων	ἀκουσᾱσῶν	ἀκουσάντων
	D.	ἀκούσᾱσι(ν)	ἀκουσάσαις	ἀκούσᾱσι(ν)
	A.	ἀκούσαντας	ἀκουσάσᾱς	ἀκούσαντα

a. ἀκούσᾱς is for ἀκουσαντς; the loss of ντ before *sigma* in both nominative singular and dative plural is compensated by the lengthening of *a* to *ᾱ* (cp. § 200).

b. λύσᾱς *having loosed* is declined like ἀκούσᾱς.

210. For the agreement of the participle with its noun, see § 53. *i.*

211. The participle is often used as an **attributive** adjective :

τὸν βασιλεύοντα[1] Ἀρταξέρξην the reigning Artaxerxes.

a. The participle may of course take one of the other attributive positions (§§ 67, 69).

212. The participle is very often used as a **substantive**, when it may be translated by a relative clause or by a noun :

οἱ παρ-όντες those who are present ;
ὁ κελεύων the man who commands ;

---

[1] Pres. partic. of βασιλεύω *be king.*

οἱ κωλύσοντες those who will hinder;

οἱ ἐθέλοντες φυγῆς ἄρχειν those that wish to begin flight;

ὁ φεύγων the fugitive, the exile;

ὁ ἄρχων the ruler;

ὁ ἄρξας the man who had (*or* has) ruled.

213. Circumstantial participle. — The participle is very often used without the article, in agreement with a noun, to define the circumstances of an action. This, the circumstantial participle, is most often equivalent to a clause expressing time or cause:

(*Of time*) Κλέαρχος δὲ λαβὼν τὸ χρυσίον στράτευμα συν-έλεξεν and when Clearchus had received the gold, he collected an army;

(*Of cause*) τὴν χώραν δι-ήρπασεν ὡς πολεμίαν οὖσαν he laid waste the country, since, as-he-alleged (= ὡς), it was hostile.

a. The word ὡς is not essential to the latter construction; but its force (lit. *as*) must be observed when it is used.

b. Particularly to be noticed is the use of ἔχων and λαβών in the sense of *with*, expressing an attendant circumstance:

καὶ ἧκε Κλέαρχος ἔχων ὁπλίτᾱς and Clearchus came with hoplites.

c. The circumstantial participle may also express condition (*if*), concession (*although*), manner, and means.

214. The time of the participle is commonly relative to that of the main verb. That is, the present participle indicates the same time with the finite verb, the aorist participle prior time, and the future participle subsequent time. But these distinctions do not always hold, particularly in case of the present and aorist participles.

215. Supplementary participle. — The participle is often used to complete the idea expressed by the main verb. This is known as the supplementary participle. Of the important constructions under this head, only one is introduced in the present lesson: the participle with τυγχάνω *happen, chance:*

ὁ δὲ παρ-ὼν ἐτύγχανε and he happened to be present, *or* and he was present, as it happened.

216. The negative with the participle is regularly οὐ; but the conditional participle takes μή.

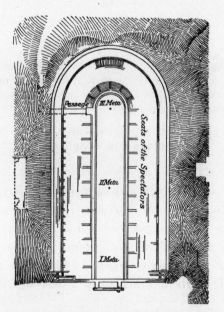

FIG. 9. — Ground Plan of the Stadium at Athens.

217.   VOCABULARY XIX

ἀπ-ῆλθον, 2 aor. indic.: *I* or *they went away*. Inf. ἀπ-ελθεῖν, partic. ἀπ-ελθών.

'Αρίστιππος, ου, ὁ: *Aristippus*.

βασίλειος, ον: *of a king, royal*. τὰ βασίλεια (neut. pl. subst.) : *the royal buildings, the palace*.

βασιλεύω, βασιλεύσω, ἐβασίλευσα: *be king, rule as king*.

εἶδον, 2 aor. indic.: *I* or *they saw*. Inf. ἰδεῖν, partic. ἰδών.

κινδῡνεύω, κινδῡνεύσω, ἐκινδῡνευσα: *incur danger, run a risk*.

λαμπρότης, ητος, ἡ: *splendor, brilliancy*.

ξένος, ου, ὁ: *guest-friend*.

πεντακόσιοι, αι, α: *five hundred*. Cp. πέντε.

πρᾱ́ττω (theme πρᾱγ-), πρᾱ́ξω, ἔπρᾱξα: *accomplish, effect, do*.

Συρίᾱ, ᾱς, ἡ: *Syria*.

τυγχάνω (theme τυχ-), fut. to be learned later, 2 aor. ἔτυχον: *hit* (with gen.); *happen, chance* (with supplementary partic.).

χρῆμα, ατος, τό: a thing of use; commonly pl., *possessions, money*.

218. NOTE. — The present of πρᾱ́ττω is formed from the theme πρᾱγ + present suffix *y*%; γ + *y* by a euphonic law becoming ττ. Cp. φυλάττω, § 182, NOTE.

The present of τυγχάνω is formed from the theme τυχ + present suffix αν%. ν, taking the form γ nasal by § 133. 2, is inserted in the theme proper before χ. A similar formation is seen in λαμβάνω (theme λαβ-). In the last verb, ν inserted before β becomes μ (§ 133. 1).

EXERCISES FOR TRANSLATION

219. I. 1. ὁ δ' ἀπ-ῆλθε κινδῡνεύσᾱς.   2. ἡ δὲ Κίλισσα ἰδοῦσα τὴν λαμπρότητα τοῦ στρατεύματος ἐθαύμασεν.   3. ὁ δὲ λαβὼν τὸ χρῡσίον στράτευμα συν-έλεξεν ἀπὸ[1] τούτων τῶν χρημάτων.   4. Πρόξενος δὲ παρ-ῆν ἔχων ὁπλίτᾱς εἰς[2] πεντακοσίους καὶ χῑλίους.   5. οἱ δὲ στρατιῶται ταῦτα ἀκούσαντες ἀπ-ῆλθον.   6. ἀγαθός ἐστιν ὁ κελεύων τὰ πλοῖα λαβεῖν.   7. ἐν-

---

[1] *I.e. with the aid of.*   [2] *to the number of.*

ταῦθα ἦν τὰ Δαρείου βασίλεια τοῦ Συρίας ἄρξαντος.
8. καὶ σὺν τοῖς παρ-οῦσι τῶν πιστῶν¹ ἦκεν ἐλαύνων εἰς
τὸ μέσον.² 9. οἱ δὲ ταῦτα ἔπραξαν, ἀγαγόντες χῑλίους
ὁπλίτᾱς. 10. καὶ ἰδὼν τὰς κώμᾱς, ἦκεν ἐλαύνων πρὸς
τοὺς ὁπλίτᾱς. 11. Ἀρίστιππος δὲ ξένος ὢν ἐτύγχανεν αὐτῷ.³ 12. ταῦτα ἔπραξε σὺν τῷ βασιλεύοντι
Ἀρταξέρξῃ.

II. 1. Aristippus happened to see the gold. 2. After
the generals had led soldiers to the number of a thousand
into the village, they went away. 3. Since Proxenus was
not present, he did not see those that were⁴ in the house.

---

¹ Subst. adj. masc. in part. gen. (§ 179), *of his trusty men.*
² Subst. *the midst.*   ³ Dat. of possession, § 119.   ⁴ that were = *being.*

FIG. 10. — Ἀσπίδες.

XX

CONSONANT DECLENSION (*Continued*). STEMS ENDING
IN A LIQUID. DECLENSION OF ADJECTIVES IN
-ων, -ον. INFINITIVE WITH δεῖ, χρή, ἔξεστιν, ETC.

STEMS ENDING IN A LIQUID

220. Sing. N. V. ἀγών, ὁ, *contest*   ἡγεμών, ὁ, *guide*
     G. ἀγῶν-ος   ἡγεμόν-ος
     D. ἀγῶν-ι   ἡγεμόν-ι
     A. ἀγῶν-α   ἡγεμόν-α

Dual N. A. V. ἀγῶν-ε   ἡγεμόν-ε
     G. D. ἀγών-οιν   ἡγεμόν-οιν

Plur. N. V. ἀγῶν-ες   ἡγεμόν-ες
     G. ἀγῶν-ων   ἡγεμόν-ων
     D. ἀγῶ-σι(ν)   ἡγεμό-σι(ν)
     A. ἀγῶν-ας   ἡγεμόν-ας

Sing. N. V. μήν, ὁ, *month*   λιμήν, ὁ, *harbor*
     G. μην-ός   λιμέν-ος
     D. μην-ί   λιμέν-ι
     A. μῆν-α   λιμέν-α

Dual N. A. V. μῆν-ε   λιμέν-ε
     G. D. μην-οῖν   λιμέν-οιν

Plur. N. V. μῆν-ες   λιμέν-ες
     G. μην-ῶν   λιμέν-ων
     D. μη-σί(ν)   λιμέ-σι(ν)
     A. μῆν-ας   λιμέν-ας

Sing. N. γείτων, ὁ, *neighbor*   κρᾱτήρ, ὁ, *mixing-bowl*
     G. γείτον-ος   κρᾱτῆρ-ος
     D. γείτον-ι   κρᾱτῆρ-ι
     A. γείτον-α   κρᾱτῆρ-α
     V. γείτον   κρᾱτήρ

Dual N. A. V. γείτον-ε   κρᾱτῆρ-ε
     G D. γειτόν-οιν   κρᾱτήρ-οιν

Plur. N. V.	γείτον-ες	κρᾱτῆρ-ες
G.	γειτόν-ων	κρᾱτήρ-ων
D.	γείτο-σι(ν)	κρᾱτῆρ-σι(ν)
A.	γείτον-ας	κρᾱτῆρ-ας

a. The nominative singular in the preceding paradigms is the stem without any case-ending; the vowel before final -ν or -ρ of the stem is always long in the nominative singular.

DECLENSION OF ADJECTIVES IN -ων, -ον

221. Adjectives in -ων with stems in -ον are declined like γείτων (§ 220). There are separate forms for the neuter in the nominative and accusative, singular and plural. The feminine is like the masculine. The accent is recessive (cp. § 44).

		MASC. AND FEM.	NEUT.
222.	Sing. N.	εὐδαίμων *prosperous*	εὔδαιμον
	G.	εὐδαίμον-ος	
	D.	εὐδαίμον-ι	
	A.	εὐδαίμον-α	εὔδαιμον
	V.	εὔδαιμον	
	Dual N. A. V.	εὐδαίμον-ε	
	G. D.	εὐδαιμόν-οιν	
	Plur. N. V.	εὐδαίμον-ες	εὐδαίμον-α
	G.	εὐδαιμόν-ων	
	D.	εὐδαίμο-σι(ν)	
	A.	εὐδαίμον-ας	εὐδαίμον-α

223. The **infinitive** may be used as the apparent subject of δεῖ or χρή *it is necessary*, ἔστι(ν) *it is possible* (§ 102), ἔξ-εστι(ν) *it is possible* or *permitted*, καλόν ἐστι(ν) *it is honorable*, and many similar expressions, particularly impersonal verbs:

δεῖ (or χρὴ) αὐτοὺς εἶναι ἀγαθούς it is necessary for them to be brave; τῆς νυκτὸς οὐκ ἔστιν ἰδεῖν τὰ πρὸ ποδῶν in the night it is not possible to see the things before one's feet;

ἔξ-εστιν αὐτοῖς πιστὰ λαβεῖν it is possible for them to receive pledges ;
οὐ καλόν ἐστι κλέπτειν it is not honorable to steal.

a. The infinitive is neuter in gender, as the last example
shows.

b. With ἔστι(ν) and ἔξ-εστι(ν) the dative is the normal
case (as αὐτοῖς above), if any noun or pronoun is needed.

c. The negative with the infinitive, when not in indirect
discourse, is μή (cp. § 98).

224.   **VOCABULARY XX**

ἀγών, ῶνος, ὁ: *gathering, contest,
games.* Agony (ἀγωνίᾱ).

γείτων, ονος, ὁ: *neighbor.*

δεῖ (contracted from δέει), fut. δεήσει, aor. ἐδέησε, impers. verb:
it is necessary.

Ἕλλην, ηνος, ὁ: *a Greek.* Cp.
Ἑλλάς.

ἔξ-εστι(ν), 3 sing. of ἔξ-ειμι: *it is
possible* or *permitted.*

ἔτι, adv.: *still, yet, besides, longer,
again.*

εὐδαίμων, ον: *fortunate, prosperous.*

ἡγεμών, όνος, ὁ: *leader, guide, commander.*

κατά (κατ᾽ and καθ᾽, § 31), prep.:
with GEN. *down from;* with
ACC. *down over, down along,*
along, opposite, against, by, in
a local sense ; *according to ; by*
in a distributive sense, as κατὰ
μῆνα: *by the month, monthly.*
Cata-strophe (στροφή *turning*).

κρᾱτήρ, ῆρος, ὁ: *mixing-bowl.*
Lat. *crātēra.* Crater. See p. 109.

λιμήν, ένος, ὁ: *harbor.*

μήν, μηνός, ὁ: *month.* Lat. *mēnsis.*

μισθός, οῦ, ὁ: *pay.*

νῦν, adv.: *now* (of time). Lat.
nunc.

προσ-ελαύνω: *drive up, ride up,*
draw near.

σωτηρίᾱ, ᾱς, ἡ: *safety.*

χρή (ἐστί is understood, never
expressed): *there is need, it
behooves, it is necessary;* one
must. Inf. χρῆναι.

EXERCISES FOR TRANSLATION

225. I. 1. ἐκ ταύτης τῆς χώρᾱς ὁ ἄρχων τοῖς Ἕλλησιν ἡγεμόνα πέμπει.   2. ὁ δ᾽ ἔφευγε κατὰ τὴν ὁδόν.
3. οἱ δὲ στρατιῶται λαμβάνουσι τὸν κατὰ μῆνα μισθόν.

4. ἔφη δὲ ἥξειν εἰς λιμένα. 5. νῦν δὲ περὶ τῆς ὑμετέ-
ρᾱς σωτηρίᾱς ὁ ἀγών ἐστιν. 6. καὶ γείτων εἰμὶ τῆς
Ἑλλάδος. 7. ἦν δὲ οἶνος ἐν κρᾱτῆρσιν. 8. ὥστε
ἔξ-εστιν ἰδεῖν τὸν ἀγῶνα. 9. χρὴ μέντοι δια-βαίνειν
τὸν Εὐφρά̄την ποταμόν. 10. δεῖ οὖν Κλέαρχον πείθειν
τοὺς στρατιώτᾱς. 11. καὶ τοὺς τῶν Ἑλλήνων στρατηγοὺς ἐκέλευσεν ὁπλί̄τᾱς ἀγαγεῖν. 12. ὁ δ᾽ ἔφη εἶναι
αὐτοῖς χώρᾱν καλὴν καὶ εὐδαίμονα. 13. ἔτυχε γὰρ ἔτι
προσ-ελαύνων. 14. οἱ δ᾽ ἡγεμόνες οὓς ἔχομεν οὔ φᾱσιν¹
εἶναι ἄλλην ὁδόν.

II. 1. It is not possible to obtain² provisions. 2. These
are brave leaders. 3. The Greeks must cross the Euphrates river. 4. It behooves the captains to be brave.

---

¹ § 156. 1. a.   ² = take.

FIG. 11. — Κνημί̄s.

XXI

PRONOUNS (*Continued*). THE INTERROGATIVE τίς. THE
    INDEFINITE τις. THE INDEFINITE RELATIVE ὅστις.
    THE PREDICATE GENITIVE. INFINITIVE WITH
    ἀνάγκη AND ὥρᾱ

THE INTERROGATIVE τίς, τί, *who? which? what?*

226. The interrogative never changes its acute accent to
the grave.

	MASC. AND FEM.		NEUT.
Sing. N.	τίς		τί
G.		τίνος, τοῦ	
D.		τίνι, τῷ	
A.	τίνα		τί
Dual N. A.		τίνε	
G. D.		τίνοιν	
Plur. N.	τίνες		τίνα
G.		τίνων	
D.		τίσι(ν)	
A.	τίνας		τίνα

THE INDEFINITE τις, τι, *any, some, anybody, somebody, anything,*
    something ; a certain

227. The indefinite is always enclitic (§§ 21, 103, 104).

	MASC. AND FEM.		NEUT.
Sing. N.	τις		τι
G.		τινός, του	
D.		τινί, τῳ	
A.	τινά		τι
Dual N. A.		τινέ	
G. D.		τινοῖν	
Plur. N.	τινές		τινά
G.		τινῶν	
D.		τισί(ν)	
A.	τινάς		τινά

THE INDEFINITE RELATIVE ὅστις, ἥτις, ὅ τι, *whoever* OR *whichever, whatever*

228. The indefinite relative is formed of the relative ὅς, ἥ, ὅ (§ 125), and the indefinite τις, τι (§ 227), both parts being declined. The combination is treated as *two words* with reference to accent. So the circumflex appears to rest on the antepenult of οὗτινος, which is accented as if οὗ τινος.

	MASC.	FEM.	NEUT.
Sing. N.	ὅστις	ἥτις	ὅ τι (or ὅ,τι)
G.	οὗτινος, ὅτου	ἧστινος	οὗτινος, ὅτου
D.	ᾧτινι, ὅτῳ	ᾗτινι	ᾧτινι, ὅτῳ
A.	ὅντινα	ἥντινα	ὅ τι (or ὅ,τι)
Dual N. A.	ὥτινε	ὥτινε	ὥτινε
G. D.	οἷντινοιν	οἷντινοιν	οἷντινοιν
Plur. N.	οἵτινες	αἵτινες	ἅτινα
G.	ὧντινων	ὧντινων	ὧντινων
D.	οἷστισι(ν)	αἷστισι(ν)	οἷστισι(ν)
A.	οὕστινας	ἅστινας	ἅτινα

229. Predicate genitive. — The genitive in any of its relations (possessive, partitive, etc.) may stand after the verb, as a part of the predicate:

αἱ δὲ κῶμαι Κύρου ἦσαν the villages belonged to Cyrus (poss. gen.) ;
ἦν δ' αὐτῶν Πρόξενος and among them was Proxenus (part. gen.).

230. With ἀνάγκη [ἐστί(ν)] *it is necessary*, ὥρα [ἐστί(ν)] *it is the proper time*, and similar expressions, the **infinitive** is used to complete the meaning. The brackets indicate that ἐστί(ν) may be omitted :

ἀνάγκη αὐτοῖς (or αὐτοὺς) λαμβάνειν τὰ ἐπιτήδεια it is necessary for them to get provisions ;
ὥρα αὐτοῖς ἥκειν it is high time for them to arrive.

231.   VOCABULARY XXI

'Aθηναῖos, ā, ον : *Athenian*.

ἀνάγκη, ης, ἡ : *necessity*. With or
   without ἐστί(ν) : *it is neces-*
   sary. Inf. ἀνάγκην εἶναι.

γυμνής, ῆτος, ὁ : *light-armed war-*
   rior, javelin-hurler, bowman, or
   slinger.

δή, postpositive particle, emphasizing the preceding word. δή
   is difficult to render adequately,
   but is sometimes translated by
   now, then, accordingly, very,
   in truth, indeed.

εἰσ-ῆλθον, 2 aor. : *I* or *they came in,*
   entered. Inf. εἰσ-ελθεῖν, partic.
   εἰσ-ελθών.

καίω or κᾱ́ω, καύσω, ἔκαυσα : *burn,*
   light, kindle. Caustic.

νεᾱνίσκος, ου, ὁ : *young man*.

ὅστις, ἥτις, ὅ τι (or ὅ,τι) : *who-*
   ever or *whichever, whatever ;*
   who, which, what ; often with
   conditional force, *if anybody*
   (= εἴ τις), *if anything* (= εἴ
   τι) ; see § 228.

σφενδόνη, ης, ἡ : *sling*.   See
   p. 112, Fig. 13.

τίς, τί : *who ? which ? what ?* see
   § 226.   τί : *what ?* often as
   adv. *why ?*

τις, τι : *any, some, anybody, some-*
   body, anything, something ; a
   certain ; see § 227.

χῑλός, οῦ, ὁ : *grass*, green *fodder*.

χρήσιμος, η, ον, and ος, ον : *useful*.

ὥρᾱ, ᾱς, ἡ : *season, hour, fit* or
   proper time. See § 230. Lat.
   hōra.

EXERCISES FOR TRANSLATION

232. I. 1. ἦν δέ τις ἐν τῇ στρατιᾷ στρατηγὸς 'Aθη-
ναῖος.   2. τίνας δὲ χρὴ φύλακας εἶναι ;   3. οὗτοι δὴ
ἔκᾱον καὶ χῑλὸν καὶ εἴ τι¹ ἄλλο χρήσιμον ἦν.   4. εἰσ-
ῆλθον δὲ παρ' αὐτὸν οἵ τε στρατηγοὶ καὶ τῶν ἄλλων
Ἑλλήνων τινές.   5. καὶ ἐνταῦθά τινες ἀπ-έθανον τῶν
στρατιωτῶν.   6. τίνες ἐστέ ;   7. τί οὐκ ἦγες τοὺς
πελταστάς ;   8. οἱ γὰρ γυμνῆτες ἔλαβόν τινας τῶν
κλωπῶν.   9. τίνες ἔχουσι σφενδόνᾱς ;   10. ταῦτα τὰ
ἔργα ἐστὶν ἀπόρων² οἵτινες ἐθέλουσι πράττειν κακόν

---

¹ εἴ τι (= *whatsoever*) might be replaced by ὅ τι, as in sentence 14.

² *characteristic of men without resources,* predicate gen. akin to possessive.

τι.   11. ἔτυχε δὲ ἐφ᾽ ἵππου[1] ἐλαύνων.   12. νεᾱνίσκος
δέ τις τῶν παρόντων συν-εβούλευσε τάδε.   13. οὐχ ὥρᾱ
ἐστὶ μέλλειν.[2]   14. ἀνάγκη δὲ Προξένῳ συμ-βουλεῦσαι
αὐτοῖς ὅ τι καλόν ἐστιν.   15. τὰ γὰρ ὅπλα Κύρου ἦν.

II.   1. Who was riding on his horse?   2. Some of the
arms belong to Cyrus.   3. He must do whatever is [3] honorable.   4. Proxenus came in with some of his friends.

XXII

THE SUBJUNCTIVE (PRESENT AND AORIST) ACTIVE
OF Ω-VERBS.   TENSES OF THE SUBJUNCTIVE.
MORE VIVID FUTURE CONDITIONS.   WARNING
FUTURE CONDITIONS.   PURPOSE CLAUSES.   HOR-
TATORY SUBJUNCTIVE

233. The thematic vowel of the subjunctive is ω before
μ and ν, otherwise η.   This is also the present tense suffix
of λύω and similar verbs.   The first aorist tense suffix is σω
before μ and ν, otherwise ση.   The primary personal endings, as seen in the present indicative, are used in *all*
subjunctive tenses.

234. The imperfect tense belongs only to the indicative
mood.   And there is no future tense in the subjunctive.

235.   PRESENT SUBJUNCTIVE ACTIVE OF λύω

	SING.	DUAL	PLUR.
1.	λΰ-ω		λΰ-ω-μεν
2.	λΰ-ῃς	λΰ-η-τον	λΰ-η-τε
3.	λΰ-ῃ	λΰ-η-τον	λΰ-ω-σι(ν)

---

[1] *on horseback.*   [2] In sense of *delay.*   [3] Use pres. indic.

FIRST AORIST SUBJUNCTIVE ACTIVE

	SING.	DUAL	PLUR.
1.	λύ-σω		λύ-σω-μεν
2.	λύ-σῃς	λύ-ση-τον	λύ-ση-τε
3.	λύ-σῃ	λύ-ση-τον	λύ-σω-σι(ν)

a. The aorist subjunctive is not augmented. Augment belongs to the secondary tenses of the indicative only (§ 77).

236. Like the present subjunctive of λύω are inflected the present subjunctives of all the other ω-verbs hitherto studied. In the formation of the first aorist subjunctive of verbs with mute themes, however, the same euphonic changes are observed at the end of the theme as in the first aorist indicative (§ 164). Thus the first aorist subjunctive of πέμπω is πέμψω, πέμψῃς, etc.; of ἁρπάζω: ἁρπάσω, ἁρπάσῃς, etc.; of πείθω: πείσω, πείσῃς, etc.

237. Verbs like ἄγω and λείπω, which have no first aorist indicative, have no first aorist subjunctive. But they have a second aorist subjunctive which does not differ in time or use from the first aorist. The inflection is the same as that of the present subjunctive.

238. SECOND AORIST SUBJUNCTIVE ACTIVE OF λείπω

(Cp. the second aorist indicative ἔλιπον, § 85)

	SING.	DUAL	PLUR.
1.	λίπ-ω		λίπ-ω-μεν
2.	λίπ-ῃς	λίπ-η-τόν	λίπ-η-τε
3.	λίπ-ῃ	λίπ-η-τον	λίπ-ω-σι(ν)

239. The second aorist subjunctive of ἄγω is ἀγάγ-ω, ἀγάγ-ῃς, etc.

240. Tenses of the subjunctive. — While the subjunctive has no future tense, both the present and the aorist may refer to future time, as will be evident from a study of the constructions in the following lessons. The difference between the two tenses is this: the present denotes continued or repeated action; the aorist denotes a simple occurrence of an action.

241. More vivid future conditions. — ἐάν (or ἤν or ἄν) *if* may introduce the subjunctive (present or aorist) to express a vivid future condition. The conclusion is expressed by the future indicative, or by the imperative, or by any other forms that *may* imply future time, such as χρή, ἔξεστι(ν), etc.:

ἐὰν ὁ στρατηγὸς κελεύῃ, ἥξει if the general orders, he will come.

a. The negative of the protasis is always μή; of the apodosis, οὐ. Cp. § 106. *a* and *b*.

242. To express something unpleasant, like a **warning** or a **threat**, the protasis may have εἰ and the future indicative:

εἰ κλέψεις τι, πράγματα ἕξεις if you steal anything, you will have trouble.

Observe that εἰ cannot introduce the subjunctive. Nor can ἐάν introduce the indicative.

243. Purpose clauses. — ἵνα, ὅπως, and ὡς, all meaning *in order that*, may introduce the subjunctive (present or aorist) to express a purpose. The subjunctive is the regular construction when the verb of the main clause, on which the purpose depends, is a primary tense (§ 39). The construction after secondary tenses will be stated later (§ 268). The negative is μή:

ὁ στρατηγὸς ἥκει, ἵνα πείσῃ τοὺς στρατιώτᾱς the general has come that he may (*i.e.* to) persuade the soldiers.

244. Hortatory subjunctive. — The subjunctive is used alone to express an exhortation in the first person. The negative is μή:

καλῶς ἀπο-θνῄσκωμεν let us die honorably.

245.   VOCABULARY XXII

ἄν (εἰ + ἄν) = ἐάν : *if*, conj. with subjv.

δᾱρεικός, οῦ, ὁ : *daric*, a Persian gold coin, worth about $5.40.

ἐάν (εἰ + ἄν), conj. with subjv. : *if*.

ἕκαστος, η, ον : *each*; used in predicate position to modify a noun with the article; used also without the article.

ἔλθω : subjv. of ἦλθον.

ἤν (εἰ + ἄν) = ἐάν : *if*, conj. with subjv.

ἴδω : subjv. of εἶδον.

ἵνα, conj. expressing purpose : *in order that, that*, § 243.

καλῶς, adv. (cp. καλός) : *beautifully, nobly, honorably*.

μᾶλλον, comp. adv. : *more, better, rather*.

οἴκαδε, adv. : *homeward, home*. Cp. οἰκία.

ὅπως, conj. : *in order that, that*, with purpose clause (§ 243).

πάσχω, fut. to be learned later, 2 aor. ἔπαθον : *suffer*. πάσχω τι (§ 181) : *suffer something*, euphemism for *be hurt* or *be killed*. Sym-pathy (συν-).

πρᾶγμα, ατος, τό : *something done* (cp. πράττω), *business, deed, matter, difficulty*; pl. sometimes *circumstances*, often *trouble*. Pragmatic.

ταχύ, adv. : *quickly*.

ὡς, rel. adv. : *as, as if*, with causal partic. (§ 213. *a*); conj. : *in order that, that*, with purpose clause (§ 243).

EXERCISES FOR TRANSLATION

246. I. 1. μὴ μέλλωμεν. 2. ἢν δέ τι μὴ πάθωμεν, ἔστιν οἴκαδε ἥκειν. 3. ἄν τινα ἴδωμεν, οὐκ ἔστιν αὐτῷ ἀπο-φυγεῖν. 4. πράγματα δ' ἕξομεν, ἐὰν κατὰ θάλατταν ἔλθωμεν. 5. ἀλλὰ κάωμεν τὴν χώρᾱν. 6. δεῖ οὖν ἔχειν φύλακάς τινας ἵνα μὴ οἱ πολέμιοι ἔλθωσι τῆς νυκτός. 7. ἄξω στρατιώτᾱς καὶ ἵππους ὅπως, ἄν τινα τῶν πολεμίων ἴδωμεν, μὴ ἀπο-φύγῃ. 8. ἵνα δὲ μᾶλλον

θαυμάσητε, πέμψω δᾱρεικὸν μισθὸν¹ ἑκάστῳ στρα-
τιώτῃ. 9. ταχὺ γάρ, ἂν ἐθέλῃς, ἥξω. 10. εἰ καύσεις
τὴν χώρᾱν, πράγματα ἕξεις. 11. ἐὰν οἱ ἡμέτεροι παῖδες καλῶς ἀπο-θνῄσκωσιν ἐν ταύτῃ τῇ μάχῃ, χρὴ χάριν
ἔχειν τοῖς θεοῖς. 12. ὁ δ᾽ ἥκει ὡς καύσῃ τὴν χώρᾱν
ὡς² πολεμίᾱν οὖσαν.

II. 1. He will have trouble, if he leads his soldiers
down the steep road. 2. Let us not take provisions from
the hostile country. 3. He will pursue the enemy quickly
in order that they may not escape.

---

¹ *as pay.* ² Cp. § 213. *a.*

Fig. 12. — Κρᾱτήρ.

XXIII

PRESENT SUBJUNCTIVE OF εἰμί. USES OF THE SUB-
JUNCTIVE (*Continued*). CONDITIONAL RELATIVE
SENTENCES: MORE VIVID FUTURE

247.   **PRESENT SUBJUNCTIVE OF** εἰμί *I am*

SING.	DUAL	PLUR.
1. ὦ		ὦμεν
2. ᾖς	ἦτον	ἦτε
3. ᾖ	ἦτον	ὦσι(ν)

248. More vivid future **conditional relative** sentences. —
1. In place of εἰ + ἄν (*i.e.* ἐάν) a relative pronoun like
ὅς, ὅστις, *whoever*, or a relative adverb like ὅπου *wherever*,
always with ἄν, may introduce the subjunctive (present or
aorist). This use of the subjunctive is known as a *conditional relative protasis*. The future indicative or an
equivalent is used in the conclusion. Thus ὅστις ἄν =
ἐάν τις *if anybody;* ὅπου ἄν = ἐάν που *if anywhere;* ὅποι
ἄν = ἐάν ποι *if anywhither.*

πράξω ἅτινα ἂν συμ-βουλεύσῃς I will do whatever you advise (*or*
    shall advise);
ἄξει στράτευμα ὅποι ἂν ἐθέλῃ he will lead an army whithersoever
    he pleases.

a. In this use the antecedent of the relative is always indefinite.
The relative with a definite antecedent has the construction of an
independent sentence, — commonly the indicative, as already has been
illustrated (§§ 138. I. 4, 145. I. 8, etc.). But not all relatives with
the indicative have definite antecedents (cp. § 232. I. 14).

2. ἐπεί, ἐπειδή, ὅτε (all meaning *when*), and similar
words, when they introduce future time, take the subjunctive with ἄν.

a. It is to be noted that ἐπεί + ἄν = ἐπήν or ἐπάν
(*when*); ἐπειδή + ἄν = ἐπειδάν (*when*); ὅτε + ἄν = ὅταν
(*when*); of these words, ἐπειδάν (or ἐπάν) meaning *when*
or *after*, when used with the aorist subjunctive, may
introduce completed future time:

ἐπειδὰν ἔλθῃ τὰ πλοῖα, τότε ἕξομεν τὰ ἐπιτήδεια when the boats
arrive (*or* after the boats have arrived), then we shall
have provisions.

249. NOTE ON ἄν. — The particle ἄν has no adequate equivalent in
English. Its uses in Greek, however, are most important. It appeared
in this book first in §§ 241, 245, as a part of the word ἐάν or ἤν or ἄν.
It makes no difference whatsoever in the *translation* of a subjunctive,
which it accompanies in a protasis. Its force with other moods will be
studied later.

The particle ἄν must not be confused with the conjunction ἄν *if*
(= εἰ + ἄν, *i.e.* ἐάν). Notice the difference in the quantity of the *alpha*.

250.   **VOCABULARY XXIII**

δέῃ, subjv. of δεῖ, impers. verb : *it
is necessary.* Cp. § 224.

ἐπειδάν (ἐπειδή + ἄν), conj. with
subjv. : *when, after.*

θύω, θύσω, ἔθυσα : *sacrifice, offer.*

ὅποι, rel. adv. : *whithersoever,
whither, where.*

ὅπου, rel. adv. : *wherever, where.*

πέρᾱν, adv. : *across, on the other*

side, with the gen.   ἐν τῷ
πέρᾱν : *on the other side* or
bank.

πρῶτος, η, ον : *first.* Adv. πρῶτον : *first.*

τάλαντον, ου, τό : *talent,* an amount
of money = about $1080.

τρέχω, 2 aor. ἔδραμον (Vocabulary XI) : *run.*

EXERCISES FOR TRANSLATION

251. I. 1. ἢν ἀνάγκη ᾖ, στράτευμα ἄξομεν εἰς τὴν
πολεμίᾱν χώρᾱν.   2. τῷ θεῷ τούτῳ θύσομεν ὅπου ἂν
πρῶτον εἰς καλὸν πεδίον ἥκωμεν.   3. Χειρίσοφος δὲ
κελεύει τοὺς πελταστὰς πράττειν ὅ τι ἂν ὁ λοχᾱγὸς

ἐθέλῃ.   4. ἐπειδὰν δὲ δράμωσιν οἱ πολέμιοι, δεῖ τοὺς
ἡμετέρους στρατιώτᾱς δια-βαίνειν τὸν ποταμόν.   5. ὃς
ἂν πρῶτος ἐν τῷ πέρᾱν τοῦ ποταμοῦ ᾖ, οὗτος ἕξει μισθὸν τάλαντον.   6. δεῖ δὲ τρέχειν, ἐπειδὰν ὁ στρατηγὸς
κελεύσῃ.   7. τοὺς ἀνθρώπους τούτους φυλάξομεν, ὅπως
ἡγεμόνες ὦσιν ὅποι ἂν δέῃ ἐλθεῖν.   8. ἀνάγκη δὲ πρᾶξαι
ἃ¹ ἂν συμ-βουλεύσῃς.   9. τούτῳ παρα-σχήσετε ὅ τι ἂν
ἄγητε.

II. 1. When you come home, you shall have a talent as
pay.   2. Whoever is first on the other bank shall lead the
soldiers.   3. We shall do whatever the general commands.

---

¹ Cognate obj. (§ 181); the antecedent ταῦτα is understood.

FIG. 13. — Slinger (σφενδονήτης).

XXIV

THE OPTATIVE (PRESENT, FUTURE, AND AORIST) ACTIVE OF Ω–VERBS. TENSES OF THE OPTATIVE. SIMPLE SENTENCES IN INDIRECT DISCOURSE AFTER VERBS THAT TAKE ὅτι **OR** ὡς *that*

252. The thematic vowel (§ 41) in the present and second aorist optative is o in all numbers and persons. The tense sign of the future optative is σο; of the first aorist, σα. There is added to these vowels, in each tense, the mood sign of the optative,[1] which is ι; in the third person plural the mood sign is ιε. Then follow the personal endings, which are mostly the same as in the imperfect indicative (secondary endings). But the first person singular ends in -μι.

253. Final -οι and -αι are long in the optative (cp. § 23).

254. PRESENT OPTATIVE ACTIVE OF λύω

SING.	DUAL	PLUR.
1. λύ-οι-μι		λύ-οι-μεν
2. λύ-οι-ς	λύ-οι-τον	λύ-οι-τε
3. λύ-οι	λῡ-οί-την	λύ-οιε-ν

FUTURE OPTATIVE ACTIVE

1. λύ-σοι-μι		λύ-σοι-μεν
2. λύ-σοι-ς	λύ-σοι-τον	λύ-σοι-τε
3. λύ-σοι	λῡ-σοί-την	λύ-σοιε-ν

FIRST AORIST OPTATIVE ACTIVE

1. λύ-σαι-μι		λύ-σαι-μεν
2. λύ-σαι-ς, -σειας [2]	λύ-σαι-τον	λύ-σαι-τε
3. λύ-σαι, -σειε(ν) [2]	λῡ-σαί-την	λύ-σαιε-ν, -σειαν [2]

[1] No account is made here of the sign ιη, which will be seen later in the book.
[2] The regular Attic Greek ending.

255. Like the present optative of λύω are inflected the present optatives of all the other ω-verbs hitherto studied. In the formation of the future and first aorist optative of verbs with mute themes, however, the same euphonic laws are observed as in the future and first aorist indicative (§§ 153, 164):

πέμψοιμι (fut. opt. of πέμπω), πέμψαιμι (aor. opt.);

λείψοιμι (fut. opt. of λείπω);

ἄξοιμι (fut. opt. of ἄγω);

πείσοιμι (fut. opt. of πείθω), πείσαιμι (aor. opt.);

ἁρπάσοιμι (fut. opt. of ἁρπάζω), ἁρπάσαιμι (aor. opt.).

256. Verbs like ἄγω and λείπω, which have no first aorist indicative or subjunctive, have no first aorist optative (cp. §§ 237, 238); but they have a second aorist optative which does not differ in time or use from the first aorist. The inflection is the same as that of the present optative.

257. SECOND AORIST OPTATIVE ACTIVE OF λείπω

	SING.	DUAL	PLUR.
1.	λίπ-οι-μι		λίπ-οι-μεν
2.	λίπ-οι-ς	λίπ-οι-τον	λίπ-οι-τε
3.	λίπ-οι	λιπ-οί-την	λίπ-οιε-ν

258. The second aorist optative active of ἄγω is ἀγά-γοιμι, ἀγάγοις, etc.

259. Tenses of the optative. — The distinction between the present and aorist optative (when not in indirect discourse) is not one of time, which is determined by the context. It is rather this: the present denotes continued or repeated action, while the aorist denotes a simple occurrence of an action. Compare the distinction between the present and aorist subjunctive (§ 240).

a. The tenses of the optative in indirect discourse, however, denote exact time, *i.e.* present, past, or future.

b. The future optative is regularly found only in indirect discourse, when it represents the future indicative of direct discourse.

SIMPLE SENTENCES IN INDIRECT DISCOURSE AFTER VERBS THAT TAKE ὅτι *that* OR ὡς *that*

260. While φησί, ἔφη, and the other forms of this verb (φημί) are followed by the infinitive in indirect discourse (§ 110), the common verb λέγω *say* takes ὅτι or ὡς *that* and a finite mood. The original mood and tense of the quoted verb are always retained after a primary tense (§ 39) of λέγω; but after a secondary tense of λέγω the mood of the quoted verb *may* be changed to the optative. The tense is regularly kept unchanged.

a. The imperfect indicative is usually retained.

261. When direct statements are made indirect, necessary changes in *person* are made as in English. The negative of the direct discourse is retained.

262. Like λέγω *say* are used εἶπον, 2 aor., *I said*, ἀκούω *hear*, μανθάνω *learn* (and several other frequent verbs that will be introduced later).

a. ἀκούω *hear* permits more than one construction; for example, it takes the infinitive also (cp. § 203. I. 10).

EXAMPLES

1. *Original statement:* οὐκ ἔχομεν τὰ ἐπιτήδεια we have no provisions.

   Quoted statement in primary sequence: λέγουσιν ὅτι (or ὡς) οὐκ ἔχουσι τὰ ἐπιτήδεια they say that they have no provisions.

Quoted statement in secondary sequence: ἔλεγον ὅτι (or ὡς) οὐκ ἔχοιεν τὰ ἐπιτήδεια they said that they had no provisions.

The original mood and tense ἔχουσι might have been retained.

2. *Original statement:* κατ-είδομεν σκηνάς we observed tents.

Quoted statement: ἔλεγον ὅτι κατ-ίδοιεν σκηνάς they said that they (had) observed tents.

The original mood and tense κατ-εῖδον might have been retained.

3. *Original statement:* αὐτὸς ταῦτα πράξω I myself will do this.

Quoted statement: εἶπεν ὅτι αὐτὸς ταῦτα πράξοι he said that he himself would do this.

The original mood and tense πράξει might have been retained.

263. **VOCABULARY XXIV**

γράφω, γράψω, ἔγραψα : *write.* Graphic.

δι-ῆλθον, 2 aor. : *I* or *they went through; spread* with λόγος (*word* or *report*) as subject; subjv. δι-έλθω, opt. δι-έλθοιμι, inf. δι-ελθεῖν, partic. δι-ελθών.

εἶπον, 2 aor. : *I* or *they said;* subjv. εἴπω, opt. εἴποιμι, inf. εἰπεῖν, partic. εἰπών.

ἔνθεν, rel. adv. : *whence, from which, where.*

Καρδοῦχοι, ων, οἱ : the *Cardūchi,* a mountain people on the left bank of the Tigris.

κατ-εῖδον, 2 aor. : *I* or *they looked down on, descried, observed;* subjv. κατ-ίδω, opt. κατ-ίδοιμι, inf. κατ-ιδεῖν, partic. κατ-ιδών.

λέγω, λέξω, ἔλεξα : *say* (to be distinguished from -λέγω of συλ-λέγω *collect*).

μανθάνω (theme μαθ- ; on the formation of the present cp. λαμβάνω and τυγχάνω, § 218), fut. to be learned later, 2 aor. ἔμαθον : *learn.*

ξύλον, ου, τό : *wood;* pl. hewn or split *wood; timbers.* Xylophone (φωνή *voice*).

ὅτι, conj., introducing a quotation : *that.*

Πέρσης, ου, ὁ : *a Persian.*

Περσικός, ή, όν (Πέρσης) : *Persian.*

σατράπης, ου, ὁ : *satrap,* Persian name for a provincial governor appointed by the king.

τότε, adv. of time : *then, at that time.*

ὑποψία, ας, ἡ : *suspicion.*

ὡς, conj., introducing a quotation : *that.* Cp. also Vocabulary XXII.

EXERCISES FOR TRANSLATION

264. I. 1. ἔλεγον ὅτι θαυμάζοιεν. 2. ὑποψίᾱ ἦν [1]
ὅτι Κῦρος ἄγοι πρὸς Ἀρταξέρξην. 3. οἱ δὲ ἔλεγον
ὅτι ἡ ὁδὸς εἰς Καρδούχους ἄγοι. 4. καὶ τότε ἔλεγον ὅτι
τυγχάνοιεν ξύλα συλ-λέγοντες. 5. ἔλεγον ὡς κατ-
ίδοιεν παῖδας καὶ νεᾱνίσκους. 6. ὁ δὲ Πέρσης ἀκούσᾱς
ὅτι Χειρίσοφος πάλιν ἥξοι ἦλθεν εἰς τὴν κώμην. 7. ὁ δ᾽
εἶπεν ὅτι ἀκούοι τοὺς βαρβάρους ἐπὶ τῷ Εὐφράτῃ ποταμῷ εἶναι.[2] 8. δι-ῆλθε λόγος ὅτι διώκει αὐτοὺς Κῦρος.
9. οἱ δ᾽ εἶπον ὅτι ὁ σατράπης ἀπ-έχει παρασάγγην.
10. ὁ δὲ γράφει ἐπιστολὴν ὅτι ἥξει. 11. ἔμαθεν ὅτι
Ἀρταξέρξης ἔχοι τὸ μέσον τοῦ Περσικοῦ στρατεύματος. 12. ἔλεγον δὲ ὅτι ἥκοιεν ἡγεμόνας ἔχοντες οἳ
αὐτοὺς ἄξουσιν ἔνθεν ἕξουσι τὰ ἐπιτήδεια.

II. 1. They said they would come into the village.
2. On the next day a man came saying that he had
observed the tents of the enemy. 3. They heard that [3]
the enemy were [3] at the Euphrates river.

---

[1] *there was a suspicion.*   [2] § 110. *a.*   [3] Use the inf.

FIG. 14.— Shield (πέλτη) carried by the πελταστής (cp. Fig. 4).

XXV

PRESENT OPTATIVE OF εἰμί. USES OF THE OPTA-
TIVE (*Continued*). POTENTIAL OPTATIVE. LESS
VIVID FUTURE CONDITIONS. PURPOSE CLAUSES
IN THE SECONDARY SEQUENCE

265.   PRESENT OPTATIVE OF εἰμί *I am*

SING.	DUAL	PLUR.
1. εἴην		εἴημεν or εἶμεν
2. εἴης	εἴητον or εἶτον	εἴητε or εἶτε
3. εἴη	εἰήτην or εἴτην	εἴησαν or εἶεν

Several of these forms show the longer optative mood
sign ιη. Cp. § 252.

266. Potential optative. — The present or aorist optative is used with ἄν (an untranslatable particle, § 249) to
indicate that something *may* or *might* happen. The degree
of probability varies according to the context. The negative is οὐ :

τοῦτο οὐκ ἂν εἴη ἀγαθόν this would not be a good thing.

a. The adverb ἄν never stands first in its sentence or
clause, but follows an emphatic word, especially a negative
or a verb.

267. Less vivid future conditions. — εἰ *if* may introduce
the optative (present or aorist) to express a less vivid (cp.
§ 241) future condition. The conclusion is expressed by
the optative with ἄν. The negative of the protasis is μή ;
of the apodosis, οὐ :

εἰ ἴδοιμι αὐτούς, ἔλθοιμι ἂν πρὸς αὐτούς if I should see them, I should
go to them.

268. Purpose clauses in the secondary sequence. — ἵνα, ὅπως, and ὡς, all meaning *in order that*, may introduce the optative (present or aorist) to express a purpose. The optative is found only when the verb of the main clause is secondary in tense; and even then the subjunctive (§ 243) is sometimes found. The negative is μή:

Κῦρος ἦλθεν ἵνα ἴδοι τοὺς στρατιώτᾱς Cyrus came in order that he might (*i.e.* to) see his soldiers.

269. VOCABULARY XXV

'Αριαῖος, ου, ὁ : *Ariaeus*, a Persian.
δίκαιος, ᾱ, ον (cp. δίκη) : *just*.
  δικαίως, adv. : *justly*.
ἐξ-ῆλθον, 2 aor. : *I* or *they went forth*. Cp. δι-ῆλθον, § 263.
κενός, ή, όν : *empty* ; *vain, ground-less*. Ceno-taph (τάφος *burial-place*).
Μένων, ωνος, ὁ : *Menon*.
οὔ-ποτε : *never*.
ταχέως, adv. : *quickly, swiftly, rapidly* ; = ταχύ.

EXERCISES FOR TRANSLATION

270. I. 1. οὗτοι ἔλεγον ὅτι 'Αριαῖος ἐν τῷ σταθμῷ[1] εἴη μετὰ τῶν ἄλλων βαρβάρων. 2. ἦγε ταχέως ὥστε δῆλον ἦν[2] ὅτι πράγματα εἴη. 3. ἔμαθον δὲ οἱ στρα-τιῶται ὅτι κενὸς ὁ φόβος εἴη. 4. οὐδὲ τοῦτο ἄν τις εἴποι. 5. χάριν αὐτοῖς ἂν ἔχοιμεν δικαίως. 6. οὐκ ἂν θαυμάζοιμι εἰ οἱ πολέμιοι φεύγοιεν. 7. τί ἂν πά-σχοιεν οἱ ἄνθρωποι; 8. τίς αὐτῶν ἔστιν ὅστις ἀγαθὸς ἐθέλοι ἂν εἶναι; 9. Μένων δ' ἤθελεν ἄρχειν ὅπως χρήματα λαμβάνοι. 10. τὴν δὲ χώρᾱν δι-αρπάσαι οὔποτε ἂν ἐθέλοιμεν. 11. ἐκ ταύτης τῆς χώρᾱς ὁ ἄρχων τοῖς Ἕλλησιν ἡγεμόνα ἔπεμψεν, ἵνα διὰ τῆς

---

[1] *halting place.*   [2] *it was evident.*

πολεμίας χώρας ἄγοι αὐτούς.   12. μετὰ ταῦτα ἐξ-ῆλθεν
ὅπως μάθοι τὰ¹ περὶ Προξένου.

II. 1. If Menon should seize the possessions, I should
not be surprised.   2. It was evident that Cyrus was² his
friend.   3. Cyrus marched rapidly, in order to take the
enemy while they were³ unguarded.

XXVI

CONSONANT DECLENSION (*Continued*).   STEMS ENDING
IN *SIGMA*.   ADJECTIVES OF TWO ENDINGS WITH
STEMS IN -εσ.   POTENTIAL OPTATIVE IN INDIRECT
DISCOURSE.   GENITIVE OF MEASURE.   ACCUSA-
TIVE OF SPECIFICATION

STEMS ENDING IN *SIGMA*

271. The nominative singular of stems ending in σ is the
mere stem, without any case-ending.   Neuter stems in -εσ
change ε to o in forming this nominative.   Thus ὀρεσ- forms
the nominative singular ὄρος.   In cases where σ comes between two vowels, it is dropped and contraction occurs.   One
σ of the dative plural -εσ + σι is also dropped.   In the following paradigms the original forms are given in brackets.

a.   RULES OF CONTRACTION

$$\epsilon + a = \eta \qquad\qquad \epsilon + o = ov$$
$$\epsilon + \epsilon = \epsilon\iota \qquad\qquad \epsilon + o\iota = o\iota$$
$$\epsilon + \iota = \epsilon\iota \qquad\qquad \epsilon + \omega = \omega$$

b. The syllable resulting from contraction receives an
accent if either one of the component syllables, in the

---

¹ *the fate of Proxenus* (§ 70. *b*).   ² In dir. disc. *is*.   ³ Say *being*.

uncontracted form, had an accent; it receives a circumflex if the *first* vowel had the acute (but it receives an
acute if the *second* vowel had the acute).

272.   Sing. N. A. V.   ὄρος, τό, *mountain* (stem ὀρεσ-)
             G.   ὄρους [ὄρεσ-ος]
             D.   ὄρει [ὄρεσ-ι]

         Dual N. A. V.   ὄρει [ὄρεσ-ε]
             G. D.   ὀροῖν [ὀρέσ-οιν]

         Plur. N. A. V.   ὄρη [ὄρεσ-α]
             G.   ὀρέων or ὀρῶν [ὀρέσ-ων]
             D.   ὄρεσι(ν) [ὄρεσ-σι(ν)]

273.   DECLENSION OF Σωκράτης (STEM Σωκρατεσ-)

         Sing N.   Σωκράτης, ὁ, *Socrates*
             G.   Σωκράτους [Σωκράτεσ-ος]
             D.   Σωκράτει [Σωκράτεσ-ι]
             A.   Σωκράτη [Σωκράτεσ-α]
             V.   Σώκρατες

a. For the accusative Σωκράτη, a form Σωκράτην after
the analogy of the ᾱ-declension is often found.

b. Xenophon declines Τισσαφέρνης : gen. Τισσαφέρνους,
dat. Τισσαφέρνει, acc. Τισσαφέρνην (cp. Σωκράτην), voc.
Τισσαφέρνη.

c. In the nominative singular final -εσ of the stem of
these nouns is changed to -ης.

274. So too the nominative singular of τριήρης is formed
from the stem τριηρεσ-.

         DECLENSION OF τριήρης (STEM τριηρεσ-)

         Sing. N.   τριήρης, ἡ, *trireme*
             G.   τριήρους [τριήρεσ-ος]
             D.   τριήρει [τριήρεσ-ι]
             A.   τριήρη [τριήρεσ-α]
             V.   τριήρες

Dual N. A. V.   τριήρει [τριήρεσ-ε]
    G. D.   τριήροιν [τριηρέσ-οιν]

Plur. N. V.   τριήρεις [τριήρεσ-ες]
    G.   τριήρων [τριηρέσ-ων]
    D.   τριήρεσι(ν) [τριήρεσ-σι(ν)]
    A.   τριήρεις

a. The accusative plural copies the nominative plural form

b. τριήροιν and τριήρων have recessive accent (§ 44).

DECLENSION OF ADJECTIVES OF TWO ENDINGS WITH STEMS IN -εσ

	Masc. and Fem.	Neut.
275. Sing. N.	ἀσφαλής *safe*	ἀσφαλές
G.	ἀσφαλοῦς [-έσ-ος]	
D.	ἀσφαλεῖ [-έσ-ι]	
A.	ἀσφαλῆ [-έσ-α]	ἀσφαλές
V.	ἀσφαλές	

Dual N. A. V.	ἀσφαλεῖ [-έσ-ε]	
G. D.	ἀσφαλοῖν [-έσ-οιν]	

	Masc. and Fem.	Neut.
Plur. N. V.	ἀσφαλεῖς [-έσ-ες]	ἀσφαλῆ [-έσ-α]
G.	ἀσφαλῶν [-έσ-ων]	
D.	ἀσφαλέσι(ν) [-έσ-σι(ν)]	
A.	ἀσφαλεῖς	ἀσφαλῆ [-έσ-α]

a It is to be observed that the masculine and feminine ἀσφαλής is declined exactly like τριήρης except as regards the accent. The neuter nominative, accusative, and vocative singular is the mere stem. The neuter nominative and accusative plural ἀσφαλῆ (for ἀσφαλέσ-α) is formed like ὄρη (for ὄρεσ-α).

POTENTIAL OPTATIVE IN INDIRECT DISCOURSE

276. When a potential optative (§ 266) is quoted after a verb that takes ὅτι or ὡς (§§ 260, 262), it is unchanged, except possibly in person; and ἄν is retained :

Original form : ἕλοιμι ἂν αὐτούς I should capture them.
Quoted after ὅτι : οὗτος Κύρῳ εἶπεν ὅτι αὐτοὺς ἂν ἕλοι this man said to Cyrus that he should capture them.

277. When a potential optative is quoted after a verb that requires the infinitive (§ 110. *a*), the optative is changed to the same tense of the infinitive, and ἄν is retained. If the subject of the infinitive is different from that of the leading verb, it must be expressed (in the accusative); but it is not expressed if it is the same (review also § 110. *c, d, e*) :

Original form : ἕλθοιμι ἂν τριήρεις ἔχων I should come with triremes.
Quoted form : νομίζω ἐλθεῖν ἂν [or νομίζω ἂν ἐλθεῖν] τριήρεις ἔχων I think I should come with triremes.

278. The **genitive** modifying a noun may express **measure** :

τεῖχος δέκα ποδῶν a wall of ten feet.

279. The **accusative** may express a **specification** (*in respect to* something) :

ἐντεῦθεν ἐξ-ελαύνει ἐπὶ τὸν ποταμόν, ὄντα τὸ εὖρος πέντε σταδίων thence he marches to the river, which is (*lit.* being) of five stades in width (= five stades wide).

σταδίων is a predicate genitive (§ 229) of measure limiting ποταμόν; while τὸ εὖρος, accusative of specification, limits πέντε σταδίων.

280.   VOCABULARY XXVI

ἀνά (elided, ἀν'), prep. with acc. only : *up, up along, up through.* (In composition also *back.*) Ana-tomy (τομή *a cutting*).

ἀνα-βαίνω (other tenses except impf. ἀν-έβαινον to be learned later) : *go up ; go inland* ("up" from the coast). Cp. δια-βαίνω.

ἀσφαλής, ές : *secure, safe.* ἐν ἀσφαλεῖ : *in safety.*

ἀφανής, ές : *invisible, out of sight.*

Ἀχαιός, οῦ, ὁ : an *Achaean,* inhabitant of Achaea.

εἴκοσι(ν), indecl. : *twenty.*

εἷλον, 2 aor. : *I* or *they took, seized ;* subjv. ἕλω, opt. ἕλοιμι, inf. ἑλεῖν, partic. ἑλών.

εὖρος, ους, τό : *breadth, width.*

καθ-ήκω (κατά + ἥκω, cp. § 31) : *come down, reach down, extend.*

κατα-λείπω (cp. λείπω) : *leave behind, leave, abandon.*

ὄρος, ους, τό : *mountain.*

παύω, παύσω, ἔπαυσα : *make to stop, stop* (trans.), *put an end to.* Pause.

πρόσθεν, adv.: *forward* (of space) ; *before, former* (of time). Cp. πρός. ἡ πρόσθεν (§ 70) νύξ : *the night before.*

Σωκράτης, ους, ὁ : *Socrates.*

τεῖχος, ους, τό : *wall ; fortress.*

Τισσαφέρνης, ους, ὁ : *Tissaphernes,* a Persian satrap. See § 273. *b.*

τριήρης, ους, ἡ : *trireme.*

ὡς, adv., introducing a comparison : *as ;* with numerals : *about.* See also Vocabularies XXII and XXIV.

EXERCISES FOR TRANSLATION

281. I. 1. Κῦρος οὖν ἀν-έβαινεν ἐπὶ τὰ ὄρη.   2. ἦν δὲ πάροδος στενὴ μεταξὺ τοῦ ποταμοῦ καὶ τῆς τάφρου ὡς εἴκοσι ποδῶν τὸ εὖρος.[1]   3. τὴν δὲ πρόσθεν νύκτα[2] ἦσαν ἐπὶ τοῦ ὄρους.   4. ἐπεὶ δ' ἦσαν ἀφανεῖς, δι-ῆλθε λόγος ὅτι διώκοι αὐτοὺς Κῦρος τριήρεσιν.   5. καὶ τὰ τείχη ἦν εἰς τὴν θάλατταν καθ-ήκοντα.[3]   6. ἀνα-βαίνει οὖν ὁ Κῦρος λαβὼν Τισσαφέρνην ὡς[4] φίλον.   7. ὁ Ἀρταξέρξης δὴ ἤκουσε Τισσαφέρνους[5] τὸν Κύρου στό-

---

[1] Abstract nouns may have the article.   [2] § 142.   [3] § 53. *i.*
[4] *as.*   [5] *from Tissaphernes,* gen. of source, § 201.

λον.   8. οἱ δὲ ἄλλοι λοχᾱγοὶ ἦσαν ἐν ἀσφαλεῖ.   9. ἔχω
γὰρ τριήρεις ὥστε ἑλεῖν τὸ ἐκείνων πλοῖον.   10. ἔφη
δ' ἂν παῦσαι ταύτᾱς τὰς ὑποψίᾱς.   11. ὁ δ' οὐκ ἂν ἔφη
ἐξ-αγαγεῖν αὐτούς.   12. ἔλεγεν ὅτι οὔποτε ἂν κατα-
λείποι αὐτούς.   13. καὶ Σωκράτην τὸν 'Αχαιόν, ξένον
ὄντα,[1] ἐκέλευσεν ἐλθεῖν.   14. τούτους δὲ ἔφασαν κᾱ́ειν
τὰς κώμᾱς τὰς[2] ἀνὰ τὰ ὄρη.

II. 1. Thence he marched to a river ten stades in width.
2. I think it would be safe[3] to cross.   3. He thought he
should never come home.   4. We heard from Tissaphernes
of the expedition of Cyrus.

---

[1] Translate by a relative clause.   [2] Cp. § 67.
[3] Use neuter adj., § 223. *a*.

FIG. 15. — Waist of a War Ship (τριήρης), from a Relief found at Athens.

XXVII

DECLENSION OF STEMS ENDING IN *IOTA* OR *UPSILON*
(INCLUDED UNDER THE CONSONANT DECLENSION).
ADVERBIAL ACCUSATIVE.   ATTRACTION OF THE
RELATIVE

STEMS ENDING IN ι OR υ

282. Stems in ι or υ present several irregularities, of
which the explanations can best be sought in the grammars, if the instructor thinks such explanations desirable
at the outset.   It is to be observed that the accusative
singular ends in -ν, and not in -α; and the accusative plural
follows the nominative plural.

Sing. N.	πόλι-s, ἡ, *city*	πῆχυ-s, ὁ, *forearm, cubit*
G.	πόλε-ως	πήχε-ως
D.	πόλει [for πόλε-ι]	πήχει [for πήχε-ι]
A.	πόλι-ν	πῆχυ-ν
V.	πόλι	πῆχυ
Dual N. A. V.	πόλει [for πόλε-ε]	πήχει [for πήχε-ε]
G. D.	πολέ-οιν	πηχέ-οιν
Plur. N. V.	πόλεις [for πόλε-ες]	πήχεις [for πήχε-ες]
G.	πόλε-ων	πήχε-ων
D.	πόλε-σι(ν)	πήχε-σι(ν)
A.	πόλεις	πήχεις

Sing. N. A. V.	ἄστυ, τό, *town*
G.	ἄστε-ως
D.	ἄστει [for ἄστε-ι]
Dual N. A. V.	ἄστει [for ἄστε-ε]
G. D.	ἀστέ-οιν
Plur. N A. V.	ἄστη [for ἄστε-α]
G.	ἄστε-ων
D.	ἄστε-σι(ν)

a. The accent of the preceding nouns (πόλις, πῆχυς, and ἄστυ) is irregular in the genitive, singular and plural (§ 17. 1)

283.
Sing.	N.	ἰχθύ-s, ὁ, *fish*
	G.	ἰχθύ-ος
	D.	ἰχθύ-ϊ
	A.	ἰχθύ-ν
	V.	ἰχθύ
Dual	N. A. V.	ἰχθύ-ε
	G. D.	ἰχθύ-οιν
Plur.	N. V.	ἰχθύ-ες
	G.	ἰχθύ-ων
	D.	ἰχθύ-σι(ν)
	A.	ἰχθῦς

284. Adverbial accusative. — The accusative in some expressions has the force of an adverb :

πρῶτον at first, first (§ 250); τί why (§ 231)? τέλος finally ; τὸ λοιπόν thereafter, in the future.

285. Attraction of the relative to the case of its antecedent. — The relative pronoun may be attracted from the accusative case to the case of its antecedent, if this is a genitive or dative :

ἐκ τῆς ἀγορᾶς ἧς [for ἥν] οὗτοι παρ-εῖχον from the market which these supplied ;

σὺν τοῖς ὅπλοις οἷς [for ἅ] ἔχομεν with the arms which we have.

286.   VOCABULARY XXVII

ἀθροίζω (theme ἀθροιδ-; cp. ἁρπάζω), ἀθροίσω, ἤθροισα : gather together, collect, assemble (trans.).

ἀρχαῖος, ᾱ, ον (ἀρχή *beginning*) : *primitive, old, of old, ancient.* τὸ ἀρχαῖον (adv. acc.) : *of old, formerly.* Archaic.

ἄστυ, εως, τό : *town.*

δασμός, οῦ, ὁ : *tribute, tax.*

δύναμις, εως, ἡ : *force, strength.* Dynamic, dynamite.

Ἑλληνικός, ή, όν ("Ελλην) : *Hellenic, Greek.*

ἰχθύς, ύος, ὁ : *fish.* Ichthyo-logy (λόγος *account*).

Ἰωνικός, ή, όν (Ἰωνίā) : *of Ionia, Ionian.*

Λακεδαίμων, ονος, ἡ : *Lacedaemon.*

λοιπός, ή, όν (cp. λείπ-ω) : *left, rest of, remaining.* τὸ λοιπόν (adv. acc.) : *thereafter, in the future.*

πεντε-καί-δεκα indecl. : *five and ten, fifteen.*

πῆχυς, εως, ὁ : *forearm ;* ɩubit, 1½ Greek feet.

πλέθρον, ου, τό : *plethrum,* 100 Greek feet.

πλήρης, ες : *full.* Cp. Lat. *plē-nus.*

πόλις, εως, ἡ : *city.* Politic, polity, etc.

πρέσβεις, εων, οἱ : *ambassadors* The nom. sing. is πρεσβευτής, οῦ, ὁ.

Σάρδεις, εων, αἱ : *Sardis,* a city in Lydia.

τέλος, ους, τό : *end.* As adv. acc. : *finally.*

Χάλος, ου, ὁ : *Chalus,* a river in Syria.

EXERCISES FOR TRANSLATION

287. I. 1. Ξενίᾱς δὴ τοὺς ἐκ τῶν πόλεων [1] λαβὼν παρ-ῆν εἰς Σάρδεις. 2. τὴν δὲ Ἑλληνικὴν δύναμιν ἤθροιζεν. 3. ἦν δὲ τεῖχος ὡς πεντεκαίδεκα πήχεων [2] τὸ εὖρος. 4. τί δεῖ λύειν αὐτοὺς τὴν γέφῡραν ; 5. καὶ γὰρ ἦσαν αἱ Ἰωνικαὶ πόλεις Τισσαφέρνους [3] τὸ ἀρχαῖον. 6. οἱ δ' ἐκ τοῦ ἄστεως [4] εἰς τὴν ἀγορὰν ἦλθον. 7. εἰς Λακεδαίμονα ἔπεμπον πρέσβεις. 8. ἐντεῦθεν ἐξ-ελαύνει σταθμοὺς δύο παρασάγγᾱς πεντεκαίδεκα εἰς πόλιν εὐδαίμονα. 9. Κῦρος δ' ἀπ-έπεμπε τοὺς δασμοὺς ἐκ τῶν πόλεων ὧν [5] ἐτύγχανεν ἔχων. 10. τέλος δ' ἀπ-ῆλθον. 11. καὶ τὸ λοιπὸν ὁ Κλέαρχος ἦρχεν. 12. ἐξ-ελαύνει ἐπὶ τὸν Χάλον ποταμόν, ὄντα τὸ εὖρος πλέθρου, [6] πλήρη δ' ἰχθύων.

---

[1] § 70. *a.*   [3] § 229.   [5] For ἅς, § 285.

[2] § 278.   [4] § 70. *a.*   [6] §§ 278, 279.

II. 1. The cities are prosperous. 2. And thereafter Cyrus sent the tributes from the cities to his brother. 3. We bought provisions from the market which the barbarians supplied. 4. The river is full of beautiful fish.

XXVIII

ADJECTIVES OF THE CONSONANT DECLENSION AND Ā-DECLENSION COMBINED. DECLENSION OF ἡδύς AND πᾶς. NOUNS WITH STEMS IN -ευ OR -ου. OMISSION OF THE COPULA. βασιλεύς WITHOUT THE ARTICLE. πᾶς IN PREDICATE POSITION, ETC.

DECLENSION OF ἡδύς *sweet*

288. Compare the masculine ἡδύς with πῆχυς (§ 282) and observe that the *endings* differ in the genitive singular only. Compare the neuter ἡδύ with ἄστυ (§ 282) and observe that the endings differ in the genitive singular and the nominative (= accusative and vocative) plural. The feminine ἡδεῖα is declined like γέφυρα, except as regards the accent.

		MASC.	FEM.	NEUT.
Sing.	N.	ἡδύς	ἡδεῖα	ἡδύ
	G.	ἡδέος	ἡδείας	ἡδέος
	D.	ἡδεῖ	ἡδείᾳ	ἡδεῖ
	A.	ἡδύν	ἡδεῖαν	ἡδύ
	V.	ἡδύ	ἡδεῖα	ἡδύ
Dual	N. A. V.	ἡδεῖ	ἡδείᾱ	ἡδεῖ
	G. D.	ἡδέοιν	ἡδείαιν	ἡδέοιν
Plur.	N. V.	ἡδεῖς	ἡδεῖαι	ἡδέα
	G.	ἡδέων	ἡδειῶν	ἡδέων
	D.	ἡδέσι(ν)	ἡδείαις	ἡδέσι(ν)
	A.	ἡδεῖς	ἡδείας	ἡδέα

DECLENSION OF πᾶς *all, every*

289. Compare this paradigm with ἀκούσᾱς (§ 209). The accent of the genitive plural πάντων and dative plural πᾱ-σι(ν) is irregular (cp. § 189).

	MASC.	FEM.	NEUT.
Sing. N. V.	πᾶς	πᾶσα	πᾶν
G.	παντός	πάσης	παντός
D.	παντί	πάσῃ	παντί
A.	πάντα	πᾶσαν	πᾶν
Plur. N. V.	πάντες	πᾶσαι	πάντα
G.	πάντων	πᾱσῶν	πάντων
D.	πᾶσι(ν)	πάσαις	πᾶσι(ν)
A.	πάντας	πάσᾱς	πάντα

NOUNS WITH STEMS ENDING IN A DIPHTHONG -ευ OR -ου

	I	2
	1	2
290. Sing. N.	βασιλεύ-ς, ὁ, *king*	βοῦ-ς, ὁ, ἡ, *ox, cow*
G.	βασιλέ-ως	βο-ός
D.	βασιλεῖ	βο-ΐ
A.	βασιλέ-ᾱ	βοῦ-ν
V.	βασιλεῦ	βοῦ
Dual N. A. V.	βασιλῆ	βό-ε
G. D.	βασιλέ-οιν	βο-οῖν
Plur. N. V.	βασιλεῖς (older -ῆς)	βό-ες
G.	βασιλέ-ων	βο-ῶν
D.	βασιλεῦ-σι(ν)	βου-σί(ν)
A.	βασιλέ-ᾱς	βοῦς

For the accent of the monosyllable βοῦς see § 189.

291. The verb ἐστί (and pl. εἰσί), commonly known as the *copula*, may be **omitted** where it can be readily supplied, as in proverbial expressions. See also § 230.

> ἀγαθὸς ὁ θεός God is good ;
> ἀγαθοὶ οἱ θεοί the gods are good.

292. The **article** is commonly **omitted** with βασιλεύς when this word means *the king* of Persia, the great king.

293. πᾶς, when modifying a noun, usually has the predicate position (§§ 68, 69). The difference in meaning between the predicate and attributive use is as follows:

> *Predicate :* πᾶσα ἡ πόλις all the city.
> *Attributive :* ἡ πᾶσα πόλις the whole city.

Sometimes the article is wanting:

> πᾶσα πόλις every city ;
> πάντες ἄνθρωποι all men.

Compare ὅλος (Vocabulary XVII), which is similarly used.

294. VOCABULARY XXVIII

ἄ-πᾶς, ᾶσα, ᾶν : *all together, all.*

βασιλεύς, έως, ὁ : *king.* Basil.

βοῦς, βοός, ὁ, ἡ : *ox, cow.* Cp. Lat. *bōs.*

δασύς, εῖα, ύ : *thickly grown, thickly wooded* ; with dat. (instrumental). Cp. Lat. *dēnsus.*

δένδρον, ου, τό : *tree.* Dat. pl. δένδροις and δένδρεσι (from τὸ δένδρος). Rhodo-dendron (ῥόδον *rose*).

ἤ, conj. : *or ; than* (after comparative ideas). ἤ . . . ἤ : *either . . . or.*

ἡδύς, εῖα, ύ : *sweet.*

ἥμισυς, εια, υ : *half.* τὸ ἥμισυ (with στρατεύματος) : *the half.* ἥμισυς takes the gender and the number of its part. gen. Cp. Lat. *sēmi-,* Eng. hemi-.

ἱππεύς, έως, ὁ (ἵππος) : *horseman ;* pl. *cavalry.*

λάθρᾳ, adv. : *secretly.* With gen. : *without the knowledge of.*

πᾶς, πᾶσα, πᾶν : *every* (in sing.), *all, whole.* See § 293. **Pan**hellenic ("Ελλην).

παχύς, εῖα, ύ : *thick* in diameter. Pachy-derm (δέρμα *hide*).

πυκνός, ή, όν : *closely set, closely standing, closely planted.*

σκότος, ους, τό : *darkness.* Also ὁ σκότος, gen. ου.

σύμ-μαχος, ον, ὁ (μάχη) : *fellow-fighter, ally.*

ὡς, prep. with acc. : *to ;* used only with names of persons and βασιλέᾱ *king* of Persia. Cp. Vocabularies XXII, XXIV, XXVI.

EXERCISES FOR TRANSLATION

295. I. 1. πάντας δ' ἀπ-έπεμπεν.   2. οἱ δ' αὐτῷ μᾶλ-λον φίλοι ἦσαν ἢ βασιλεῖ.   3. φᾱσὶν οὖν δασέα τὰ ὄρη ταῦτα εἶναι.   4. οἶνον ἡδὺν εἶχεν.   5. ὁ Χειρί-σοφος δι-έβαινεν ἔχων τὸ ἥμισυ τοῦ στρατεύματος.[1] 6. ἦν δὲ οὗτος ὁ λόφος δασὺς δένδρεσι παχέσι μὲν οὔ,[2] πυκνοῖς δέ.   7. οὐδὲ ἱππέᾱ σύμμαχον[3] ἔχομεν.   8. ἅμα δὲ τῇ ἡμέρᾳ εἶδον ἱππέᾱς πέρᾱν τοῦ ποταμοῦ.   9. ἔθῡ-σαν δὲ ἢ βοῦς ἢ ἵππους.   10. τὴν δὲ Ἑλληνικὴν δύνα-μιν Κῦρος λάθρᾳ ἤθροιζεν, ὅπως ἀφύλακτον λάβοι βασιλέᾱ.   11. Τισσαφέρνης δὲ ἦλθεν ὡς βασιλέᾱ, ἱπ-πέᾱς ἔχων ὡς πεντακοσίους.   12. πᾶσα ἡ ὁδὸς διὰ σκότους ἐστίν.   13. πᾶς δὲ ποταμὸς ἄπορος.[4]   14. αἱ σπονδαί εἰσιν ἅπασιν.

II. 1. On the following day they all came to a river full of fish.   2. He says that this river is thickly grown with trees.   3. All the satraps sent sweet wine to the king.

---

[1] § 179.   [2] § 99.   [3] § 53. *j*.   [4] Supply ἐστίν.

Fig. 16. — Prow of a War Ship.

XXIX

THE IMPERATIVE ACTIVE OF Ω–VERBS. IMPERATIVE OF
εἰμί. TENSES OF THE IMPERATIVE. DECLENSION
OF ἐγώ AND σύ. USES OF PERSONAL PRONOUNS.
ACCENT OF SUCCESSIVE ENCLITICS. PREDICATE
POSITION OF THE POSSESSIVE GENITIVE OF
PERSONAL PRONOUNS. PROHIBITIONS. ἐπεί AND
ὅτι CAUSAL

296. The thematic vowel (§ 41) and tense suffix of the
present imperative and the tense suffix (σα) of the first
aorist imperative are the same as in the indicative mood.
The imperative has special personal endings, however;
and the second person singular of the first aorist has a
peculiar ending, -σον.

297.   PRESENT IMPERATIVE ACTIVE OF λύω

	SING.	DUAL	PLUR.
2.	λῦ-ε *loose*	λύ-ε-τον	λύ-ε-τε *loose*
3.	λῡ-έ-τω *let him loose*	λῡ-έ-των	λυ-ό-ντων *let them loose*

FIRST AORIST IMPERATIVE ACTIVE

2.	λῦ-σον *loose*	λύ-σα-τον	λύ-σα-τε *loose*
3.	λῡ-σά-τω *let him loose*	λῡ-σά-των	λῡ-σά-ντων *let them loose*

298. Like the present imperative of λύω are inflected
the present imperatives of all the other ω-verbs hitherto
studied.

299. In the formation of the first aorist imperative of
verbs with mute themes, the same euphonic laws are observed as in the first aorist indicative, subjunctive, and

optative (§§ 153, 164). Thus πέμψον (πέμπω), πεῖσον (πείθω), ἅρπασον (ἁρπάζω), φύλαξον (φυλάττω).

300. Verbs which, like λείπω, lack a first aorist indicative, also lack a first aorist imperative (and all other first aorist forms). They have, instead, a second aorist imperative, with the inflection of the present.

301. SECOND AORIST IMPERATIVE ACTIVE OF λείπω

	SING.	DUAL	PLUR.
2.	λίπ-ε *leave*	λίπ-ε-τον	λίπ-ε-τε *leave*
3.	λιπ-έ-τω *let him leave*	λιπ-έ-των	λιπ-ό-ντων *let them leave*

a. Some second aorist imperatives are irregularly accented on the ultima (instead of the penult) in the second person singular: thus εἰπέ *say*.[1]

302.   PRESENT IMPERATIVE OF εἰμί *I am*

	SING.	DUAL	PLUR.
2.	ἴσ-θι *be thou*	ἔσ-τον	ἔσ-τε *be ye*
3.	ἔσ-τω *let him be*	ἔσ-των	ἔσ-των[2] *let them be*

303. Tenses of the imperative. — The distinction between the present and aorist imperative is the same as that between the present and aorist subjunctive (§ 240). The present denotes a continued or repeated act; the aorist a single act.

a. The aorist imperative refers to future time, and is therefore regarded as a primary tense.

DECLENSION OF THE PERSONAL PRONOUNS ἐγώ *I* AND σύ *you*

304.	Sing. N.	ἐγώ *I*	N.V.	σύ *you* (*thou*)
	G.	ἐμοῦ, μου		σοῦ, σου
	D.	ἐμοί, μοι		σοί, σοι
	A.	ἐμέ, με		σέ, σε

---

[1] So, too, ἐλθέ *come*, εὑρέ *find* (εὑρίσκω), ἰδέ *see, behold*, λαβέ *seize*.

[2] Also ἔσ-τω-σαν and ὄντων.

Dual N. A.	νώ		σφώ
G. D.	νῷν		σφῷν
Plur. N.	ἡμεῖς *we*	N. V.	ὑμεῖς *you*
G.	ἡμῶν		ὑμῶν
D.	ἡμῖν		ὑμῖν
A.	ἡμᾶς		ὑμᾶς

a. Enclitic forms (§ 21) are μου, μοι, με, σου, σοι, σε; emphatic forms, not enclitic, are ἐμοῦ, ἐμοί, ἐμέ, σοῦ, σοί, σέ. After prepositions the accented forms are regularly used.

Review the rules about enclitics (§§ 103–105).

305. If two or more **enclitics** occur **in succession**, each has an acute accent except the last, which remains unaccented:

εἴ τίς τί μοί φησιν if anybody says anything to me.

306. A **personal pronoun** as subject nominative is expressed only for emphasis:

ταῦτα ἤκουσα ἐγώ it was I who heard this.

307. The personal pronoun of the third person is αὐτοῦ *of him*, αὐτῆς *of her*, αὐτοῦ *of it* (§ 123. 3). The nominative, when required to be expressed, may be ὁ δέ (§ 99), ἡ δέ (§ 99), ἐκεῖνος, οὗτος, ὅδε (§§ 175–177).

308. αὐτοῦ, μου, σου, etc., when denoting *possession*, have the predicate position (cp. § 127):

ὁ ἀδελφός μου my brother (cp. § 126).

309. A **prohibition** is expressed by:

1. μή with the present imperative (§ 303):

μὴ θαυμάζετε don't wonder (*i.e.* keep from wondering *or* cease to wonder).

2. μή with the second person of the aorist subjunctive (§ 240):

μὴ θαυμάσητε don't be astonished (*for once*).

310. ἐπεί and ὅτι causal, *since*, are followed by tenses of the indicative. The negative is οὐ. Other causal conjunctions take the same construction :

πέμψατε Πρόξενον, ἐπεὶ στρατηγός ἐστιν send Proxenus, since he is a general.

311.   VOCABULARY XXIX

ἄ-βατος, ον (ἀ- priv. and stem βα-, cp. δια-βαίνω) : not to be trodden on, *impassable.*

ἄγε, imv. of ἄγω used as an interjection : *come !* ἄγε (or ἄγετε) δή : *come now !*

βλέπω, fut. to be learned later, ἔβλεψα : *look.*

γνώμη, ης, ἡ : *opinion, judgment ; plan, proposition ; understanding.* Gnome.

ἐγώ : *I,* § 304. Lat. *ego.*

ἐπεί, conj. : *since.* Strengthened, ἐπεί-περ : *since indeed.* Cp. Vocabulary XIV.

ὅσ-περ, ἥ-περ, ὅ-περ (strengthened ὅς) : *the very one which, the very thing which.*

ὅταν = ὅτε + ἄν (§ 248. 2), conj. with subjv. : *when.*

πατρίς, ίδος, ἡ : *fatherland.*

πρός, prep. : with GEN. *from the side of, from ; toward ;* πρὸς (τῶν) θεῶν : *before the gods, in the sight of the gods ;* with DAT. *near, beside, in addition to ;* with ACC. *to, toward, against.* Cp. Vocabulary II.

στρατό-πεδον, ου, τό : *camp.* Cp. στράτευμα, στρατιά.

σύ : *you* (sing.), § 304.

σύνθημα, ατος, τό : *agreement ; watchword.*

ὑπέρ, prep. : with GEN. *over, above ; on behalf of ;* with ACC. *over, beyond.* Hyper-bole (βολή *a throw*).

EXERCISES FOR TRANSLATION

312. I. 1. ἥκετε εἰς τὸ μέσον τοῦ στρατοπέδου καὶ τοὺς ἄρχοντας ἄγετε. 2. ἀπό-πεμπε δὲ ἢ ἡμᾶς ἢ αὐτούς. 3. νομίζω γὰρ ὑμᾶς ἐμοὶ[1] εἶναι καὶ πατρίδα καὶ φίλους καὶ συμμάχους. 4. ἀκούσατε οὖν μου πρὸς θεῶν. 5. τὰ δὲ ἐπιτήδεια λαμβάνετε ἐκ τῶν ἐν τῷ πεδίῳ[2] κωμῶν. 6. σὺ δέ, ὦ Σώκρατες, ἐλθὼν[3] εἰπὲ ὅτι

---

[1] § 119.   [2] § 70.   [3] Freely : *go and say.*

ἐγὼ κελεύω αὐτοὺς κατα-λιπεῖν τὰ ὅπλα.   7. ὅταν δὲ
ταύτᾱς τὰς πόλεις ἔχητε, μὴ ἀπ-έλθητε.   8. ἄγε δή, ὦ
'Αριαῖε, ἐπείπερ ὁ αὐτὸς στόλος ἐστὶν ὑμῖν[1] καὶ ἡμῖν,
εἰπὲ τὴν σὴν γνώμην.   9. λέξον δὲ πᾶσι, ὦ Πρόξενε,
ἅπερ ἔλεξας καὶ[2] πρὸς ἡμᾶς.   10. βλέψον πρὸς τὰ
ὄρη καὶ ἴδε ὡς[3] ἄβατα πάντα ἐστίν.   11. εἰ δέ τις
ἄλλος πάρ-εστι, λεξάτω.   12. συμ-πέμψατε μέντοι μοί
τινας, οἵτινες καὶ[4] λέξουσιν ὑπὲρ ἐμοῦ καὶ πρᾱ́ξουσιν.
13. παρ-έστω δ' ἡμῖν καὶ[2] ὁ κῆρυξ.   14. τοῦτο ἔστω
τὸ σύνθημα.

II. 1. But do you[5] send others to the mountains.
2. Do not take[6] supplies from the villages in the plain.
3. Let the herald attend me, when I come[7] to the camp.

---

[1] *I.e.* you and your followers.   [2] *also.*   [3] *how.*
[4] *both.*   [5] Sing.   [6] Single act.   [7] Aor. subjv.

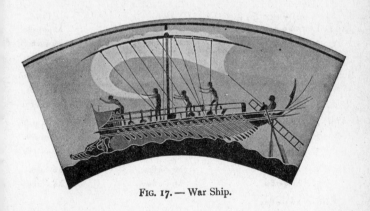

FIG. 17. — War Ship.

XXX

THE PRESENT MIDDLE SYSTEM OF Ω–VERBS.   MEAN-
INGS OF THE MIDDLE VOICE.   DEPONENT VERBS.
DATIVE OF ASSOCIATION

313. In the inflection of the present and imperfect
middle (§ 37) there are to be seen the same thematic vowel,
mood signs, and augment (in the imperfect indicative) as
in the corresponding active tenses.   Only a new series of
personal endings has to be learned.   The primary endings
are seen in the present indicative and the subjunctive;
the secondary endings, in the imperfect indicative and the
optative.   The ending of the second person singular, primary -σαι and secondary -σο, does not, however, appear
intact in any of these forms.

314.   PRESENT MIDDLE SYSTEM OF λύω

	SING.	DUAL	PLUR.
Indic. 1.	λύ-ο-μαι *I loose for myself, I ransom*		λῡ-ό-μεθα
2.	λύ-ῃ or λύ-ει	λύ-ε-σθον	λύ-ε-σθε
3.	λύ-ε-ται	λύ-ε-σθον	λύ-ο-νται
Subjv. 1.	λύ-ω-μαι		λῡ-ώ-μεθα
2.	λύ-ῃ	λύ-η-σθον	λύ-η-σθε
3.	λύ-η-ται	λύ-η-σθον	λύ-ω-νται
Opt. 1.	λῡ-οί-μην		λῡ-οί-μεθα
2.	λύ-οι-ο	λύ-οι-σθον	λύ-οι-σθε
3.	λύ-οι-το	λῡ-οί-σθην	λύ-οι-ντο
Imv. 2.	λύ-ου	λύ-ε-σθον	λύ-ε-σθε
3.	λῡ-έ-σθω	λῡ-έ-σθων	λῡ-έ-σθων
Inf.	λύ-ε-σθαι		
Partic.	λῡ-ό-μενος, η, ον (declined like ἀγαθός, but with accent like		
	πολέμιος, §§ 116, 117)		

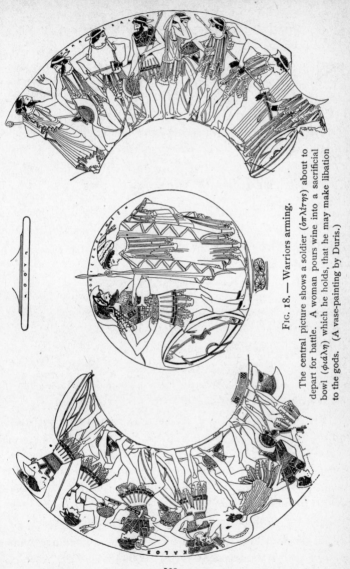

Fig. 18. — Warriors arming.

The central picture shows a soldier (ὁπλίτης) about to depart for battle. A woman pours wine into a sacrificial bowl (φιάλη) which he holds, that he may make libation to the gods. (A vase-painting by Duris.)

The imperfect indicative belongs to the present system:

	SING.	DUAL	PLUR.
Impf. 1.	ἐ-λῡ-ό-μην *I loosed for myself, I ransomed*		ἐ-λῡ-ό-μεθα
Indic. 2.	ἐ-λύ-ου	ἐ-λύ-ε-σθον	ἐ-λύ-ε-σθε
3.	ἐ-λύ-ε-το	ἐ-λῡ-έ-σθην	ἐ-λύ-ο-ντο

Review the present active system of λύω, *i.e.* the present and imperfect indicative, the present subjunctive, optative, imperative, infinitive, and participle (§§ 45, 81, 206. *a*, 235, 254, 297).

MEANINGS OF THE MIDDLE VOICE

315. The middle voice of the Greek verb represents the subject

I. As acting directly on himself (*direct middle*):

οἱ Ἕλληνες παρ-εσκευάζοντο the Greeks made themselves ready;
πορεύονται they make themselves go, they proceed;
ἀθροίζονται they gather themselves together, they muster;
φυλάττονται they guard themselves, they are on their guard [against];
σῴζονται they save themselves.

II. As acting for himself or for his own interests in some way (*indirect middle*):

τὰς ἁμάξᾱς παρα-σκευάζεται he prepares the wagons *for himself;*
Κῦρον μετα-πέμπεται he sends for Cyrus *to come to himself;*

It is often impossible to translate the middle, in this use, differently from the active.

a. There is also a *reciprocal* use of the middle voice, which represents the subjects as acting mutually. Thus δια-λέγονται *they converse*, μάχονται (μάχη) *they fight*, ἀγωνίζονται (ἀγών) *they struggle*.

316. Many verbs are found in the middle voice only, either in some or in all of their tenses. They are commonly known as **deponent verbs.** Thus οἴχομαι *be gone.*

317. Converse *with* and fight *with* somebody are expressed by the dative without a preposition. The dative so used with these and similar verbs is included under the dative of association :

δια-λέγονται τοῖς στρατηγοῖς they converse with the generals.

318. VOCABULARY XXX

ἀθροίζομαι, mid. of ἀθροίζω (Vocabulary XXVII) : *gather* (intr.), *muster*, with εἰς and acc.

βούλομαι : *wish*.

δια-λέγομαι (cp. λέγω *say*) : *converse*, with dat. Dialect.

ἑρμηνεύς, έως, ὁ : *interpreter*. Hermeneutics.

ἔρχομαι, 2 aor. ἦλθον (Vocabulary XVIII) : *come, go*.

μετα-πέμπομαι (cp. πέμπω) : *send after to come to oneself, summon*.

οἴχομαι : *be gone, have gone* (pres. with pf. meaning). Often with supplementary partic. ; cp. § 215.

παρα-σκευάζω (theme σκευαδ-), παρα-σκευάσω, παρ-εσκεύασα : *prepare, equip* ; MID. *make oneself ready, prepare oneself ; prepare* something *for oneself*.

πορεύομαι : *go, proceed*. Cp. ἄ-πορος.

προ-πέμπω (cp. πέμπω) : *send forward* or *ahead*.

σώζω (themes σωδ- and σω-), σώσω, ἔσωσα : *save* ; MID. *save oneself*.

φυλάττομαι, mid. of φυλάττω (Vocabulary XV) : *guard oneself, be on one's guard* (*against*, with acc.).

EXERCISES FOR TRANSLATION

319. I. 1. ὁ δὲ Δαρεῖος ἐβούλετο τοὺς παῖδας παρεῖναι.   2. οἱ δὲ στρατιῶται εἰς τὸ πεδίον ἀθροίζονται. 3. Ἀρίστιππος ἔρχεται πρὸς τὸν Κῦρον.   4. πορεύεται δὲ ὡς βασιλέā.   5. μετὰ ταῦτα ἐξ-ῆλθον φυλαττόμενοι στρατηγοὶ τῶν Ἑλλήνων.   6. δεῖ δὲ ἡμᾶς παρα-σκευά-ζεσθαι ὅπως σωζώμεθα.   7. οἱ δὲ ἤθροιζον τὰς τριήρεις, ὡς ἐν ταῖς τριήρεσι σώζοιντο.   8. εἰ δὲ ἐθέλεις, πορεύου ἐπὶ τὸ ὄρος.   9. παρα-σχήσω αὐτῷ ὅ τι ἂν

βούληται.   10. οἱ δὲ στρατιῶται ἔλεγον ὡς ὁ λοχᾱγὸς
οἴχοιτο.   11. καὶ προ-πέμψᾱς ἑρμηνέᾱ εἶπεν ὅτι βούλοιτο δια-λέγεσθαι τοῖς ἄρχουσιν.   12. ὁ δ᾽ ἑρμηνεὺς
εἶπεν ὅτι παρὰ βασιλέως πορεύονται πρὸς τὸν σατράπην.   13. Κῦρος δὲ μετ-επέμπετο τὸν Κλέαρχον.
14. καὶ βασιλεὺς δὴ ἐπεὶ ἤκουσε Τισσαφέρνους τὸν
Κύρου στόλον, παρ-εσκευάζετο.   15. καὶ εἰς τὸ πρόσθεν[1] οἴχονται διώκοντες.

II. 1. Cyrus summoned the generals (to come to him).
2. The leaders said that they wished to converse with
us.   3. Guarding ourselves, we proceeded through the
night.   4. Take whatever you wish.

XXXI

SYNCOPATED NOUNS.   DATIVE OF RESPECT

320. Some frequently occurring nouns of the consonant
declension, with stems in ερ-, drop ε before ρ in the genitive and dative singular and the dative plural: πατήρ
(πατερ-) *father*, μήτηρ (μητερ-) *mother*, θυγάτηρ (θυγατερ-)
daughter.   One noun, ἀνήρ (ἀνερ-) *man*, drops ε before ρ in
all its cases except the nominative and vocative singular;
δ is inserted where ε is dropped from forms of ἀνήρ.   The
dative plural of all these nouns has the auxiliary sound *a*
added to the stem before the case ending.

The accent is to be carefully noted.   It is recessive in
the vocative singular.

---

[1] *to the front.*

321.

Sing.	N.	πατήρ, ὁ, *father*	μήτηρ, ἡ, *mother*
	G.	πατρ-ός [for πατέρ-ος]	μητρ-ός [for μητέρ-ος]
	D.	πατρ-ί [for πατέρ-ι]	μητρ-ί [for μητέρ-ι]
	A.	πατέρ-α	μητέρ-α
	V.	πάτερ	μῆτερ
Dual N. A. V.		πατέρ-ε	μητέρ-ε
G. D.		πατέρ-οιν	μητέρ-οιν
Plur. N. V.		πατέρ-ες	μητέρ-ες
G.		πατέρ-ων	μητέρ-ων
D.		πατρά-σι(ν)	μητρά-σι(ν)
A.		πατέρ-ας	μητέρ-ας

Sing.	N.	θυγάτηρ, ἡ, *daughter*	ἀνήρ, ὁ, *man*
	G.	θυγατρ-ός	ἀνδρ-ός [for ἀνέρ-ος]
	D.	θυγατρ-ί	ἀνδρ-ί etc.
	A.	θυγατέρ-α	ἄνδρ-α
	V.	θύγατερ	ἄνερ
Dual N. A. V.		θυγατέρ-ε	ἄνδρ-ε
G. D.		θυγατέρ-οιν	ἀνδρ-οῖν
Plur. N. V.		θυγατέρ-ες	ἄνδρ-ες
G.		θυγατέρ-ων	ἀνδρ-ῶν
D.		θυγατρά-σι(ν)	ἀνδρά-σι(ν)
A.		θυγατέρ-ας	ἄνδρ-ας

322. Dative of respect. — The instrumental dative (§ 141) may indicate *in respect to what* an expression is used :

γένει προσ-ήκων βασιλεῖ in respect to birth related to the king.

a. The accusative of specification (§ 279) is far more commonly used.

323. VOCABULARY XXXI

'Αβροκόμᾱς, ᾱ (Doric gen., for ου), ὁ: *Abrocomas.*

ἀνήρ, ἀνδρός, ὁ: *man; husband.* ὦ ἄνδρες στρατιῶται (or ῞Ελλη-νες) : *fellow soldiers* (or *Greeks*).

γένος, ους, τό: *kinship, family, birth.* Lat. *genus, gēns.*

δώ-δεκα (δύο + δέκα), indecl.:
twelve. Dodeca-gon (γωνία
angle).

ἐχθρός, ά, όν: hostile. ἐχθρός
(subst.) οὗ, ὁ: personal enemy.
To be distinguished from
πολέμιος and οἱ πολέμιοι the
enemy in war.

θυγάτηρ, θυγατρός, ἡ: daughter.

μήτηρ, μητρός, ἡ: mother. Lat.
māter.

Ὀρόντᾱς, ᾱ (Doric gen., for ου), ὁ:
Orontas.

Παρύσατις, ιδος, ἡ: Parysatis,
wife of Darius II, king of Per-

sia, and mother of Artaxerxes II
and Cyrus the Younger.

πατήρ, πατρός, ὁ: father. Lat.
pater.

προσ-ήκω: come to, reach to, pertain to; pres. partic. related,
with dat.

στρατεύω, στρατεύσω, ἐστράτευσα:
make an expedition; dep. MID.
take the field, serve in war. Cp.
στράτευ-μα, etc.

συ-στρατεύω (σύν + στρατεύω, § 133.
4), usually dep. MID. συ-στρατεύομαι: take the field with, serve
in war with, with dat.

EXERCISES FOR TRANSLATION

324. I. 1. ἐγώ, ὦ ἄνδρες Ἕλληνες, γείτων εἰμὶ τῇ
Ἑλλάδι. 2. οἱ δ' ἔλεγον ὅτι ἄνδρες περὶ σπονδῶν
ἥκοιεν. 3. ἀγαθοὶ δὴ φίλοι εἰσὶ χρήσιμοι ἀνδρί.[1]
4. Κῦρος οὖν ἀνα-βαίνει παρὰ τὸν πατέρα. 5. οἱ δὲ
στρατιῶται κατ-έλιπον πατέρας καὶ μητέρας ἐπεὶ συν-
εστρατεύοντο Κύρῳ. 6. ἐντεῦθεν ἐπορεύοντο εἰς τὰς
Παρυσάτιδος κώμᾱς τῆς Κύρου καὶ βασιλέως μητρός.
7. Ὀρόντᾱς δ' ἤγετο[2] τὴν θυγατέρα τὴν[3] βασιλέως.
8. ἡ δὲ μήτηρ αὐτὸν ἀπο-πέμπει πάλιν ἐπὶ τὴν ἀρχήν. 9. ἐκέλευσε δὲ τοὺς λοχᾱγοὺς λαμβάνειν[4] ἄνδρας.
10. ἔλεξε γὰρ ὅτι ἀκούοι Ἀβροκόμαν, ἐχθρὸν ἄνδρα,
ἐπὶ τῷ Εὐφράτῃ ποταμῷ εἶναι, ἀπ-έχοντα δώδεκα σταθμούς. 11. πρὸς τοῦτον οὖν ἔφη βούλεσθαι στρα-

---

[1] § 111.
[3] §§ 67, 69.
[2] ἄγω in mid. sometimes means marry.
[4] take = enlist.

τεύεσθαι.   12. Ὀρόντας δέ, Πέρσης ἀνήρ, γένει τε
προσ-ήκων βασιλεῖ,[1] ἐπι-βουλεύει Κύρῳ.

II. 1. I advise you to abandon this man.   2. Men have
come[2] with reference to[3] a truce.   3. The father summoned his daughters (to his side).[4]   4. Cyrus ordered
his generals to enlist men, in order that they might take
the field with him against the king.

XXXII

THE SECOND AORIST MIDDLE AND THE FUTURE
MIDDLE SYSTEMS OF Ω–VERBS.   FUTURE SYSTEM
OF εἰμί.   FUTURE PARTICIPLE EXPRESSING PUR-
POSE.   ὡς WITH FUTURE PARTICIPLE.   INFINI-
TIVE WITH ADJECTIVES OF *FITNESS* AND
ABILITY

325. The second aorist middle of λείπω and similar
verbs (§§ 83–88) differs from the second aorist active in
the personal endings only.   The second aorist indicative
is inflected with the endings of the imperfect; while the
second aorist subjunctive, optative, and imperative have
the endings of the present tense in these moods.

The second person singular of the second aorist middle
imperative in -οῦ always has the circumflex on the ultima;
and the second aorist middle infinitive is always accented
on the penult.

---

[1] § 111.   [2] ἥκω.   [3] *about*.   [4] Omit.

326. SECOND AORIST SYSTEM OF λείπω IN THE MIDDLE VOICE

	SING.	DUAL	PLUR.
Indic. 1.	ἐ-λιπ-ό-μην		ἐ-λιπ-ό-μεθα
2.	ἐ-λίπ-ου	ἐ-λίπ-ε-σθον	ἐ-λίπ-ε-σθε
3.	ἐ-λίπ-ε-το	ἐ-λιπ-έ-σθην	ἐ-λίπ-ο-ντο
Subjv. 1.	λίπ-ω-μαι		λιπ-ώ-μεθα
2.	λίπ-ῃ	λίπ-η-σθον	λίπ-η-σθε
3.	λίπ-η-ται	λίπ-η-σθον	λίπ-ω-νται
Opt. 1.	λιπ-οί-μην		λιπ-οί-μεθα
2.	λίπ-οι-ο	λίπ-οι-σθον	λίπ-οι-σθε
3.	λίπ-οι-το	λιπ-οί-σθην	λίπ-οι-ντο
Imv. 2.	λιπ-οῦ	λίπ-ε-σθον	λίπ-ε-σθε
3.	λιπ-έ-σθω	λιπ-έ-σθων	λιπ-έ-σθων
Inf.	λιπ-έ-σθαι		
Partic.	λιπ-ό-μενος, η, ον		

Review the second aorist active system of λείπω, *i.e.* the second aorist indicative, subjunctive, optative, imperative, infinitive, and participle (§§ 85, 208, 238, 257, 301).

327. The **future middle** differs from the future active in personal endings only. The subjunctive and imperative have no future tense in any voice.

328. The future middle of mute themes is formed with the same euphonic changes at the end of the theme as the future active (§ 153). Thus μετα-πέμπομαι *summon*, fut. μετα-πέμψομαι, δέχομαι *receive*, fut. δέξομαι, ἁρπάζω *plunder*, fut. mid. ἁρπάσομαι.

329. FUTURE SYSTEM OF λύω IN THE MIDDLE VOICE

	SING.	DUAL	PLUR.
Indic. 1.	λύ-σο-μαι { *I shall loose for myself* / *I shall ransom* }		λῡ-σό-μεθα
2.	λύ-σῃ, λύ-σει	λύ-σε-σθον	λύ-σε-σθε
3.	λύ-σε-ται	λύ-σε-σθον	λύ-σο-νται

	Sing.	Dual	Plur.
Opt. 1.	λῡ-σοί-μην		λῡ-σοί-μεθα
2.	λύ-σοι-ο	λύ-σοι-σθον	λύ-σοι-σθε
3.	λύ-σοι-το	λῡ-σοί-σθην	λύ-σοι-ντο
Inf.	λύ-σε-σθαι		
Partic.	λῡ-σό-μενος, η, ον		

Review the future active system of λύω, *i.e.* the future indicative, optative, infinitive, and participle (§§ 151, 207, 254).

FUTURE SYSTEM OF εἰμί *I am*

330. The future of εἰμί is ἔσομαι *I shall be,* inflected like λύ-σο-μαι except in the third person singular of the indicative, which irregularly lacks the thematic vowel (ε).

	Sing.	Dual	Plur.
Indic. 1.	ἔσομαι		ἐσόμεθα
2.	ἔσῃ, ἔσει	ἔσεσθον	ἔσεσθε
3.	ἔσται	ἔσεσθον	ἔσονται
Opt. 1.	ἐσοίμην		ἐσοίμεθα
2.	ἔσοιο	ἔσοισθον	ἔσοισθε
3.	ἔσοιτο	ἐσοίσθην	ἔσοιντο
Inf.	ἔσεσθαι		
Partic.	ἐσόμενος, η, ον		

331. The circumstantial **participle** may be used in the future to express a **purpose** (cp. § 213):

ἄνδρα πέμπει κελεύσοντα κτλ. he sends a man to command, etc.

332. ὡς often accompanies the participle of purpose as well as the causal participle (§ 213. *a*). It sometimes means *as, as if,* etc., and sometimes it can hardly be translated:

κελεύει τοὺς πελταστὰς πορεύεσθαι εἰς τὸν ποταμὸν ὡς δια-βησομένους[1]
he orders the peltasts to proceed into the river as if to cross (*i.e.* as if with the purpose of crossing);

καὶ ὑμεῖς παρα-σκευάζεσθε ὡς ἀνα-βησόμενοι[2] and do you make yourselves ready in order to go inland.

---

[1] Fut. of δια-βαίνω, § 144.   [2] Fut. of ἀνα-βαίνω, § 280.

333. The **infinitive** is used to complete the meaning of certain adjectives, especially such as denote *fitness*, *ability*, and the like :

ἱκανοὶ τὰς ἀκροπόλεις φυλάττειν sufficient [troops] to guard the citadels ;

ἄρχειν δὲ καλῶν καὶ ἀγαθῶν ἱκανὸς ἦν he was able to govern honorable and brave men.

334.   VOCABULARY XXXII

ἀκρό-πολις, εως, ἡ : high part of a city, *citadel*. Acropolis.

ἄκρος, ᾱ, ον : *top of*, *highest point of* ; τὸ ἄκρον (subst.) : *the height*. Cp. Lat. *acus*, *acūtus*, *aciēs*.

Βαβυλών, ῶνος, ἡ : *Babylon*.

βουλεύω, βουλεύσω, ἐβούλευσα : *plan*, *devise* ; but the simple verb is commonly dep. mid. βουλεύομαι : *take counsel with oneself, plan*. Cp. ἐπι-βουλεύω and συμ-βουλεύω.

γίγνομαι (for γι-γεν-ο-μαι, theme γεν-), fut. γενήσομαι (the increase of the theme to γενη- is to be noted), 2 aor. ἐγενόμην : *become, be born, be* ; *happen, arise, take place, turn out*. Cp. γένος. Genesis.

δέχομαι, δέξομαι, aor. to be learned later : *receive, accept*.

δια-βήσομαι, fut. of δια-βαίνω (Vocabulary XI), theme βα- : *shall go across, shall cross*.

εἱλόμην, 2 aor. mid. of εἷλον (Vocabulary XXVI) : *I took for myself, I chose*. Subjv. ἕλωμαι, opt. ἑλοίμην, imv. ἑλοῦ, inf. ἑλέσθαι, partic. ἑλόμενος, η, ον.

εἶπον (Vocabulary XXIV), meaning *commanded, proposed, urged*, is followed by the inf. Cp. § 98.

ἱκανός, ή, όν : *sufficient, able*.

κατα-λαμβάνω (cp. λαμβάνω, λήψομαι, ἔλαβον) : *seize, occupy, overtake, come upon*, with acc.

λήψομαι (theme ληβ-), fut. of λαμβάνω (Vocabulary V) : *shall take* or *receive*.

παρα-γίγνομαι (cp. γίγνομαι) : *come (to)* ; *be at hand, be present*. Cp. πάρ-ειμι.

παύομαι, mid. of παύω (Vocabulary XXVI) : *stop oneself, cease*.

πείσομαι : either (1) fut. of πάσχω *suffer* (Vocabulary XXII), or (2) fut. mid. of πείθω (Vocabulary I) in mid. meaning *obey* (with dat.).

πηγή, ῆς, ἡ : *spring* of water ; generally pl. *source*.

ῥᾴδιος, ᾱ, ον : *easy*.

EXERCISES FOR TRANSLATION

335. I. 1. ἢν δὲ φύγῃ, ἡμεῖς πρὸς[1] ταῦτα βουλευσό-
μεθα.   2. καὶ Κῦρος ἔλεγεν ὅτι ἡ ὁδὸς ἔσοιτο πρὸς
βασιλέα εἰς Βαβυλῶνα.   3. Δαρείου[2] καὶ Παρυσάτιδος[2]
γίγνονται παῖδες δύο.   4. τὰς πηγὰς τοῦ ποταμοῦ,
ἢν βούλωνται, δια-βήσονται.   5. οὐκ ἔφη παύσεσθαι.
6. ἔλεγε δ᾽ ὅτι μισθὸν τάλαντον λήψοιντο.   7. ἀπ-
ελθεῖν ῥᾴδιον ἔσται, ἢν βουλώμεθα.   8. οἱ Ἕλληνες
παρ-εσκευάζοντο ὡς δεξόμενοι βασιλέα.   9. πάντες
οὗτοι οἱ βάρβαροι πολέμιοι ἡμῖν ἔσονται.   10. οὐ
γὰρ ἱκανοὶ ἦσαν οἱ ἐν τῇ ἀκροπόλει σχεῖν[3] τοὺς ἄνδρας.   11. Πρόξενον δὲ ἐκέλευσε λαβόντα ἄνδρας
παρα-γενέσθαι, ὡς[4] εἰς Πῑσίδᾱς βουλόμενος στρατεύεσθαι.   12. Ξενίᾱς δὴ τοὺς ἐκ τῶν πόλεων λαβὼν παρ-
εγένετο εἰς Σάρδεις.   13. ἐνόμισεν εἶναι ἱκανὸς[5]
ἄρχειν.   14. σὺν ὑμῖν ὅ τι ἂν δέῃ πείσομαι.[6]   15. τῷ
ἀνδρὶ ὃν ἂν ἕλησθε πείσομαι.[7]   16. στρατιώτης δέ τις
εἶπεν ἑλέσθαι ἄλλους στρατηγούς, καὶ πέμψαι ἄνδρας
κατα-ληψομένους[8] τὰ ἄκρα.

II. 1. Clearchus proposed to choose leaders, and to send
them with soldiers to occupy the mountains.   2. He will
not be able to control[9] bad men.

---

[1] *with reference to.*   [2] *from* gen., § 201.
[3] In sense of *restrain*, § 88.   [4] § 213. *a.*
[5] § 110. *d.*   [6] Fut. of πάσχω.
[7] Fut. mid. of πείθω.   [8] § 331.   [9] ἄρχειν.

XXXIII

CONSONANT DECLENSION (*Continued*).   SOME IMPOR-
TANT IRREGULAR NOUNS. μέγας AND πολύς

336.   **IRREGULAR NOUNS**

I.   Sing. N. γυνή, ή, *woman*   2. χείρ, ή, *hand*
           G. γυναικ-ός   χειρ-ός
           D. γυναικ-ί   χειρ-ί
           A. γυναῖκ-α   χεῖρ-α
           V. γύναι   χείρ

     Dual N. A. V. γυναῖκ-ε   χεῖρ-ε
          G. D. γυναικ-οῖν   χερ-οῖν and χειρ-οῖν

     Plur. N. V. γυναῖκ-ες   χεῖρ-ες
           G. γυναικ-ῶν   χειρ-ῶν
           D. γυναιξί(ν)   χερ-σί(ν)
           A. γυναῖκ-ας   χεῖρ-ας

3. Sing. N. A. V. πῦρ, τό, *fire*   4. ὕδωρ, τό, *water*
           G. πυρ-ός   ὕδατ-ος
           D. πυρ-ί   ὕδατ-ι

     Plur. N. A. V. πυρ-ά, τά (o-decl.), *watch fires*   ὕδατ-α
           G. πυρ-ῶν   ὑδάτ-ων
           D. πυρ-οῖς   ὕδα-σι(ν)

5. Sing. N. A. V. δόρυ, τό, *spear*   6. γόνυ, τό, *knee*
           G. δόρατ-ος   γόνατ-ος
           D. δόρατ-ι   γόνατ-ι

     Dual N. A. V. δόρατ-ε   γόνατ-ε
          G. D. δοράτ-οιν   γονάτ-οιν

     Plur. N. A. V. δόρατ-α   γόνατ-α
           G. δοράτ-ων   γονάτ-ων
           D. δόρα-σι(ν)   γόνα-σι(ν)

337. TWO IMPORTANT IRREGULAR ADJECTIVES

			MASC.	FEM.	NEUT.
I.	Sing.	N.	μέγας *great*	μεγάλη	μέγα
		G.	μεγάλου	μεγάλης	μεγάλου
		D.	μεγάλῳ	μεγάλῃ	μεγάλῳ
		A.	μέγαν	μεγάλην	μέγα
	Plur.	N.	μεγάλοι	μεγάλαι	μεγάλα
		G.	μεγάλων	μεγάλων	μεγάλων
		D.	μεγάλοις	μεγάλαις	μεγάλοις
		A.	μεγάλους	μεγάλᾱς	μεγάλα
2.	Sing.	N.	πολύς *much*	πολλή	πολύ
		G.	πολλοῦ	πολλῆς	πολλοῦ
		D.	πολλῷ	πολλῇ	πολλῷ
		A.	πολύν	πολλήν	πολύ
	Plur.	N.	πολλοί	πολλαί	πολλά
		G.	πολλῶν	πολλῶν	πολλῶν
		D.	πολλοῖς	πολλαῖς	πολλοῖς
		A.	πολλούς	πολλᾱ́ς	πολλά

338. VOCABULARY XXXIII

ἀπο-λαμβάνω (cp. λαμβάνω, λήψο-μαι, ἔλαβον) : *take* or *receive back* ; *take off, cut off.*

γόνυ, γόνατος, τό : *knee.* Lat. *genū.*

γυνή, γυναικός, ἡ : *woman, wife.*

δόρυ, δόρατος, τό : *spear.*

ἤδη, adv. : *now, already, straightway.*

Κελαιναί, ῶν, αἱ : *Celaenae,* a city in Phrygia.

μέγας, μεγάλη, μέγα : *great, large.* Mega-phone (φωνή *voice*).

νύκτωρ, adv. (cp. νύξ) : *by night.*

πολύς, πολλή, πολύ : *much, many; extensive, large.* οἱ πολλοί : *the many, the most.* οἱ πολλοὶ τῶν

Ἑλλήνων : *the most of the Greeks.* τὸ πολὺ τοῦ στρατεύ-ματος : *the most of the army.* Poly-, poly-gon (γωνία *angle*), poly-technic (τέχνη *art*), etc.

πῦρ, πυρός, τό : *fire.* πυρά, τά : *watch fires.* Cp. pyre, pyro-technic (τέχνη *art*), etc.

Ταρσοί, ῶν, οἱ : *Tarsus,* the chief city of Cilicia.

τόξον, ον, τό : *bow.* Cp. τοξότης, τόξευμα.

χείρ, χειρός, ἡ : *hand.* Chiro-graphy (γράφω).

ὕδωρ, ὕδατος, τό : *water ; rain.* Hydro-, hydro-phobia (φόβος), etc.

EXERCISES FOR TRANSLATION

339. I. 1. ἔστι δὲ μεγάλου βασιλέως βασίλεια ἐν
Κελαιναῖς. 2. ἦν γὰρ πολὺς σῖτος ἐν ταῖς κώμαις.
3. μεγάλα δὲ τὰ τόξα τὰ Περσικά¹ ἐστιν. 4. οἱ δ᾽
ἀπο-λήψονται καὶ παῖδας καὶ γυναῖκας. 5. ἐν τῇ χειρὶ
Κλέαρχος εἶχε τὸ δόρυ. 6. ἐπὶ τῷ πυρὶ κατ-έλαβον
φυλακὴν τῆς νυκτός.² 7. ἔλεγόν τινες ὅτι κατ-ίδοιεν
νύκτωρ πολλὰ πυρά. 8. καὶ ὕδωρ πολὺ ἦν.³ 9. εἶχον
δὲ δόρυ ὡς πεντεκαίδεκα πήχεων.⁴ 10. τῷ δὲ δόρατι⁵
παίει αὐτὸν κατὰ τὸ γόνυ. 11. διὰ τούτου τοῦ πεδίου
ἤλασε σταθμοὺς πέντε παρασάγγας δύο καὶ εἴκοσιν εἰς
Ταρσούς, τῆς Κιλικίᾱς πόλιν μεγάλην καὶ εὐδαίμονα.
12. οὗτος δ᾽ ὁ ποταμὸς ἦν καλὸς μέν, μέγας δ᾽ οὔ.⁶
κῶμαι δὲ πολλαὶ περὶ αὐτὸν ἦσαν. 13. Τισσαφέρνης καὶ ὁ τῆς βασιλέως γυναικὸς ἀδελφὸς ἤδη παρ-
ῆσαν. 14. εὐθὺς δ᾽ ἔλαβε τὰ παλτὰ εἰς τὰς χεῖρας.

II. 1. The wife of the king of Cilicia arrived⁷ at⁸ the
camp. 2. On coming up⁹ they kindled a fire. 3. The
general marched five days' journey to Celaenae, a large
and prosperous city. 4. The most of the barbarians had
spears in their hands.

---

¹ §§ 67, 69.   ² § 155.   ³ *there was.*
⁴ §§ 278, 282.   ⁵ § 141.   ⁶ § 99.
⁷ Use proper tense of παρα-γίγνομαι.   ⁸ εἰς.
⁹ Use aor. partic. and omit *on.*

FIG. 19. — Greek Spears.

XXXIV

THE FIRST AORIST MIDDLE SYSTEM OF Ω–VERBS.
INDIRECT QUESTIONS INTRODUCED BY THE IN-
TERROGATIVE τίς, THE INDEFINITE RELATIVE
ὅστις, AND OTHER INTERROGATIVE WORDS

340. The first aorist middle differs from the first aorist
active (§ 160) only in the personal endings. The personal
endings of the first aorist indicative middle are the same as
in the imperfect middle; in the second person singular of
the first aorist indicative, -σα + [σ]ο contracts to -σω. The
other moods have in the first aorist middle the same personal endings as in the present middle. But the second
person singular of the middle imperative in -σαι (λῦσαι) is
peculiar in form, as is the second person singular of the
active imperative in -σον (λῦσον).

341. A verb of three syllables naturally has recessive
accent in the second person singular of the first aorist
middle imperative. Thus συμ-βούλευσαι *consult*. From
this form must be carefully distinguished the first aorist
infinitive active συμ-βουλεῦσαι *to advise* (§ 166); and the
third person singular of the first aorist optative active
συμ-βουλεύσαι (or -σειε), final -αι being long in the optative mood (§ 253).

342.   FIRST AORIST MIDDLE SYSTEM OF λύω

	SING.	DUAL	PLUR.
Indic. 1.	ἐ-λῡ-σά-μην *I loosed for myself, I ransomed*		ἐ-λῡ-σά-μεθα
2.	ἐ-λύ-σω	ἐ-λύ-σα-σθον	ἐ-λύ-σα-σθε
3.	ἐ-λύ-σα-το	ἐ-λῡ-σά-σθην	ἐ-λύ-σα-ντο

	SING.	DUAL	PLUR.
Subjv. 1.	λύ-σω-μαι		λῡ-σώ-μεθα
2.	λύ-σῃ	λύ-σῃ-σθον	λύ-σῃ-σθε
3.	λύ-σῃ-ται	λύ-σῃ-σθον	λύ-σω-νται
Opt. 1.	λῡ-σαί-μην		λῡ-σαί-μεθα
2.	λύ-σαι-ο	λύ-σαι-σθον	λύ-σαι-σθε
3.	λύ-σαι-το	λῡ-σαί-σθην	λύ-σαι-ντο
Imv. 2.	λῦ-σαι	λύ-σα-σθον	λύ-σα-σθε
3.	λῡ-σά-σθω	λῡ-σά-σθων	λῡ-σά-σθων
Inf.	λύ-σα-σθαι		
Partic.	λῡ-σά-μενος, η, ον		

Review the first aorist active system of λύω, *i.e.* the first aorist indicative, subjunctive, optative, imperative, infinitive, and participle (§§ 162, 209. *b*, 235, 254, 297).

INDIRECT QUESTIONS

343. The same words that introduce direct questions may also introduce indirect questions. Thus τίς *who?* τί *what* (ποῦ *where?* etc.). Or the corresponding indefinite relative pronoun (or adverb) may be used. Thus ὅστις for τίς (and ὅπου for ποῦ, etc.). Examples are provided under §§ 344, 345.

a. εἰ after an interrogative verb may mean *whether*.

344. An indirect question after a primary tense of the verb of *asking* keeps its original mood and tense unchanged:

δια-λέγου καὶ μάθε (§ 303. *a*) τίνες εἰσίν [or οἵ τινές εἰσιν] converse (with them) and learn who they are.

345. After a secondary tense of the verb of *asking* the verb of the indirect question may be changed to the optative. The tense used in the direct question must be retained, but the change of mood is optional:

ἤρετο ὅ τι [or τί] εἴη τὸ σύνθημα he asked what the watchword was. *In the direct form:* τί ἐστι τὸ σύνθημα; what is the watchword?

The original verb ἐστί might have been retained in the indirect question.

346. **VOCABULARY XXXIV**

ἀληθής, ές : *true*.

ἄρχομαι, ἄρξομαι, ἠρξάμην (mid. of ἄρχω, Vocabulary VIII) : *begin*, with gen. or inf.

δια-πράττομαι (cp. πράττω), δια-πράξομαι, δι-επραξάμην : carry through to the end, *bring about*, *accomplish, effect* (for oneself) ; *manage* that (with acc. and inf.).

δυνατός, ή, όν : *able, strong*. Cp. δύναμις.

εἰ, after an interr. verb : *whether*.

ἠρόμην, 2 aor. : *I asked* (a question) or *inquired* ; subjv. ἔρωμαι, opt. ἐροίμην, imv. ἐροῦ, inf. ἐρέσθαι, partic. ἐρόμενος.

θύομαι, θύσομαι, ἐθῡσάμην (mid. of θύω, Vocabulary XXIII) : *sac-rifice, offer* for oneself or from one's own resources.

κατα-βαίνω, κατα-βήσομαι : *go down, descend*. Cp. ἀνα-βαίνω (Vocabulary XXVI).

σκέπτομαι, σκέψομαι, ἐσκεψάμην, dep. mid. : *view, observe, con-sider*. The pres. and impf. are rare in Attic. Skeptic.

συ-σκευάζω (σύν + σκευάζω, cp. παρα-σκευάζω), συ-σκευάσω, συν-εσκεύασα : *make ready* (by get-ting things together, συν-), *pack up*, with acc. ; MID. *pack up one's own baggage, pack up*.

χαρίζομαι (theme χαριδ-), fut. to be learned later, ἐχαρισάμην, dep. mid. : *show a favor* to somebody (dat.), *gratify, grant* something (acc.) to somebody (dat.) *as a favor*. Cp. χάρις.

χιών, όνος, ἡ : *snow*.

EXERCISES FOR TRANSLATION

347. I. 1. Πρόξενος αὐτὸν μετ-επέμψατο, ξένος ὢν ἀρχαῖος. 2. ταῦτα δ᾽ εἰπὼν ἐπαύσατο. 3. ἐπὶ τού-τοις¹ ἐθύσαντο. 4. τούτους ἐκέλευε σκέψασθαι τί εἴη τὸ κωλῦον.² 5. ἤρξαντο δὲ κατα-βαίνειν ἀπὸ τοῦ λόφου πρὸς τοὺς ἄλλους. 6. οἱ δὲ πολέμιοι οὐκ ἐδέξαντο αὐτούς. 7. αὐτὸς δὲ δυνατὸς³ ἦν παρα-σκευάσασθαι

---

¹ *upon this, thereupon.*   ² *the hindrance* (§ 212).   ³ § 333.

χῑλόν.   8. λεγέτω τί ἔσται τοῖς στρατιώταις,[1] ἐὰν αὐτῷ
ταῦτα τὰ ὅπλα χαρίσωνται.   9. συν-έλεξα ὑμᾶς ὅπως
βουλευσαίμεθα ὅ τι χρὴ πρᾱ́ττειν.   10. συ-σκευασά-
μενοι δ᾽ εὐθὺς ἐπορεύοντο διὰ χιόνος πολλῆς, ἡγεμόνας
ἔχοντες πολλούς.   11. καὶ τᾱ̀ς ἁμάξᾱς, ᾱ̀ς παρ-εσκευά-
σατο Κῦρος, οἱ σὺν βασιλεῖ δι-ήρπασαν.   12. ὁ δὲ
Κλέαρχος δι-επρᾱ́ξατο πέντε μὲν στρατηγοὺς ἥκειν,
εἴκοσι δὲ λοχᾱγούς.   13. ταῦτα δὲ δια-πρᾱξάμενοι οἱ
βάρβαροι ἧκον ἐπὶ λόφον.   14. ἤρετο τὸν ἄνθρωπον εἰ
ἀληθῆ ταῦτ᾽ εἴη.

II. 1. Cyrus wondered what the watchword was.   2. We
asked why they had taken the field against the king.
3. The barbarians plundered all the wagons, full of wine
and grain, which Cyrus had prepared.

---

[1] § 119.

FIG. 20. — Helmet with Movable Cheek Pieces.

XXXV

COMPARISON OF ADJECTIVES.   DECLENSION OF COM-
PARATIVES IN -ων.   GENITIVE OF COMPARISON.
CCUSATIVE OF THE *WAY BY WHICH*.   SUPER-
LATIVE TRANSLATED BY *VERY*

348. The comparative degree of an adjective in -ος is
commonly formed by adding -τερος to the stem of the
adjective as seen in the positive degree. Thus δίκαιος
just; comparative δικαιό-τερος (ᾱ, ον) *more just.* Similarly
the superlative degree is commonly formed by the suffix
-τατος. Thus δικαιό-τατος (η, ον) *most just.*

a. All comparatives and superlatives have recessive
accent.

349. If the penult of the adjective is short in the positive degree, the ο of the stem is lengthened to ω before the
comparative and superlative suffixes. Thus ἄξιος *worthy*,
comparative ἀξιώ-τερος, superlative ἀξιώ-τατος.

350. A penult is counted long, although its vowel is
short, if its vowel is followed by two consonants or a double
consonant (§ 6). Thus the penult of πιστός *faithful* is
long, and the comparative and superlative are therefore
πιστό-τερος, πιστό-τατος.

351. AN ILLUSTRATIVE LIST OF ADJECTIVES COMPARED

POSITIVE	COMPARATIVE	SUPERLATIVE
a. δίκαιος, ᾱ, ον, *just*	δικαιότερος, ᾱ, ον	δικαιότατος, η, ον
ἰσχῡρός, ά, όν, *strong*	ἰσχῡρότερος, ᾱ, ον	ἰσχῡρότατος, η, ον
μακρός, ά, όν, *long*	μακρότερος, ᾱ, ον	μακρότατος, η. ον
πιστός, ή, όν, *faithful*	πιστότερος, ᾱ, ον	πιστότατος, η, ον

POSITIVE	COMPARATIVE	SUPERLATIVE
ᵇ. ἄξιος, ᾱ, ον, *worthy*	ἀξιώτερος, ᾱ, ον	ἀξιώτατος, η, ον
φοβερός, ά, όν, *fearful*	φοβερώτερος, ᾱ, ον	φοβερώτατος, η, ον
χαλεπός, ή, όν, *hard,*	χαλεπώτερος, ᾱ, ον	χαλεπώτατος, η, ον
difficult, harsh, severe		

Similarly are compared:

c. βραχύς, εῖα, ύ, *short*	βραχύτερος, ᾱ, ον	βραχύτατος, η, ον
[πρέσβυς, poetic, *old* [1]]	πρεσβύτερος, ᾱ, ον,	πρεσβύτατος, η, ον
	older, elder	
d. ἀληθής, ές, *true*	ἀληθέσ-τερος, ᾱ, ον	ἀληθέσ-τατος, η, ον
ἀσφαλής, ές, *safe*	ἀσφαλέσ-τερος, ᾱ, ον	ἀσφαλέσ-τατος, η, ον
e. εὐδαίμων, ον, *prosperous*	εὐδαιμον-έσ-τερος, ᾱ, ον	εὐδαιμον-έσ-τατος, η, ον

352. The following are compared by the suffixes -*ίων*, *ιον*, comparative, and -*ιστος, η, ον*, superlative:

POSITIVE	COMPARATIVE	SUPERLATIVE
a. ἡδύς, εῖα, ύ, *sweet*	ἡδίων, ἥδῑον	ἥδιστος, η, ον
ταχύς, εῖα, ύ, *swift,*	[ταχ-ίων =] θάττων,	τάχιστος, η, ον
quick	θᾶττον	
b. αἰσχρός, ά, όν, *shameful*	αἰσχίων, αἴσχῑον	αἴσχιστος, η, ον
ἐχθρός, ά, όν, *hostile*	ἐχθίων, ἔχθῑον	ἔχθιστος, η, ον

These drop -*ρός* and add -*ίων, -ιστος*.

DECLENSION OF COMPARATIVE ADJECTIVES IN -ων, GENITIVE -ονος

353. Comparatives in -*ων*, neut. -*ον*, gen. -*ονος*, are declined like εὐδαίμων (§ 222), with these exceptions: the accusative singular masculine and feminine and the nominative, accusative, and vocative plural, masculine and feminine, may contract. The contracted accusative plural masculine and feminine copies the nominative plural. The nominative, accusative, and vocative neuter plural may be similarly contracted.

---

[1] Cp. pl. πρέσβεις, Vocabulary XXVII.

a. The contracted forms come from stems in -οσ, as ἡδίοσ-α, ἡδίοσ-ες ; *sigma* dropping between two vowels, $o + a = \omega$, and $o + \epsilon = ov$.

		MASC. AND FEM.		NEUT.
354.	Sing. N.	ἡδίων *sweeter*		ἥδῑον
	G.		ἡδίονος	
	D.		ἡδίονι	
	A.	ἡδίονα or ἡδίω		ἥδῑον
	V.		ἥδῑον	
	Dual N. A. V.		ἡδίονε	
	G. D.		ἡδῑόνοιν	
	Plur. N. V.	ἡδίονες or ἡδίους		ἡδίονα or ἡδίω
	G.		ἡδῑόνων	
	D.		ἡδίοσι(ν)	
	A.	ἡδίονας or ἡδίους		ἡδίονα or ἡδίω

355. Genitive of comparison. — The genitive case follows a comparative when ἤ *than* is omitted. This is the *from* use of the genitive. (Similarly in Latin the ablative follows a comparative when *quam*, "than," is omitted.)

οἶνος τούτου ἡδίων wine sweeter than this.

356. Akin to the cognate accusative (§ 181) is the **accusative** of the *way by which* found with a verb of *motion :*

ὁδὸν πορεύεσθαι to travel a road.

357. The **superlative** degree may be sometimes translated by *very*. Thus ἥδιστος *sweetest* or *very sweet*.

358.   VOCABULARY XXXV

Learn the adjectives in §§ 351, 352. They are not repeated in the following list.

Ἀρταπάτης, ου, ὁ: *Artapates*, a friend of Cyrus.

βασιλικός, ή, όν (cp. βασιλεύς and

βασίλειος) : *kinglike, fit to be king; royal.*

εἰσ-άγω (cp. ἄγω) : *lead in.*

ἐπι-τυγχάνω, ἐπι-τεύξομαι (dep. fut.), ἐπ-έτυχον : *chance upon, happen upon, find*, with dat.

νέος, ā, ον : *new, fresh, young*. Comp. νεώτερος, sup. νεώτατος. Cp. Lat. *novus*. Neo-lithic (λίθος *stone*).

οὔ-πω, adv. : *not yet, never yet*.

ὄχλος, ου, ὁ : *crowd, throng*; *annoyance, bother*.

ὡς : adv. with sup. to express the very highest degree. Cp. Lat. *quam* with sup. Thus ὡς μακρότατος : *as long as possible*. See also previous Vocabularies (XXII, XXIV, XXVI, XXVIII).

EXERCISES FOR TRANSLATION

359. I. 1. Δαρείου καὶ Παρυσάτιδος γίγνονται παῖδες δύο, πρεσβύτερος μὲν Ἀρταξέρξης, νεώτερος δὲ Κῦρος. 2. χαλεπώτατος δὲ ἐχθρός[1] ἐστιν. 3. πάντες οὗτοι οἱ βάρβαροι πολεμιώτεροι ἡμῖν ἔσονται τῶν παρὰ βασιλεῖ ὄντων. 4. οἴνῳ τούτου ἡδίονι οὔπω ἐπ-έτυχον ἐγώ. 5. τοὺς δὲ ἰσχῡροτάτους τῶν πελταστῶν ἐκέλευε σκέψασθαι τί εἴη τὸ κωλῦον. 6. ἐπορεύοντο δὲ μακροτέρᾱν ὁδόν. 7. οὗτοι οἱ ἄνδρες αἰσχίους εἰσὶ τῶν πρόσθεν.[2] 8. δεῖ ἡμᾶς πορεύεσθαι δέκα σταθμοὺς ὡς μακροτάτους. 9. φεύγειν αὐτοῖς ἀσφαλέστερόν ἐστιν ἢ ἡμῖν. 10. ἐντεῦθεν Κῦρος τὴν Κίλισσαν εἰς τὴν Κιλικίᾱν ἀπο-πέμπει τὴν ταχίστην ὁδόν.[3] 11. ὁ Ἀριαῖος φίλος ἐστὶ τοῖς Κύρου ἐχθίστοις.[4] 12. μετὰ ταῦτα εἰσ-ῆγον Ὀρόντᾱν εἰς τὴν Ἀρταπάτου σκηνήν, τοῦ πιστοτάτου τῶν Κύρου φίλων. 13. Κῦρος δὲ ἤδη ἦν βασιλικώτατός τε καὶ ἄρχειν ἀξιώτατος. 14. πᾶς δὲ ὄχλος φοβερώτατος.

---

[1] The noun, § 323.
[2] Supply *men*, § 70. *b*.
[3] §§ 284, 356.
[4] Used as noun : *most bitter enemies*.

II. 1. They proceeded home by the quickest way. 2. It is necessary for a soldier to be as faithful as possible if he is about to do guard duty.[1] 3. I think that road is safer than this.[2]

XXXVI

COMPARISON OF ADJECTIVES (*Continued*). IRREGULAR COMPARISON. DOUBLE QUESTIONS

360. The following common adjectives show irregularities of comparison:

POSITIVE	COMPARATIVE	SUPERLATIVE
1. ἀγαθός, ή, όν, *good*, etc.	ἀμείνων, ἄμεινον, *braver, better*	ἄριστος, η, ον
(morally *better*)	βελτίων, βέλτῖον	βέλτιστος, η, ον
(*stronger, better*)	κρείττων, κρεῖττον	κράτιστος, η, ον
2. κακός, ή, όν, *bad, cowardly*, etc.	κακίων, κάκῖον	κάκιστος, η, ον
	χείρων, χεῖρον	χείριστος, η, ον
	ἥττων, ἧττον	ἥκιστα, adv., *least of all, by no means*
3. καλός, ή, όν, *beautiful, noble*, etc.	καλλίων, κάλλῖον	κάλλιστος, η, ον
4. μέγας, μεγάλη, μέγα, *big*	μείζων, μεῖζον	μέγιστος, η, ον
5. μῑκρός, ά, όν, *small*	μῑκρότερος, ᾱ, ον μείων, μεῖον, *smaller, fewer* (in pl.)	μῑκρότατος, η, ον
6. ὀλίγος, η, ον, *little, few*	ἐλάττων, ἔλαττον	ἐλάχιστος, η, ον

(The comparative and superlative may be given with μῑκρός also.)

7. πολύς, πολλή, πολύ, *much, many*	πλείων, πλεῖον and πλέον	πλεῖστος, η, ον
8. ῥᾴδιος, ᾱ, ον, *easy*	ῥᾴων, ῥᾷον	ῥᾷστος, η, ον

---

[1] §§ 156. 2, 181.   [2] Be careful about the gender.

For the declension of the comparatives in -ων, -ον, cp. ἡδίων, § 354.

361. The following lack the positive:

πρότερος, ᾱ, ον, *former* πρῶτος, η, ον, *first*
ὕστερος, ᾱ, ον, *later* ὕστατος, η, ον, *latest*

a. ἔσχατος, η, ον, *last, extreme*, is found in the superlative only.

362. A **double question**, direct or indirect, may be introduced by πότερον (or πότερα) . . . ἤ *whether . . . or*. In the double indirect question the same rules apply as in single indirect questions (§§ 344, 345).

πότερον οἱ στρατηγοὶ βούλονται πορεύεσθαι ἢ μέλλειν; do the generals wish to proceed or to delay?

ἤρετο πότερον οἱ στρατηγοὶ βούλοιντο πορεύεσθαι ἢ μέλλειν he asked whether the generals wished to proceed or to delay.

The original verb βούλονται might have been retained in the indirect question.

363. The double *indirect* question may also be introduced by εἰ . . . ἤ *whether . . . or*:

ἤρετο εἰ οἱ στρατηγοὶ βούλοιντο πορεύεσθαι ἢ μέλλειν he asked whether the generals wished to proceed or to delay.

364.   VOCABULARY XXXVI

Learn the meanings of all the adjectives in §§ 360, 361. They are not repeated in the following list

ἔπειτα, adv.: *thereupon, then, next*.

πότερον (πότερα) . . . ἤ, introducing a double question, direct or indirect: *whether . . . or*.

προσ-έρχομαι (cp. ἔρχομαι): *go to, come to, come up*; may take dat. of pers. or εἰς and acc.

πρόβατον, ου, τό: *cattle, sheep*.

EXERCISES FOR TRANSLATION

365. I. 1. ὥστε ὥρᾱ λέγειν ὅ τι τις νομίζει ἄριστον εἶναι. 2. δεῖ δὲ ἡμᾶς μὴ κακίους εἶναι τῶν πρόσθεν.[1] 3. κακίους εἰσὶ περὶ ἡμᾶς ἢ ἡμεῖς περὶ ἐκείνους. 4. ἐκέλευσε τοὺς περὶ αὐτὸν Πέρσᾱς τοὺς κρατίστους κάεω τὰς ἁμάξᾱς. 5. ἤρετο δὲ εἰ οἱ πλεῖστοι τῶν ἱππέων εἶεν Θρᾷκες ἢ οὔ. 6. ἔτυχε γὰρ ὕστερος προσ-ερχόμενος. 7. ὁ δ' Ὀρόντᾱς γράφει ἐπιστολὴν παρὰ βασιλέᾱ ὅτι ἥξει ἔχων ἱππέᾱς ὡς πλείστους. 8. ὦ ἄνδρες Ἕλληνες, νομίζων ὑμᾶς ἀμείνους καὶ κρείττους πολλῶν βαρβάρων εἶναι, διὰ τοῦτο συμμάχους ὑμᾶς ἄγω. 9. οὗτοι οἱ ἵπποι μείονές εἰσι τῶν Περσικῶν ἵππων. 10. ῥᾷόν ἐστι πορεύεσθαι ἢ μέλλειν; 11. Πρόξενος δ' οὐκ ἤρετο πότερον βέλτῑον εἴη αὐτῷ πορεύεσθαι ἢ μέλλειν. 12. ἀλλ' ὑμεῖς, ὦ ἄνδρες στρατηγοί, τούτοις λέγετε ὅ τι κάλλιστόν τε καὶ ἄριστον ἔχετε.[2] 13. ἦσαν δὲ τάφροι, αἱ μὲν πρῶται μεγάλαι, ἔπειτα δὲ ἐλάττους· αἱ δὲ ἔσχαται ἦσαν μῑκρόταται. 14. εἰ βούλοιό τῳ[3] φίλος εἶναι, ὡς μέγιστος φίλος ἂν εἴης. 15. χρὴ τοὺς στρατιώτᾱς ὡς ἐλάχιστα πρόβατα ἁρπάσαι.

II. 1. There were very many[4] horses in the plain. 2. This grain was very abundant[5] in the land. 3. If there is any other, better way, speak out.[6] 4. He commanded his generals to enlist as many and as brave men as possible.

---

[1] Cp. § 359. I. 7.   [2] *consider*.   [3] § 227.

[4] § 357.   [5] Sup. of πολύς.   [6] Omit *out*.

XXXVII

FORMATION AND COMPARISON OF ADVERBS. IRREGU-
LAR ADVERBS. GENITIVE AFTER ADVERBS OF
PLACE

366. The positive degree of an adverb is commonly
formed from any adjective in the positive degree by
changing final **ν** of the genitive plural neuter to **s**. The
accent of the adjective is retained in the adverb. Thus

GENITIVE PLURAL NEUTER ADJECTIVE	CORRESPONDING ADVERB
δικαίων (from δίκαιος)	δικαίως *justly*
ἰσχυρῶν (from ἰσχυρός)	ἰσχυρῶς *strongly, exceedingly, harshly*
ἀσφαλῶν (from ἀσφαλής)	ἀσφαλῶς *safely*
ἡδέων (from ἡδύς)	ἡδέως *gladly*

367. Not infrequently the neuter singular accusative
(adverbial accusative, § 284) of the adjective in the positive degree is used for the corresponding adverb. Thus
ταχύ quickly.

368. The *neuter singular accusative* of the comparative
degree of an adjective is used for the comparative degree
of the adverb; and the *neuter plural accusative* of the
superlative degree of an adjective is used for the superlative degree of the adverb.

EXAMPLES OF COMPARISON OF ADVERBS

POSITIVE	COMPARATIVE	SUPERLATIVE
δικαίως *justly*	δικαιότερον	δικαιότατα
ἰσχυρῶς *strongly, exceedingly, harshly*	ἰσχυρότερον	ἰσχυρότατα

POSITIVE	COMPARATIVE	SUPERLATIVE
φοβερῶς *fearfully*	φοβερώτερον	φοβερώτατα
ἀσφαλῶς *safely*	ἀσφαλέστερον	ἀσφαλέστατα
ταχέως ⎫ *swiftly,* or irregular **τάχα** ⎭ *quickly*	θᾶττον	τάχιστα
κακῶς *badly*	κάκῑον *worse*	κάκιστα
καλῶς *beautifully*	κάλλῑον	κάλλιστα
ἡδέως *gladly*	ἥδῑον	ἥδιστα

369. A LIST OF IRREGULAR ADVERBS

	POSITIVE	COMPARATIVE	SUPERLATIVE
I.	**ἄνω** *up*	ἀνωτέρω *higher*	ἀνωτάτω *highest*
2.	**ἐγγύς** *near*	ἐγγύτερον ἐγγυτέρω	ἐγγύτατα ἐγγυτάτω
3.	**εὖ** *well* (adv. of **ἀγαθός**)	ἄμεινον *better*	ἄριστα *best*
		βέλτῑον κρεῖττον	βέλτιστα κράτιστα
4.	**μάλα** *very*	μᾶλλον *more*	μάλιστα *most*

370. Adjectives may be compared by using μᾶλλον and μάλιστα with the positive degree. Thus μᾶλλον φίλοι *more friendly.*

371. Various other adverbial endings may be best learned with the words themselves, as οἴκαδε *homeward.*

372. An **adverb of place** is followed by the genitive case :

ἐγγὺς τοῦ χωρίου near the stronghold.

Under this head comes also πέρᾱν (Vocabulary XXIII).

373. Note ὡς (or ὅτι) τάχιστα (cp. § 358) *as quickly as possible ;* ὡς μάλιστα *as much as possible.*

374.   VOCABULARY XXXVII

Learn the adverbs in §§ 366–369.   Except ἄνω, they are not repeated in this list.

ἄνω, adv.: *up*; up from the sea, inland, *into the interior*. Cp. ἀνά.

ἀ-παράσκευος, ον: *unprepared*. Cp. παρα-σκευάζω.

ἀρετή, ῆς, ἡ (cp. ἄρ-ιστος): *fitness, excellence, bravery*; *virtue, noble-mindedness, magnanimity*.

δέοι, pres. opt. of δεῖ: *it is necessary* (Vocabulary XX).

κολάζω (theme κολαδ-), κολάσω, ἐκόλασα: *chastise, punish*.

μάχομαι (cp. μάχη), fut. to be learned later, ἐμαχεσάμην (aor. with lengthened theme): *fight*. The enemy is expressed by the dat. or πρός (*against*) and acc.[1] Cp. § 317.

ὄνομα, ατος, τό: *name*. Syn-onym (συν-).

ὅσος, η, ον, rel. pron.: *as great as, as much as, as many as, all that*;

how great, how much, how many. ὅσα: *as many things as, all that*.

ὅτι, as adv., strengthens a superlative, like ὡς (Vocabulary XXXV). Thus ὅτι ἀπαρασκευότατος: *as unprepared as possible*.

οὕτω and οὕτως (cp. οὗτος), adv.: *thus, in this way* (usually with reference to what goes before), *so*.

πόλεμος, ου, ὁ (cp. πολέμιος): *war*.

πολύ, adv. (cp. πολύς): *much, by far*. See § 367.

προθύμως (adv. of πρόθυμος *ready, eager*): *readily, eagerly, zealously*. Comp. προθυμότερον, sup. προθυμότατα.

τὸ πρόσθεν (adv. acc.): *before, formerly*. Cp. Vocabulary XXVI.

συμ-πορεύομαι: *proceed with, accompany*.

EXERCISES FOR TRANSLATION

375. I. 1. Κῦρος καὶ οἱ σὺν αὐτῷ ἐπορεύοντο ἄνω. 2. κάκῑον δὲ ἔπρᾱξαν.[2]   3. ἄλλος δὲ εἶπε[3] στρατηγοὺς ἐλέσθαι ὡς τάχιστα.   4. οἱ δὲ Ἕλληνες, ἀκούσαντες τὴν Κύρου ἀρετήν, ἥδῑον καὶ προθῡμότερον συνεπορεύοντο.   5. ἔτρεχον γὰρ πολὺ θᾶττον τῶν ἵππων.[4]

---

[1] μάχεσθαι σύν τινι, on the other hand, means to *fight with the aid of somebody*, who is an ally, not an enemy.

[2] *did = fared*.   [3] § 334.   [4] § 355.

6. ἥδιστα ἂν ἀκούσαιμι τὸ ὄνομα τούτου τοῦ ἀνδρὸς καὶ ὅσα ἔπραξεν.   7. εἰς τὰς ἐγγυτάτω[1] κώμᾱς ἧκεν ἔχων τοὺς πρώτους.[2]   8. δικαίως ἄν μοι χαρίζοιτο.   9. Κλέαρχος δὲ ἐκόλαζεν ἰσχῡρῶς.   10. οἱ δὲ βάρβαροι μᾶλλον φίλοι Κύρῳ ἦσαν ἢ βασιλεῖ.   11. ὁ δὲ Κῦρος θᾶττον ἐπορεύετο, ὅπως ὅτι ἀπαρασκευότατον λάβοι βασιλέᾱ.   12. οὕτως πορευοίμεθα ἂν ὡς ἀσφαλέστατα, καὶ εἰ μάχεσθαι δέοι, ὡς κράτιστα ἂν μαχοίμεθα. 13. ἦσαν γὰρ ἐγγὺς τοῦ ποταμοῦ οὔτε πόλεις οὔτε κῶμαι διὰ τοὺς πολέμους τοὺς πρὸς τοὺς Καρδούχους. 14. ἐξ-ήλαυνον ἐπὶ τοὺς πολεμίους πολὺ ἔτι προθῡμότερον ἢ τὸ πρόσθεν.   15. λέγει ὅτι κάλλιστα διελέγοντο περὶ ἀρετῆς.

II. 1. The king collected his army quickly, in order that he might fight with the enemy while they were [3] as unprepared as possible.   2. The enemy ran more swiftly than before.   3. We marched as quickly as possible that we might be first on the other side of the river.

---

[1] § 70.   [2] the van.   [3] Omit while they were.

XXXVIII

REFLEXIVE PRONOUNS.   THE RECIPROCAL PRONOUN.
THE   INDIRECT   REFLEXIVE   οἷ.   ATTRIBUTIVE
POSITION OF THE POSSESSIVE GENITIVE OF RE-
FLEXIVE PRONOUNS

Review the paradigms of personal pronouns (§ 304) and of αὐτός
(§ 122).   For ἑαυτοῦ cp. also § 378.

THE REFLEXIVE PRONOUNS ἐμαυτοῦ, σεαυτοῦ, AND ἑαυτοῦ

376. The reflexive pronouns are made up, in the singular, from the stems of the personal pronouns and the forms
of αὐτός in the oblique (§ 123. 3) cases.

		Masc.	Fem.	Neut.
1.	Sing. G.	ἐμαυτοῦ *of myself*	ἐμαυτῆς	
	D.	ἐμαυτῷ	ἐμαυτῇ	
	A.	ἐμαυτόν	ἐμαυτήν	
	Plur. G.	ἡμῶν αὐτῶν *of ourselves*		
	D.	ἡμῖν αὐτοῖς	ἡμῖν αὐταῖς	
	A.	ἡμᾶς αὐτούς	ἡμᾶς αὐτάς	
2.	Sing. G.	σεαυτοῦ[1] *of yourself*	σεαυτῆς	
	D.	σεαυτῷ	σεαυτῇ	
	A.	σεαυτόν	σεαυτήν	
	Plur. G.	ὑμῶν αὐτῶν *of yourselves*		
	D.	ὑμῖν αὐτοῖς	ὑμῖν αὐταῖς	
	A.	ὑμᾶς αὐτούς	ὑμᾶς αὐτάς	
3.	Sing. G.	ἑαυτοῦ[2] *of himself*	ἑαυτῆς	ἑαυτοῦ
	D.	ἑαυτῷ	ἑαυτῇ	ἑαυτῷ
	A.	ἑαυτόν	ἑαυτήν	ἑαυτό

---

[1] Or, contracted, σαυτοῦ, σαυτῆς, etc.

[2] Or, contracted, αὐτοῦ, αὐτῆς, αὐτοῦ, etc.

	Masc.	Fem.	Neut.
Plur. G.	ἑαυτῶν[1] *of themselves*	ἑαυτῶν	ἑαυτῶν
D.	ἑαυτοῖς	ἑαυταῖς	ἑαυτοῖς
A.	ἑαυτούς	ἑαυτάς	ἑαυτά

Plur. also:	G.	σφῶν αὐτῶν *of themselves*	
	D.	σφίσιν αὐτοῖς	σφίσιν αὐταῖς
	A.	σφᾶς αὐτούς	σφᾶς αὐτάς

THE RECIPROCAL PRONOUN, *one another*

		Masc.	Fem.	Neut.
377.	Dual G. D.	ἀλλήλοιν	ἀλλήλαιν	ἀλλήλοιν
	A.	ἀλλήλω	ἀλλήλᾱ	ἀλλήλω
	Plur. G.	ἀλλήλων	ἀλλήλων	ἀλλήλων
	D.	ἀλλήλοις	ἀλλήλαις	ἀλλήλοις
	A.	ἀλλήλους	ἀλλήλᾱς	ἄλληλα

THE INDIRECT REFLEXIVE OF THE THIRD PERSON

378. Sing. G. [οὗ], [οὑ][2]   Plur. N. σφεῖς

D. οἷ, οἱ, *to* or *for himself*   G. σφῶν

or *herself*   D. σφίσι(ν)

A. [ἕ], [ἑ]   A. σφᾶς

a. This pronoun is an *indirect* reflexive in Attic Greek; that is, used in a subordinate clause, it refers to the subject of the *main* clause:

ἐκέλευον αὐτὸν πέμπειν σφίσι πλοῖα they ordered him to send boats to them.

379. The **genitive** of the reflexive pronoun, when denoting possession, has the attributive (§ 67) position:

συν-έλεξε τοὺς αὑτοῦ στρατιώτᾱς he collected his own soldiers.

---

[1] Or, contracted, αὑτῶν, αὑτῶν, αὑτῶν, etc.

[2] Enclitic forms are [οὑ], οἱ, [ἑ]. Bracketed forms are very rare in Attic prose.

a. It will be recalled that the possessive genitive of the *personal* pronoun has the predicate position (§§ 127, 308).

380. In such expressions as that just described, the noun is often understood (cp. § 70. *b*) :

οἱ ἑαυτοῦ (supply στρατιῶται) his own soldiers ; τὰ ἑαυτῶν their own affairs *or* their own possessions.

381. VOCABULARY XXXVIII

For ἀλλήλοιν, ἐμαυτοῦ, σεαυτοῦ and σαυτοῦ, ἑαυτοῦ and αὑτοῦ, and οὖ see the preceding paradigms.

αἰσθάνομαι (theme αἰσθ-, pres. tense suffix αν%), fut. αἰσθήσομαι (with lengthened theme), 2 aor. ᾐσθόμην, subjv. αἴσθωμαι, etc.: *perceive.* An-aesthetic (ἀν- privative).

εἰσ-ελαύνω (cp. ἐλαύνω) : *drive in, ride* or *march in*, with εἰς and acc.

ἐκκλησίᾱ, ᾱς, ἡ: *assembly.* [In a later age, *church.*] Ecclesiastic.

ἐπι-βουλή, ῆς, ἡ: *plot* (against). Cp. ἐπι-βουλεύω.

ἕτοιμος, η, ον, or ἕτοιμος, ον: *ready, prepared.*

οἴομαι (often οἶμαι), fut. οἰήσομαι (with lengthened theme) : *think, suppose.*

Συέννεσις, ιος (non-Attic gen.), ὁ: *Syennesis*, king of Cilicia.

τάξις (ταγ + σι + s), εως, ἡ : *order, arrangement* ; military *line, column, division*. Cp. τάττω.

τάττω (theme ταγ-, pres. tense suffix *y*%, cp. φυλάττω. § 182, NOTE), τάξω, ἔταξα : *arrange, draw up, marshal* troops. Tactics, etc.

χωρίς, adv. : *apart* ; prep. with gen. : *apart from.*

ὧδε, adv. (cp. ὅδε) : *thus, as follows.*

EXERCISES FOR TRANSLATION

382. I. 1. πρῶτον[1] γὰρ καὶ μέγιστον[1] οἱ θεῶν ὅρκοι[2] κωλύουσιν ἡμᾶς πολεμίους εἶναι[3] ἀλλήλοις. 2. ὥστε βασιλεὺς τὴν πρὸς ἑαυτὸν ἐπιβουλὴν οὐκ ᾐσθάνετο. 3. εἶχε δὲ ἡ Κίλισσα φυλακὴν περὶ αὐτήν. 4. Κῦρος

---

[1] § 284.   [2] *oaths by the gods.*   [3] hinder us *from being*, etc.

FIG. 21. — Monument of Dexileos, an Athenian Knight (ἱππεύς).

δὲ ἐπεὶ εἰσ-ήλασεν εἰς τὴν πόλιν, μετ-επέμψατο τὸν
Συέννεσιν πρὸς ἑαυτόν.   5. Κλέαρχος δὲ συν-ήγαγεν
ἐκκλησίᾱν τῶν αὑτοῦ στρατιωτῶν.   6. μετὰ δὲ ταῦτα
συν-αγαγὼν τούς θ᾽[1] ἑαυτοῦ στρατιώτᾱς καὶ τῶν ἄλλων[2]
τὸν βουλόμενον,[3] ἔλεξεν ὧδε.   7. αὐτὸς δὲ τοὺς ἑαυτοῦ
ἤδη ἔταξεν.   8. τῇ δὲ αὐτῇ ἡμέρᾳ Κλέαρχος ἀπ-ῆλθεν
ἐπὶ τὴν ἑαυτοῦ σκηνὴν διὰ τοῦ Μένωνος στρατεύματος.
9. Ὀρόντᾱς δὴ νομίσᾱς ἑτοίμους εἶναι αὐτῷ τοὺς ἱππέᾱς
γράφει ἐπιστολὴν παρὰ βασιλέᾱ.   10. ὁ δ᾽ Ὀρόντᾱς
ᾤετο τὸν ἄνδρα πιστόν οἱ εἶναι.   11. ἤξω δ᾽ αὐτὸς
ἐπὶ τὴν ἐμαυτοῦ ἀρχήν.   12. τότε ἔμαθες τὴν σαυτοῦ
δύναμιν.   13. ὥστε τῇ ὑστεραίᾳ Κῦρος ἐπορεύετο
ὀλίγους ἐν τάξει ἔχων πρὸ αὐτοῦ.   14. Μένων συν-
έλεξε τὸ αὑτοῦ στράτευμα χωρὶς τῶν ἄλλων.

II. 1. Cyrus commanded each general to draw up his
own men.   2. Clearchus wished his own soldiers to proceed first.[4]   3. The king's wife rode past in her own
carriage.

---

[1] For τ᾽ = τε (§ 31).   [2] § 179.   [3] § 212.
[4] Put *first* in pred. position.

XXXIX

THE PASSIVE VOICE OF Ω–VERBS. FIRST AORIST
PASSIVE SYSTEM. EUPHONIC LAWS OF MUTES
BEFORE MUTES. DECLENSION OF PARTICIPLES
IN -εἰς. DEPONENT PASSIVES. AGENT EXPRESSED
BY ὑπό AND GENITIVE. CONSTRUCTION AFTER
PASSIVE OF λέγω *say*

383. The present, imperfect, perfect, pluperfect, and
future perfect passive tenses are the same in form as the
corresponding tenses of the middle voice. The perfect
tenses will be studied later (§§ 452 ff.). Only the aorist
passive and the future passive have forms distinct from
the middle. The sign of the first aorist passive and of the
first future passive is θη or θε. This sign is added to the
verb theme before the usual suffixes.

THE FIRST AORIST PASSIVE

384. The aorist passive uses the active personal endings
throughout. In the aorist indicative, imperative, and infinitive the endings are added directly to the passive sign θη.[1]
In the other moods θε is the form of the passive sign. The
aorist subjunctive, as usual, has the long thematic vowel
$^{\omega}/\eta$ as its mood sign, before which ε (of θε) is absorbed.
The aorist optative has the mood sign ιη (after θε) in the
singular, but regularly (in classical Greek) the short mood
sign ι in the dual and plural. As before noted (§ 252), the
sign in the third person plural is ιε.

---

[1] θε in 3 pl. imperative.

385. FIRST AORIST PASSIVE SYSTEM OF λύω

	SING.	DUAL	PLUR.
Indic. 1.	ἐ-λύ-θη-ν *I was loosed*		ἐ-λύ-θη-μεν
2.	ἐ-λύ-θη-s	ἐ-λύ-θη-τον	ἐ-λύ-θη-τε
3.	ἐ-λύ-θη	ἐ-λυ-θή-την	ἐ-λύ-θη-σαν
Subjv. 1.	λυ-θῶ [for λυ-θέ-ω]		λυ-θῶ-μεν
2.	λυ-θῇs [for λυ-θέ-ῃs]	λυ-θῆ-τον	λυ-θῆ-τε
3.	λυ-θῇ [for λυ-θέ-ῃ]	λυ-θῆ-τον	λυ-θῶ-σι(ν)
Opt. 1.	λυ-θείη-ν		λυ-θεῖ-μεν
2.	λυ-θείη-s	λυ-θεῖ-τον	λυ-θεῖ-τε
3.	λυ-θείη	λυ-θεί-την	λυ-θεῖε-ν

	Less common	1.		λυ-θείη-μεν
		2.	λυ-θείη-τον	λυ-θείη-τε
		3.	λυ-θειή-την	λυ-θείη-σαν

	SING.	DUAL	PLUR.
Imv. 2.	λύ-θη-τι [1]	λύ-θη-τον	λύ-θη-τε
3.	λυ-θή-τω	λυ-θή-των	λυ-θέ-ντων
Inf.	λυ-θῆ-ναι [2]		
Partic.	λυ-θείς, εῖσα, έν		

386. The first aorist passive formation ἐ-λύ-θην is typical of all vowel themes. But mute themes suffer euphonic changes before the passive suffix θη (θε).

MUTES BEFORE MUTES

387. 1. A labial mute (π β φ) or a palatal mute (κ γ χ) before a lingual mute (τ δ θ) must be of the same order (§ 28); *i.e.* smooth before smooth, middle before middle, and rough before rough. The *class* of the mute remains unchanged:

π + θ = φθ	κ + θ = χθ	τ + τ = ττ
β + θ = φθ	γ + θ = χθ	γ + τ = κτ

---

[1] For λύ-θη-θι : -θι, the imv. suffix, is changed to τ (*smooth*) to avoid repetition of the rough mute θ at the beginning of successive syllables.

[2] All infinitives in -ναι are accented on the penult.

ἐ-πεμπ-θην (1 aor. pass. of πέμπω) becomes ἐπέμφθην.

ἐ-λειπ-θην (λείπω) becomes ἐλείφθην.

ἐ-ληβ-θην (λαμβάνω, themes λαβ- and ληβ-) becomes ἐλήφθην.

ἐ-φυ-λακ-θην (φυλάττω, theme φυλακ-) becomes ἐφυλάχθην.

ἐ-λεγ-θην (λέγω *say*) becomes ἐλέχθην.

ἐ-πρᾱγ-θην (πρᾱττω, theme πρᾱγ-) becomes ἐπρᾱχθην.

ἐ-ταγ-θην (τάττω, theme ταγ-) becomes ἐτάχθην.

2. A lingual mute (τ δ θ) before another lingual mute is changed to *sigma*.

ἐ-πειθ-θην (1 aor. pass. of πείθω) becomes ἐπείσθην.

ἡρπαδ-θην (ἁρπάζω, theme ἁρπαδ-) becomes ἡρπάσθην.

DECLENSION OF PARTICIPLES IN -εἰς, -εῖσα, -έν

λυθείς (STEM λυθεντ-) *having been loosed*, 1 AOR. PASS. PARTIC.
OF λῡω

		MASC.	FEM.	NEUT.
388.	Sing. N. V.	λυθείς	λυθεῖσα	λυθέν
	G.	λυθέντος	λυθείσης	λυθέντος
	D.	λυθέντι	λυθείσῃ	λυθέντι
	A.	λυθέντα	λυθεῖσαν	λυθέν
	Dual N. A. V.	λυθέντε	λυθείσᾱ	λυθέντε
	G. D.	λυθέντοιν	λυθείσαιν	λυθέντοιν
	Plur. N. V.	λυθέντες	λυθεῖσαι	λυθέντα
	G.	λυθέντων	λυθεισῶν	λυθέντων
	D.	λυθεῖσι(ν)	λυθείσαις	λυθεῖσι(ν)
	A.	λυθέντας	λυθείσᾱς	λυθέντα

a. In the nominative singular masculine and dative plural masculine and neuter, ε preceding ντ is lengthened to ει in compensation for the loss of ντ before σ (cp. § 200).

389. Certain deponent verbs (§ 316) lack the aorist middle, and have, instead, the aorist passive in the deponent use. For this reason they are commonly called **deponent passive** verbs. Thus βούλομαι, aor. ἐβουλήθην *I wished;* δια-λέγομαι, aor. δι-ελέχθην *I conversed;* οἴο-μαι, aor. ᾠήθην *I thought;* πορεύομαι, aor. ἐπορεύθην *I proceeded.*

Take care never to write the aorist of πορεύομαι as ἐπο-ρευσάμην. The future is πορεύσομαι (middle).

390. The **agent,** with a passive verb, is expressed by ὑπό *by* with the genitive.

391. The **passive of λέγω** *say* is followed by the infinitive in indirect discourse (cp. § 110). This passive has both a *personal* and an *impersonal* use :

ἐλέγετο ἐλθεῖν he was said to have come (personal use) ;

ἐλέγετο αὐτὸν ἐλθεῖν it was said that he came (impersonal use) ;

ἐλέγετο δὲ καὶ Συέννεσις εἶναι ἐπὶ τῶν ἄκρων and Syennesis, too, was said to be on the heights.

392. VOCABULARY XXXIX

ἀν-άγω (ἀνά + ἄγω): *lead up;* lead "up" from the coast.

ἄν-οδος, ου, ἡ (ἀνά + ὁδός): *road up, way up.*

τὸ Ἑλληνικόν (cp. Ἑλληνικός, Vocabulary XXVII): *the Greek force* (neut. subst.).

κατα-πέμπω (cp. πέμπω): *send down,* especially to the sea.

Λῡδίᾱ, ᾱς, ἡ; *Lydia,* a district of Western Asia Minor, of which Sardis was the chief city.

νόμος, ου, ὁ: *custom, law.* Deutero-nomy (δεύτερος *second*).

ὀκτώ, indecl.: *eight.* Cp. Lat. *octō.*

ὅπως, rel. adv.: *how, in what way* (cp. Vocabulary XXII).

πάνυ, adv. (cp. πᾶς): *wholly, alto-gether, very.*

πείθω, in mid. and pass.: *obey* (be persuaded or convinced by somebody), with dat. Cp. Vocabulary I.

πυνθάνομαι (theme πυθ-, pres. tense suffix αν%, cp. λαμβάνω, τυγ-χάνω, § 218), fut. πεύσομαι (for πευθ-, a longer form of the theme, + σομαι), 2 aor. ἐπυθόμην: *inquire, ask ; learn, perceive.*

τῑμή, ῆς, ἡ: *honor.*

τοι-γαρ-οῦν: *therefore* (a strong particle of inference).

ὑπηρέτης, ου, ὁ: *servant, helper, supporter.*

ὑπό (also ὑπ before smooth breathing, and ὑφ' before rough breathing, § 31), prep. : with GEN.
from under, by (with pass.
verb), *because of, from*; with
DAT. *under, beneath* (with

verbs of rest) ; with ACC. *under*
(with verbs of motion). Hypo-
dermic (δέρμα *skin*), etc.

χρόνος, ου, ὁ : *time.* Chrono-meter
(μέτρον *measure*), chrono-logy
(λόγος *account*).

EXERCISES FOR TRANSLATION

393. Give the meaning of the following passive forms :
λείπεται, ἐλείποντο, τάττονται, λυθῆναι, λέγεται, λεγόμενος,
ἤγετο, ἁρπάζεται, πεμπόμενος, κολάζονται, ἄρχεσθαι.

394. I. 1. ὦ ἄνδρες, ἐάν μοι πεισθῆτε, ἐν μεγάλῃ
τιμῇ ἔσεσθε. 2. εἰς τὴν Ἀρταπάτου σκηνὴν εἰσ-ήχθη.
3. Κῦρος δ' οὔποτε ἐξ-ήχθη [1] διώκειν. [2] 4. πάνυ ὀλίγοι
ἀμφ' αὐτὸν κατ-ελείφθησαν. 5. κατ-επέμφθη ὑπὸ τοῦ
πατρὸς σατράπης [3] Λυδίας. 6. τοιγαροῦν κράτιστοι
δὴ ὑπηρέται Κύρῳ ἐλέχθησαν γενέσθαι. 7. οὕτως οὖν
ἠθροίσθη Κύρῳ τὸ Ἑλληνικόν. 8. ταῦτα ἐν τῇ ἀνόδῳ
ἐπράχθη. 9. ἐκέλευσε δὲ τοὺς Ἕλληνας, ὡς νόμος
αὐτοῖς ἦν εἰς [4] μάχην, οὕτω ταχθῆναι. 10. ἐντεῦθεν
δ' ἐπορεύθησαν σταθμοὺς δύο, παρασάγγᾶς ὀκτώ.
11. ὁ δὲ Ξενίᾶς ἐπυνθάνετο ὅπως ἂν κάλλιστα [5]
πορευθείη. 12. πρὸς [6] ταῦτα οἱ βάρβαροι πολὺν
χρόνον [7] δια-λεχθέντες ἀλλήλοις ἀπ-ῆλθον. 13. οἱ
δὲ στρατηγοὶ οὕτω ληφθέντες ἀν-ήχθησαν ὡς βασιλέᾶ.
14. πορευθεὶς δὲ τὰ πυρὰ οὐκ ἔφη [8] ἰδεῖν.

---

[1] From ἐξ-άγω in sense of *induce.*
[2] Complementary infinitive.
[3] *as satrap*, in apposition to the subject, § 53. *j.*
[4] *for.*
[5] *most successfully.*
[6] *with reference to.*
[7] § 142.
[8] § 156. 1. *a.*

II. 1. Cyrus ordered the soldiers to be marshaled for[1] battle.   2. The general inquired in what way he should travel,[2] in order to reach home safely.[3]   3. The very[4] timbers had been plundered[5] from[6] the houses by the king's army.

XL

THE FIRST FUTURE PASSIVE SYSTEM.   PRESENT GENERAL CONDITIONS.   CONDITIONAL RELATIVE PROTASIS IN PRESENT TIME.   GENITIVE ABSO- LUTE.   GENITIVE OF VALUE.   DATIVE OF CAUSE

395. The first future passive indicative is formed from the verb theme as it appears in the first aorist passive, plus the first passive suffix $\theta\eta$ (§ 383), plus the future tense sign $\sigma\%$, plus the passive personal endings, which are the same as the middle.   The optative has its usual mood sign.

Observe that the first future passive is exactly like the future middle with the insertion of $\theta\eta$ before the future tense sign.

396.   FIRST FUTURE PASSIVE SYSTEM OF λύω

	SING.	DUAL	PLUR.
Indic. 1.	λυ-θή-σο-μαι *I shall be loosed*		λυ-θη-σό-μεθα
2.	λυ-θή-σῃ or -σει	λυ-θή-σε-σθον	λυ-θή-σε-σθε
3.	λυ-θή-σε-ται	λυ-θή-σε-σθον	λυ-θή-σο-νται
Opt. 1.	λυ-θη-σοί-μην		λυ-θη-σοί-μεθα
2.	λυ-θή-σοι-ο	λυ-θή-σοι-σθον	λυ-θή-σοι-σθε
3.	λυ-θή-σοι-το	λυ-θη-σοί-σθην	λυ-θή-σοι-ντο
Inf.	λυ-θή-σε-σθαι		
Partic.	λυ-θη-σό-μενος, η, ον		

---

[1] εἰς.   [a] Cp. I. 11.   [3] Say *be saved homeward.*
[4] Say *the timbers themselves,* § 123. 1.   [5] Use aor. pass.   [6] ἀπό.

397. Like λυθήσομαι are inflected : πεμφθήσομαι (πέμπω), πεισθήσομαι (πείθω), λειφθήσομαι (λείπω), ἀχθή-σομαι (ἄγω), ἁρπασθήσομαι (ἁρπάζω); ληφθήσομαι (λαμ-βάνω); πρᾱχθήσομαι (πρᾱττω); σωθήσομαι (σώζω).

For the euphonic changes in the mutes before the passive suffix θη compare the first aorist passive and § 387.

GENERAL CONDITIONS

398. The conditions studied thus far have been par-ticular ; that is, they have referred to definite and usually single acts.   But when the *if* clause (protasis) refers to a repeated act, or to any one of a number of acts, the condition is called *general.*

Thus *if he says this, he speaks the truth* is a particular condition in present time, for in the protasis a single present act is indicated : εἰ ταῦτα λέγει, ἀληθῆ λέγει (cp. § 106).   But *if ever he says anything* (or *whenever he says anything*), *he speaks the truth* is a general condition in present time, for the protasis and apodosis indicate a repeated act or any one of a number of acts.

While the Greek makes no distinction between particu-lar and general conditions in future time, so far as form is concerned, it does make a most important distinction between such conditions in present time and in past time.

399. **Present general conditions.** — ἐάν (or ἤν or ἄν) intro-duces the subjunctive in the protasis of a present general condition ; the apodosis has the present indicative or its equivalent to express continued or repeated action in pres-ent time.   This form of condition differs from the more vivid future (§ 241) in the apodosis only.

ἐάν τι λέγῃ, ἀληθῆ λέγει if ever he says anything, he speaks the truth.

400. The conditional relative protasis in present time. —
In place of ἐάν (or ἤν or ἄν) with the subjunctive the protasis of a present general condition is often introduced by a
relative or temporal word plus ἄν, exactly like the protasis
of a more vivid future condition (§ 248):

ὅταν τι λέγῃ, ἀληθῆ λέγει whenever he says anything, he speaks the
truth ;

ἅ τινα ἂν λέγῃ, ἀληθῆ λέγει whatever he says, he speaks the truth.

401. Genitive absolute. — A circumstantial participle
(generally present or aorist) and its subject may stand
together in the genitive case in a construction grammati-
cally independent of the rest of the sentence. This
construction corresponds to the Latin *ablative absolute.*

ἐξ-ήλαυνον τῶν πολεμίων οὐ κωλυόντων they marched forth without
hindrance from the enemy (*lit.* the enemy not hindering).

a. The genitive absolute may express any of the relations (time, cause, etc.) of the circumstantial participle.

b. ὡς sometimes accompanies the participle in the genitive absolute. For its force compare § 213. *a.*

Κῦρος συν-έλεξε στράτευμα, ὡς ἐπι-βουλεύοντος Τισσαφέρνους ταῖς πόλεσιν Cyrus collected an army on the ground that Tissaphernes
was plotting against his cities (*cause*).

402. The **genitive** is used to denote **value** or price. This
construction is regular with ἄξιος :

φίλος πολλοῦ ἄξιος a friend worth much (*i.e.* valuable).

403. The instrumental **dative** may denote **cause** :

ἀνάγκῃ λαμβάνομεν τὰ ἐπιτήδεια from necessity (on account of necessity) we take provisions.

404. VOCABULARY XL

ακων, ουσα, ον: *unwilling.* Declined like λύων (cp. § 206. *a*). Used like a partic. in the gen. abs. const.

κίνδῡνος, ου, ό: *danger.* κίνδῡνός ἐστι(ν): *there is danger.* Cp. :ινδῡνεύω.

ὅπῃ, rel. adv.: *where, wherever ; how, in what way.* Cp. πῃ, Vocabulary XVII.

στρατοπεδεύω (στρατόπεδον) and mid. dep. στρατοπεδεύομαι, aor. ἐστρατοπεδευσάμην: *encamp.*

φιλίᾱ, ᾱς, ἡ (φίλος): *friendship.*

EXERCISES FOR TRANSLATION

405. I. 1. οὗτος συλ-ληφθήσεται, εἰ παίσει¹ τὸν στρατιώτην. 2. καὶ ἐνόμισαν συλ-ληφθήσεσθαι. 3. οὐ γὰρ ἔστιν² ὅστις³ ἀνθρώπων σωθήσεται. 4. παρ-ῆν δὲ ὁ σατράπης βουλόμενος μαθεῖν τί πρᾱχθήσεται. 5. ἀγαθοὶ δὲ ἄνδρες εἰσὶν οἱ πρᾱττοντες⁴ ὅτι ἂν ἐν ταῖς μάχαις γίγνηται. 6. ὁ δ' ἀνὴρ πολλοῦ μὲν ἄξιος φίλος ἐστὶν ᾧ ἂν φίλος ᾖ, χαλεπώτατος δ' ἐχθρὸς ᾧ ἂν πολέμιος ᾖ. 7. ὅποι δ' ἂν ἐλθόντες ἀγορᾱν μὴ ἔχωμεν, ἀνάγκῃ λαμβάνομεν τὰ ἐπιτήδεια. 8. οὐ κολασθήσεται ὑπὸ Κύρου διὰ φιλίᾱν. 9. τοῦτο τὸ πεδίον κάλλιστον τρέχειν,⁵ ὅπου ἄν τις βούληται. 10. νῦν ῡμῖν ἔξ-εστιν πορεύεσθαι ὅπῃ ἂν ἔλησθε. 11. οὐκ ἂν βουλοίμην ἀπ-ελθεῖν Κύρου ἄκοντος. 12. εἰς Πῑσίδᾱς Κῦρος ἐβούλετο στρατεύεσθαι, ὡς πρᾱγματα⁶ παρεχόντων τῶν Πῑσιδῶν τῇ ἑαυτοῦ χώρᾳ. 13. στρατοπεδευομένων δ' αὐτῶν γίγνεται τῆς νυκτὸς χιὼν πολλή. 14. κίνδῡνος οὖν ἐστιν, ἢν πορεύησθε ἐπὶ⁷ τὰ ἐπιτήδεια.

---

¹ § 242. ² § 102. ³ *there is not who = nobody.*
⁴ § 212. ⁵ *for running,* § 333.
ᵛ πρᾱγματα παρ-έχω: *cause trouble.* ⁷ *after.*

II. 1. They thought they should be abandoned by the other soldiers.   2. They will be led up to the king.   3. If ever the barbarians do not provide a market, we take provisions ourselves, from necessity.   4. Wherever the Greeks go, they plunder the land.

XLI.

THE SECOND AORIST PASSIVE SYSTEM. DATIVE OF DEGREE OF DIFFERENCE

406. Some verbs have aorists and futures in the passive voice formed without the letter θ of the first passive suffix (§ 383).   Otherwise they are like the first aorist and the first future passive, and do not usually differ in meaning. Mute themes naturally suffer no euphonic change before the suffix, which is η (or ε).   λύω has no second aorist or second future passive.

THE SECOND AORIST PASSIVE

407. The second aorist passive adds the second passive sign η to the theme in the indicative, imperative,[1] and infinitive; and the second passive sign ε to the theme in other moods.   The inflection is like the first aorist.

408. SECOND AORIST PASSIVE SYSTEM OF βλάπτω (THEME βλαβ-) *hurt*

	SING.	DUAL	PLUR.
Indic. 1.	ἐ-βλάβ-η-ν *I was hurt*		ἐ-βλάβ-η-μεν
2.	ἐ-βλάβ-η-s	ἐ-βλάβ-η-τον	ἐ-βλάβ-η-τε
3.	ἐ-βλάβ-η	ἐ-βλαβ-ή-την	ἐ-βλάβ-η-σαν

---

[1] Except the 3 pl. imv., which has ε.

	SING.		DUAL	PLUR.
Subjv 1.	βλαβ-ῶ [for βλαβ-έ-ω]			βλαβ-ῶ-μεν
2.	βλαβ-ῇς	etc.	βλαβ-ῆ-τον	βλαβ-ῆ-τε
3.	βλαβ-ῇ		βλαβ-ῆ-τον	βλαβ-ῶ-σι(ν)
Opt. 1.	βλαβ-είη-ν			βλαβ-εῖ-μεν
2.	βλαβ-είη-s		βλαβ-εῖ-τον	βλαβ-εῖ-τε
3.	βλαβ-είη		βλαβ-εί-την	βλαβ-εῖε-ν

			PLUR.
Less common	1.		βλαβ-είη-μεν
	2.	βλαβ-είη-τον	βλαβ-είη-τε
	3.	βλαβ-ειή-την	βλαβ-είη-σαν

		DUAL	PLUR.
Imv. 2.	βλάβ-η-θι	βλάβ-η-τον	βλάβ-η-τε
3.	βλαβ-ή-τω	βλαβ-ή-των	βλαβ-έ-ντων

Inf.   βλαβ-ῆ-ναι

Partic.   βλαβ-είς, εῖσα, έν [1]

409. Similarly are inflected:

συν-ε-λέγ-η-ν (συλ-λέγω *collect*)   ἐ-κόπ-η-ν (κόπτω *cut* [3])

ἐ-τράπ-η-ν [2] (τρέπω *turn*)   ἐ-γράφ-η-ν (γράφω *write*)

ἐ-τράφ-η-ν (τρέφω *nourish*)   ἐ-στράφ-η-ν [2] (στρέφω *turn*)

410. The instrumental dative (§ 141) is used to denote the **degree of difference** (corresponding to the Latin ablative):

πέντε ἡμέραις πρότερον earlier by five days, five days before ; πολλῷ ὕστερον much later (*lit.* later by much).

a. But πολύ (adv. acc., § 284) is more common than the dative πολλῷ in this sense.

---

[1] For the declension cp. λυθείς, § 388.

[2] Used commonly in intr. or mid. sense: *turned*.

[3] κόπτω *cut* is formed by adding τ%ϵ to the theme κοπ- in the pres. system. The τ does not appear outside of the pres. system. The fut. is κόψω, aor. ἔκοψα, 2 aor. pass. ἐκόπην.

411. VOCABULARY XLI

ἀνα-στρέφω : *turn back, turn about*
(intr.) ; PASS. in mid. sense,
turn about, face about, rally.

ἀπο-κόπτω : *cut off*. See § 409.

βλάπτω (theme βλαβ-),[1] fut.
βλάψω, aor. ἔβλαψα, 1 aor.
pass. ἐβλάφθην, 2 aor. pass.
ἐβλάβην : *hurt, harm*.

δια-κόπτω: *cut through, cut in pieces,
break through*. See § 409.

ἐκ-πλήττω (πλήττω *strike*, theme
πληγ- or πλαγ-, πλήξω, ἔπληξα,
2 aor. pass. ἐπλήγην), with 2 aor.
pass. ἐξ-επλάγην : *strike out* of
one's wits, *terrify utterly, bewilder*.

ἔνδον, adv.: *within*. οἱ ἔνδον :
those within.

ἔξω, adv. : *without, outside*, sometimes with gen. οἱ ἔξω : *those
without*.

ἔφ-οδος, ου, ἡ (ἐπί + ὁδός) : *way
to, approach*.

κατα-κόπτω : *cut down*. See § 409.

Κίλιξ, ικος, ὁ : *Cilician*, a native
of Cilicia.

στρέφω (themes στρεφ-, στραφ-),
στρέψω, ἔστρεψα, 2 aor. pass.
(intr.) ἐστράφην : *turn; wheel
about*. Cp. τρέπω.

τρέφω (themes τρεφ-, τραφ-, for
θρεφ-, etc.), fut. θρέψω, aor.
ἔθρεψα, 2 aor. pass. ἐτράφην :
feed, support, rear.

ὥσπερ, rel. adv. : *just as, as, as if,
like*.

EXERCISES FOR TRANSLATION

412. I. 1. οἱ δὲ στρατιῶται συλ-λεγέντες ἐβουλεύοντο.
2. οἱ δὲ πολέμιοι ἐτράπησαν εἰς φυγήν. 3. οὐκ ἂν
σωθεῖμεν, εἰ δια-κοπείη ἡμῶν ἡ φάλαγξ. 4. ἐβλάβητε
ὑπὸ τῶν Λακεδαιμονίων. 5. καὶ οἱ Ἕλληνες στραφέντες
παρ-εσκευάζοντο ὡς δεξόμενοι βασιλέᾱ. 6. οὐ πολλῷ
δὲ ὕστερον οἵ τ' ἔνδον συν-ελαμβάνοντο καὶ οἱ ἔξω κατ-
εκόπησαν. 7. ὑπὲρ γὰρ τῆς κώμης λόφος ἦν, ἐφ' οὗ
ἀν-εστράφησαν οἱ ἀμφὶ βασιλέᾱ. 8. ἐξ-επλάγη δὲ
βασιλεὺς τῇ ἐφόδῳ[2] τοῦ στρατεύματος. 9. καὶ λέγει
ὡς ἀπ-εκόπησαν ἀπὸ τοῦ λόφου. 10. ἐν ταύταις ταῖς
πόλεσιν ὑμεῖς ἐγένεσθε καὶ ἐτράφητε. 11. ἀλλ' ἐτρά-

---

[1] Cp. κόπτω (theme κοπ-) for the formation of the pres. stem.   [2] § 403.

φησαν τοῖς προβάτοις[1] ἃ ἐκ τῶν πολεμίων ἔλαβον.
12. ἐπεὶ δὲ οὗτοι ἔφυγον, ἐτράπησαν δὴ καὶ οἱ ἄλλοι.
13. ἔφασαν τοὺς στρατιώτᾱς ἁρπάζοντάς τι κατα-
κοπῆναι ὑπὸ τῶν Κιλίκων. 14. ἔστι δ' ὅστις[2] κατ-
ελήφθη ἐν τῇ μάχῃ ὥσπερ ὑπὸ τῶν ἱππέων ἐκ-πλαγείς.

II. 1. The Greeks rallied, and received[3] (the attack of)[4]
the enemy. 2. We admire the cities in which the Greeks
were born and reared. 3. The Cilician woman came to
these cities five days before[5] Cyrus.[6]

XLII

THE SECOND FUTURE PASSIVE SYSTEM. PAST GEN-
ERAL CONDITIONS. CONDITIONAL RELATIVE
PROTASIS IN PAST TIME. IMPERFECT INDICATIVE
IN PROTASIS OF PAST GENERAL RELATIVE CON-
DITION

413. Verbs that have a second aorist passive, like ἐβλάβην, ἐκόπην, συν-ελέγην, and ἐγράφην, usually form a second
future passive by adding the future suffix σ% and the
personal endings of the middle voice to the second
passive stem, which consists of the theme plus η. The
inflection is like that of the first future passive, and the
meanings are identical.

---

[1] Dat. of means, § 141.
[2] *there is who = somebody.*
[3] The aor. of δέχομαι is ἐδεξάμην.
[4] Omit.
[5] Use the feminine προτέρᾱ in agreement with the subject.
[6] § 355.

414. SECOND FUTURE PASSIVE SYSTEM OF βλάπτω
(THEME βλαβ-) *hurt*

	SING.	DUAL	PLUR.
Indic. 1.	βλαβ-ή-σο-μαι *I shall be hurt*		βλαβ-η-σό-μεθα
2.	βλαβ-ή-ση or -σει	βλαβ-ή-σε-σθον	βλαβ-ή-σε-σθε
3.	βλαβ-ή-σε-ται	βλαβ-ή-σε-σθον	βλαβ-ή-σο-νται
Opt. 1.	βλαβ-η-σοί-μην		βλαβ-η-σοί-μεθα
2.	βλαβ-ή-σοι-ο	βλαβ-ή-σοι-σθον	βλαβ-ή-σοι-σθε
3.	βλαβ-ή-σοι-το	βλαβ-η-σοί-σθην	βλαβ-ή-σοι-ντο
Inf.	βλαβ-ή-σε-σθαι		
Partic.	βλαβ-η-σό-μενος, η, ον		

415. Similarly are inflected:

γραφ-ή-σο-μαι, 2 fut. pass. of γράφω *write*.

συλ-λεγ-ή-σο-μαι, 2 fut. pass. of συλ-λέγω *collect*.

416. Past general conditions. — εἰ introduces the optative
in the protasis of a past general condition; the apodosis
has the imperfect indicative (or an equivalent) to express
repeated action in past time.

This form of condition differs from the less vivid future
(§ 267) in the apodosis only:

εἴ τι λέγοι, ἀληθῆ ἔλεγεν if he [ever] said anything, he [always]
spoke the truth.

417. The conditional relative protasis in past time. — In
place of εἰ with the optative, the protasis of a past general condition is often introduced by a relative pronoun or
adverb (cp. § 400):

ὁπότε τι λέγοι, ἀληθῆ ἔλεγεν whenever he said anything, he spoke the
truth ;

ἅ τινα λέγοι, ἀληθῆ ἔλεγεν whatever he said [at any time], he spoke
the truth.

418. Not uncommonly the **imperfect indicative** introduced by a *relative* is used for the optative in the protasis of a past general condition. The following sentence shows both uses combined:

ἐπορευόμεθα διὰ ταύτης τῆς χώρας ὅποι ἐβουλόμεθα (where βουλοίμεθα might also be used), ἣν μὲν χώραν ἐθέλοιμεν δι-αρπάζοντες, ἣν δ' ἐθέλοιμεν κάοντες we proceeded through this country whithersoever we would, sacking whatever land we wished, and burning whatever we wished.

a. The negative of the protasis, as always, is μή.

419. **VOCABULARY XLII**

ἀεί, adv.: *always, continually, in succession.*

ἀπο-λείπω (cp. λείπω): *leave behind, desert, abandon.*

γυμνάζω (theme γυμναδ-), γυμνάσω, etc. (like ἁρπάζω): *exercise.* Cp. γυμνής. Gymnastic.

δεινός, ή, όν: *fearful, terrible, frightful; skillful.* τὸ δεινόν (subst.): *danger.*

ἕπομαι (for σέπομαι), ἕψομαι, 2 aor. ἑσπόμην, impf. with irreg. aug. εἱπόμην (cp. εἶχον): *follow*, with dat. of association (§ 317). Cp. Lat. *sequor.*

θηρεύω, θηρεύσω, etc.: *hunt; catch* (by hunting). Cp. θηρίον.

θηρίον, ου, τό: *wild beast.*

κατ-άγω (cp. ἄγω), *lead down; bring* a ship (especially a captured one) *into harbor; restore* exiles.

ὁπόσος, η, ον, indef. rel. pron. and indir. interr.: *as many as; how great,* (pl.) *how many.* Cp. ὅσος.

ὁπότε, rel. adv.: *when, whenever, as often as; since.* Cp. ὅτε.

παρ-έρχομαι (cp. ἔρχομαι), 2 aor. παρ-ῆλθον: *go by, go past.*

πολλάκις, adv. (πολύς): *often.*

σπεύδω (theme σπευδ-), σπεύσω, ἔσπευσα: *urge on, hasten.*

τέκνον, ου, τό: *child.*

EXERCISES FOR TRANSLATION

420. I. 1. οἱ δὲ στρατιῶται πάντες συλ-λεγήσονται. 2. ἐν ταύτῃ τῇ ἐπιστολῇ γραφήσεται τάδε. 3. ὁ δὲ στρατηγὸς τῷ ἄρχοντι τῆς κώμης ταύτης ἔλεξεν ὅτι οὐ βλαβήσοιτο. 4. καὶ εἰ δέοι γέφυραν δια-βαίνειν, ἔσπευδεν ἕκαστος, βουλόμενος δια-βαίνειν πρῶτος. 5. Κῦρος δὲ ἐθήρευε θηρία ἀφ᾽ ἵππου,¹ ὁπότε γυμνάσαι βούλοιτο ἑαυτόν τε καὶ τοὺς ἵππους. 6. Κῦρος γὰρ ἔπεμπεν οἶνον πρὸς τοὺς φίλους πολλάκις, ὁπότε πάνυ ἡδὺν λάβοι. 7. σταθμοὺς δὲ πάνυ μακροὺς ἤλαυνεν, ὁπότε ἢ πρὸς ὕδωρ βούλοιτο ἐλθεῖν ἢ πρὸς χιλόν. 8. ἐλάμβανε δὲ ὅ τι βούλοιτο. 9. ὅπου δέ τινα τῶν φίλων ἴδοι, πρὸς ἑαυτὸν ἀεὶ αὐτὸν ἐλάμβανεν. 10. ἐπεὶ δὲ παρ-έλθοιεν οἱ Ἕλληνες, οἱ βάρβαροι εἵποντο αὐτοῖς. 11. τοιγαροῦν πολλοὶ ἤθελον κινδυνεύειν, ὅπου τις οἴοιτο Κῦρον αἰσθήσεσθαι. 12. τὰ ἐπιτήδεια ἐλάμβανον, ὅπου τις αὐτοῖς ἐπι-τυγχάνοι. 13. ὁπόσα λαμβάνοι πλοῖα, κατ-ῆγεν ἐπὶ τὸ στρατόπεδον. 14. ἀπ-έλειπον τὸν στρατηγὸν πάντες ὅσοι συν-επορεύοντο, ὅτε² ἔξω³ τοῦ δεινοῦ γένοιντο.

II. 1. He will be hurt, if he goes⁴ into this danger. 2. Whenever they had to cross a river, all hastened. 3. Cyrus used to hunt wild animals on horseback whenever he went to the mountains.

---

¹ *from horseback = on horseback,* the attention being directed away *from* the horse while a man is hunting.

² *whenever.*   ³ *out of.*

⁴ Use the proper form of πορεύομαι.

XLIII

NUMERALS.   DECLENSION OF NUMERALS.   ARTICLE
WITH "ROUND" NUMBERS.   EMPHATIC NEGATIONS

421. Commit to memory the numerals from 1 to 21
(inclusive); the others are to be memorized as they are
needed.   Some, as ἑκατόν and χίλιοι, have already occurred
in the special vocabularies.

1	εἷς, μία, ἕν	19	ἐννεακαίδεκα
2	δύο	20	εἴκοσι(ν)
3	τρεῖς, τρία	21	εἷς καὶ εἴκοσι(ν) or
4	τέτταρες, τέτταρα		εἴκοσι (καὶ) εἷς
5	πέντε	30	τριάκοντα
6	ἕξ	40	τετταράκοντα
7	ἑπτά	50	πεντήκοντα
8	ὀκτώ	60	ἑξήκοντα
9	ἐννέα	70	ἑβδομήκοντα
10	δέκα	80	ὀγδοήκοντα
11	ἕνδεκα	90	ἐνενήκοντα
12	δώδεκα	100	ἑκατόν
13	τρεῖς (τρία) καὶ δέκα or	200	διᾱκόσιοι, αι, α
	τρισκαίδεκα	300	τριᾱκόσιοι, αι, α
14	τέτταρες καὶ δέκα or	400	τετρακόσιοι, αι, α
	τετταρεσκαίδεκα	500	πεντακόσιοι, αι, α
15	πεντεκαίδεκα	600	ἑξακόσιοι, αι, α
16	ἑκκαίδεκα	700	ἑπτακόσιοι, αι, α
17	ἑπτακαίδεκα	800	ὀκτακόσιοι, αι, α
18	ὀκτωκαίδεκα	900	ἐνακόσιοι, αι, α

1,000	χίλιοι, αι, α
2,000	δισχίλιοι, αι, α (δίς *twice*)
3,000	τρισχίλιοι, αι, α (τρίς *three times*)
4,000	τετρακισχίλιοι, αι, α (τετράκις *four times*)
5,000	πεντακισχίλιοι, αι, α (πεντάκις *five times*)
6,000	ἑξακισχίλιοι, αι, α (ἑξάκις *six times*)
7,000	ἑπτακισχίλιοι, αι, α (ἑπτάκις *seven times*)

8,000	ὀκτακισχίλιοι, αι, α (ὀκτάκις *eight times*)
9,000	ἐνακισχίλιοι, αι, α (ἐνάκις *nine times*)
10,000	μύριοι, αι, α, or μυριάς (gen. άδος) myriad
20,000	δισμύριοι, αι, α, or δύο μυριάδες (gen. -ων)
30,000	τρισμύριοι, αι, α, or τρεῖς μυριάδες
	etc.

422.   **DECLENSION OF** εἷς *one*

	MASC.	FEM.	NEUT.
N.	εἷς	μία	ἕν
G.	ἑνός	μιᾶς	ἑνός
D.	ἑνί	μιᾷ	ἑνί
A.	ἕνα	μίαν	ἕν

423. δύο *two* sometimes is declined :

     N. A.   δύο   G. D.   δυοῖν

a. Often it is used as indeclinable.

424. DECLENSION OF τρεῖς   **425. DECLENSION OF** τέτταρες
        three   *four*

	MASC. AND FEM.	NEUT.	MASC. AND FEM.	NEUT.
N.	τρεῖς	τρία	τέτταρες	τέτταρα
G.	τριῶν		τεττάρων	
D.	τρισί(ν)		τέτταρσι(ν)	
A.	τρεῖς	τρία	τέτταρας	τέτταρα

426.   **DECLENSION OF** οὐδείς *nobody*

	MASC.	FEM.	NEUT.		MASC.
Sing. N.	οὐδείς	οὐδεμία	οὐδέν *nothing*	Plur. N.	οὐδένες
G.	οὐδενός	οὐδεμιᾶς	οὐδενός	G.	οὐδένων
D.	οὐδενί	οὐδεμιᾷ	οὐδενί	D.	οὐδέσι(ν)
A.	οὐδένα	οὐδεμίαν	οὐδέν	A.	οὐδένας

a. μηδείς, μηδεμία, μηδέν, *nobody*, *nothing*, is similarly declined. μηδείς is used wherever μή is the appropriate negative.

427. The **article** often accompanies " round " numbers. It is not to be translated :

ἀμφὶ τοὺς ἑκατόν about one hundred.

428. **Emphatic negations.** — If a simple or a compound negative is followed by one or several *compound* negatives in the same clause, the negation is made more emphatic. The negatives must be of the same sort (*i.e.* all οὐ and its compounds, or all μή and its compounds):

οὐδ' ἄλλος ἔπαθεν οὐδεὶς οὐδέν nor did anybody else suffer any injury.

429.   VOCABULARY XLIII

Numerals are not repeated (from § 421) in this Vocabulary and the following Vocabularies.

δῶρον, ου, τό: *gift*. Cp. Lat. dōnum.

μη-δέ: *and not, nor, not even*. Used like μή. Cp. οὐδέ.

μηδ-είς, μηδε-μία, μηδ-έν: *nobody, no one, no, nothing*.

μή-τε ... μή-τε: *neither ... nor*. Used like μή. Cp. οὔτε ... οὔτε

οὐδ-είς, οὐδε-μία, οὐδ-έν (οὐδέ + εἷς). *nobody, no one, no, nothing*.

Πασίων, ωνος, ὁ: *Pasion*.

Σοφαίνετος, ου, ὁ: *Sophaenetus*.

σύμ-πᾱς, πᾶσα, παν (σύν + πᾶς): *all together, all, whole*. Cp.ἅ-πᾱς.

συν-έρχομαι (cp. ἔρχομαι), 2 aor. συν-ῆλθον: *go* or *come together, assemble*.

EXERCISES FOR TRANSLATION

430. 1. I. καὶ ἤγαγον αὐτοὺς ἐν τρισὶν ἡμέραις ἐπὶ τὴν θάλατταν.   2. Κῦρος δ' οὖν ἀν-έβαινεν ἐπὶ τὰ ὄρη οὐδενὸς κωλύοντος.   3. τῇ δ' οὖν στρατιᾷ τότε παρ-έσχε[1] Κῦρος μισθὸν τεττάρων μηνῶν.   4. καὶ ἧκε Κλέαρχος ἔχων ὁπλίτᾱς χιλίους καὶ πελταστὰς Θρᾷκας ὀκτακοσίους καὶ τοξότᾱς διᾱκοσίους.   5. καὶ ἐγέ-νοντο[2] οἱ σύμπαντες[3] ὁπλῖται[4] μὲν μύριοι καὶ χίλιοι,

---

[1] From παρ-έχω.   [2] *amounted to.*   [3] Subj.   [4] Pred. nom.

πελτασταὶ δὲ ἀμφὶ τοὺς δισχῑλίους. 6. καὶ ἐγένοντο
οἱ συν-ελθόντες στρατηγοὶ καὶ λοχᾱγοὶ ἀμφὶ τοὺς
ἑκατόν. 7. καὶ οὐδὲν μέντοι οὐδὲ Κλέαρχον παθεῖν
ἔφασαν. 8. μηδὲ σὺ δια-λέγου¹ μηδενί, μήτε στρα-
τηγῷ μήτε ἄλλῳ ἄρχοντι. 9. παρ' οὐδενὸς οὔτε δῶρα
οὔτε μισθὸν δέχομαι. 10. Ξενίᾱς μὲν δὴ τοὺς ἐκ τῶν
πόλεων λαβὼν παρ-εγένετο εἰς Σάρδεις, ὁπλίτᾱς εἰς
τετρακισχῑλίους, Πρόξενος δὲ παρ-ῆν ἔχων ὁπλίτᾱς μὲν
εἰς πεντακοσίους καὶ χῑλίους, γυμνῆτας δὲ πεντακοσίους, Σοφαίνετος δὲ ὁπλίτᾱς ἔχων χῑλίους, Σωκράτης
δὲ ὁπλίτᾱς ἔχων ὡς πεντακοσίους, Πᾱσίων δὲ τριᾱκοσίους μὲν ὁπλίτᾱς, τριᾱκοσίους δὲ πελταστᾱς ἔχων
παρ-εγένετο.

II. 1. The general arrived with three hundred hoplites
and a thousand bowmen. 2. There were two thousand
and five hundred peltasts, and about ten thousand light-
armed troops of the barbarians. 3. Then the Greeks came
to the Harpasus² river, which was³ four plethra wide.⁴

---

¹ § 309.   ² Ἅρπασος, ου, ὁ.   ³ Say being.   ⁴ § 279.

XLIV

THE FIRST PERFECT AND FIRST PLUPERFECT IN THE
ACTIVE VOICE.   REDUPLICATION.   DECLENSION
OF THE PERFECT PARTICIPLE.   OBJECT CLAUSES
AFTER VERBS OF *FEARING*.   SUPPLEMENTARY
PARTICIPLE AFTER VERBS OF *BEGINNING*, ETC.;
AFTER VERBS OF *PERCEPTION*.   SUPPLEMENTARY
PARTICIPLE IN INDIRECT DISCOURSE

431. The perfect active tense stem consists of the reduplicated theme, to which is added the perfect active tense
suffix.

The first perfect active tense suffix is κα in the perfect
indicative (which becomes κε in the third person singular).
Its forms in the pluperfect indicative (κε) and elsewhere
may best be learned by inspection of the paradigms.

432. **Reduplication** is a sign of all perfect tenses (including the pluperfect and future perfect) throughout the
moods.

a. Verbs that begin with a single consonant reduplicate
the theme by prefixing its initial consonant followed by ε.

λέ-λυ-κα, perfect active of λύω; βέ-βη-κα, perfect of βαίνω (theme
βα- or βη-).

b. Verbs that begin with a rough mute prefix the smooth
mute of the same class (§§ 27, 28) in reduplicating the
theme :

τέ-θυ-κα, perfect of θύω; τέ-θνη-κα, perfect of θνῄσκω (cp. § 137).

c. Verbs that begin with two or more consonants or
a double consonant (§ 6) or the letter ῥ have *syllabic*

augment (§ 77. 1) throughout the perfect in place of reduplication :

ἐ-στράτευ-κα, perfect of στρατεύω.

d. But verbs that begin with a mute and a liquid (§ 27) generally reduplicate in the regular way :

τέθνη-κα, perfect of θνήσκω.

e. Verbs that begin with a vowel (or diphthong) have the *temporal* augment (§ 77. 2) throughout the perfect in place of reduplication :

ἥρπα-κα, perfect of ἁρπάζω (theme ἁρπαδ-).

f. A lingual mute (τ δ θ) at the end of the theme is dropped before the perfect suffix κα :

ἥρπα-κα for ἥρπαδ-κα ; πέπει-κα for πεπειθ-κα (from πείθω).

g. The accent can never recede back of the reduplication or augment (cp. § 131). Compound verbs are reduplicated, as they are augmented, after the prefix (§ 130):

δια-βέβηκα, perfect of δια-βαίνω.

433. The pluperfect, like the imperfect (§ 234), belongs only to the indicative mood. It has syllabic augment, too, in addition to reduplication, if the theme begins with a consonant :

ἐ-λε-λύ-κη, pluperfect active of λύω.

434. PERFECT ACTIVE SYSTEM OF λύω

SING.

Pf. Indic. 1.   λέ-λυ-κα *I have loosed*
        2.   λέ-λυ-κα-s *you have loosed*
        3.   λέ-λυ-κε(ν) *he has loosed*

DUAL

        2.   λε-λύ-κα-τον
        3.   λε-λύ-κα-τον

PLUR.

1. λε-λύ-κα-μεν *we have loosed*
2. λε-λύ-κα-τε *you have loosed*
3. λε-λύ-κᾱ-σι(ν) [1] *they have loosed*

Inf. λε-λυ-κέ-ναι [2] *to have loosed*

Partic. λε-λυ-κώς, [3] -κυῖα, -κός, *having loosed*

SING.

Plup. Indic. 1. ἐ-λε-λύ-κη *I had loosed*
2. ἐ-λε-λύ-κη-s *you had loosed*
3. ἐ-λε-λύ-κει(ν) *he had loosed*

DUAL

2. ἐ-λε-λύ-κε-τον
3. ἐ-λε-λυ-κέ-την

PLUR.

1. ἐ-λε-λύ-κε-μεν *we had loosed*
2. ἐ-λε-λύ-κε-τε *you had loosed*
3. ἐ-λε-λύ-κε-σαν *they had loosed*

435. DECLENSION OF THE PERFECT PARTICIPLE

	MASC.	FEM.	NEUT.
Sing. N. V.	λελυκώς *having loosed*	λελυκυῖα	λελυκός
G.	λελυκότος	λελυκυίᾱς	λελυκότος
D.	λελυκότι	λελυκυίᾳ	λελυκότι
A.	λελυκότα	λελυκυῖαν	λελυκός
Dual N. A. V.	λελυκότε	λελυκυίᾱ	λελυκότε
G. D.	λελυκότοιν	λελυκυίαιν	λελυκότοιν
Plur. N. V.	λελυκότες	λελυκυῖαι	λελυκότα
G.	λελυκότων	λελυκυιῶν	λελυκότων
D.	λελυκόσι(ν)	λελυκυίαις	λελυκόσι(ν)
A.	λελυκότας	λελυκυίᾱς	λελυκότα

a. *Having loosed, having heard*, etc., are more frequently expressed in Greek by the aorist than by the perfect participle.

---

[1] For λε-λυ-κα-νσι(ν).   [2] For accent see § 385, footnote 2.

[3] All perfect active participles, like second aorist active participles, are accented on the ultima

436 Periphrastic forms of the perfect subjunctive and optative, made up of the perfect active participle and the proper forms of εἰμί (subjunctive, § 247; optative, § 265), are more common than the simple forms, which are purposely omitted from this lesson.

	SING.	DUAL	PLUR.
Pf. Subjv. 1.	λελυκὼς ὦ		λελυκότες ὦμεν
2.	λελυκὼς ᾖς	λελυκότε ἦτον	λελυκότες ἦτε
3.	λελυκὼς ᾖ	λελυκότε ἦτον	λελυκότες ὦσι(ν)
Pf. Opt. 1.	λελυκὼς εἴην		λελυκότες εἴημεν
2.	λελυκὼς εἴης	λελυκότε εἴητον	λελυκότες εἴητε
3.	λελυκὼς εἴη	λελυκότε εἰήτην	λελυκότες εἴησαν

a. The shorter forms εἶτον, εἶμεν, etc., also occur.

437. The perfect imperative active almost never occurs.

438. **Object clauses after verbs of fearing.** — After a verb of fearing in a primary tense (§ 39) μή *lest* introduces the subjunctive (present or aorist) to express the object of fear (provided this is future). *Lest not* is expressed by μὴ οὐ:

δέδοικα μὴ κακῶς πράξωσιν I fear lest they do (= fare) ill;

δέδοικα μὴ οὐκ ἔχω (pres. subjv.) ἱκανοὺς φίλους I fear lest I shall not have enough friends.

a. After a secondary tense μή *lest* may introduce the optative (or subjunctive, cp. § 268):

ἐδεδοίκη μὴ κακῶς πράξειαν (or πράξωσιν) I feared lest they should fare ill.

439. The **supplementary participle** (§ 215) is used in agreement with the subject of verbs meaning *begin, continue, cease, be pleased*, etc. :

ἥδομαι, ὦ Κλέαρχε, ἀκούων σου δικαίους λόγους I am pleased, Clearchus, to hear just words from you.

440. The **supplementary participle** is used in agreement with the object of verbs of *perception* (of the mind or senses):

εἶδε Κλέαρχον ἐλαύνοντα he saw Clearchus riding.

441. Supplementary participle in indirect discourse. — In the use of § 440 the participle often represents a finite verb of the main clause of a quotation ; and if so, the participle is said to be in the construction of indirect discourse. The tenses of the participle in indirect discourse are used in exactly the same way as the tenses of the infinitive in indirect discourse (§§ 110. *a*, *b*; 156. 1; 277). That is, the present participle represents the present tense (and imperfect tense) of the finite verb; the perfect, aorist, and future participles represent respectively the perfect, aorist, and future tenses of the finite verb. If ἄν accompanied the finite verb (*e.g.* in the potential optative), it is retained with the equivalent participle in indirect discourse :

πυνθάνεται (or αἰσθάνεται) Κῦρον προσ-ελαύνοντα he learns (*or* he perceives) that Cyrus is drawing near ;

Direct form : Κῦρος προσ-ελαύνει Cyrus is drawing near.

εἶδον ῥᾳδίως[1] ἂν τὸ τεῖχος ληφθέν they saw that the wall might be easily taken ;

Direct form : ῥᾳδίως ἂν τὸ τεῖχος ληφθείη the wall may be easily taken.

For an example of the perfect participle, see § 442. *a*.

442. Verbs of *perception* commonly admit the construction with ὅτι as well :

πυνθάνεται (or αἰσθάνεται) ὅτι Κῦρος προσ-ελαύνει he learns (*or* he perceives) that Cyrus is drawing near.

---

[1] Adv. of ῥᾴδιος, § 360. 8.

a. ἀκούω *hear* allows either a ὅτι clause (§ 262) or the infinitive (§ 262. *a*) or the participle in indirect discourse:

ἤκουσαν Κῦρον τεθνηκότα they heard that Cyrus was dead;

Direct form: Κῦρος τέθνηκεν Cyrus is dead.

Examples of the other constructions have already oc- curred (§§ 203. I. 10; 264. I. 6).

443. VOCABULARY XLIV

δέδοικα, pf. with pres. meaning (from δείδω): *fear;* I aor. ἔδεισα. Cp. δεινός.

ἔνθα, rel. adv.: *where;* dem.: *there;* of time, ἔνθα δή: *then indeed.*

εὑρίσκω, fut. εὑρήσω, 2 aor. ηὗρον, pf. act. ηὕρηκα, pf. mid. to be learned later, aor. pass. ηὑρέθην: *find.* Eureka.

ἥδομαι (theme ἡδ-): *be pleased;* ἡσθήσομαι: *shall be pleased;* ἥσθην: *was pleased; with* some- thing (dat. § 403). See § 439. Cp. ἡδύς.

καιρός, οῦ, ὁ: *the right measure, right time, right place; proper time; opportunity, crisis.*

κράτος, ους, τό: *strength, might.* ἀνὰ κράτος: *to the limit of strength, at full speed.*

λανθάνω (themes λαθ-, ληθ-, cp. λαμ- βάνω, τυγχάνω, § 218), fut. λήσω, 2 aor. ἔλαθον (other parts to be learned later): *lie hid, escape notice of;* with supplementary partic., in construction like τυγ- χάνω (§ 215): thus ἔλαθεν ἐλθών *he went secretly,* lit. *he escaped notice going.*

μή, conj.: *lest,* after verbs of *fear- ing.* μὴ οὐ: *lest not.* See § 438.

Μιθραδάτης, ου, ὁ: *Mithradātes.*

τέθνηκα, pf. of θνῄσκω: *be dead, be slain.* Cp. ἀπο-θνῄσκω(§ 137). The simple verb is common in the perfect.

ὑπερβολή, ῆς, ἡ: *passing over, pass.* Hyperbole.

χαράδρᾱ, ᾱς, ἡ: *ravine.*

EXERCISES FOR TRANSLATION

444. I. 1. καὶ τὰς σπονδὰς παρὰ τοὺς ὅρκους λελύ- κᾱσιν.[1] 2. πολλοὺς δὲ ἄνδρας καὶ πολλὰ χρήματα ἡρπάκαμεν. 3. Κῦρος δ᾽ ἐπεὶ ᾔσθετο αὐτοὺς δια- βεβηκότας, ᾔσθη. 4. Κῦρος δὲ ᾔσθη τὸν ἐκ[2] τῶν

---

[1] Cp. § 121. I. 7.　　　　[2] *inspired by.*

Ἑλλήνων εἰς τοὺς βαρβάρους φόβον ἰδών. 5. ἀλλὰ δέδοικα μὴ οὐχ εὕρωμεν τὴν οἴκαδε ὁδόν. 6. καὶ ἐδεδοίκη μὴ οὐχ ἥδοιτο τῷ ἵππῳ.[1] 7. Ἀβροκόμας ἤκουσε Κῦρον ἐν Κιλικίᾳ ὄντα. 8. νῦν οὖν καιρός ἐστι φυλάξασθαι μὴ ληφθῶμεν, ἵνα μὴ κολασθῶμεν. 9. οὗτοι ἔλεγον ὅτι Κῦρος τέθνηκεν. 10. ἐπεὶ δὲ οἱ Ἕλληνες διαβεβηκότες ἀπεῖχον τῆς χαράδρας ὅσον[2] ὀκτὼ σταδίους, ἔνθα δὴ διέβαινε καὶ[3] ὁ Μιθραδάτης. 11. τοῦτο τὸ στράτευμα ἐλάνθανε τρεφόμενον αὐτῷ.[4] 12. δείσαντες μὴ ἀποληφθείησαν ἔφευγον ἀνὰ κράτος. 13. Χειρίσοφος δ᾽ ἐπεὶ εἶδε τοὺς πολεμίους ἐπὶ τῇ ὑπερβολῇ, ἐπαύσατο πορευόμενος. 14. ὁ δὲ Ξενίας πέπεικε τοῦτον τὸν ἄνθρωπον λέγειν ὧδε.

II. 1. We were glad to see the army of Cyrus. 2. We heard that the soldiers had crossed[5] the ravine. 3. A man came riding at full speed and said that Cyrus was dead. 4. Our soldiers captured the height unobserved.[6] 5. He fears that[7] the enemy will come secretly[8] in the night.

---

[1] § 403.
[2] Adv. acc., *as far as, about.*
[3] *also.*
[4] § 53. *d.*
[5] Use all possible constructions.
[6] Say *escaped notice taking,* etc.
[7] *lest.*
[8] Say *escape notice coming.*

XLV

THE SECOND PERFECT AND THE SECOND PLUPERFECT
ACTIVE. ATTIC REDUPLICATION. REDUPLICATION
WITH εἰ-. SUPPLEMENTARY PARTICIPLE WITH
δῆλός ἐστιν, ETC.

445. There is a second form of the perfect and pluperfect active made with the suffix α (also ε) instead of κα (κε).
It is like the first perfect except for the want of the letter
κ. This **second perfect** belongs only to certain verbs:
some with themes ending in a mute and some with themes
ending in a liquid. The theme itself often undergoes
modification of its vowel sound; and a smooth mute (π, κ)
or middle mute (β, γ, cp. § 28) before the suffix α (or ε)
is usually (but not always) changed to the corresponding
rough.

πέ-πομφ-α (πέμπ-ω) I have sent;
πέ-ποιθ-α (πείθ-ω) I trust;
πέ-πονθ-α (πάσχω, themes παθ-, πενθ-) I have suffered;
πέ-φευγ-α (φεύγ-ω) I have fled;
λέ-λοιπ-α (λείπ-ω) I have left;
ἦχ-α (ἄγ-ω) I have led;
γέ-γον-α (γίγνομαι, theme γεν-) I have been born, become,
    I am;
γέ-γραφ-α (γράφ-ω) I have written.

a. Some verbs like πείθω have both perfects, but with
different meanings:

πέ-πει-κα *means* I have persuaded (πέποιθα, *second perfect*,
    I trust).

446. SECOND PERFECT SYSTEM OF λείπω

	SING.	DUAL	PLUR.
Pf. Indic. 1.	λέ-λοιπ-α *I have left*		λε-λοίπ-α-μεν *we have left*
2.	λέ-λοιπ-α-s *you have left*	λε-λοίπ-α-τον	λε-λοίπ-α-τε *you have left*
3.	λέ-λοιπ-ε *he has left*	λε-λοίπ-α-τον	λε-λοίπ-ᾱσι(ν) *they have left*

Subjv. 1. λε-λοιπ-ὼs ὦ (cp. § 436), etc.

Opt. 1. λε-λοιπ-ὼs εἴην (cp. § 436), etc.

Imv. Almost never occurs in the perfect active (§ 437)

Inf. λε-λοιπ-έ-ναι *to have left*

Partic. λε-λοιπ-ώs, -υῖα, -όs, *having left* (Cp. § 435)

Plup. Indic. 1.	ἐ-λε-λοίπ-η *I had left*		ἐ-λε-λοίπ-ε-μεν *we had left*
2.	ἐ-λε-λοίπ-η-s *you had left*	ἐ-λε-λοίπ-ε-τον	ἐ-λε-λοίπ-ε-τε *you had left*
3.	ἐ-λε-λοίπ-ει(ν) *he had left*	ἐ-λε-λοιπ-έ-την	ἐ-λε-λοίπ-ε-σαν *they had left*

447. Attic reduplication. — Some verbs beginning with a short vowel followed by a consonant prefix the first two letters and lengthen the initial vowel of the theme:

ἐλ-ήλυθ-α [2 pf. from theme ἐλυθ-, of which a shorter form is seen in ἦλθον (ἐλθ-)] I have come [1];

ἐλ-ήλα-κα [1 pf. from theme ἐλα- (ἐλαύνω)] I have driven *or* marched.

448. A few verbs have εἰ- prefixed to the theme for reduplication:

εἴ-ληφ-α (2 pf. of λαμβάνω, themes ληβ-, λαβ-) I have taken;
συν-εἴ-λοχ-α (2 pf. of συλ-λέγω, theme λεγ-) I have collected;
εἴ-ρη-κα (1 pf. from theme ῥη-) I have said.

---

[1] This verb supplies the 2 pf. of ἔρχομαι. But ἥκω (§ 137) is commonly used for the *simple* ἐλήλυθα.

449. The **supplementary participle** in indirect discourse is common in agreement with the subject of δῆλός ἐστι(ν) *he is evident* and similar expressions, such as:

$$\left. \begin{array}{l} \text{φανερός ἐστι}(ν) \\ \text{and φανερὸς γέγονε}(ν) \end{array} \right\} \text{he is evident.}$$

δῆλος ἦν Κῦρος σπεύδων πᾶσαν τὴν ὁδόν Cyrus was clearly hastening (*lit.* was evident hastening) all the way.

a. The construction δῆλόν (ἐστιν) ὅτι *it is evident that* also occurs (§ 270. I. 2).

450.   VOCABULARY XLV

ἄγγελος, ου, ὁ: *messenger.* Angel.

εἴρηκα, pf [1]: *I have said, I have mentioned.*

ἔνιοι, αι, α: *some.*

ἱερός, ά, όν: *sacred, holy.* Hierarchy (ἄρχω).

προ-έρχομαι (cp. ἔρχομαι), 2 aor. προ-ῆλθον, 2 pf. προ-ελήλυθα (§ 447): *go before, go forward, proceed.*

τοσοῦτος, τοσαύτη, τοσοῦτο (declined like οὗτος, § 171), dem. pron : *so much, so great, so many;* often followed by correlative word like ὅσος *as.* The neut. is also τοσοῦτον as well as τοσοῦτο. Cp. Lat. *tantus.*

φανερός, ά, όν: *visible, clear, evident.*

EXERCISES FOR TRANSLATION

451. I. 1. οἱ δὲ στρατηγοὶ κακὰ πεπόνθασιν.   2. πεπόμφασι δὲ εἰς τὴν Ἑλλάδα πρέσβεις ἐπ᾽ [2] ἄλλην στρατιάν.   3. ἀπο-λελοίπασιν ἡμᾶς Ξενίας καὶ Πασίων. 4. νῦν δ᾽ ἐπι-βουλεύων μοι φανερὸς γέγονας. 5. οὗτοι ἔλεγον ὅτι Ἀριαῖος πεφευγὼς εἴη μετὰ τῶν ἄλλων βαρβάρων.   6. τῇ δ᾽ ὑστεραίᾳ ἧκεν ἄγγελος λέγων ὅτι λελοιπὼς εἴη Συέννεσις τὰ ἄκρα.   7. βασιλεὺς δὲ καὶ Τισσαφέρνης ἐνίους συν-ειλήφασιν ἡμῶν.   8. ὑμεῖς τοσοῦτοι [3] ὄντες ὅσοι [4] νῦν συν-εληλύθατε μέγιστον

---

[1] Supplies the pf. act. of λέγω *say.*   [2] *to fetch, after.*

[3] *so many.*   [4] *as.*

ἔχετε καιρόν. 9. οὐ πολὺ δὲ προ-εληλυθότων αὐτῶν·
ἧκε πάλιν ὁ Μιθραδάτης. 10. καὶ κατ-ειληφότες φυ-
λάττουσι τὴν ὁδόν. 11. καὶ τοῦτον τὸν λόφον παρ-
εληλύθεσαν οἱ Ἕλληνες. 12. συν-εληλυθότες δ᾽ ἦσαν
ἐνταῦθα καὶ ἄνδρες καὶ γυναῖκες καὶ πρόβατα πολλά.
13. ἐν τούτῳ τῷ χρόνῳ ἦλθεν ὁ λοχᾱγὸς πεφευγώς.
14. Μένων δὲ δῆλος ἦν ἐπι-βουλεύων τῷ φίλῳ. 15. ὁ δὲ
στρατηγὸς ἔχων οὓς² εἴρηκα ἐξ-ῆλθεν ἐκ τοῦ ἱεροῦ
χωρίου.

II. 1. It has become clear that Cyrus is³ plotting against
his brother. 2. You have evidently come together⁴ in
order to advise us. 3. They have seized our generals and
captains.

XLVI

THE PERFECT AND PLUPERFECT MIDDLE AND PASSIVE
OF VOWEL THEMES. INFINITIVE WITH μέμνημαι
remember how, ETC. DATIVE OF AGENT

452. The middle and passive voices have identical forms
in the perfect, pluperfect, and future perfect tenses as well
as in the present and imperfect (cp. § 383).

453. The perfect middle (passive) tenses reduplicate the
theme in the same way as the perfect active tenses, and
have augment for reduplication under similar circumstances
(§§ 432, 447, 448).

---

¹ § 401.
² Supply τούτους as antecedent.
³ Say *Cyrus has become clear*.
⁴ *you are evident having come together* (cp. I. 12).

454. In the perfect middle indicative (and pluperfect), imperative, infinitive, and participle, the endings are added directly to the theme without any connecting vowels. The perfect subjunctive and optative are periphrastic forms, made up of the perfect middle (passive) participle and the proper forms of εἰμί (cp. the perfect subjunctive and optative active, § 436).

a. There are no second perfect or second pluperfect tenses in the middle and passive voices.

455. PERFECT MIDDLE OR PASSIVE SYSTEM OF λύω

	SING.	DUAL	PLUR.
Pf. Indic. 1.	λέ-λυ-μαι { *I have ransomed* (Pass. *I have been loosed*)		λε-λύ-μεθα
2.	λέ-λυ-σαι	λέ-λυ-σθον	λέ-λυ-σθε
3.	λέ-λυ-ται	λέ-λυ-σθον	λέ-λυ-νται
Imv. 2.	λέ-λυ-σο	λέ-λυ-σθον	λέ-λυ-σθε
3.	λε-λύ-σθω	λε-λύ-σθων	λε-λύ-σθων
Inf.	λε-λύ-σθαι [1]		
Partic.	λε-λυ-μένος,[2] η, ον		
Plup. Indic. 1.	ἐ-λε-λύ-μην { *I had ransomed* (Pass. *I had been loosed*)		ἐ-λε-λύ-μεθα
2.	ἐ-λέ-λυ-σο	ἐ-λέ-λυ-σθον	ἐ-λέ-λυ-σθε
3.	ἐ-λέ-λυ-το	ἐ-λε-λύ-σθην	ἐ-λέ-λυ-ντο

PERIPHRASTIC FORMS

Pf. Subjv. 1.	λε-λυ-μένος ὦ		λε-λυ-μένοι ὦμεν
2.	λε-λυ-μένος ᾖς	λε-λυ-μένω ἦτον	λε-λυ-μένοι ἦτε
3.	λε-λυ-μένος ᾖ	λε-λυ-μένω ἦτον	λε-λυ-μένοι ὦσι(ν)
Opt. 1.	λε-λυ-μένος εἴην		λε-λυ-μένοι εἴημεν
2.	λε-λυ-μένος εἴης	λε-λυ-μένω εἴητον	λε-λυ-μένοι εἴητε
3.	λε-λυ-μένος εἴη	λε-λυ-μένω εἰήτην	λε-λυ-μένοι εἴησαν

a. The shorter forms εἶτον, εἶμεν, etc., also occur.

---

[1] The pf. mid. (pass.) inf. is always accented on the penult.
[2] The pf. mid. (pass.) partic. is always accented on the penult.

456. The perfect middle of γίγνομαι is γε-γέν-η-μαι (cp. the fut. γεν-ή-σο-μαι for the lengthened theme).

The perfect middle of στρατοπεδεύω is ἐ-στρατοπέδευ-μαι (§ 432. c).

457. The **infinitive** is used with verbs of *remembering, learning*, etc., when they mean *remember how, learn how*:

εὐθὺς παῖδες ὄντες μανθάνουσιν ἄρχειν τε καὶ ἄρχεσθαι straightway from boyhood they learn how to rule and to be ruled.

a. Such verbs take a ὅτι clause or a participle in indirect discourse in the sense *remember that, learn that*, as has already been described (§§ 441, 442).

458. Dative of agent. — The dative case may be used to express the agent with the perfect and pluperfect passive :

ἡ γέφῡρα λέλυται Κύρῳ the bridge has been destroyed by Cyrus.

459. VOCABULARY XLVI

ἄ-δικος, ον (ἀ- priv. and δίκη ; cp. δίκαιος) : *unjust.*

εἴσω, adv. : *within*, with gen.

κατα-κλείω : *shut up, confine, inclose.*

κλείω, fut. κλείσω, I aor. ἔκλεισα, I pf. κέκλεικα, pf. mid. κέκλειμαι, I aor. pass. ἐκλείσθην (σ is irregularly inserted) : *shut.*

Κρής, Κρητός, ὁ : *Cretan*, a native of Crete.

κωμ-άρχης, ου, ὁ (κώμη + ἄρχω) : *ruler* or *head man of a village, village chief.*

μέμνημαι : *remember*, a pf. with pres. meaning ; fut. to be learned later ; aor. ἐμνήσθην (σ is irregularly inserted). The pres. act. is μι-μνή-σκω

remind, which form is made up of the reduplication μι- plus the theme μνη- (long form of μνα-) plus the pres. suffix ισκ% ; fut. μνήσω, I aor. ἔμνησα. Lat. *meminī.* Mnemonic.

πύλη, ης, ἡ : *gate.* Cp. Θερμο-πύλαι, lit. " Hot Gates."

τιτρώσκω (theme τρω-, reduplicated in pres. τι-τρω, and with the pres. suffix σκ%), fut. τρώσω, I aor. ἔτρωσα, pf. mid. τέτρωμαι, I aor. pass. ἐτρώθην : *wound.*

τοξεύω (cp. τόξον), fut. τοξεύσομαι, I aor. ἐτόξευσα. pf. pass. τετόξευμαι, I aor. pass. ἐτοξεύθην : *shoot* with bow and arrow.

ψῑλός, ή, όν : *bare, unprotected ; light-armed.*

EXERCISES FOR TRANSLATION

460. I. 1. ἀκούων δὲ οὐ μέμνησαι. 2. ἦγε δ' αὐτοὺς ὁ κωμάρχης λελυμένος[1] διὰ χιόνος. 3. καὶ εἶπε πάντα τὰ γεγενημένα. 4. ὁ δὲ τοξότης ἧκε φεύγων τετρωμένος εἰς τὴν χεῖρα. 5. πολλοὶ γὰρ ἦσαν οἱ τετρωμένοι. 6. αἱ δὲ πύλαι ἐκέκλειντο. 7. φησὶν οὖν περὶ ἐμὲ ἄδικος γεγενῆσθαι. 8. ἐτύγχανε γὰρ Ἀριαῖος ἐφ' ἁμάξης πορευόμενος ὅτι[2] ἐτέτρωτο. 9. μετὰ ταῦτα μετ-επέμψαντο Τισσαφέρνην οἵ τε Ἕλληνες καὶ ὁ Ἀριαῖος, ἐγγὺς ἀλλήλων ἐστρατοπεδευμένοι ἡμέρᾱς πλείους ἢ εἴκοσιν. 10. λελυμένης[3] δὲ τῆς γεφύρᾱς οὐχ ἕξουσιν ἐκεῖνοι τὰ ἐπιτήδεια. 11. ἐγώ, ὦ Τισσαφέρνη, μέμνημαι ἡμῖν[4] ὅρκους γεγενημένους.[5] 12. μεμνήσθω ἀγαθὸς ἀνὴρ εἶναι.[6] 13. μεμνήσθω ὅτι ἀγαθὸς ἀνήρ ἐστιν. 14. μεμνήσθω ἀγαθὸς ἀνὴρ ὤν.[7] 15. οἱ γὰρ Κρῆτες βραχύτερα[8] τῶν Περσῶν ἐτόξευον καὶ ἅμα ψῑλοὶ ὄντες εἴσω τῶν ὁπλῑτῶν κατ-εκέκλειντο.

II. 1. The barbarians had encamped near the Greeks. 2. The village chief has been loosed (from shackles)[9] by Cheirisophus. 3. The crowd (of camp followers)[9] has been shut up within the (ranks of)[9] hoplites. 4. Let him remember that Cyrus is a brave man.[10]

---

[1] *loosed* from shackles.   [2] § 310.
[3] *broken down, destroyed.*   [4] § 458.
[5] = *have been made* (§§ 440, 441).   [6] § 457.
[7] When the subject of the participle in indirect discourse (§ 441) is the same as that of the verb on which the participle depends, it agrees in case.— Sentences 13 and 14 mean the same thing.
[8] *a shorter distance* (§ 351. *c*).   [9] Omit.
[10] Express in two ways.

XLVII

PERFECT MIDDLE AND PASSIVE OF MUTE THEMES.
EUPHONIC RULES: MUTES BEFORE μ. *SIGMA*
DROPPED BETWEEN TWO CONSONANTS.

461. Themes that end in a mute (§§ 27, 28) naturally
suffer euphonic changes in the perfect and pluperfect
middle before the personal endings, which are added
directly to the theme.

The following rules of euphony therefore must be added
to those already learned (§§ 153, 387):

MUTES BEFORE μ

462. 1. A labial mute (π β φ) before μ becomes μ:

λέ-λειμ-μαι for λε-λειπ-μαι (λείπω).

2. A palatal mute (κ χ) before μ becomes γ:

πε-φύλαγ-μαι for πε-φυλακ-μαι (φυλάττω, theme φυλακ-).

a. γ before μ is naturally kept unchanged:

τέ-ταγ-μαι (pf. mid. of τάττω, theme ταγ-).

3. A lingual mute (τ δ θ) before μ becomes σ:

πέ-πεισ-μαι for πε-πειθ-μαι (πείθω).

463. **Sigma** coming between two consonants is dropped:

λέ-λειφ-θε for λε-λειπ-σθε.

464. The **third person plural** of the perfect and pluperfect indicative middle of mute themes is a periphrastic
form made up of the perfect participle and εἰσί(ν) (perfect) or ἦσαν (pluperfect).

a. With a neuter plural subject ἐστί(ν) and ἦν are used
for εἰσί(ν) and ἦσαν respectively; or the regularly formed
third person singular of the verb is used.

465. PERFECT AND PLUPERFECT MIDDLE OR PASSIVE
OF λείπω (THEME λειπ-)

	SING.	DUAL	PLUR.
Pf. Indic. 1.	λέ-λειμ-μαι¹ (Pass.) *I have been left*		λε-λείμ-μεθα¹
2.	λέ-λειψαι²	λέ-λειφ-θον⁴	λέ-λειφ-θε⁴
3.	λέ-λειπ-ται³	λέ-λειφ-θον⁴	λε-λειμ-μένοι¹ εἰσί(ν)
Subjv. 1.	λε-λειμ-μένος¹ ὦ		
2.	λε-λειμ-μένος¹ ᾖς, etc.		
Opt. 1.	λε-λειμ-μένος¹ εἴην		
2.	λε-λειμ-μένος¹ εἴης, etc.		
Imv. 2.	λέ-λειψο²	λέ-λειφ-θον⁴	λέ-λειφ-θε⁴
3.	λε-λείφ-θω⁴	λε-λείφ-θων⁴	λε-λείφ-θων⁴
Inf.	λε-λεῖφ-θαι⁴		
Partic.	λε-λειμ-μένος¹		
Plup. Indic. 1.	ἐ-λε-λείμ-μην¹		ἐ-λε-λείμ-μεθα¹
2.	ἐ-λέ-λειψο²	ἐ-λέ-λειφ-θον⁴	ἐ-λέ-λειφ-θε⁴
3.	ἐ-λέ-λειπ-το³	ἐ-λε-λείφ-θην⁴	λε-λειμ-μένοι¹ ἦσαν

a. All other labial mute (π β φ) themes are inflected
on the model of λέ-λειμ-μαι:

γέ-γραμ-μαι, pf. mid. of γράφω (theme γραφ-) ;
συν-είλημ-μαι, pf. mid. of συλ-λαμβάνω (themes λαβ-, ληβ-).

b. But πέμπω (theme πεμπ-) forms the pf. mid. or pass.
πε-πεμμ-μαι (§ 462. 1); and one μ of the unpronounceable
combination is dropped (πέ-πεμ-μαι):

	SING.	DUAL	PLUR.
Pf. Indic. 1.	πέ-πεμ-μαι (Pass.) *I have been sent*		πε-πέμ-μεθα
2.	πέ-πεμψαι	πέ-πεμφ-θον	πέ-πεμφ-θε
3.	πέ-πεμπ-ται	πέ-πεμφ-θον	πε-πεμ-μένοι εἰσί(ν)

---

¹ § 462. 1.   ² § 153. 1.   ³ § 387. 1.   ⁴ §§ 463; 387. 1.

466. PERFECT AND PLUPERFECT MIDDLE OR PASSIVE
OF τάττω *arrange* (THEME ταγ-)

	SING.	DUAL	PLUR.
Pf. Indic. 1.	τέ-ταγ-μαι[1] (Pass.) *I have been arranged* or *marshaled*		τε-τάγ-μεθα[1]
2.	τέ-ταξαι[2]	τέ-ταχ-θον[4]	τέ-ταχ-θε[4]
3.	τέ-τακ-ται[3]	τέ-ταχ-θον[4]	τε-ταγ-μένοι[1] εἰστ(ν)
Subjv. 1.	τε-ταγ-μένος[1] ὦ		
2.	τε-ταγ-μένος[1] ᾖς, etc.		
Opt. 1.	τε-ταγ-μένος[1] εἴην		
2.	τε-ταγ-μένος[1] εἴης, etc.		
Imv. 2.	τέ-ταξο[2]	τέ-ταχ-θον[4]	τέ-ταχ-θε[4]
3.	τε-τάχ-θω[4]	τε-τάχ-θων[4]	τε-τάχ-θων[4]
Inf.	τε-τάχ-θαι[4]		
Partic.	τε-ταγ-μένος,[1] η, ον		
Plup. Indic. 1.	ἐ-τε-τάγ-μην[1]		ἐ-τε-τάγ-μεθα[1]
2.	ἐ-τέ-ταξο[2]	ἐ-τέ-ταχ-θον[4]	ἐ-τέ-ταχ-θε[4]
3.	ἐ-τέ-τακ-το[3]	ἐ-τε-τάχ-θην[4]	τε-ταγ-μένοι[1] ἦσαr

a. Like τέταγμαι are inflected all other verbs with themes
ending in a palatal mute (κ γ χ):

ἦγ-μαι, pf. mid. of ἄγω (theme ἀγ-) ;
ἐκ-πέ-πληγ-μαι, pf. mid. of ἐκ-πλήττω (theme πληγ-) ;
πέ-πρᾱγ-μαι, pf. mid. of πράττω (theme πρᾱγ-).

467. PERFECT AND PLUPERFECT MIDDLE OR PASSIVE
OF πείθω (THEME πειθ-)

	SING.	DUAL	PLUR.
Pf. Indic. 1.	πέ-πεισ-μαι[5] (Pass.) *I have been persuaded*		πε-πείσ-μεθα[5]
2.	πέ-πει-σαι[6]	πέ-πει-σθον[6]	πέ-πει-σθε[6]
3.	πέ-πεισ-ται[7]	πέ-πει-σθον[6]	πε-πεισ-μένοι[5] εἰσί(ν)

---

[1] § 462. 2. *a.*　　[2] § 153. 2.　　[3] § 387. 1.
[4] §§ 463; 387. 1.　　[5] § 462. 3.　　[6] § 153. 3.　　[7] § 387, 2.

	SING.	DUAL	PLUR.
Subjv. 1.	πε-πεισ-μένος¹ ὦ		
2.	πε-πεισ-μένος¹ ῇς, etc.		
Opt. 1.	πε-πεισ-μένος¹ εἴην		
2.	πε-πεισ-μένος¹ εἴης, etc.		
Imv. 2.	πέ-πει-σο²	πέ-πει-σθον²	πέ-πει-σθε²
3.	πε-πεί-σθω²	πε-πεί-σθων²	πε-πεί-σθων²
Inf.	πε-πεῖ-σθαι²		
Partic.	πε-πεισ-μένος¹		
Plup. Indic. 1.	ἐ-πε-πείσ-μην¹		ἐ-πε-πείσ-μεθα¹
2.	ἐ-πέ-πει-σο²	ἐ-πέ-πει-σθον²	ἐ-πέ-πει-σθε²
3.	ἐ-πέ-πει-το³	ἐ-πε-πεί-σθην²	πε-πεισ-μένοι¹ ἦσαν

a. Like πέ-πεισ-μαι are inflected all other verbs with themes ending in a lingual mute (τ δ θ):

ἥρπασ-μαι, pf. mid. of ἁρπάζω (theme ἁρπαδ-) ;

παρ-εσκεύασ-μαι, pf. mid. of παρα-σκευάζω (theme σκευαδ-).

468.   VOCABULARY XLVII

ἄλλῃ, adv. (dat. fem. of ἄλλος, with ὁδῷ or χώρᾳ understood) : *elsewhere, in another place* or *direction.*

ἀ-πορία, ᾶς, ἡ (cp. ἄ-πορος, πο-ρεύομαι) : lack of way out, *em-barrassment, difficulty.*

ἔμ-προσθεν, adv. (ἐν + πρόσθεν) : *in front, before.* It may take the gen.

ἐν-τυγχάνω (cp. τυγχάνω) : *chance upon, happen upon, come upon by chance, encounter,* with dat.

ἐπι-τάττω (cp. τάττω) : *enjoin* something (acc.) *on* somebody (dat.), *direct, command.*

κατά-βασις, εως, ἡ (κατα-βαίνω) : *descent, way down* a mountain side ; the *descent* from the interior to the sea.

μόνος, η, ον : *alone, only.* **Mon**-archy (ἄρχω), mono-gamy (γά-μος *marriage*), etc.

ὁποῖος, ᾱ, ον, indef. rel. pron. and indir. interr. : *of what sort, what sort of.*

ποτόν, οῦ, τό : *drink.*

που, indef. adv., enclitic : *some-where, anywhere.*

προ-κατα-λαμβάνω (cp. κατα-λαμ-βάνω, Vocabulary XXXII) : *seize* or *occupy beforehand.*

σιτίον, ου, τό (diminutive of σῖ-τος) : *grain, food.*

---

¹ § 462. 3.   ² § 153. 3.   ³ § 387. 2.

EXERCISES FOR TRANSLATION

469. I. 1. βασιλεὺς σὺν στρατεύματι πολλῷ προσέρχεται ὡς εἰς μάχην παρ-εσκευασμένος. 2. οὐδεὶς
αὐτῷ ἐμάχετο οὐδὲ τοῖς ἔμπροσθεν αὐτοῦ τεταγμένοις.
3. κατα-λαμβάνουσι δὲ τῶν τε ἄλλων χρημάτων τὰ
πλεῖστα δι-ηρπασμένα καὶ εἴ τι[1] σῑτίον ἢ ποτὸν ἦν.
4. δι-ήρπαστο ὑπὸ τοῦ βασιλικοῦ στρατεύματος καὶ[2]
αὐτὰ[3] τὰ ἀπὸ τῶν οἰκιῶν ξύλα.[4] 5. καὶ δῆλον ἦν ὅτι
ἐγγύς που βασιλεὺς ἦν ἢ ἄλλος τις ᾧ ἐπ-ετέτακτο[5]
ταῦτα πράττειν. 6. καὶ ἐγὼ μόνος τῶν κατὰ τοὺς
Ἕλληνας τεταγμένων οὐκ ἔφυγον. 7. τὸ στράτευμα
πολὺ ἦν, ὥστε τὸν Πέρσην ἐκ-πεπλῆχθαι. 8. καὶ
ὁποίοις λόγοις Κλέαρχος ἔπεισε Κῦρον ἄλλῃ γέγρα-
πται.[6] 9. ἐπεὶ δὲ οἱ στρατηγοὶ συν-ειλημμένοι ἦσαν,
ἐν πολλῇ δὴ ἀπορίᾳ ἦσαν οἱ Ἕλληνες. 10. μόνοι δὲ
κατα-λελειμμένοι ἦσαν, οὐδὲ ἱππέᾱ οὐδένα[7] σύμμαχον
ἔχοντες. 11. προ-κατ-είληπται γὰρ ἡμῖν[8] ὁ ὑπὲρ τῆς
καταβάσεως λόφος. 12. Χειρίσοφος δὲ εἶδε προ-κατ-
ειλημμένην τὴν ἀκρόπολιν. 13. καλόν τι[9] πρὸς τοὺς
ἐν Σάρδεσι βαρβάρους ἐπέπρᾱκτο ὑμῖν.[10] 14. πορευό-
μενοι δ᾽ ἐν-τυγχάνουσι λόφῳ ὑπὲρ τῆς ὁδοῦ κατ-ειλημμένῳ
ὑπὸ τῶν πολεμίων.

II. 1. Cyrus, prepared for battle, advanced against the
enemy. 2. Most of the possessions had been plundered
by the king's army. 3. These soldiers have been led up
to the king..

---

[1] Cp. § 232. I. 3. [2] *even.* [3] *very,* § 123. 1; cp. § 394. II. 3.
[4] Subject of δι-ήρπαστο. [5] *it had been directed.*
[6] *it has been written.* [7] § 428.
[8] § 53. *d.* [9] *a noble deed* (cp. § 232. I. 10). [10] § 458.

XLVIII

THE FUTURE PERFECT MIDDLE AND PASSIVE.   MEAN‑
   ING OF FUTURE PERFECT.   VERBAL ADJECTIVES
   IN -τός AND -τέος.   DATIVE OF AGENT WITH
   VERBALS IN -τέος

470. There is but one form for the future perfect middle
and passive (§ 383); the meaning is generally passive; but
the form is uncommon in either the middle or passive use.

471. The future perfect passive (middle) is formed from
the reduplicated (perfect) theme, plus the future suffix σ%,
to which the endings of person (indicative) or mood and
person (optative) are added.   The middle endings are
used.   The forms are like the future middle, with redupli‑
cation of the theme.

unimportant

472.   FUTURE PERFECT PASSIVE (MIDDLE) OF λύω

	SING.	DUAL	PLUR.
Indic. 1.	λε-λύ-σο-μαι *I shall have been loosed*		λε-λῡ-σό-μεθα
2.	λε-λύ-ση, -σει	λε-λύ-σε-σθον	λε-λύ-σε-σθε
3.	λε-λύ-σε-ται	λε-λύ-σε-σθον	λε-λύ-σο-νται
Opt. 1.	λε-λῡ-σοί-μην		λε-λῡ-σοί-μεθα
2.	λε-λύ-σοι-ο	λε-λύ-σοι-σθον	λε-λύ-σοι-σθε
3.	λε-λύ-σοι-το	λε-λῡ-σοί-σθην	λε-λύ-σοι-ντο
Inf.	λε-λύ-σε-σθαι		
Partic.	λε-λῡ-σό-μενος, η, ον		

473. Like λε-λύ-σο-μαι are inflected:

λε-λείψο-μαι (λείπω) I shall have been left;
κε-κόψο-μαι (κόπτω) I shall have been cut;
με-μνή-σο-μαι (μέμνημαι) I shall remember (see Vocabulary **XLVI**).

474. The future perfect passive may be used to denote a future act as *sure to occur*. It is then an emphatic future:

κατα-κεκόψονται they shall be surely cut down;
λελείψεται he will be left.

VERBAL ADJECTIVES

475. Their form. — Verbal adjectives end in -τός, ή, όν,[1] and -τέος, ᾱ, ον. These endings are generally added to that form of the verb theme which is used in the first aorist passive (without the augment). If the theme ends in a mute, the necessary euphonic changes must be made (§ 387. 1 and 2).

476. Their meaning. — The adjective with the suffix -τός may denote (1) a completed act like the Latin perfect passive participle; or (2) a possible act, like Latin adjectives in *-bilis*, English *-able*:

λυ-τός that may be loosed, looseable;
ἄ-βα-τος that may not be trodden on, impassable (ἐ-βά-θην, from βαίνω);
ἀ-διά-βα-τος not to be crossed, impassable (δι-ε-βά-θην);
ἀ-φύλακ-τος unguarded (ἐ-φυλάχ-θην).

477. The adjective with the suffix -τέος denotes a necessity, like the Latin gerundive:

διωκτέος (necessary) to be pursued (ἐ-διώχ-θην was pursued);
δια-βατέος (necessary) to be crossed (δι-ε-βά-θην was crossed);
πρᾱκτέος (necessary) to be done (ἐ-πράχ-θην was done).

---

[1] Compound verbals in -τος have recessive accent and two endings: -τος (masc. and fem.), -τον (neut.). But prepositional compounds denoting *possibility* are usually of three endings and accented like simple verbals. Thus δια-βατός. ή, όν, *able to be crossed, fordable* (of a river).

Such verbal adjectives may be used:

1. *Personally*: ποταμὸς δια-βατέος ἐστίν *a river must be crossed.*

2. *Impersonally*[1]: πειστέον (πείθομαι *obey*) ἐστίν *it must be obeyed, obedience must be rendered* (with dat.); πορευτέον (πορεύομαι) ἐστίν *it must be proceeded, one must proceed;* σκεπτέον (σκέπτομαι *consider*) ἐστίν *it must be considered.*

ἐστί(ν) may be omitted (§ 291).

478. With the verbal in -τέος the **agent** is regularly expressed by the **dative** (cp. § 458):

ταῦτα πρᾱκτέα μοι this must be done by me.

479. It must be observed that *necessity* is far more commonly expressed by δεῖ and the infinitive (§ 223) with subject accusative, and by similar expressions, than by the verbal adjective in -τέος.

480. VOCABULARY XLVIII

βαθύς, εῖα, ύ: *deep.*

δεσπότης, ου, ὁ: *master.* Despot.

δια-βατέος, ᾱ, ον (verbal adj. of δια-βαίνω): necessary *to be crossed.*

δια-βατός, ή, όν (verbal adj. of δια-βαίνω): *able to be crossed, fordable* (of a river). Cp. ἀ-διά-βατος (§ 108).

διωκτέος, ᾱ, ον (verbal adj. of διώκω): necessary *to be pursued.*

θαυμαστός, ή, όν (verbal adj. of θαυμάζω): *admirable, wonderful, strange.*

μετά-πεμπτος, ον (verbal adj. of μετα-πέμπομαι): *sent after, summoned.*

πειστέον (verbal adj. of πείθομαι), impers.: *one must obey*, with dat.

πορευτέος, ᾱ, ον (verbal adj. of πορεύομαι): necessary *to be passed over, to be traversed;* neut. impers.: *one must proceed.*

σκεπτέον (verbal adj. of σκέπτομαι), impers.: *it must be considered, one must consider.*

τρω-τός, ή, όν (verbal adj. of τιτρώσκω): *able to be wounded, vulnerable.*

ὑπο-ζύγιον, ου, τό (ζυγόν *yoke*): *something under the yoke, beast of burden.*

---

[1] The impersonal verbal may even take an object. Thus διωκτέον ἐστὶ τὰ θηρία *one must pursue the wild beasts.*

EXERCISES FOR TRANSLATION

481. I. 1. ἂν δὲ εὖ γένηταί τι, οὐ μεμνήσεσθαί σέ φᾶσιν.   2. ὥστε φίλος ἡμῖν οὐδεὶς λελείψεται.   3. νῦν δὲ διωκτέον ἐστίν.   4. ἐὰν γὰρ ἀλλήλοις μαχέσησθε, νομίζετε[1] ἐν τῇδε τῇ ἡμέρᾳ ἐμέ τε κατα-κεκόψεσθαι καὶ ὑμᾶς οὐ πολὺ ἐμοῦ ὕστερον.   5. πορευτέον ἐστὶν ὅτι τάχιστα.   6. ὁ δὲ λοχᾱγὸς ἔμαθεν ὅτι ἀφύλακτον εἴη τὸ ἱερὸν χωρίον.   7. καὶ πειστέον ἐστὶ τῷ δεσπότῃ.   8. παρ-ῆν δὲ καὶ[2] Χειρίσοφος, μετά-πεμπτος ὑπὸ Κύρου.   9. πορευτέον δ' ἡμῖν τοὺς πρώτους στα-θμοὺς[3] ὡς μακροτάτους.   10. ποταμὸς δὲ βαθὺς ἡμῖν ἐστι δια-βατέος.   11. οἱ δὲ πολέμιοι τρωτοί εἰσι μᾶλλον ἡμῶν.   12. εἰ δὲ μὴ ἀγαθός ἐστιν, οὐδὲν[4] θαυμαστόν.[5]   13. σκεπτέον ἐστὶν ὅπως ὡς πλεῖστα ὑποζύγια ἁρπάσωμεν.   14. κατὰ γὰρ μέσον[6] τὸν σταθμὸν τοῦτον ποταμὸν ηὗρον[7] διαβατόν.

II. 1. The horses will certainly[8] be loosed.   2. We must proceed five days' journey to Celaenae, that large and prosperous city.   3. If he should not be brave, it would not be at all[9] strange.   4. A messenger reported[10] that the river was impassable.

---

[1] Imv.   [2] *also.*   [3] § 181.   [4] *in no respect* (§ 284).
[5] § 291.   [6] § 192.   [7] § 443.   [8] § 474.
[9] *not at all* = οὐδέν (§ 284).   [10] ἔφη.

XLIX

SYNOPSIS OF THE Ω–VERB. PRINCIPAL PARTS OF
TYPICAL VERBS. SOME COMMON SUFFIXES OF
NOUNS AND ADJECTIVES

482.   SYNOPSIS OF λύω *loose*; THEME $\begin{cases} λῡ- \\ λυ- \end{cases}$

ACTIVE

	INDIC.	SUBJV.	OPT.	IMV.	INF.	PARTIC.
Pres.	λύω	λύω	λύοιμι	λῦε	λύειν	λύων
Impf.	ἔλῡον					
Fut.	λύσω		λύσοιμι		λύσειν	λύσων
Aor.	ἔλῡσα	λύσω	λύσαιμι	λῦσον	λῦσαι	λύσᾱς
Pf.	λέλυκα	§ 436	§ 436		λελυκέναι	λελυκώς
Plup.	ἐλελύκη					

MIDDLE

	INDIC.	SUBJV.	OPT.	IMV.	INF.	PARTIC.
Pres.	λύομαι	λύωμαι	λῡοίμην	λύου	λύεσθαι	λῡόμενος
Impf.	ἐλῡόμην					
Fut.	λύσομαι		λῡσοίμην		λύσεσθαι	λῡσόμενος
Aor.	ἐλῡσάμην	λύσωμαι	λῡσαίμην	λῦσαι	λύσασθαι	λῡσάμενος
Pf.	λέλυμαι	λελυμένος ὦ	λελυμένος εἴην	λέλυσο	λελύσθαι	λελυμένος
Plup.	ἐλελύμην					
Fut. Pf.	λελύσομαι		λελῡσοίμην		λελύσεσθαι	λελῡσόμενος

PASSIVE

	INDIC.	SUBJV.	OPT.	IMV.	INF.	PARTIC
Pres. Impf.	} like the	Middle				
Fut.	λυθήσομαι		λυθησοίμην		λυθήσεσθαι	λυθησόμινος
Aor.	ἐλύθην	λυθῶ	λυθείην	λύθητι	λυθῆναι	λυθείς
Pf.						
Plup. Fut. Pf.	} like the	Middle				

483. SYNOPSIS OF λείπω *leave* IN THE SECOND AORIST
AND SECOND PERFECT; THEMES
λειπ-, λοιπ-, λιπ-

ACTIVE

	INDIC.	SUBJV.	OPT.	IMV.	INF.	PARTIC.
2 Aor.	ἔλιπον	λίπω	λίποιμι	λίπε	λιπεῖν	λιπών
2 Pf.	λέλοιπα	§ 446	§ 446		λελοιπέναι	λελοιπώς
2 Plup.	ἐλελοίπη					

MIDDLE

	INDIC.	SUBJV.	OPT.	IMV.	INF.	PARTIC.
2 Aor.	ἐλιπόμην	λίπωμαι	λιποίμην	λιποῦ	λιπέσθαι	λιπόμενος

484. SYNOPSIS OF βλάπτω *hurt* IN THE SECOND AORIST PASSIVE AND SECOND FUTURE PASSIVE; THEME βλαβ-

PASSIVE

	INDIC.	SUBJV.	OPT.	IMV.	INF.	PARTIC.
2 Fut.	βλαβήσομαι		βλαβησοίμην		βλαβήσεσθαι	βλαβησόμενος
2 Aor.	ἐβλάβην	βλαβῶ	βλαβείην	βλάβηθι	βλαβῆναι	βλαβείς

PRINCIPAL PARTS OF VERBS

485. The following tense systems have now been studied — all the tense systems of the ordinary Greek verb:

1. Present (including imperfect): Active, Middle (Passive).

2. Future: Active, Middle.

3. First Aorist: Active, Middle.

4. Second Aorist: Active, Middle.

5. First Perfect (including first pluperfect): **Active.**

6. Second Perfect (including second pluperfect): Active.

7. Perfect Middle (including pluperfect and future perfect).

8. First Passive (first aorist and first future passive).

9. Second Passive (second aorist and second future passive).

a. If one knows the first form in each of these systems (the first person singular of the indicative mood), he can by the rules already mastered produce the complete inflection of the ω-verb. Therefore the first forms in these systems are together known as the **principal parts** of the verb

486. It is not usual for a *single* verb to be inflected in all of the above tense systems. Most verbs are in this sense defective.

487. The following list (page 219) includes the principal parts of some typical verbs already studied. Vacant places indicate that the tense system is wanting. For the principal parts of the other verbs that have been introduced into the work thus far, consult the general VOCABULARY at the end of the book.

488. The **second perfect active** πέπομφα illustrates the tendency to change an ε sound in the theme to ο in this tense. Cp. also λέλοιπα (λείπω).

489. The **second aorist passive** ἐστράφην illustrates the tendency to change an ε sound in the theme to α in this tense. Cp. also ἐτράπην (τρέπω).

490. The verbs στρέφω *turn*, τρέπω *turn*, and τρέφω *nourish*, change ε of the theme to α in the perfect middle: ἔστραμμαι, τέτραμμαι, τέθραμμαι.

SOME COMMON SUFFIXES USED IN FORMING NOUNS AND ADJECTIVES

NOUNS

491. Indicating the AGENT:

-ευ-: ἱππεύς (ἵππος *horse*) *horseman.*
-τα-: τοξότης (τόξον *bow*) *bowman ;*
πελταστής (πελτάζω *be a peltast*) *peltast.*
-τηρ-: σωτήρ (σῴζω *save*) *savior.*
-τορ-, nom. -τωρ: ῥήτωρ, gen. ῥήτορος (εἴ-ρη-κα *I have spoken*), *orator.*

PRES.	MEANING	THEME	FUT.	1 AOR.	2 AOR.	1 PF. ACT.	2 PF. ACT.	PF. MID.	1 AOR. PASS.	2 AOR. PASS.
ἄγω	lead	ἀγ-	ἄξω		ἤγαγον		ἦχα	ἦγμαι	ἤχθην	
ἁρπάζω	seize	ἁρπαδ-	ἁρπάσω	ἥρπασα		ἥρπακα		ἥρπασμαι	ἡρπάσθην	
βλάπτω	hurt	βλαβ-	βλάψω	ἔβλαψα			βέβλαφα	βέβλαμμαι	ἐβλάφθην	ἐβλάβην
ἔχω	have	[σ]εχ- σχη-	ἕξω σχήσω	ἔσχον	ἔσχον	ἔσχηκα		ἔσχημαι		
θύω	sacrifice	θυ- θυ-	θύσω	ἔθυσα		τέθυκα		τέθυμαι	ἐτύθην (for ἐθύθην)	
λαμβάνω	take	λαβ- ληβ-	λήψομαι		ἔλαβον		εἴληφα	εἴλημμαι	ἐλήφθην	
λείπω	leave	λειπ- λοιπ- λιπ-	λείψω	ἔλειψα	ἔλιπον		λέλοιπα	λέλειμμαι	ἐλείφθην	
λύω	loose	λυ- λυ-	λύσω	ἔλυσα		λέλυκα		λέλυμαι	ἐλύθην	
πείθω	persuade	πειθ- ποιθ-	πείσω	ἔπεισα		πέπεικα	πέποιθα, § 445. a	πέπεισμαι	ἐπείσθην	
πέμπω	send	πεμπ- πομπ-	πέμψω	ἔπεμψα			πέπομφα	πέπεμμαι	ἐπέμφθην	
στρέφω	turn	στρεφ- στραφ-	στρέψω	ἔστρεψα				ἔστραμμαι		ἐστράφην
συλ-λέγω	collect	λεγ- λογ-	συλ-λέξω	συν-έλεξα			συν-είλοχα	συν-είλεγμαι	συν-ελέχθην	συν-ελέγην

492. Indicating QUALITY or an ABSTRACT IDEA:

-ῐᾱ-: σωτηρίᾱ (σωτήρ savior) safety;
ὑποψίᾱ (ὑπ-όψομαι I shall suspect) suspicion;
φιλίᾱ (φίλος friend) friendship.

493. Indicating ACTION:

-σι-: κατάβασις (καταβαίνω descend) descent;
τάξις (τάττω arrange) arrangement
(cp. § 381).

494. Indicating RESULT of action:

-ματ-: πρᾶγμα, gen. πράγματος (πράττω do), deed,
etc.;
στράτευμα (στρατεύω make an expedition)
expedition, army.

495. Indicating SMALLNESS, etc., although the diminutive idea is not always preserved:

-ιο-: χρῡσίον (χρῡσός gold) piece of gold;
παιδίον (παῖς child) little child;
χωρίον (χῶρος place) place, stronghold

ADJECTIVES

496.
-ιο-: πολέμιος (πόλεμος war) hostile;
Λακεδαιμόνιος (Λακεδαίμων Lacedaemon)
Lacedaemonian;
δίκαιος (δίκη justice) just;
ἀρχαῖος (ἀρχή beginning) ancient.
-ικο-: βασιλικός (βασιλεύς king) kinglike;
Ἑλληνικός (Ἕλλην a Greek) Greek;
πολεμικός (πόλεμος war) warlike.

L

CONTRACT NOUNS OF THE Ā–DECLENSION AND OF
THE O–DECLENSION. CONTRACT ADJECTIVES.
THE INFINITIVE WITH THE ARTICLE USED AS
A NOUN

497. Learn the declension of γῆ *earth*, μνᾶ *mina* (§ 594);
νοῦς *mind* (§ 596); χρῦσοῦς, ῆ, οῦν, *golden*, ἀργυροῦς, ᾶ, οῦν,
silver, ἀπλοῦς, ῆ, οῦν, *simple* (§ 609); εὔνους, ουν, *well-disposed* (§ 610).

498.   **RULES OF CONTRACTION**

$$\epsilon + o = ov$$
$$o + o = ov$$

Any short vowel before a long vowel (or diphthong) or
before *a* is absorbed.

But, in the singular of the **ā**-declension,

$$\epsilon + \bar{a} = \eta \ (\dot{a} \text{ after } \rho).$$

a. The syllable resulting from contraction is always
long, — a long vowel or a diphthong.

b. Contract nouns and adjectives are regularly cir-
cumflexed on the ultima throughout. But forms of the
o-declension have the acute accent (*not* the circumflex) on
the ultima of the nominative, accusative, and vocative dual,
when the ultima is accented.

499. Compounds of νοῦς *mind* and πλοῦς *voyage* keep
the accent throughout on the same syllable as in the nominative singular. Thus εὔνων, genitive plural (for εὐνόων).
Such compounds also do not contract in the neuter plural
nominative and accusative. Thus εὔνοα.

500. The **infinitive** preceded by a neuter article (τό, τοῦ, τῷ) may be **used as a noun**, in the various constructions of a noun :

τὸ ἀποθνῄσκειν (nom. or acc.) death ;

φόβος τοῦ στρατεῦσαι fear of taking the field ;

ἐκώλυσεν αὐτοὺς τοῦ κάειν (gen. of separation) τὴν χώρᾱν he hindered them from burning the land.

a. This construction of the infinitive is common after prepositions. Frequent is διὰ τό followed by an infinitive :

διὰ τὸ στενὴν εἶναι τὴν ὁδόν on account of the fact that the road was narrow.

501.   VOCABULARY L

ἁπλοῦς, ῆ, οῦν : *simple, sincere.*

ἀργύριον, ου, τό : *silver, money.*

ἀργυροῦς, ᾶ, οῦν : *of silver, silver.*

γῆ, ῆς, ἡ : *earth, land.*   Geometry (μέτρον *measure*).

ἔκ-βασις, εως, ἡ (ἐκ-βαίνω) : passage out, mountain *pass.*

εὔ-νους, ουν : *well-disposed.*

μνᾶ, ᾶς, ἡ : *mina,* one sixtieth of a talent ; *i.e.* about $18.

νοῦς, οῦ, ὁ : *mind.*

πλοῦς, οῦ, ὁ : *voyage ; a sailing, sailing weather.* Cp. πλοῖον.

ποτέ, enclitic adv. of time : *ever, at any time, at some time, once on a time.*

προσ-έχω, with τὸν νοῦν : *direct* the mind *to,* with dat.

Τίγρης, ητος, ὁ : *Tigris,* a great river of western Asia.

τόπος, ου, ὁ : *place.* Topic.

χρῡσοῦς, ῆ, οῦν : *golden, of gold, gold.*

EXERCISES FOR TRANSLATION

502. I. 1. ἐν τούτῳ δὲ τῷ τόπῳ ἦν ἡ γῆ πεδίον ἅπαν ὥσπερ θάλαττα.   2. καὶ λέγεται[1] ὡς καλοὶ πλοῖ εἰσιν εἰς τὴν Ἑλλάδα.   3. ἦρξαν τοῦ διαβαίνειν τὸν Τίγρητα ποταμόν.   4. οἱ πολέμιοι ἐθαύμαζον τί οἱ Ἕλληνες ἐν νῷ ἔχοιεν.[2]   5. ὁ δὲ στρατηγὸς ἦγε πρὸς τὴν φανερὰν

---

[1] Impers.   [2] § 345.

ἔκβασιν ὅπως ταύτῃ τῇ ὁδῷ οἱ πολέμιοι προσέχοιεν τὸν
νοῦν. 6. ἐξήλαυνον ὡς τάχιστα διὰ τὸ ἀνάγκην εἶναι
λαμβάνειν τὰ ἐπιτήδεια. 7. νῦν ὑμῖν ἔξεστι πορεύεσθαι, ὅπῃ ἂν ἔλησθε,[1] καὶ κατὰ γῆν καὶ κατὰ θάλατταν.
8. ἔπεμψε δὲ σάλπιγγά τε ἀργυρᾶν καὶ σκηνὴν ἀξίᾱν
δέκα μνῶν.[2] 9. φίλους δὲ ἁπλοῦς τε καὶ εὔνους Κῦρος
εἶχεν. 10. οἱ καλοί τε καὶ ἀγαθοὶ εὖνοι αὐτῷ ἦσαν.
11. φόβον βασιλεὺς παρέσχε[3] τοῦ στρατεῦσαί ποτε ἐπ’
αὐτόν. 12. ἐκώλυσε τοὺς ἱππέᾱς τοῦ διαρπάζειν τὴν
χώρᾱν.

II. 13. δυνατὸς ἦν χῑλὸν παρασκευάζεσθαι διὰ τὸ
πολλοὺς ἔχειν ὑπηρέτᾱς. 14. καὶ ὑμεῖς παρασκευ-
άζεσθε[4] ὡς ἅμα τῇ ἡμέρᾳ ἀναξόμενοι,[5] ἐὰν πλοῦς ᾖ.
15. βασιλέᾱ δ’ ἔφασαν ἔχειν θώρᾱκα χρῡσοῦν καὶ
ἀσπίδα χρῡσῆν. 16. ὁ δ’ εἶχε δέκα μνᾶς ἀργυρίου.[6]
17. ὁ δὲ κωμάρχης τὰς πύλᾱς ἔκλεισε διὰ τὸ μὴ
ἐθέλειν δέχεσθαι τοὺς Ἕλληνας.

III. 1. What have you in mind? 2. They had fear[7]
of marching against the king. 3. All the soldiers were
well-disposed to Cyrus.

---

[1] § 248. 1 or § 400. [2] § 402. [3] *caused.* [4] Imv.
[5] ἀν-άγομαι sometimes, as here, means *put to sea;* for the construction
see §§ 331, 332.
[6] *Of* gen. (§ 53. *f*), denoting material. [7] Use the noun.

LI

CONTRACT VERBS. PRESENT SYSTEM OF ποιέω. DIS-
SYLLABIC VERBS IN -έω. TWO ACCUSATIVES
AFTER VERBS OF *MAKING, APPOINTING; ASK-
ING, DEPRIVING.* CONSTRUCTION OF δοκέω

503. The inflection of contract verbs differs from that
of regular ω-verbs in the present system only. In all other
systems these verbs, if regular, are inflected like the corresponding tenses of λύω.

504. The syllable resulting from contraction receives an
accent if either one of the component syllables, in the uncontracted form, had an accent; it receives a circumflex, if
the *first* vowel had the acute; but it receives an acute,
if the *second* vowel had the acute.

505. Examples of accentuation of contract verbs:

ποιέω	contracts to	ποιῶ	ἐποίεον	contracts to ἐποίουν
ποιέομεν	"	" ποιοῦμεν	ἐποίεε	" " ἐποίει
ἑσταώς	"	" ἑστώς		

PRESENT SYSTEM OF ποιέω

506. Learn the inflection in the present system of the
active and middle (= passive) voices of ποιέω *do, make*
(§ 643).

a. Similarly are inflected αἱρέω *take,* mid. *choose;* ἀφ-
ικνέομαι *arrive;* ἡγέομαι *lead* (with gen. or dat.) or *think.*

507.   RULES OF CONTRACTION

ε + ε = ει

ε + ο = ου

ε before a long vowel or diphthong is absorbed.

508. Verbs in -έω of two syllables, like πλέω *sail*, contract only when ει results; otherwise they are uncontracted :

πλέω, πλεῖς, πλεῖ, πλέομεν, πλεῖτε, πλέουσι ;
δέῃ, subjv. of δεῖ (it is necessary).

509. Outside of the present system the final ε of the theme is regularly lengthened to η :

ποιῶ (-έω), ποιήσω, ἐποίησα, πεποίηκα, πεποίημαι, ἐποιήθην.

Exceptions must be learned as they occur. Thus ἡρέθην *I was chosen*, not ἡρήθην (from αἱρέω).

510. Verbs of *making, appointing*, and similar meanings may take **two accusatives**, one of which stands in a predicate relation to the other :

σατράπην αὐτὸν ἐποίησεν he made him satrap ;
εὔνουν αὐτὸν ἐνόμισεν he thought him well-disposed.

511. Verbs of *asking* and *depriving* may take **two accusatives**, one of the *person*, the other of the *thing* :

αἰτεῖ αὐτὸν μισθόν he asks him for pay ;
ἀφαιρεῖσθαι τοὺς Ἕλληνας τὴν γῆν to deprive the Greeks of their land.

512. Δοκῶ (-έω) *seem* is commonly used personally (cp. § 391) with the infinitive in indirect discourse :

δοκεῖ οὐχ ὥρα εἶναι παύεσθαι it seems not to be an hour for resting (*lit.* the hour seems not, etc.) ;
ἐδόκουν ταχὺ ποιεῖν ταῦτα they seemed to do this quickly.

a. There is also a less common but nevertheless frequent use of δοκεῖ as an impersonal verb, in the meaning *it seems good* or *best*. The accompanying infinitive is the subject of the impersonal verb :

ἐδόκει αὐτῷ πορεύεσθαι ἄνω it seemed best to him to proceed **inland**.

b. Δοκῶ (-έω) sometimes means *I think* like νομίζω :

ἐδόκει βασιλέα ἥξειν he thought the king would come.

513. VOCABULARY LI

αἰρέω, αἱρήσω, εἷλον, ᾕρηκα, ᾕρημαι, ᾑρέθην: *take, capture, seize;* MID. *choose.* See Vocabularies XXVI, XXXII. Heresy.

αἰτέω, αἰτήσω, ᾔτησα, ᾔτηκα, ᾔτημαι, ᾐτήθην: *ask a favor, beg, ask for* something *from* somebody (two accusatives); MID. *ask for oneself.*

ἀπο-πλέω: *sail away.*

ἀφ-αιρέομαι (mid. of αἰρέω): *take away for oneself, deprive, rob* somebody *of* something (two accusatives).

ἀφ-ικ-νέ-ομαι (theme ἱκ-; νε- appears only in pres. system), ἀφίξομαι, ἀφ-ῑκόμην, ἀφ-ῖγμαι: *arrive, come.*

ὁοκέω (theme δοκ-, but δοκε- in pres. system), δόξω, ἔδοξα, δέδογμαι, ἐδόχθην: *seem, be reputed; seem best; think.* Dogma.

ἡγέομαι, ἡγήσομαι, ἡγησάμην, ἥγημαι: *lead, guide* (with gen. or dat.); *think, believe.* Cp. ἡγεμών.

θέω, θεύσομαι: *run.*

ὅθεν, rel. adv.: *whence, from which place, from what source.*

πλέω, πλεύσομαι, ἔπλευσα, πέπλευκα, πέπλευσμαι (σ is irregularly inserted): *sail.* Cp. πλοῖον, πλοῦς.

ποιέω, ποιήσω, ἐποίησα, πεποίηκα, πεποίημαι, ἐποιήθην: *do, make;* the mid. is translated like the act., but implies *in* or *for one's own interest.* Poet (ποιητής).

πολεμικός, ή, όν (πόλεμος): *suited to war, warlike; hostile.*

πώ-ποτε, adv. of time: *ever yet, ever.*

πῶς, interr. adv.: *how? in what way?* Cp. ὅπως.

στρατείᾱ, ᾱς, ἡ (στρατεύω): *expedition.*

τρόπος, ου, ὁ (τρέπω): *turn, manner, method, character.* Tropic.

φοβέω (φόβος), φοβήσω, ἐφόβησα, πεφόβημαι, ἐφοβήθην: *frighten;* MID. with dep. aor. pass., *be afraid, fear.* The mid. forms are common (φοβέομαι, φοβήσομαι, πεφόβημαι, ἐφοβήθην).

EXERCISES FOR TRANSLATION

514. I. 1. καὶ τῷ αὐτῷ τρόπῳ[1] τοῦτον τὸν λόφον αἱροῦσιν. 2. αἱροῦνται αὐτὸν ἄρχοντα τῆς στρατείᾱς. 3. ἐδόκει δὲ δῆλον εἶναι ὅτι αἱρήσονται αὐτὸν στρατηγόν. 4. εἷς δὲ εἶπε[2] Κῦρον αἰτεῖν πλοῖα, ὡς ἀποπλέοιεν.

---

[1] § 141.   [2] *proposed* (§ 334).

5. Κλέαρχος δὴ ἐδόκει γενέσθαι ἀνὴρ πολεμικός.   6. ὁ
λοχᾱγὸς ἐβουλεύετο τί χρὴ ποιεῖν περὶ τοῦ ἄνω στρατεύεσθαι.   7. πάνυ χαλεπὸν ἐδόκει εἶναι μὴ πλεῖν οἴκαδε.
8. καὶ ἐποίουν οὕτως οὗτοι.   9. καὶ στρατηγοὺς αἱροῦνται ἑαυτῶν δέκα.   10. τοὺς δ' ἀνθρώπους τὰ χρήματα
ἀφαιροῦνται.   11. ἐνταῦθα ἀφικνεῖται ἡ Συεννέσιος
γυνὴ παρὰ Κῦρον.   12. συνεβουλεύετο[1] πῶς ἂν τὴν
μάχην ποιοῖτο.   13. οὗτοι δὲ ἐφοβοῦντο αὐτόν.   14. οὐδένα πώποτε τὴν χώρᾱν Κῦρος ἀφείλετο.

II.   15. ἡγεῖτο δ' αὐτοῖς ὁ κωμάρχης λελυμένος[2] διὰ
χιόνος.   16. καὶ[3] πάντες δὲ ἔθεον.   17. φοβοίμην δ'
ἂν τῷ ἡγεμόνι ἕπεσθαι, μὴ ἡμᾶς ἀγάγῃ ὅθεν[4] οὐκ ἔσται[5]
ἐξελθεῖν.   18. καὶ ἡγεῖσθαι ἐκέλευον αὐτὸν ὅπου τὸν
δρόμον[6] πεποιηκὼς εἴη.[7]   19. αἱρήσομαι δ' οὖν ὑμᾶς,
καὶ σὺν ὑμῖν ὅ τι ἂν δέῃ πείσομαι.   20. τούτους ἄρχοντας ἐποίει τῆς χώρᾱς.

III.   1. We chose him general of the expedition.   2. I
should fear to ask[8] him for pay.   3. Cyrus was reputed to
have been[9] a kingly man.

---

[1] Mid. *he consulted.*   [2] Cp. § 460. I. 2.   [3] *also.*
[4] To a place *from which.*   [5] *it will not be possible.*   [6] *race course.*
[7] The optative is due to implied indirect discourse, the direct form being
ὅπου . . . πεποίηκας.   [8] Cp. sentence 17 above.   [9] γενέσθαι.

LII

PRESENT SYSTEM OF τῑμάω. IRREGULAR CONTRACT
VERBS IN -άω. INFINITIVE AFTER VERBS OF
PROMISING, *HOPING*, AND *SWEARING*. CLAUSES
INTRODUCED BY CONJUNCTIONS MEANING *WHILE*,
UNTIL, AND *BEFORE*

515. Learn the inflection in the present system of the
active and middle (= passive) voices of τῑμάω *honor* (§ 643).

a. Similarly are inflected ἐρωτάω *ask*, impf. ἠρώτων ; ἐάω
permit, impf. εἴων (with irregular augment); πειράομαι *try*.

516.   **RULES OF CONTRACTION**

a + an ε-sound (ε, η, ει, ῃ) = $\bar{a}$ (or ᾳ).
a + an o-sound (o, ω, οι, ου) = ω (or ῳ).
ι in the uncontracted form is *subscript* in the contracted
   form.

517. Some verbs, including χράομαι *use*, and ζάω *live*,
irregularly have η wherever $\bar{a}$ would naturally occur in the
contracted forms; they likewise have ῃ for ᾳ :

> χρῆσθαι (pres. inf.), not χρᾶσθαι ;
> ζῆν (pres. inf.), not ζᾶν ;
> ζῇ (3 sing. pres. indic.), not ζᾷ.

518. Outside of the present system the final **α** of the
theme is regularly lengthened to **η** :

> τῑμῶ (τῑμάω), τῑμήσω, ἐτίμησα, τετίμηκα, τετίμημαι, ἐτῑμήθην.

a. But after ε, ι, or ρ (cp. §§ 114, 139) the final **α** of the
theme is retained in its long form, outside of the present
system :

ἐῶ (ἐάω), ἐάσω, εἴασα,[1] εἴακα, εἴαμαι, εἰάθην ;
πειράομαι, πειράσομαι, etc.

χράομαι, however, has χρήσομαι, etc.

519. The **infinitive** (commonly future) is used after verbs
of *promising, hoping,* and *swearing :*

περὶ τούτων ὑπέσχετο βουλεύσεσθαι about these matters he promised
   to take counsel.

a. The future infinitive used as above represents the
future indicative of direct discourse :

περὶ τούτων βουλεύσομαι about these matters I will take counsel.

b. The negative used with this infinitive is μή, although
οὐ was used in direct discourse (cp. § 110. *e*):

ὑπέσχετο μὴ παύσεσθαι he promised not to stop (*direct :* οὐ παύ-
   σομαι).

520. The **supplementary participle** in indirect discourse
§ 441) is especially common after forms of ὁρῶ (ὁράω)
see :

ὁρῶ ἵππους ὄντας ἐν τῷ στρατεύματι I see there are horses in the
   army (*direct :* ἵπποι εἰσίν).

521. Besides the temporal conjunctions meaning *when*
§§ 168, 202), there are other conjunctions of time meaning *so long as, while, until :* ἔστε, ἔως, μέχρι (*until*); and
meaning *until* or *before :* πρίν.

522. ἔστε, ἔως, and μέχρι (§ 521) take the same constructions as ἐπεί *when* (§§ 167, 248. 2 and *a*, 400, 417).
That is to say :

---

[1] The augment is irregular.

1. When they introduce a definite past act, they take a past tense of the indicative (negative οὐ):

τί οὐκ ἐποίησεν, ἔστε σπονδῶν ἔτυχεν; what did he not do, until[1] he obtained a truce?

ἕως πόλεμος ἦν, ἡδόμην so long as[1] there was war, I rejoiced.

2. When they introduce a future or a repeated act, they take the subjunctive (with ἄν) after a primary tense or the optative after a secondary tense:

ταῦτα ποιεῖτε ἔστ᾽ ἂν ἐγὼ ἔλθω do this until[1] I come;

ἔστε δ᾽ ἂν πολεμῆτε, ὑπισχνοῦμαι ὑμῖν τὸν μισθόν and so long as[1] you are at war, I promise you your pay.

523. πρίν *until* when following a negative clause usually takes:

1. The indicative of a definite past act:

οὐκ ἐπορεύετο πρὶν Σωκράτει συνεβουλεύσατο he did not proceed until he had consulted Socrates;

οὐκ ἐλθεῖν ἤθελε, πρὶν ἡ γυνὴ αὐτὸν ἔπεισεν he did not wish to come, until his wife persuaded him.

2. The subjunctive (with ἄν) of a future act:

μὴ ἀπέλθητε πρὶν ἂν ἀκούσητε, κτλ. do not go away until you hear, etc.

524. πρίν *before* depending on an affirmative clause takes the infinitive alone or with subject accusative:

ἔφυγον πρὶν ἡμᾶς ἐλθεῖν they fled before we arrived.

---

[1] The context must determine between *while* (*so long as*) and *until* as translations of ἔστε and ἕως.

525.   VOCABULARY LII

ἐάω, ἐάσω, εἴᾱσα, εἴᾱκα, εἴᾱμαι, εἰάθην: *permit, allow, let*. For
impf. εἴων, etc., see §§ 515. *a*,
518. *a*.

ἐπι-θῡμέω, ἐπι-θῡμήσω, ἐπ-εθΰμησα:
*have one's heart set on, yearn,
desire*, with inf. or gen.

ἐρωτάω, ἐρωτήσω, ἠρώτησα, ἠρώτηκα, ἠρώτημαι, ἠρωτήθην: *ask
a question, inquire*. To be
distinguished from αἰτέω (Vocabulary LI).   Cp. ἠρόμην
(Vocabulary XXXIV), which
is often used for ἠρώτησα.
See also §§ 343–345.

ἔστε, temporal conj.: *while, so long
as, until*.

ἕως, temporal conj.: *while, so long
as, until*.

ζάω, ζήσω: *live*.

θεάομαι, θεάσομαι, ἐθεᾱσάμην, τεθέᾱμαι: *look on, gaze at, see*.
Theater.

μέχρι, temporal conj.: *until*.

νῑκάω (νίκη), νῑκήσω, ἐνίκησα, νενίκηκα, νενίκημαι, ἐνῑκήθην: *conquer, surpass*.

ὁράω (impf. ἑώρων[1]), fut. ὄψομαι,
2 aor. εἶδον (Vocabulary XIX),
ἑώρᾱκα or ἑόρᾱκα, ἑώρᾱμαι or
ὦμμαι, ὤφθην: *see, behold*.

πειράομαι, πειρᾱσομαι, ἐπειρᾱσάμην,
πεπείρᾱμαι, and ἐπειρᾱ́θην: *try,
attempt*. Pirate.

πολεμέω (πόλεμος), πολεμήσω, ἐπολέμησα, πεπολέμηκα, πεπολέμημαι, ἐπολεμήθην: *wage war,
make war on*, with dat. (§ 317),
or πρός and acc.

πρίν, temporal conj.: *before, until*.
πρόσθεν (Vocabulary XXVI)
. . . πρίν = Lat. *prius* . . .
quam: earlier than, before.

τῑμάω (τῑμή), τῑμήσω, ἐτίμησα,
τετίμηκα, τετίμημαι, ἐτῑμήθην:
honor.

ὑπ-ισχνέομαι (ἴσχω, strong form
of ἔχω, with pres. suffix νε-),
ὑπο-σχήσομαι, ὑπ-εσχόμην, ὑπ-
έσχημαι: *undertake, promise*.

χράομαι, χρήσομαι, ἐχρησάμην, κέχρημαι, with pass. aor. ἐχρήσθην: *use*, with dat. of means;
cp. Lat. *ūtor* with abl.

EXERCISES FOR TRANSLATION

526. I. 1. ἕως [2] ἂν παρῇ τις, χρῶμαι αὐτῷ. 2. καὶ
ταῦτα ἐποίουν, μέχρι σκότος ἐγένετο.   3. οἱ δὲ βάρβαροι φεύγουσι πρὶν ὁρᾶν τὰς τάξεις τὰς τῶν πολεμίων.

---

[1] This imperfect is irregular in having *double* augment, both syllabic ἐ- and
temporal -ω-; cp. also pf. ἑώρᾱκα and ἑώρᾱμαι.   [2] *while*.

4. καὶ ὑπῖσχνεῖτο μὴ κακὸς ἔσεσθαι.　5. πειράσομαι δὲ τοῖς πολεμίοις πολεμεῖν ἔστ᾽ [1] ἂν δοκῇ αὐτοῖς πολέμου [2] παύσασθαι.　6. Μένων δῆλος ἦν ἐπιθῡμῶν τῑμᾶσθαι.　7. ὅστις ζῆν ἐπιθῡμεῖ, πειράσθω νῑκᾶν. 8. Κῦρος εἴα τὸν Κλέαρχον ἔχειν τοὺς στρατιώτᾱς. 9. ταύτην τὴν γέφῡραν ἐπειρῶντο διαβαίνειν οἱ Ἕλληνες.　10. τὰ ὅπλα ἔχοντες οἰόμεθα ἂν [3] καὶ τῇ ἀρετῇ χρῆσθαι.　11. ὑπῖσχνεῖτο δὲ αὐτῷ φίλον αὐτὸν Κύρῳ ποιήσειν.　12. εἰ δέ τινα ὁρῴη ἀγαθὸν ὄντα, οὐδένα τὴν χώρᾱν πώποτε ἀφῃρεῖτο.　13. κἂν [4] ὑμᾶς ὁρῶσιν ὄντας κακούς, πάντες κακοὶ ἔσονται.　14. ἠρώτων δ᾽ αὐτὸν τί χρὴ ποιεῖν.

II.　15. οἱ γὰρ πολέμιοι οὐ πρόσθεν ἐπολέμησαν πρὸς ἡμᾶς πρὶν τοὺς στρατηγοὺς ἡμῶν συνέλαβον. 16. βασιλεὺς δ᾽ ἤκουσε Τισσαφέρνους [5] ὅτι οἱ Ἕλληνες νῑκῷεν τὸ καθ᾽ αὑτούς. [6]　17. οὓς ἑώρᾱ ἐθέλοντας κινδῡνεύειν, τούτους [7] ἄρχοντας τῆς χώρᾱς ἐποίει καὶ ἄλλοις δώροις ἐτῑμᾱ.　18. θεῶνται οἱ παῖδές τινας τῑμωμένους ὑπὸ βασιλέως.　19. οἱ Ἕλληνες ἐνίκων τοὺς Πέρσᾱς καὶ κατὰ γῆν καὶ κατὰ θάλατταν.

III.　1. Before they advanced ten stadia, the Greeks tried to cross this river.　2. While there was war, we kept using the provisions of both friends and enemies.　3. We saw that the soldiers were honoring Cyrus.

---

[1] *until.*　　　　　　[2] § 201.
[3] With the inf. (§ 277).　　[4] § 30.
[5] Gen. of source (§ 201).　　[6] *the division opposite themselves.*
[7] Antecedent of **οὕς** at the beginning : *those whom.*

LIII

PRESENT SYSTEM OF δηλόω. COMPLEX SENTENCES IN INDIRECT DISCOURSE

527. Learn the inflection in the present system of the active and middle (= passive) voices of δηλόω *show* (§ 643).

a. Similarly are inflected ἀξιόω *demand*, σκηνόω (a parallel form of σκηνάω) *encamp*.

528.   RULES OF CONTRACTION

$o + \epsilon$ or o or $ov = ov$.

$o + \eta$ or $\omega = \omega$.

$o + $ a diphthong containing ι ($\epsilon\iota$, $o\iota$, η) $= o\iota$.

529. Outside of the present system the final **o** of the theme is regularly lengthened to **ω**:

δηλῶ (δηλόω), δηλώσω, ἐδήλωσα, δεδήλωκα, δεδήλωμαι, ἐδηλώθην.

COMPLEX SENTENCES IN INDIRECT DISCOURSE

530. When a complex sentence is quoted, whether after a verb that requires ὅτι, or after a verb that requires the infinitive or the participle, the verb of the main clause of the quotation comes under the rules already explained (§§ 110, 260, 276, 277, 441, 519).

The only new principle involved concerns the verb of the *subordinate* clause. This verb is retained in the original mood and tense after a primary tense of the introductory verb of *saying* or *thinking;* but it may be changed to the same tense of the optative after a secondary tense of the introductory verb; *except* that, even in the secondary sequence, dependent secondary tenses of the indicative (*i.e.* imperfect, aorist, and pluperfect) are regularly kept unchanged.

a. Dependent optative clauses of the direct discourse are of course retained in the indirect discourse after both primary and secondary tenses. ἄν with the optative in direct discourse is retained in indirect discourse.

b. The verb of a dependent clause can not be changed to the infinitive.

c. Changes of person are made as the sense requires.

d. The negative of the direct discourse is, as usual, retained in the indirect.

EXAMPLES

1. *Sentence quoted after primary tense :* ἂν δὲ εὖ γένηταί τι, οὐ μεμνήσεσθαί σέ φᾶσιν (*direct :* οὐ μεμνήσῃ) and if anything turns out successfully, they say you will not remember. (Here the dependent clause ἂν . . . γένηται is retained unchanged, since the introductory verb is φᾶσίν.)

2. *Sentence quoted after secondary tense :*

   a. Original sentence : εἰ μή τις προκαταλήψεται τὸ ἄκρον, οὐκ ἔσται δυνατὸν παρελθεῖν unless somebody shall seize the height in advance, it will not be possible to go past.

   b. Quoted sentence : ἔφη εἰ μή τις προκαταλήψοιτο τὸ ἄκρον, οὐκ ἔσεσθαι δυνατὸν παρελθεῖν he said that unless somebody should seize the height in advance, it would not be possible to go past. (In the dependent clause, προκαταλήψεται might be retained.)

3. *Dependent secondary tenses of indicative retained :* ἧκεν ἄγγελος λέγων ὅτι λελοιπὼς εἴη Συέννεσις τὰ ἄκρα ἐπεὶ ᾔσθετο . . . καὶ ὅτι ἤκουε, κτλ. a messenger came saying that Syennesis had left the heights since he had perceived . . . and because he heard, etc. (Here λελοιπὼς εἴη represents the original λέλοιπε *has left* of the messenger's

language ; but neither ἤσθετο nor ἤκονε could be changed to the optative, since in the direct discourse they were *dependent secondary* tenses of the indicative. The tense that determines the sequence is seen in ἦκεν.)

531. When a subjunctive introduced by ἐάν or ἐπάν, or ὅστις ἄν, or similar words, is changed to the optative after a secondary tense of the introductory verb of *saying* or *thinking*, ἄν is omitted; that is, ἐάν becomes εἰ, ἐπάν becomes ἐπεί, ὅστις ἄν becomes ὅστις, etc. :

a. *Original sentence :* οἱ Ἕλληνες διαβήσονται ἐὰν (or ἐπὰν) μηδεὶς κωλύσῃ the Greeks will cross if (*or* when) nobody hinders.

b. *Quoted sentence in secondary sequence :* ἔφη τοὺς Ἕλληνας διαβήσεσθαι εἰ (or ἐπεὶ) μηδεὶς κωλύσειεν he said the Greeks would cross if (*or* when) nobody should hinder.

Of course the original subjunctive introduced by ἐάν or ἐπάν might have been retained in the last sentence.

532. VOCABULARY LIII

ἀξιόω (ἄξιος), ἀξιώσω, ἠξίωσα, ἠξίωκα, ἠξίωμαι, ἠξιώθην : *deem worthy ; claim as one's right, demand, ask.*

δηλόω (δῆλος), δηλώσω, ἐδήλωσα, δεδήλωκα, δεδήλωμαι, ἐδηλώθην : *show, make evident.*

ἔρημος, η, ον, and ἔρημος, ον : *deserted.* σταθμοὶ ἔρημοι : *marches through the desert.* Eremite.

πλῆθος, ους, τό : *crowd, throng, host, multitude.*

σκηνόω (σκηνή), ἐσκήνωσα, ἐσκήνωκα : *stay in a tent, camp.*

τελευτάω (τελευτή *end*), τελευτήσω, ἐτελεύτησα, τετελεύτηκα, ἐτελευτήθην : *end, finish, die.*

τοίνυν, inferential particle, postpositive : *therefore, then.*

EXERCISES FOR TRANSLATION

533. I. 1. ταῦτ᾽ οὖν οὐκ ἀξιοῦμεν. 2. τῑμᾶσθαι δ᾽ ἠξίου. 3. ὡς ὁρᾶτε, σκηνοῦμεν ἐν τῇ τάξει.[1] 4. ἄλλοι

---

[1] *in our order.*

δέ τινες ἔλεξαν ὅτι εἰ βασιλεὺς ἐθέλοι ἐπὶ τὴν Κιλικίαν στρατεύειν, πορεύοιντο ἂν σὺν αὐτῷ.[1]   5. καὶ αὐτὸς ἐν τῷ πεδίῳ ἐσκήνου.   6. καὶ ἔχων τὰ χωρία πειρᾶται σκηνοῦν.   7. εἶπε δὲ Κῦρος ὅτι ἐπειδὰν τάχιστα[2] παύσηται τῆς στρατείας,[3] εὐθὺς ἀποπέμψει τὸν στρατηγόν. 8. καὶ νῦν τοίνυν ἐπεὶ πόλεμός ἐστιν, ἀξιοῦν δεῖ ὑμᾶς αὐτοὺς ἀμείνους τοῦ πλήθους[4] εἶναι.   9. ἀκούομεν ὑμᾶς σκηνοῦν ἐν ταῖς οἰκίαις.   10. καὶ ἠξίουν αὐτοὺς τὰ βέλτιστα συμβουλεύειν.   11. εἶπε δ' ὅτι οὗτος ἄριστος ἔσοιτο ὃς ἂν πρῶτος ἐν τῷ πέρᾱν τοῦ ποταμοῦ γένηται.[5] 12. εἰ δὲ δή ποτε Κῦρος πορεύοιτο, καὶ πλεῖστοι[6] μέλλοιεν ὄψεσθαι,[7] μετεπέμπετο τοὺς φίλους, ὡς δηλοίη οὓς τιμᾷ.

II. 13. καὶ σοὶ δηλώσω ὅθεν ἐγὼ περὶ σοῦ ἀκούω. 14. καὶ ὡς[8] ἡ μάχη ἐγένετο καὶ ὡς Κῦρος ἐτελεύτησεν, ἐν τῷ πρόσθεν λόγῳ[9] δεδήλωται.   15. ἐντεῦθεν ἐξελαύνει σταθμοὺς ἐρήμους δέκα · οἱ δὲ στρατιῶται κακῶς σκηνοῦσιν.   16. δηλοῖ δὲ τοῖς φύλαξι πέντε μνᾶς ἀργυρίου καὶ θώρᾱκα χρῡσοῦν.   17. ἔλεξεν ὅτι οἱ στρατιῶται τὸν μισθὸν λάβοιεν ἐπεὶ ἀφίκοντο εἰς Σάρδεις.

III. 1. Cyrus promised[10] to provide[11] a market as soon as[12] he should arrive at Sardis.   2. He kept demanding that these gifts should be sent[13] to the king.

---

[1] Note that λέγουσιν might be used for ἔλεξαν without affecting the following construction (§ 530. a).

[2] ἐπειδὴ (ἐπειδὰν) τάχιστα = as soon as.   [3] § 201.   [4] § 355.

[5] The dependent clause might also read ὃς . . . γένοιτο (without ἄν).

[6] very many men.   [7] § 156. 2.   [8] how.   [9] the previous account.

[10] Always compose complicated indirect discourse in the direct form first.

[11] Cp. § 526. I. 11 for construction after ὑπισχνέομαι.

[12] Cp. sentence 7 above.   [13] Use acc. with inf. : these gifts to be sent.

LIV

DECLENSION OF CONTRACT PARTICIPLES. ὅπως WITH
FUTURE INDICATIVE. VARIOUS IDIOMS

534. Learn the declension of ποιῶν, τῑμῶν, δηλῶν (§ 622
and *a*).

a. Similarly are declined ζῶν *living*, νῑκῶν *conquering*,
ὁρῶν *seeing*, etc.

535. Object clauses introduced by ὅπως. — Verbs signifying *to strive for*, *to care for*, or *to effect*, may be followed by
ὅπως (meaning *how*) with the future indicative, which is
almost always retained even after a secondary tense. The
negative is μή :

βουλεύεται ὅπως μήποτε ἔτι ἔσται ἐπὶ τῷ ἀδελφῷ he plans how he
shall never again be in the power of his brother.

a. But such verbs are often followed by ὅπως or ὡς with
the present or aorist subjunctive or (after a secondary
tense) optative, like ordinary purpose clauses (§§ 243, 268) :

διεπράξατο ὅπως εἰς τὸ τεῖχος εἰσέλθοι he contrived how to enter into
the fortification (*i.e.* that he might enter).

536. Worthy of special attention is the construction of
ἔχω with an adverb :

> καλῶς ἔχειν to be handsome *or* well ;
> κακῶς ἔχειν to be bad ;
> οὕτως ἔχειν to be thus *or* so ;
> ἄλλως ἔχειν to be otherwise.

537. Also noteworthy are the expressions : κακῶς ποιεῖν
to do ill to, *to injure*, with the accusative ; and its passive

κακῶς πάσχειν ὑπό τινος *to be injured by anybody*. Other
adverbs like εὖ *well* may be similarly used with ποιεῖν
and πάσχειν: εὖ πάσχειν ὑπό τινος = *to be treated kindly
by anybody*.

ἱκανώτατος ἔσται ὑμᾶς καὶ εὖ καὶ κακῶς ποιεῖν he will be most competent both to benefit and to injure you.

538. Used in a different sense are:

κακῶς πράττειν to fare badly (cp. examples, § 438);
εὖ or καλῶς πράττειν to fare well.

539.   VOCABULARY LIV

ἀθυμία, ᾱς, ἡ: *discouragement, despondency*.

ἄλλως (adv. of ἄλλος): *otherwise*.

ἀπ-άγω: *lead away, lead back*.

γε, enclitic particle, regularly following the emphatic word:
certainly, surely, at least.

ἐξ-απατάω (ἀπατάω *deceive*, ἀπατήσω, ἠπάτησα, ἠπάτηκα, ἠπάτημαι, ἠπατήθην): *utterly deceive, cheat*.

ἐπι-μελέομαι, ἐπι-μελήσομαι, ἐπι-
μεμέλημαι, ἐπ-εμελήθην, dep.
pass.: *take care of, care for*,
with gen.

ἡττάομαι (ἥττων), ἡττήσομαι, ἥττημαι, ἡττήθην: *be inferior, be conquered*. Used as pass. of νῑκάω.

μή-ποτε: *never*; used like μή *not*.

Ξενοφῶν, ῶντος, ὁ: *Xenophon*.
The word is declined like τῑμῶν (§ 622) in the masc. sing.

οἷος, ᾱ, ον, rel. pron.: *of what sort,
what sort of*, (*such*) *as*. οἷός
τε: *able*; οἷόν τ' ἐστίν: *it is
possible*. Lat. *quālis*.

ὅπως, conj.: *how*, introducing an
obj. clause, § 535. Cp. Vocabularies XXII, XXXIX.

ποιητέος, ᾱ, ον (verbal adj. of ποιέω,
with ἐστί or εἰσί expressed or
understood): *necessary to be
done, must be done*.

τοιοῦτος, τοιαύτη, τοιοῦτο (declined
like οὗτος, § 171), dem. pron.:
of such a sort, such; often
understood or expressed as
antecedent of οἷος. τοιοῦτος οἷος
= *such as*. The neut. is also
τοιοῦτον as well as τοιοῦτο.
Lat. *tālis*.

φωνή, ῆς, ἡ (cp. φα-, φησί): *voice*.
Mega-phone.

EXERCISES FOR TRANSLATION

540. I. 1. βασιλεὺς νῑκῶν τυγχάνει. 2. οἱ δὲ ὁρῶντες ταῦτα ἐθαύμαζον. 3. οἱ δὲ ἄνδρες εἰσὶν οἱ ποιοῦντες [1] ὅ τι ἂν ἐν ταῖς μάχαις γίγνηται. 4. ἡμᾶς, τοὺς Ξενοφῶντος φίλους, κακῶς ποιεῖν πειρᾶται. 5. οἱ δ' ἀπήγαγον τὸν ἄνδρα διὰ τῆς ἀγορᾶς μάλα μεγάλῃ τῇ φωνῇ δηλοῦντα οἷα [2] ἔπασχεν. 6. σκεπτέον μοι δοκεῖ εἶναι ὅπως τὰ ἐπιτήδεια ἕξομεν. 7. ἐνταῦθα δὴ πολλὴ ἀθῡμίᾱ ἦν τοῖς Ἕλλησιν, ὁρῶσι [3] μὲν τὸ εὖρος τοῦ ποταμοῦ, ὁρῶσι [3] δὲ τοὺς διαβαίνειν κωλύσοντας.[4] 8. ἐφοβούμην μὴ Κῦρος ἐξαπατῴη ἡμᾶς· καὶ εἶχεν [5] οὕτως. 9. εἰ οὖν τις ἄλλο βέλτῑον ὁρᾷ, ἄλλως ἐχέτω. 10. ἡμῖν γε οἶμαι πάντα ποιητέα [6] ὡς μήποτε ἐπὶ τοῖς βαρβάροις γενώμεθα. 11. κακῶς γὰρ τῶν ἡμετέρων [7] ἐχόντων πάντες οὗτοι οὓς ὁρᾶτε βάρβαροι πολεμιώτεροι ἡμῖν ἔσονται τῶν παρὰ βασιλεῖ ὄντων.[8] 12. εὖ ἐπάθομεν ὑπ' ἐκείνου.

II. 13. τῶν παρ' ἑαυτῷ βαρβάρων Κῦρος ἐπεμελεῖτο ὡς πολεμεῖν [9] ἱκανοὶ εἴησαν. 14. Ξενοφῶν δ' ἔλεξεν ὅτι οὐχ οἷόν τ' εἴη διώκειν τοὺς πολεμίους. 15. τῶν γὰρ νῑκώντων [10] ἐστὶ καὶ τὰ ἑαυτῶν [11] σῴζειν καὶ τὰ τῶν ἡττωμένων λαμβάνειν. 16. οἱ δ' ἥρπαζον τὸ στρατόπεδον ὡς ἤδη πάντα νῑκῶντες. 17. ἀλλὰ δεῖ πειρᾶσθαι ὅπως καλῶς νῑκῶντες σῳζώμεθα. 18. ὅτῳ [12] οὖν ταῦτα

---

[1] Cp. § 405. I. 5.
[2] The antecedent is τοιαῦτα understood: *such things as, what sort of things.*
[3] A participle.   [4] § 212.   [5] Impers.   [6] § 477.
[7] *our affairs.*   [8] §§ 212, 355.   [9] § 333.
[10] *it is the right of,* etc., § 229.   [11] § 380.   [12] § 228.

δοκεῖ καλῶς ἔχειν, λεξάτω ὡς τάχιστα.   19. τούτων δὲ
τοιούτων ὄντων[1] πάντα ποιητέα ὅπως μὴ ἐπ᾽ ἐκείνῳ
γενησόμεθα.

III. 1. They evidently honor us.   2. They have been
treated kindly by us.   3. We planned never, while living,
to fall[2] into the power of the enemy.

LV

THE FUTURE AND AORIST OF LIQUID THEMES. SOME OTHER VERBS THAT CONTRACT IN THE FUTURE, INCLUDING VERBS IN -ίζω. UNREAL SUPPOSITIONS

541. Verbs whose themes end in a liquid (§ 27), like
φαίνω *show* and μένω *remain*, use for the future tense suffix
ε% and not σ%.   As contraction results, the future of these
verbs is like the present indicative, optative, infinitive, and
participle of verbs in -έω.   Learn the inflection of the
future active and middle of φαίνω (§ 644), theme φαν- :

φανῶ, φανοίην, φανεῖν, φανῶν ; φανοῦμαι, φανοίμην, φανεῖσθαι, φανούμενος.

φανῶν is declined like ποιῶν (§ 622).

542. Verbs with liquid themes form the first aorist with
the suffix **a** instead of σα.   At the same time they lengthen
the theme vowel: a becomes η[3]; ε becomes ει ; ι becomes ῑ ;
υ becomes ῡ:

φαίνω (theme φαν-), first aorist active ἔφηνα ;
μένω (theme μεν-), first aorist ἔμεινα.

This first aorist is inflected like ἔλῡσα.

---

[1] *Quae cum ita sint.*   [2] *become in the power of.*
[3] But a becomes ᾱ in the first aorist after ι or ρ.

Learn the inflection in the first aorist active and middle of φαίνω (§ 645):

ἔφηνα, φήνω, φήναιμι, φῆνον, φῆναι, φήνᾱς, -ᾱσα, -αν (declined like ἀκούσᾱς, § 209); ἐφηνάμην, φήνωμαι, φηναίμην, φῆναι, φήνασθαι, φηνάμενος.

543. Verbs in -ίζω of more than two syllables form their futures in -ιέω, -ιέεις, etc., with resulting contraction: -ιῶ, -ιεῖς, etc. These future forms are contracted like the futures of liquid themes (§ 644) or the presents of verbs in -έω (§ 643):

νομιῶ, νομιοίην, νομιεῖν, νομιῶν; νομιοῦμαι, νομιοίμην, νομιεῖσθαι, νομιούμενος; futures of νομίζω *think.*

ἀγωνιούμεθα, future of ἀγωνίζομαι *contend.*

544. Some verbs drop σ of the future suffix between two vowels and then contract. Thus the future of καλέω *call* is καλῶ (*i.e.* καλέω for καλέσω), which is inflected like ποιῶ (ποιέω, § 643). This means that the future indicative, optative, infinitive, and participle of καλέω are like the present of this same verb in the corresponding moods. Similarly the future of μάχομαι *fight* is μαχοῦμαι (*i.e.* μαχέομαι for μαχέσομαι), μαχοίμην, μαχεῖσθαι, μαχούμενος.

a. The future of ἐλαύνω *drive, ride* is ἐλῶ (*i.e.* ἐλάω for ἐλάσω), which is inflected like τῑμάω (§ 643).

545. Unreal (or contrary to fact) suppositions. — εἰ is used with the imperfect indicative to express an unreal supposition in *present* time; with the aorist indicative to express an unreal supposition in *past* time; the verb of the conclusion (apodosis) may be either the imperfect indicative with ἄν, representing *present* time, or the aorist indicative with ἄν, representing *past* time.

Therefore these conditions may be distinguished, in form, from simple present and past suppositions by the single fact that ἄν accompanies the conclusion :

εἰ ἐπὶ τοῖς πολεμίοις ἦσαν, κακῶς ἂν ἔπασχον if they were in the power of the enemy, they would be suffering harm ;

εἰ ἐπὶ τοῖς πολεμίοις ἐγένοντο, κακῶς ἂν ἔπαθον if they had got into the power of the enemy, they would have suffered harm ;

εἰ μὴ ὑμεῖς ἤλθετε, ἐπορευόμεθα ἂν ἐπὶ βασιλέα if you had not come, we should now be proceeding against the king.

546. When a supposition contrary to fact occurs in indirect discourse, neither the verb of the protasis nor that of the apodosis may be changed to the optative, even after a secondary tense. But the verb of the main clause (apodosis) must be changed to the infinitive or participle if the introductory verb requires the infinitive or participle; ἄν is always retained :

ἐνόμισαν εἰ ἐπὶ τοῖς πολεμίοις ἐγένοντο, κακῶς ἂν παθεῖν they supposed that if they had got into the power of the enemy, they would have suffered harm.

547. VOCABULARY LV

ἀγγέλλω (for ἀγγελ + yω, theme ἀγγελ-), ἀγγελῶ, ἤγγειλα, ἤγγελκα, ἤγγελμαι, ἠγγέλθην : *announce, report,* with ὅτι or partic. in indir. disc. Cp. ἄγγελος.

ἀγωνίζομαι (theme ἀγωνιδ-), ἀγωνιοῦμαι, ἠγωνισάμην, ἠγώνισμαι : *contend* as in games, *struggle.* Cp. ἀγών. Agonize.

ἀδικέω (cp. ἄδικος), ἀδικήσω, ἠδίκησα, ἠδίκηκα, ἠδίκημαι, ἠδικήθην : *do wrong to, injure, be in the wrong.*

ἀπ-αγγέλλω : *bring back a message, report.*

ἀπο-κρίνομαι (mid. of ἀπο-κρίνω, see κρίνω) : *give one's decision, answer, reply,* with ὅτι clause.

ἀπο-κτείνω (for κτεν + yω, theme κτεν-), -κτενῶ, -έκτεινα, -έκτονα : *put to death, slay, kill.* The pass. is supplied by ἀποθνῄσκω.

γιγνώσκω (reduplicated pres. from theme γνο-, with pres. suffix σκ%), γνώσομαι, 2 aor. to be learned later, ἔγνωκα, ἔγνωσμαι,[1] ἐγνώσθην[1] : *learn, know,* with ὅτι or partic. in indir. disc. Cp. Lat. (g)nōscō, ī-gnōtus, Eng. know.

---

[1] With *sigma* irregularly inserted.

ἐπι-σῑτίζομαι (theme σῑτιδ-), -σῑ-
τιοῦμαι, -εσῑτισάμην : get provisions for oneself. Cp. σῖτος.

καλέω, καλῶ (fut.), ἐκάλεσα (with
the final short vowel of the
theme retained before the tense
suffix), κέκληκα, κέκλημαι, ἐκλήθην : call, summon, invite. Cp.
ἐκ-κλησίᾱ.

κρίνω (for κριν + yω, theme κριν-),
κρινῶ, ἔκρῑνα, κέκρικα, κέκριμαι,
ἐκρίθην : separate, judge, decide.
Cp. Lat. cernō. Critic.

μένω (themes μεν-, μενη-), μενῶ,
ἔμεινα, μεμένηκα : remain, wait
for. Cp. Lat. maneō.

παρ-αγγέλλω : give directions to,
direct, command, with dat. of
pers. or acc. of pers. and inf.

συγ-καλέω (σύν + καλέω) : call together.

φαίνω (for φαν + yω, theme φαν-),
φανῶ, ἔφηνα, πέφηνα (have
appeared), πέφασμαι, ἐφάνθην
(was shown) and ἐφάνην (appeared) : bring to light, show ;
MID. and PASS. usually appear.
In mid. and pass. the verb may
take a supplementary partic.
like δῆλός ἐστι (§ 449). Phe-
nomenon.

EXERCISES FOR TRANSLATION

548. I. 1. ἐνταῦθα ἔμεινεν ἡμέρᾱς ἑπτά. 2. καὶ
ἕως¹ μένομεν ἐν τούτῳ τῷ τόπῳ, σκεπτέον μοι δοκεῖ
εἶναι ὅπως ὡς ἀσφαλέστατα μενοῦμεν. 3. Κλέαρχος
ἤρετο τὸν Κῦρον· Οἴει σοι μαχεῖσθαι, ὦ Κῦρε, τὸν
ἀδελφόν ; 4. καὶ Κῦρος λέγεται ἀποκτεῖναι αὐτὸς τῇ
ἑαυτοῦ χειρὶ² τὸν ἄρχοντα. 5. ὁ δὲ συλλαμβάνει
Κῦρον ὡς ἀποκτενῶν.³ 6. ταῦτα δὴ ἀπαγγελοῦμεν.
7. παρήγγειλε τοῖς στρατηγοῖς ἑκάστοις λαμβάνειν
ἄνδρας.⁴ 8. ὁ δ' ἀπεκρίνατο ὅτι ἀκούοι Ἀβροκόμᾱν,
ἐχθρὸν ἄνδρα, ἐπὶ τῷ Εὐφράτῃ ποταμῷ εἶναι. 9. χρὴ
οὖν ὑμᾶς διαβαίνειν πρὶν δῆλον εἶναι ὅ τι οἱ ἄλλοι
Ἕλληνες ἀποκρινοῦνται Κύρῳ. 10. τότε ἔφηναν οἷα⁵

---

¹ while, with present indicative of a definite present act.
² § 141.
³ §§ 331, 332.
⁴ Cp. § 324. I. 9.
⁵ The antecedent is τοιαῦτα understood.

περὶ ὑμῶν ἐγίγνωσκον. 11. εἰ δὲ ἡγεμὼν μηδεὶς ἡμῖν
φανεῖται,[1] ἐρωτήσομεν αὐτοὶ ἥτις ἡ πάροδός ἐστιν.
12. οὐκ ἂν ἐποίησεν ὁ λοχαγὸς ταῦτα, εἰ μὴ ἐγὼ
αὐτὸν ἐκέλευσα.   13. ὥρα[2] δὲ βουλεύεσθαι ὅπως ὡς
κάλλιστα ἀγωνιούμεθα.   14. ἐκάλεσέ τις αὐτὸν τῶν
ὑπηρετῶν.

II. 15. ἔπειτα συγκαλοῦμεν[3] τοὺς ἄλλους στρατιώτᾱς.   16. ὁ δὲ Κλέαρχος ἔκρῑνε τὸν Μένωνος στρατιώτην ἀδικεῖν.   17. ἀγορὰν οὐδεὶς πώποτε παρέξει ἡμῖν,
οὐδὲ ὅθεν[4] ἐπισῑτιούμεθα.   18. καὶ ἡμῖν[5] γ᾽ ἂν ἡδέως
ταῦτ᾽ ἐποίει, εἰ ἑώρα ἡμᾶς μένειν παρασκευαζομένους.
19. Κλέαρχος, ἐπεὶ ἐφάνη τὰς σπονδὰς λύων, ἔχει τὴν
δίκην.   20. ἤγγειλεν οὖν ὅτι ὁ στρατηγὸς μενεῖ.

III. 1. He will call the soldiers together[6] if no guides
shall appear.[7] 2. We should have gone back if the guide
had not shown[8] us this road.

LVI

THE INFLECTION OF MI–VERBS: ἵστημι, ἐπριάμην, ἔβην, ἀπ-έδρᾱν

549. By "μι-verbs" are meant those whose present
indicative, first person, singular, ends in -μι.   Thus ἵστημι
I set or *place;* τίθημι *I put;* δίδωμι *I give;* and δείκνῡμι
I show.

---

[1] Cp. § 242.   [2] § 230.   [3] Fut.
[4] A place *from which.*   [5] *for us.*   [6] Cp. II. **15.**
[7] Cp. I. **11.**   [8] Use **φαίνω.**

The essential difference between μι-verbs and ω-verbs is that μι-verbs lack the thematic vowel $^o/_e$ used by ω-verbs before the personal endings in the present and second aorist tense systems. The thematic vowel $^ω/_η$ is retained in the subjunctive, however. In other tense systems [1] μι-verbs and ω-verbs are inflected alike.

550. Learn the inflection of ἵστημι in the present system active and middle (= passive), in the second aorist active (§ 646), and in the second perfect active (§ 647). No second aorist middle of ἵστημι exists ; and in its stead the second aorist ἐπριάμην (which has no present) *I bought* should be learned (§ 646).

551. ἵστημι is a reduplicated present, built on the theme στα- thus : σι-στη-μι. The initial *sigma* is dropped, and is represented by the rough breathing. The vowel of the theme is long (η) in the active voice in the following places : in the singular of the present and imperfect indicative ; in the second person singular of the present imperative ; and throughout the second aorist indicative, imperative (except the third person plural), and infinitive. In all other active forms of these tenses (present and second aorist), and in *all* middle forms of these tenses the theme vowel is short (α).

552. In the subjunctive α contracts with the thematic vowel $^ω/_η$:

$$a + \omega = \omega.$$
$$a + \eta = \eta.$$
$$a + \mathcal{y} = \mathcal{y}.$$

---

[1] Except a few second perfects and pluperfects of the μι-form, like ἕστατον *they* (two) *stand*, ἕστασαν *they stood*.

553. Some ω-verbs have second aorists that are inflected like those of μι-verbs:

ἔβην I went (from βαίνω); subjv. βῶ; opt. βαίην; imv. βῆθι; inf. βῆναι; partic. βάς, βᾶσα, βάν.

ἀπ-έδρᾶν I ran away *by stealth*, ἀπέδρᾱς, ἀπέδρᾱ, etc. (from ἀπο-διδράσκω); subjv. ἀποδρῶ, ἀποδρῇς, ἀποδρᾷ, etc.; opt. ἀπο-δραίην; imv. wanting; inf. ἀποδρᾶναι; partic. ἀποδράς, ᾶσα, άν.

554. Learn the declension of ἱστάς and στάς, which are declined alike (§ 617). Cp. ἀκούσᾱς (§ 209). Learn the declension of ἑστώς (§ 624).

555. MEANINGS OF THE TENSES AND VOICES OF ἵστημι
set OR *place* OR *stand*

	TRANSITIVE			INTRANSITIVE
	ACT.	MID.	PASS.	
Pres.	ἵστημι *I set*	ἵσταμαι *I set for myself*	ἵσταμαι *I am set* or *placed*	ἵσταμαι *I take my place*
Fut.	στήσω *I shall set*	στήσομαι *I shall set for myself*	σταθήσομαι *I shall be set* or *placed*	στήσομαι *I shall take my place*
Aor.	ἔστησα *I set* or *placed*	ἐστησάμην *I set* or *placed for myself*	ἐστάθην *I was set* or *placed*	ἔστην *I stood*
Pf.				ἕστηκα *I stand*
Plup.				εἱστήκη *I stood*
Fut. Pf.				ἑστήξω *I shall stand*

a. The transitive and intransitive tenses of compounds of ἵστημι are similarly distinguished.

556. **VOCABULARY LVI**

ἀναγκάζω (theme ἀναγκαδ-, cp.
ἀνάγκη), ἀναγκάσω, ἠνάγκασα,
ἠνάγκακα, ἠνάγκασμαι, ἠναγκά-
σθην : *compel, force.*

ἄνευ, prep. with gen. only: *without.*

ἀν-ίστημι : *make stand up, start
up ;* (intr.) *stand up.* For
intr. tenses see § 555.

ἀντί, prep. with gen. only: *instead of, for.* In comp. :
against. Anti-dote, etc.

ἀπο-διδράσκω (δι-δρά-σκω, δράσο-
μαι, ἔδρᾱν, δέδρᾱκα) : *run away*
by stealth; *run away from,*
with acc.

ἅρμα, ατος, τό : *chariot* for use in
battle. See p. 252, Fig. 22.

βασιλείᾱ, ᾱς, ἡ (βασιλεύω) : *kingdom.* Do not confuse this
word with βασίλεια, τά, *royal
buildings, palace* (§ 217).

δύναμαι, δυνήσομαι, δεδύνημαι, ἐδυ-
νήθην (or ἠδυνήθην), dep. pass. :

be able. Cp. δύναμις. Dynast,
dynamite.

ἐπί-σταμαι, ἐπιστήσομαι, ἠπιστήθην, dep. pass. : *understand.*

ἐπριάμην (2 aor.) : *I bought.* No
pres. from this verb.

ἱππικός, ή, όν (ἵππος) : *of horse, of
cavalry.*

ἵστημι, στήσω, ἔστησα and ἔστην,
ἕστηκα and ἕστατον, ἐστάθην :
set, place, make stand, halt ;
intr. tenses : *stand, stand still,
stop.* See § 555. Cp. Lat.
stō, Eng. stand.

καθ-ίστημι : *set* or *place down, station ;* intr. tenses : *be placed,
stationed,* or *established ; statio⁓
oneself, take one's place.* Fo⁓
intr. tenses cp. ἵστημι, § 555.

κεφαλή, ῆς, ἡ : *head.* Cp. Lat.
caput.

Λύδιος, ᾱ, ον (Λῡδίᾱ) : *Lydian.*

ὄνος, ου, ὁ : *ass.* Lat. *asinus.*

Φρυγίᾱ, ᾱς, ἡ : *Phrygia.*

EXERCISES FOR TRANSLATION

557. I. 1. ἐνταῦθα ἔστησαν οἱ Ἕλληνες. 2. καὶ οἱ
μετὰ Ἀριαίου [1] οὐκέτι ἵστανται. 3. καὶ ἀνίστασαν τοὺς
στρατιώτᾱς. 4. φύλακας δὲ καθίστασαν. 5. Κῦρος
δὲ ψῑλὴν ἔχων τὴν κεφαλὴν εἰς τὴν μάχην καθίστατο.
6. ὁ δὲ Κῦρος βουλεύεται ὅπως μήποτε ἔσται ἐπὶ τῷ
ἀδελφῷ, ἀλλά, ἢν δύνηται, βασιλεύσει ἀντ᾽ ἐκείνου.
7. ἐπειρῶντο δ᾽ ἀποδρᾶναι· καὶ οὗτος ἀποδρὰς ᾤχετο.[2]

---

[1] *Ariaeus and his men.*   [2] § 318.

8. Ξενοφῶν δ' ἐφοβεῖτο μὴ οὐ δύναιτο[1] ἐκ τῆς χώρᾱς
ἐξελθεῖν τῆς βασιλέως. 9. Κῦρος δ' οὖν ἀνέβη ἐπὶ τὰ
ὄρη, οὐδενὸς κωλύοντος. 10. τοῦτον τὸν ποταμὸν δια-
βὰς ἐξελαύνει διὰ Φρυγίᾱς. 11. ὥστε ἠναγκάσθη ὁ
Ξενοφῶν ἀναστῆναι καὶ εἰπεῖν τάδε. 12. ἐπειδὴ δὲ
πάντας παρήλασεν, ἔστησε τὸ ἅρμα πρὸ τῆς φάλαγγος
μέσης.[2] 13. καὶ πρίασθαι τὸν σῖτον οὐκ ἦν[3] εἰ μὴ[4] ἐν
τῇ Λῡδίᾳ ἀγορᾷ. 14. καὶ οἱ ὄνοι, ἐπεί τις διώκοι,[5] ἐπὶ
πολὺ[6] δραμόντες ἔστασαν.

II. 15. καὶ ἔμεινε πολὺν χρόνον ἑστώς. 16. ἐπεὶ δὲ
Ἀρταξέρξης κατέστη εἰς τὴν βασιλείᾱν, μετεπέμψατο
Κῦρον τὸν ἑαυτοῦ ἀδελφόν. 17. ἐν μέσῳ ἡμῶν καὶ
βασιλέως ὁ Τίγρης ποταμός ἐστιν, ὃν οὐκ ἂν δυναί-
μεθα ἄνευ πλοίων διαβῆναι. 18. τὰς δὲ ὄρνῑθας ἄν τις
ταχὺ ἀνιστῇ,[7] ἔστι[8] λαμβάνειν. 19. ἔχει δὲ Κῦρος
δύναμιν καὶ πεζὴν καὶ ἱππικήν, ἣν πάντες ὁρῶμέν τε καὶ
ἐπιστάμεθα.

III. 1. The soldiers cannot cross[9] this river without
boats. 2. Cyrus after halting[10] his chariot took his place
in the battle.

---

[1] § 438. a.	[2] § 192.	[3] *it was not possible.*
[4] *except.*	[5] § 417.	[6] *for a long distance.*
[7] § 399.	[8] § 102.	[9] 2 aor.
[10] *having halted.*		

LVII

THE INFLECTION OF MI–VERBS (*Continued*): τίθημι, ἵημι.
DELIBERATIVE SUBJUNCTIVE. ACCUSATIVE ABSO–
LUTE

558. Learn the inflection of τίθημι in the present system
active and middle (= passive), and in the second aorist,
active and middle (§ 646).

559. τίθημι is a reduplicated present, built on the theme
θε- (cp. § 551) thus : τί-θη-μι. The vowel of the theme is
long (η) in the singular of the present indicative active,
and in the first person singular of the imperfect indicative
active. The second and third persons singular of the
imperfect indicative active are formed like the corresponding persons of contract verbs in -έω thus : ἐτίθεις, ἐτίθει.
Similarly the second person singular of the present imperative active is τίθει.

560. The second aorist indicative active of τίθημι is
wanting in the singular number; its place is supplied by
first aorist forms with the irregular suffix -κα, -κας, -κε. So
the inflection of the aorist indicative active is as follows :

ἔθηκα	⎫		ἔθεμεν	⎫	
ἔθηκας	⎬ 1 Aor.	ἔθετον	ἔθετε	⎬ 2 Aor.
ἔθηκε(ν)	⎭	ἐθέτην	ἔθεσαν	⎭

561. Learn the inflection of ἵημι (§ 649), which is
nearly like τίθημι. This is also a reduplicated present,
from the theme ἑ-. The theme when augmented becomes
εἱ-, which is its form in the second aorist (but see the
paradigm below, § 562) and perfect tenses.

562. The second aorist indicative active, like that of
τίθημι, is wanting in the singular; and these forms are
supplied by an irregular first aorist in -κα, etc., as follows:

ἧκα			εἷμεν	
ἧκας	1 Aor.	εἷτον	εἷτε	2 Aor.
ἧκε(ν)		εἵτην	εἷσαν	

563. Learn the declension of τιθείς and θείς, which are
declined alike (§ 620).   Similarly are declined ἱείς and εἵς.
Cp. λυθείς (§ 388).

564. Deliberative subjunctive. — The subjunctive of the
first person may be used in a deliberative question.   The
negative is μή.

ποῖ φύγω; whither shall I flee?

τί μὴ μένω τὸ τέλος; why shall I not wait for the end?

565. Such a subjunctive, in an indirect question, is
retained after a primary tense of the verb of *asking;* but
the subjunctive may be changed to the same tense of the
optative if the sequence is secondary:

ἤρετο τὸν παῖδα εἰ παίσειεν αὐτόν he asked the boy whether he
should strike him.

The direct question was παίσω (aor. subjv.) *αὐτόν; shall
I strike him?*

566. Accusative absolute. — The participles of impersonal verbs may be used in the accusative singular neuter
in an absolute construction (cp. the genitive absolute,
§ 401).   The use is generally concessive (*although*):

ἐξὸν τοῖς βαρβάροις φίλους εἶναι, τοὺς Ἕλληνας αἱρήσονται though it
is possible (*lit.* it being possible, cp. ἔξ-εστι) for them to be
friends to the barbarians, they will choose the Greeks.

567.   VOCABULARY LVII

ἀνδράποδον, ου, τό (ἀνήρ and πούς):   λίθος, ου, ὁ: *stone.* Litho-graphy
  slave taken in war.   (γράφω).
ἀφ-ίημι: *let go away, dismiss.*   ποῖ; interr. adv.: *whither? where?*
βάλλω (for βαλ + yω, themes βαλ-,   συν-τίθημι: *place* or *set together*;
  βλη-), βαλῶ, ἔβαλον, βέβληκα,   MID. place oneself in agree-
  βέβλημαι, ἐβλήθην: *throw, hurl,*   ment with somebody, *agree*
  pelt.* Often with acc. of pers.   with somebody (dat.), *make a*
  and dat. of means.   compact.* May be followed by
εἰρήνη, ης, ἡ: *peace.* Irene.   inf. of indir. disc.
ἐπι-τίθημι: *put* or *place upon*; *put*   τίθημι, θήσω, ἔθηκα and ἔθετον, τέ-
  or *inflict* punishment (δίκην)   θηκα, ἐτέθην: *put, set.* τίθε-
  on somebody (τινί); MID. *set*   σθαι τὰ ὅπλα: *set down one's*
  oneself upon, attack,* with dat.   arms, rest one's arms on the
ἵημι, ἥσω, ἧκα and εἷτον, εἷκα, εἷμαι,   ground;* therefore (1) *take a*
  εἵθην: *send, hurl* (with some-   military position, take one's*
  thing, in dat.); MID. *hurl one-   post;* (2) *halt.*
  self, hasten.*

            EXERCISES FOR TRANSLATION

568. I. 1. τοὺς δ' ὁπλίτᾱς θέσθαι ἐκέλευσε τὰ ὅπλα.
2. οἱ δ' ὁπλῖται ἔθεντο τὰ ὅπλα.   3. καὶ ἵενται πολλοὶ
εἴσω καὶ νῑκῶσι τοὺς πολεμίους.   4. ἐπεὶ δ' εἶδον
ἀλλήλους, οἱ Ἕλληνες ἵεντο ἐπὶ τοὺς ἀνθρώπους.   5. καὶ
ἀφίεσαν τοὺς Ἕλληνας.   6. τοῖς δὲ στρατηγοῖς τῶν
Ἑλλήνων ἔδοξε πάντα τὰ ἀνδράποδα ἐν τῇ στρατιᾷ
ἀφεῖναι.   7. ὁ δὲ συντίθεται αὐτοῖς εἰς τὴν ὑστεραίᾱν[1]
παρέσεσθαι[2] ἔχων σῑτία καὶ ποτά.   8. Κῦρος ἔφη
ἐθέλειν[3] ἐπιθεῖναι τὴν[4] δίκην Ἀβροκόμᾳ.   9. οὐκ ἐθέλω
ἐλθεῖν πρὸς αὐτόν, δεδιὼς[5] μὴ λαβών με δίκην μοι
ἐπιθῇ.   10. καὶ Ἀριαῖος κελεύει ὑμᾶς φυλάττεσθαι

---

[1] *on the morrow.*   [2] In dir. disc. παρέσομαι (§ 110. *a* and *c*).
[3] § 110. *a* and *c*.   [4] Cp. § 281. I. 2, footnote 1.
[5] *fearing;* from δέδια = δέδοικα.

μὴ ὑμῖν ἐπιθῶνται τῆς νυκτὸς[1] οἱ βάρβαροι. 11. καὶ οὔτε ἐπέθετο αὐτοῖς οὐδεὶς οὔτε πρὸς τὴν γέφῡραν οὐδεὶς ἦλθεν. 12. ποῖ φύγωμεν; 13. οὐχ ἕξουσιν ὅποι φύγωσιν. 14. ἐξὸν εἰρήνην ἔχειν Κλέαρχος αἱρεῖται πολεμεῖν.

II. 15. ἐξὸν δὲ χρήματα ἔχειν, Κλέαρχος αἱρεῖται τούτοις εἰς[2] πόλεμον χρῆσθαι. 16. οἱ δ' Ἕλληνες ἐφοβοῦντο μὴ οἱ πολέμιοι ἐπιθεῖντο αὐτοῖς. 17. δοκεῖ δέ μοι ἀξιοῦν Κῦρον ἀφιέναι ἡμᾶς. 18. πέμπωμεν ἄνδρας τινὰς ἢ πάντας; 19. ἐβουλεύοντο δὲ εἰ πέμποιεν ἄνδρας τινὰς ἢ πάντας. 20. οἱ δ' ἐπὶ τῶν ἄκρων βάρβαροι ἔβαλλον λίθοις τοὺς ἐπιτιθεμένους.

III. 1. Although it is possible for the general to inflict punishment on the slaves, he wishes to let them go. 2. The soldiers used to hurl their spears[3] a long way.[4]

---

[1] § 155.

[2] *for*, *i.e.* to spend this *on*.

[3] §§ 141; 336. 5.

[4] μακρᾱν (§ 142) agreeing with ὁδόν understood.

Fig. 22. — ἅρμα.

LVIII

THE INFLECTION OF MI–VERBS (*Continued*): δίδωμι, ἑάλων OR ἥλων, ἔγνων

569. Learn the inflection of δίδωμι *give* in the present system active and middle (= passive) and in the second aorist, active and middle (§ 646).

570. δίδωμι is a reduplicated present, like ἵστημι and τίθημι, built on the theme δο- thus: δί-δω-μι. The vowel of the theme is long (ω) in the singular of the present indicative active. The singular of the imperfect indicative active is formed like the corresponding singular of a contract verb in -όω thus: ἐδίδουν, ἐδίδους, ἐδίδου. Similarly the second person singular of the present imperative active is δίδου.

571. The second aorist indicative active of δίδωμι is wanting in the singular number; its place is supplied by first aorist forms with the irregular suffix -κα, -κας, -κε (cp. ἔθηκα and ἧκα). So the inflection of the aorist indicative active is as follows:

ἔδωκα		ἔδομεν	
ἔδωκας ⎱ 1 Aor.	ἔδοτον	ἔδοτε ⎱ 2 Aor.	
ἔδωκε(ν) ⎰	ἐδότην	ἔδοσαν ⎰	

572. It is convenient to group together four irregular forms of the second aorist active imperative, in the second person singular: θές (τίθημι, § 646), ἕς (ἵημι, § 649), δός (δίδωμι, § 646), and σχές (ἔχω, 2 aor. ἔσχον). The last named resembles the other forms only in using -ς for -θι as the personal ending.

573. As mentioned before (§ 553), some ω-verbs have second aorists inflected like those of μι-verbs. Here are included the second aorists of ἀλίσκομαι *be captured*, and γιγνώσκω *know*. Following are the synopses:

	a.		*b.*
Indic.	ἑάλων or ἥλων		ἔγνων
Subjv.	ἁλῶ		γνῶ
Opt.	ἁλοίην		γνοίην
Imv.	wanting		γνῶθι
Inf.	ἁλῶναι		γνῶναι
Partic.	ἁλούς, ἁλοῦσα, ἁλόν		γνούς, γνοῦσα, γνόν
G.	ἁλόντος, ἁλούσης, ἁλόντος		γνόντος, γνούσης, γνόντος
	etc.		etc.

574. These two verbs (ἀλίσκομαι and γιγνώσκω), differing from δίδωμι, retain ω throughout the second aorist indicative, imperative (except the third person plural), and infinitive (cp., on the contrary, ἔδοσαν, δότω, etc.):

SECOND AORIST INDICATIVE OF γιγνώσκω

1.	ἔγνων		ἔγνωμεν
2.	ἔγνως	ἔγνωτον	ἔγνωτε
3.	ἔγνω	ἐγνώτην	ἔγνωσαν

IMPERATIVE

2.	γνῶθι	γνῶτον	γνῶτε
3.	γνώτω	γνώτων	γνόντων

The subjunctive and optative are inflected like δῶ and δοίην.

575. Learn the declension of διδούς and δούς, which are declined alike (§ 621). Similarly are declined ἁλούς and γνούς.

576.   VOCABULARY LVIII

ἁλ-ίσκομαι (themes ἁλ- and ἁλο-),
ἁλώσομαι, ἑάλων or ἤλων, ἑάλωκα
or ἤλωκα : *be taken, be captured.*
Used as pass. of αἱρέω.

ἀπο-σῴζω : *save from* something ;
bring safely back.

βαρβαρικός, ή, όν (βάρβαρος) : *foreign, barbarian, not Greek.* Bar-
baric.

δεξιός, ά, όν : *right, on the right
hand* or *side.* δεξιά, ᾶς, ἡ (supply χείρ) : *the right hand,* as a
pledge. Lat. *dexter.*

δια-βάλλω : *accuse falsely, slander.*
Diabolic (δια-βολικός).

δια-δίδωμι : *give from hand to
hand, distribute.*

δίδωμι, δώσω, ἔδωκα and ἔδοτον,
δέδωκα, δέδομαι, ἐδόθην : *give ;*
sometimes *offer* (in pres. and
impf.). δίκην διδόναι : *give
satisfaction, suffer punishment.* Cp. δῶρον. Lat. *dō,
dōnum.*

ἐκ-λείπω : *leave out, abandon ;*
(intr.) *leave off, fail.* Eclipse.

λόγχη, ης, ἡ : *spear point, spear.*

παρα-δίδωμι : *give over, surrender ;
pass along* (a watchword : σύνθημα).

EXERCISES FOR TRANSLATION

577. I. 1. ὁ δὲ Κῦρος δίδωσιν αὐτῷ ἐξ μηνῶν[1] μισθόν. 2. καὶ ἡ Κίλισσα ἐλέγετο Κύρῳ δοῦναι διὰ
φιλίᾱν χρήματα πολλά. 3. φίλος τε ἐβούλετο εἶναι
τοῖς μέγιστον δυναμένοις,[2] ἵνα ἀδικῶν μὴ διδοίη δίκην.
4. συμβουλεύω ὑμῖν μὴ παραδοῦναι τὰ ὅπλα. 5. ἐπεὶ
δὲ Κῦρος οὐκ ἔδωκε πιστά, Τισσαφέρνης διαβάλλει
αὐτὸν πρὸς τὸν ἀδελφόν. 6. ἔγνωσαν οἱ στρατιῶται
ὅτι κενὸς ὁ φόβος εἴη. 7. ταύτην τὴν πόλιν ἐξέλιπον
οἱ ἄνθρωποι, καὶ οὕτως ἑάλω. 8. Κλέαρχος δ᾽ εἶπεν ὅτι οὐ τῶν νῑκώντων[3] εἴη τὰ ὅπλα παραδιδόναι.
9. ταῦτα τὰ δῶρα τοῖς φίλοις διεδίδου. 10. φοβοίμην

---

[1] § 278.
[2] *the most powerful.*
[3] *the part of,* etc.; cp. §§ 229, 232. I. 10, 540. II. 15.

δ' ἂν τῷ ἡγεμόνι ἕπεσθαι ᾧ[1] Κῦρος δοίη.[2] 11. ἐντεῦθεν διδόᾱσιν οἱ μὲν Πέρσαι βαρβαρικὴν λόγχην τοῖς Ἕλλησιν, οἱ δὲ Ἕλληνες ἐκείνοις Ἑλληνικήν. 12. ἐὰν δὲ μὴ διδῷ ταῦτα τὰ πλοῖα, ἡγεμόνα αἰτῶμεν[3] Κῦρο .

II. 13. Συέννεσις ἔδωκε Κύρῳ χρήματα πολλὰ εἰς[4] τὴν στρατιάν. 14. καὶ τῷ κωμάρχῃ ἐδίδοσαν λαμβάνειν[5] ὅ τι βούλοιτο. 15. ταῦτα δὲ γνοὺς ἠτούμην βασιλέᾱ δοῦναι ἐμοὶ ἀποσῶσαι[6] ὑμᾶς εἰς τὴν Ἑλλάδα. 16. καὶ Τισσαφέρνης καὶ ὁ τῆς βασιλέως γυναικὸς ἀδελφὸς δεξιᾱς ἔδοσαν τοῖς τῶν Ἑλλήνων στρατηγοῖς. 17. ὁ δ' ἀνὴρ οὐχ ἥλω ἐν τῇ κώμῃ. 18. καὶ μισθὸν οὐκ ἐδίδου ὁ σατράπης. 19. ἀνέστησαν οἱ Ἕλληνες καὶ εἶπον ὅτι ὥρᾱ[7] φύλακας καθιστάναι καὶ σύνθημα παραδιδόναι.

III. 1. Then the generals knew[8] that it was not safe to remain. 2. We gave pledges to the captains of the Greeks. 3. I should fear to embark[9] on the boats which Cyrus might give us.

---

[1] § 285.

[2] This relative clause has the construction of the protasis of a less vivid future condition (§ 267), the conclusion being expressed by **φοβοίμην ἄν**. In this sentence **ᾧ**, attracted from **ὅν** to the case of its antecedent **ἡγεμόνι**, is equivalent to **εἴ τινα**. The less vivid future type of the conditional relative protasis (introduced by **ὅς, ὅτε, ἐπεί**, etc.) is comparatively rare.

[3] § 244.   [4] Cp. § 568. II. 15.   [5] *permission to take.*

[6] *permission to bring* you *safely back.*

[7] § 230.   [8] 2 aor.   [9] **ἐμ-βαίνειν** with **εἰς** and acc.

Fig. 23. — λόγχη.

LIX

THE INFLECTION OF MI–VERBS *(Continued)*: δείκνῡμι,
ἔδῡν, κεῖμαι. WISHES

578. Learn the inflection of δείκνῡμι *show* in the present
system active and middle (= passive), § 648.

579. The final vowel of the theme is long (ῡ) in the
singular of the present and imperfect indicative active, and
in the second person singular of the present imperative
active.

580. This verb has a regular first aorist (ἔδειξα), but no
second aorist. A second aorist of the μι-form, however, is
seen in ἔδῡν from δύω *enter, set, sink* (used of the sun).
Its second aorist synopsis is as follows:

Indic. ἔδῡν; subjv. δύω; opt. wanting; imv. δῦθι; inf. δῦναι; partic.
δύς, δῦσα, δύν (gen. δύντος, δύσης, δύντος).

Learn the inflection of this second aorist (§ 648).

581. The subjunctive and optative of verbs in -ῡμι are
formed exactly like the corresponding moods of ω-verbs,
without contraction. And even in the other moods thematic forms (*i.e.* ω-forms) also occur. Thus δεικνύει is
found along with δείκνῡσι; ἐδείκνυε with ἐδείκνῡ; and δει-
κνύων as well as δεικνύς.

582. Learn the declension of δεικνύς and δύς, which are
declined alike (§ 619).

583. Learn the inflection of κεῖμαι *lie, be placed, be situated* (§ 654). This verb and its compounds are used as
perfect passives of τίθημι *place* and its compounds.

584. Possible wishes. — Wishes that refer to future time are expressed by the present or aorist optative *without* ἄν. This optative is sometimes introduced by εἴθε or εἰ γάρ *if only, would that*. The negative is μή:

> μὴ οἱ θεοὶ ταῦτα δοῖεν may the gods not grant this.
> σῴζοισθε or εἴθε σῴζοισθε may you be saved.

585 Impossible wishes. — Wishes that cannot be realized refer to present or past time. They may be expressed by the imperfect indicative (of *present* time) or the aorist indicative (of *past* time); these tenses must be introduced by εἴθε or εἰ γάρ. The negative is μή:

εἴθε οἱ θεοὶ ταῦτα μὴ ἔδοσαν would that the gods had not granted this.

586. A wish that cannot be realized may also be expressed by ὤφελον, ες, ε (2 aor. of ὀφείλω *owe*), *I, you,* or *he ought* with the present or aorist infinitive:

ὤφελε Κῦρος ζῆν would that Cyrus were alive (*lit.* Cyrus ought to be living).

587. VOCABULARY LIX

ἀνα-παύω : *make cease* ; MID. *rest.*

ἀπ-όλλυμι (ὄλλυμι for ὄλ-νυ-μι, themes ὀλ-, ὀλε- ; ὀλῶ, ὤλεσα, ὀλώλεκα [§ 447] and 2 pf. ὄλωλα, ὠλόμην) : *destroy, lose* ; MID. and 2 pf. act., *perish, be lost.*

αὐτοῦ (cp. αὐτός), adv. : *in the very place, here, there.*

δείκνῡμι (and δεικνύω, theme δεικ-), δείξω, ἔδειξα, δέδειχα, δέδειγμαι, ἐδείχθην : *show, point out.*

δέομαι, δεήσομαι, δεδέημαι, ἐδεήθην, dep. pass. : *want, need* ; *desire, ask, beg.* Often with gen. or

with gen. of pers. and inf. Cp. δεῖ.

δύω (and δύνω), δύσω, ἔδῡσα (trans.), ἔδῡν (intr.), δέδῡκα, δέδυμαι, ἐδύθην : *enter, set* (used of the sun).

ἐπι-δείκνῡμι : *show, point out* ; mid. in sense of act. and also *distinguish oneself.*

ἐπί-κειμαι : *lie upon, attack,* with dat.

ἥλιος, ου, ὁ : *sun.* Helio-trope (τρέπω *turn*).

κατά-κειμαι : *lie down.*

κεῖμαι, κείσομαι : *lie, lie outstretched*
as the dead on the battlefield.
This verb is used as the pass.
of the pf. tenses of τίθημι, in
the meaning *be placed, be set*.
With τὰ ὅπλα κεῖται cp. the
act. θέσθαι τὰ ὅπλα.

κοινός, ή, όν : *common, in common,
general*.

Μῆδοι, ων, οἱ : the *Medes*.

μήν, postpositive adv. : *in truth,*

certainly. γε μήν : *to be sure,
at any rate*.

νεκρός, οῦ, ὁ : *dead body, corpse*.
Cp. Lat. *necō*. Necro-logy (λόγος *account*).

ὄμ-νῡ-μι (and ὀμ-νύω, themes ὀμ-,
ὀμο), ὀμοῦμαι, ὤμοσα, ὀμώμοκα
(§ 447), ὀμώμο(σ)μαι, ὠμό-
(σ)θην : *swear, promise with
an oath, take oath*.

EXERCISES FOR TRANSLATION

588. I. 1. ὁ δὲ τὴν ἐπιστολὴν λαβὼν Κύρῳ δείκνῡ-
σιν.   2. ταῦτα εἰπὼν ἐδείκνυε πολλὰ καὶ καλὰ χρήματα.   3. τὰς δὲ κεφαλὰς τῶν νεκρῶν ἐπεδείκνυσαν
τοῖς Ἕλλησιν.   4. ἦν οὖν τῆς ὥρας [1] μικρὸν πρὸ δύντος
ἡλίου.   5. Κῦρος δὲ τὸν θώρακα ἐνέδῡ,[2] καὶ ἀναβὰς
ἐπὶ τὸν ἵππον τὰ παλτὰ εἰς τὰς χεῖρας ἔλαβεν.   6. ἐνταῦθα λέγεται ἡ βασιλέως γυνὴ φυγεῖν, ὅτε ἀπώλλυσαν
τὴν ἀρχὴν ὑπὸ Περσῶν Μῆδοι.   7. ὤμνυτε δὲ ἡμῖν
τοὺς αὐτοὺς φίλους [3] καὶ ἐχθροὺς νομιεῖν.[4] 8. εἴς γε
μὴν ἀρετὴν ἐπιδείκνυσ᾽αι ἐβούλετο.   9. ἐκ δὲ τούτου [5]
ἄλλοι ἀνίσταντο ἐπιδεικνύντες οἷα εἴη [6] ἡ ἀπορία.
10. μὴ γενοίμεθα ζῶντες ἐπὶ τοῖς πολεμίοις.   11. οἱ
δὲ πολέμιοι εὐθὺς ἐπέκειντο αὐτοῖς.   12. Χειρίσοφος
ἡγοῖτο.   13. πολλά μοι καὶ ἀγαθὰ γένοιτο.   14. ἔκειντο
δὲ πολλοὶ ἐν τῷ πεδίῳ.

II. 15. καὶ τῶν ὑποζυγίων καὶ τῶν ἀνδραπόδων πολλὰ

---

[1] *the time was*, lit. *it was of the hour*, part. gen. with the following words.
[2] *put on*, lit. *entered*, 2 aor. of ἐν-δύω.
[3] *the same men as friends.*   [4] § 519.
[5] *and thereupon.*   [6] § 345.

ἀπώλετο.   16. ἤρξαντο καταβαίνειν πρὸς τοὺς ἄλλους
ἔνθα τὰ ὅπλα ἔκειτο.   17. καὶ λέγεται δεηθῆναι ἡ
Κίλισσα Κύρου ἐπιδεῖξαι τὸ στράτευμα αὐτῇ.   18. κα-
τακείμεθα ὥσπερ ἐξὸν[1] ἀναπαύεσθαι.   19. ἕως δ' ἂν
αὐτοῦ μένωμεν, πάντες δεόμεθα κοινῆς σωτηρίας· πολλοὶ γὰρ ἀπόλλυνται.

III. 1. We took oaths[2] not[3] to be enemies[4] to one
another.   2. Many men lay prostrate on the plain after
the battle.   3. They gladly show[5] their possessions to
Cyrus.

LX

IRREGULAR MI-VERBS: εἶμι, φημί, οἶδα, AND εἰμί
(Completed and Reviewed)

589. Learn the inflection of εἶμι *I am going, I shall go*
(§ 651); φημί *I say* (§ 652); and οἶδα *I know* (§ 655).
Review the inflection of εἰμί *I am* (§ 650).

590.   VOCABULARY LX

ἀ δύνατος, ον (δύναμαι): *impos-*
  sible.

ἄπ-ειμι (εἶμι): *go away; go back,*
  return.

δι-δά-σκω (theme διδαχ-), διδάξω,
  ἐδίδαξα, δεδίδαχα, δεδίδαγμαι, ἐδι-
  δάχθην: *teach.* Didactic.

εἶ-μι, impf. ᾖα: *go, shall go*; pres.
  serving as fut. of ἔρχομαι. Lat.
  eō, īre.

ἔξ-ειμι (εἶμι): *go out, go forth.*

ἔπ-ειμι (εἶμι): *go or come on, ap-*
  proach.

θόρυβος, ου, ὁ: *noise.*

---

[1] § 566; this use of the acc. absolute is conditional, as is proved by ὥσπερ
use as if.   [2] Use impf.

[3] § 519. *b.*   [4] Nom. (§ 110. *d*).   [5] Use δείκνυμι.

κάμ-νω (theme καμ-), fut. καμοῦμαι, 2 aor. ἔκαμον, pf. κέκμηκα : *labor, be weary*.

κραυγή, ῆς, ἡ : *outcry*.

οἶδα (2 pf. with pres. meaning), ᾔδη (2 plup.) or ᾔδειν, εἴσομαι (fut.) : *know*.

φέρω (themes φερ-, οἰ-, ἐνεκ-, ἐνεγκ-),

οἴσω, ἤνεγκα or ἤνεγκον, ἐνήνοχα, ἐνήνεγμαι, ἠνέχθην : *bear, carry; carry away, receive* (as pay). Cp. Lat. *ferō*.

φη-μί (theme φα-), φήσω, ἔφησα : *say, declare*. οὔ φημι (cp. Lat. *negō*): *deny, say . . . not* (§ 156. 1. *a*). Cp. Lat. *fārī*.

EXERCISES FOR TRANSLATION

591. I. 1. οἶδα δεξιᾶς δεδομένᾱς.[1] 2. αὐτὸς δ' οὐκ ἔφη ἰέναι. 3. ἔδοξεν αὐτοῖς ἀπιέναι. 4. ἀλλὰ ἰόντων, εἰδότες ὅτι[2] κακίους εἰσὶ περὶ ἡμᾶς ἢ ἡμεῖς περὶ ἐκείνους. 5. ἢν οὖν ἴητε σὺν ἡμῖν, δᾱρεικὸν ἕκαστος ὑμῶν οἴσει τοῦ[3] μηνός.[4] 6. σκεπτέον μοι δοκεῖ εἶναι ὅπως ὡς ἀσφαλέστατα ἄπιμεν καὶ ὅπως τὰ ἐπιτήδεια ἕξομεν. 7. ἐγὼ οὖν φημι ὑμᾶς χρῆναι διαβῆναι τὸν Εὐφρᾱτην ποταμὸν πρὶν δῆλον εἶναι ὅ τι οἱ ἄλλοι Ἕλληνες ἀποκρινοῦνται Κύρῳ. 8. καὶ τοὺς Ἕλληνας ἔφασαν οἴχεσθαι · ὅποι δέ, οὐκ ἔφασαν εἰδέναι. 9. τὸν δ' οὖν Εὐφρᾱτην ἴσμεν ὅτι ἀδύνατον[5] διαβῆναι κωλυόντων πολεμίων. 10. κραυγῇ πολλῇ ἐπίᾱσιν. 11. ὅπως δὲ εἰδῆτε εἰς οἷον ἔρχεσθε ἀγῶνα ὑμᾶς εἰδὼς διδάξω. 12. καὶ αὐτοὶ ἐβουλεύοντο εἰ αὐτοῦ μένοιεν[6] ἢ ἀπίοιεν ἐπὶ τὸ στρατόπεδον.

II. 13. ταῦτα δὲ λέγων θορύβου ἤκουσε[7] διὰ τῶν τάξεων ἰόντος. 14. ὅτῳ δὲ Μένων φαίη[8] φίλος εἶναι, τούτῳ δῆλος ἐγίγνετο ἐπιβουλεύων. 15. τοὺς δ' ἀνθρώπους ἠρώτων εἴ τινα εἰδεῖεν ἄλλην ὁδὸν ἢ τὴν φανερᾱν.

---

[1] § 441.   [2] § 442.   [3] *each*.   [4] § 155.
[5] §§ 223, 291.   [6] §§ 363, 564, 565.   [7] § 193.   [8] § 417.

16. Κλέαρχε καὶ Πρόξενε καὶ οἱ ἄλλοι οἱ παρόντες
Ἕλληνες, οὐκ ἴστε ὅ τι ποιεῖτε.   17. ἐγὼ τοίνυν, ὦ
ἄνδρες, κάμνω ἤδη συσκευαζόμενος¹ καὶ τρέχων καὶ τὰ
ὅπλα φέρων καὶ ἐν τάξει ἰὼν καὶ φυλακὰς² φυλάττων
καὶ μαχόμενος.   18. ἅμα ἡλίῳ δύνοντι³ οἱ Ἕλληνες
ἐξῄεσαν ἐκ τῶν κωμῶν.

III. 1. Clearchus deliberated whether they should send⁴
some men⁵ or should all go to the camp.   2. They said
they did not know in what direction⁶ the barbarians had
gone.

---

¹ § 439.   ² § 181.   ³ *at sunset* (cp. § 157).
⁴ §§ 362, 564, 565.   ⁵ Omit *men*.   ⁶ ὅποι.

Fig. 24. — Sparta.

SELECTIONS FROM THE *ANABASIS*

[The following selections are from Xenophon's *Anabasis of Cyrus*. In places they are somewhat simplified, chiefly by the omission of unessential details.]

THE SUBJECT OF THE *ANABASIS*

Cyrus, a young and ambitious prince of Persia, plotted to wrest the throne from his elder brother Artaxerxes II, the reigning king (401 B.C.). So far as possible, he disguised his real purpose. But information of the plot was nevertheless laid before the Great King by his crafty satrap Tissaphernes.

Cyrus enlisted in his enterprise about thirteen thousand Greek soldiers, who were attracted by the desire to serve under so noble a leader and by the promise of large pay. The larger part of these assembled, under Cyrus's orders, at Sardis; and from this city they set forth in the spring of 401 B.C. Only after they had marched well into the interior were they informed of the real object of the expedition. Cyrus had also a host of Persians, said to have numbered a hundred thousand. They proved utterly unreliable. The leader of this "barbarian" force was the Persian Ariaeus.

The young prince was generous; he had persuasive manners and the enthusiasm of youth. He dazzled the common soldiers with his promises, and he commanded the loyalty of his officers by rich presents and favors. So he was able to win to his cause many really noble spirits among both Persians and Greeks. Not a few of these, as the sequel showed, were ready to prove their devotion by sacrificing their lives. Of his Greek generals the most prominent was the Spartan Clearchus, a fearless and exceedingly stern disciplinarian. The other Greek generals were faithful and in their way good men, also; but exception must be made of the Thessalian Menon, who was faithless and unprincipled.

By the village of Cunaxa, near Babylon, Cyrus met the royal army, which was commanded by the king in person (late in the summer of 401 B.C.). Cyrus's force was outnumbered eight times over, if reliance may be placed on the figures that are mentioned. Yet the issue of the battle might have been favorable to Cyrus, owing to the valor and success of his Greek mercenaries, if only he had not risked his own life. He was slain. And the Greeks, far from wishing any pretext for staying longer in the Persian empire, had only the desire to get back to Greek lands again.

They accomplished their wearisome and dangerous retreat during the winter of 401–400 B.C., striking through the country northward over mountains and, for the most part, through wild and hostile tribes. But almost at the beginning of their retreat, before they had passed out of the reach of Persia, they lost the leadership of their generals, including the intrepid Clearchus. These were entrapped and put to death through the agency of Tissaphernes.

At this point Xenophon, the Athenian, the author of the history, put himself forward as a leader. He had previously accompanied the expedition merely as a gentleman in search of adventure. He was now elected a general and appointed to the difficult position of commander of the rear guard, while Cheirisophus was chosen

to command the van. And under this leadership the
Greeks who have become known in history as " The Ten
Thousand" came, with losses, to Trebizond, one of the
Greek settlements on the Black Sea. After further adven-
tures they arrived finally in Ionia again (Cheirisophus had
meantime died).

Xenophon was the author of several interesting works
besides the *Anabasis of Cyrus*. And in addition to his
literary interests he was an ardent sportsman, fond of
horses, dogs, and hunting. He has left us a description
of his pleasant country-place in Elis, where later in life he
settled to enjoy his good fortune, surrounded by his family.
Here he engaged in the composition of his books and in
the delights of country life.

I. *The Greek soldiers and the inducements to join Cyrus's army*

οἱ πλεῖστοι τῶν στρατιωτῶν ἦσαν οὐ σπάνει βίου
ἐκπεπλευκότες ἐπὶ ταύτην τὴν μισθοφοράν, ἀλλὰ
τὴν Κύρου ἀρετὴν ἀκούοντες, οἱ μὲν καὶ ἄνδρας
ἄγοντες, οἱ δὲ καὶ προσανηλωκότες χρήματα, καὶ
5 τούτων ἕτεροι ἀποδεδρακότες πατέρας καὶ μητέρας,

I. 1. ἦσαν ἐκπεπλευκότες (ἐκ-
πλέω): *had sailed off* from their
homes.

οὐ σπάνει βίου: *not on account
of lack of means, not from lack
of livelihood.* σπάνει is dative of
cause (§ 403).

2. ἐπὶ ταύτην τὴν μισθοφοράν:
after this pay, i.e. to earn money
by service in Cyrus's army.

3. ἀκούοντες: expresses cause
(§ 213).

οἱ μὲν ... οἱ δέ: see § 99; the
words are appositives to οἱ πλεῖστοι.

ἄνδρας ἄγοντες: *bringing men
along, i.e.* enlisting soldiers with
the aid of the money that Cyrus
furnished.

4. προσανηλωκότες: *having
spent in addition* money of their
own; see προσαναλίσκω.

5. τούτων: partitive genitive
with ἕτεροι *others.*

οἱ δὲ καὶ τέκνα καταλιπόντες ὡς χρήματ' αὐτοῖς
κτησάμενοι ἥξοντες πάλιν, ἀκούοντες καὶ τοὺς ἄλλους τοὺς παρὰ Κύρῳ πολλὰ καὶ ἀγαθὰ πράττειν.
(vi. 4. 8.) ὁ δὲ Κῦρος στρατεύματι ἀληθινῷ ἐχρή-
10 σατο. καὶ γὰρ στρατηγοὶ καὶ λοχᾱγοί, οἳ χρημάτων
ἕνεκα πρὸς ἐκεῖνον ἔπλευσαν, ἔγνωσαν κερδαλεώτερον
εἶναι Κύρῳ καλῶς ὑπάρχειν ἢ τὸ κατὰ μῆνα κέρδος.
(i. 9. 17.)

II. *Cyrus leads his army into the heart of the Persian empire before
he meets serious resistance. The king's apparent unwilling-
ness to fight throws the invaders off their guard*

ἦν δὲ παρὰ τὸν Εὐφράτην πάροδος στενὴ μεταξὺ
τοῦ ποταμοῦ καὶ τῆς τάφρου ὡς εἴκοσι ποδῶν τὸ
εὖρος · ταύτην δὲ τὴν τάφρον βασιλεὺς ποιεῖ ἀντὶ
ἐρύματος, ἐπειδὴ πυνθάνεται Κῦρον προσελαύνοντα.
5 ταύτην δὴ τὴν πάροδον Κῦρός τε καὶ ἡ στρατιὰ

---

6. ὡς χρήματ' αὐτοῖς κτησάμενοι ἥξοντες πάλιν : *with the purpose
of returning again* (§ 332) *after
they had gained wealth for them*.

7. τοὺς ἄλλους τοὺς παρὰ Κύρῳ :
= τοὺς παρὰ Κύρῳ ἄλλους (§§ 67,
70), subject of πράττειν.

8. πολλὰ καὶ ἀγαθὰ πράττειν
(§ 110): *were making great for-
tunes*.

9. ἀληθινῷ : *trusty*.
ἐχρήσατο : *had the services of*.

11. κερδαλεώτερον εἶναι (§ 110) :
it was more profitable.

12. τὸ κατὰ μῆνα κέρδος :
monthly pay.

II. 2. εἴκοσι ποδῶν : see § 278.
τὸ εὖρος : see § 279.

3. ποιεῖ : *had made*.
ἀντὶ ἐρύματος : *for a defense*.

4. ἐπειδὴ πυνθάνεται : *when he
learned*. The present is frequently used by Xenophon when
a past tense is required by good
English style. ποιεῖ and πυνθάνεται are illustrations of the so-
called "historical present."

προσελαύνοντα : see § 441.

παρῆλθε καὶ ἐγένοντο εἴσω τῆς τάφρου. ταύτῃ μὲν
οὖν τῇ ἡμέρᾳ οὐκ ἐμαχέσατο βᾰσιλεύς, ἀλλ᾽ ὑποχωρούντων φανερὰ ἦσαν καὶ ἵππων καὶ ἀνθρώπων ἴχνη
πολλά. ἐνταῦθα Κῦρος Σῑλᾱνὸν καλέσᾱς τὸν Ἀμπρα-
10 κιώτην μάντιν ἔδωκεν αὐτῷ δᾱρεικοὺς τρισχῑλίους,
ὅτι τῇ ἑνδεκάτῃ ἀπ᾽ ἐκείνης ἡμέρᾳ προθῡόμενος εἶπεν
αὐτῷ ὅτι βασιλεὺς οὐ μαχεῖται δέκα ἡμερῶν, Κῦρος
δ᾽ εἶπεν, Οὐκ ἄρα ἔτι μαχεῖται, εἰ ἐν ταύταις οὐ μαχεῖται ταῖς ἡμέραις· ἐὰν δ᾽ ἀληθεύσῃς, ὑπισχνοῦμαί σοι
15 δέκα τάλαντα. τοῦτο τὸ χρῡσίον τότε ἀπέδωκεν, ἐπεὶ
παρῆλθον αἱ δέκα ἡμέραι. ἐπεὶ δ᾽ ἐπὶ τῇ τάφρῳ οὐκ
ἐκώλῡε βασιλεὺς τὸ Κύρου στράτευμα διαβαίνειν,
ἔδοξε καὶ Κύρῳ καὶ τοῖς ἄλλοις ἀπεγνωκέναι τοῦ
μάχεσθαι· ὥστε τῇ ὑστεραίᾳ Κῦρος ἐπορεύετο ἡμε-
20 λημένως μᾶλλον. τῇ δὲ τρίτῃ ἐπί τε τοῦ ἅρματος

---

6. **ταύτῃ τῇ ἡμέρᾳ**: see § 180.

7. **ὑποχωρούντων**: *retreating*, agrees with ἵππων and ἀνθρώπων.

8. **ἦσαν**: the subject is the neuter plural ἴχνη. This deviation from the rule (§ 71) occurs occasionally in the *Anabasis* and in other Greek.

9. **Ἀμπρακιώτην**: *Ambracian*, from the town Ambracia in Epirus.

11. **τῇ ἑνδεκάτῃ ἀπ᾽ ἐκείνης ἡμέρᾳ** (§ 180): *on the eleventh day before*, i.e. (in our idiom) *ten days before*. The Greeks, like the Romans, counted in the days at both ends of the reckoning. With ἀπ᾽ ἐκείνης supply τῆς ἡμέρᾱς.

12. **δέκα ἡμερῶν**: see § 155.

13. **Οὐκ ἄρα κτλ.**: the direct quotation is introduced by a capital letter (without quotation marks), § 2.

εἰ ... οὐ μαχεῖται: this apparently irregular negative (§ 106. *b*) is used because Cyrus quotes the exact words of the soothsayer above (l. 12).

14. **ἐὰν ἀληθεύσῃς**: see § 241.

17. **ἐκώλῡε ... διαβαίνειν**: see § 382. I. 1.

18. **ἔδοξε . . . ἀπ-εγνωκέναι** (from ἀπο-γιγνώσκω) **τοῦ μάχε-σθαι**: *he seemed to have abandoned the idea of fighting*.

19. **ἡμελημένως μᾶλλον**: *more carelessly*.

καθήμενος τὴν πορείᾶν ἐποιεῖτο καὶ ὀλίγους ἐν τάξει
ἔχων πρὸ αὐτοῦ, τὸ δὲ πολὺ αὐτῷ ἀνατεταραγμένον
ἐπορεύετο καὶ τῶν ὅπλων τοῖς στρατιώταις πολλὰ ἐπὶ
ἀμαξῶν ἤγετο καὶ ὑποζυγίων. (i. 7. 15–20.)

III. *The battle of Cunaxa, in which Cyrus encounters the Persian*
king and is slain

Καὶ ἤδη τε ἦν ἀμφὶ ἀγορὰν πλήθουσαν καὶ πλησίον ἦν ὁ σταθμὸς ἔνθα ἔμελλε καταλύειν, ἡνίκα
Πατηγύᾶς ἀνὴρ Πέρσης τῶν ἀμφὶ Κῦρον πιστῶν
προφαίνεται ἐλαύνων ἀνὰ κράτος ἱδροῦντι τῷ ἵππῳ,
5 καὶ εὐθὺς πᾶσιν οἷς ἐνετύγχανεν ἐβόᾱ καὶ βαρβαρικῶς καὶ Ἑλληνικῶς ὅτι βασιλεὺς σὺν στρατεύματι
πολλῷ προσέρχεται ὡς εἰς μάχην παρεσκευασμένος.
ἔνθα δὴ πολὺς τάραχος ἐγένετο · Κῦρός τε καταπη-
δήσᾱς ἀπὸ τοῦ ἅρματος τὸν θώρᾱκα ἐνέδῦ καὶ ἀνα-

---

21. **καθήμενος**: *sitting*, participle of κάθημαι, which is inflected
in § 653.

22. **τὸ δὲ πολύ**: supply τοῦ
στρατεύματος.

αὐτῷ: *for him*, dative of disadvantage (§ 53. *d*).

23. The order of the Greek
words rearranged for translation
is : πολλὰ τῶν ὅπλων ἤγετο (*were
carried*) τοῖς στρατιώταις (§ 53. *d*)
ἐπὶ ἀμαξῶν καὶ ὑποζυγίων.

III. 1. **ἀμφὶ ἀγορὰν πλήθου-**
σαν: *about the time of full market*,
the middle of the forenoon.

2. **σταθμός**: *stopping place* or

station (cp. ἵστημι) is the meaning here.

κατα-λύειν: *to unyoke* the pack
animals for the rest from the midday heat. **ἔμελλε** takes a present
infinitive as well as the future
(§ 156. 2).

3. **τῶν ἀμφὶ Κῦρον πιστῶν**:
partitive genitive. Cyrus had a
devoted bodyguard.

4. **ἱδροῦντι τῷ ἵππῳ**: *with his
horse in a sweat*, properly a dative
of means (§ 141).

5. **βαρβαρικῶς**: *in Persian*.

7. **ὡς … παρεσκευασμένος**: *apparently prepared*.

10 βὰς ἐπὶ τὸν ἵππον τὰ παλτὰ εἰς τὰς χεῖρας ἔλαβε,
τοῖς τε ἄλλοις πᾶσι παρήγγελλεν ἐξοπλίζεσθαι καὶ
καθίστασθαι εἰς τὴν ἑαυτοῦ τάξιν ἕκαστον. ἔνθα
δὴ σὺν πολλῇ σπουδῇ καθίσταντο, Κλέαρχος μὲν τὰ
δεξιὰ τοῦ κέρατος ἔχων πρὸς τῷ Εὐφράτῃ ποταμῷ,
15 Πρόξενος δὲ ἐχόμενος, οἱ δ᾽ ἄλλοι μετὰ τοῦτον, Μένων
δὲ τὸ εὐώνυμον κέρας ἔσχε τοῦ Ἑλληνικοῦ. Κῦρος
δὲ καὶ οἱ ἱππεῖς τούτου ὅσον ἐξακόσιοι ἔστησαν κατὰ
μέσον τοῦ βαρβαρικοῦ, ὡπλισμένοι θώραξι μὲν αὐτοὶ
καὶ παραμηριδίοις καὶ κράνεσι πάντες πλὴν Κύρου·
20 Κῦρος δὲ ψιλὴν ἔχων τὴν κεφαλὴν εἰς τὴν μάχην
καθίστατο. καὶ ἤδη τε ἦν μέσον ἡμέρᾶς καὶ οὔπω
καταφανεῖς ἦσαν οἱ πολέμιοι· ἡνίκα δὲ δείλη ἐγίγνετο, ἐφάνη κονιορτὸς ὥσπερ νεφέλη λευκή, χρόνῳ
δὲ συχνῷ ὕστερον ὥσπερ μελανίᾶ τις ἐν τῷ πεδίῳ ἐπὶ
25 πολύ. ὅτε δὲ ἐγγύτερον ἐγίγνοντο, τάχα δὴ αἱ λόγ-
χαι καὶ αἱ τάξεις καταφανεῖς ἐγίγνοντο. καὶ ἦσαν
ἱππεῖς μὲν λευκοθώρᾱκες ἐπὶ τοῦ εὐωνύμου τῶν πολε-
μίων· Τισσαφέρνης ἐλέγετο τούτων ἄρχειν· ἐχόμενοι
δὲ γερροφόροι, ἐχόμενοι δὲ ὁπλῖται σὺν ποδήρεσι

---

12. **ἕκαστον**: *each*, in apposition to the subject of καθίστασθαι;
ordered them each to take his place.

13. **τὰ δεξιὰ τοῦ κέρᾱτος** (§ 179):
the right wing. For the declension
of κέρᾱτος see § 602.

14. **πρός**: *beside.*

15. **ἐχόμενος**: *next.*

17. **ὅσον**: *about.*

20. **ψιλὴν ἔχων τὴν κεφαλήν**:
with his head unprotected by a
helmet. But Cyrus doubtless wore
the tiāra, the usual Persian head-
dress, which was a sort of turban.

22. **δείλη**: *early afternoon.*

23. **ἐφάνη**: *appeared*, 2 aor.
pass. of φαίνω.

χρόνῳ (§ 410) **συχνῷ ὕστερον**:
a considerable time later.

24. **ἐπὶ πολύ**: *over a long distance.*

29. **γερροφόροι**: supply ἦσαν.

30 ξυλίναις ἀσπίσιν. Αἰγύπτιοι δ' οὗτοι ἐλέγοντο εἶναι·
ἄλλοι δ' ἱππεῖς, ἄλλοι τοξόται. πάντες δ' οὗτοι κατὰ

FIG. 25. — δρεπανηφόρον ἅρμα.

ἔθνη ἐπορεύοντο. πρὸ δὲ αὐτῶν ἅρματα διαλείποντα
συχνὸν ἀπ' ἀλλήλων τὰ δὴ δρεπανηφόρα καλούμενα.
οἱ δὲ βάρβαροι ἐν ἴσῳ καὶ βραδέως προσῇσαν.
35 καὶ ἐν τούτῳ Κῦρος παρελαύνων αὐτὸς σὺν Πίγρητι
τῷ ἑρμηνεῖ καὶ ἄλλοις τρισὶν ἢ τέτταρσι τῷ Κλεάρχῳ
ἐβόα ἄγειν τὸ στράτευμα κατὰ μέσον τὸ τῶν πολεμίων, ὅτι ἐκεῖ βασιλεὺς εἴη · κἂν τοῦτ', ἔφη, νῑκῶμεν,
πάνθ' ἡμῖν πεποίηται. ἀλλ' ὁ Κλέαρχος οὐκ ἤθελεν
40 ἀποσπάσαι ἀπὸ τοῦ ποταμοῦ τὸ δεξιὸν κέρας, φοβού-

---

31. ἄλλοι: *besides*, lit. *other*.
Observe the omission of a conjunction before the second ἄλλοι; this
is due to a desire for a vivid and
concise style at this point.

    κατὰ ἔθνη: *nation by nation*.

32. ἅρματα: supply ἦν.

    διαλείποντα συχνόν: *distant a
considerable space*.

33. τὰ . . . καλούμενα: *the so-
called scythe-bearing* chariots.

34. ἐν ἴσῳ: *in step*.

37. κατὰ μέσον τὸ τῶν πολεμίων: *against the center of the
enemy*.

38. εἴη: this causal clause introduced by ὅτι *because* is really a
subordinate clause in indirect dis-

μένος μὴ κυκλωθείη ἑκατέρωθεν, τῷ δὲ Κύρῳ ἀπεκρίνατο ὅτι αὐτῷ μέλοι ὅπως καλῶς ἔχοι. καὶ ἐν τούτῳ
τῷ καιρῷ τὸ μὲν βαρβαρικὸν στράτευμα ὁμαλῶς
προῄει, τὸ δὲ Ἑλληνικὸν ἔτι ἐν τῷ αὐτῷ μένον συνε-
45 τάττετο ἐκ τῶν ἔτι προσιόντων. καὶ ὁ Κῦρος παρελαύνων οὐ πάνυ πρὸς αὐτῷ τῷ στρατεύματι κατεθεᾶτο
ἑκατέρωσε ἀποβλέπων εἴς τε τοὺς πολεμίους καὶ τοὺς
φίλους. ἰδὼν δὲ αὐτὸν ἀπὸ τοῦ Ἑλληνικοῦ Ξενοφῶν
Ἀθηναῖος, πελάσᾱς ὡς συναντῆσαι ἤρετο εἴ τι παραγ-
50 γέλλοι. ὁ δ' ἐπιστήσᾱς εἶπε καὶ λέγειν ἐκέλευε
πᾶσιν ὅτι καὶ τὰ ἱερὰ καλὰ καὶ τὰ σφάγια καλά.
ταῦτα δὲ λέγων θορύβου ἤκουσε διὰ τῶν τάξεων
ἰόντος, καὶ ἤρετο τίς ὁ θόρυβος εἴη. ὁ δὲ εἶπεν ὅτι
σύνθημα παρέρχεται δεύτερον ἤδη. καὶ Κῦρος ἐθαύ-

---

course, representing the thought
of Cyrus; therefore the optative
εἴη replaces the indicative
(§ 530).

κᾶν . . . νῑκῶμεν: protasis of
the more vivid future condition;
the apodosis is emphatically expressed as already accomplished,
πεποίηται. **πάνθ'** is for πάντα
(§§ 29, 31). For ἡμῖν see § 458.

41. **μὴ κυκλωθείη:** see § 438. *a.*

42. **ὅτι αὐτῷ μέλοι** (§ 260) **ὅπως
καλῶς ἔχοι** (§ 535. *a*): *that he was
taking care that all should be well;*
lit. *that it was a care to him how
it should be well.*

44. **ἐν τῷ αὐτῷ μένον:** *remaining in the same place;* μένον is a
pres. partic. neut. agreeing with
στράτευμα.

συν-ετάττετο: *was forming in
line.*

46. **οὐ πάνυ πρός:** *not very
near to.*

49. **πελάσᾱς ὡς συναντῆσαι:**
approaching so as to meet him.

50. **ἐπιστήσᾱς:** supply τὸν ἵππον.

51. **τὰ ἱερά:** *the* usual or ordinary *sacrifices;* **τὰ σφάγια:** *the
propitiatory offerings,* an extraor-
dinary service for the occasion.
Supply εἴη (§§ 260, 291) in the
predicate.

52. **θορύβου:** object of ἤκουσε,
which sometimes takes the *thing
heard* in the genitive.

53. **εἴη:** see § 345.

54. **παρέρχεται:** might have
been changed to what form? § 260.

55 μασε τίς παραγγέλλει καὶ ἤρετο ὅ τι εἴη τὸ σύνθημα.
ὁ δ' ἀπεκρίνατο Ζεὺς σωτὴρ καὶ νίκη. ὁ δὲ Κῦρος
ἀκούσᾱς 'Αλλὰ δέχομαί τε, ἔφη, καὶ τοῦτο ἔστω.
ταῦτα δ' εἰπὼν εἰς τὴν αὑτοῦ χώρᾱν ἀπήλαυνε. καὶ
οὐκέτι τρία ἢ τέτταρα στάδια διειχέτην τὼ φάλαγγε
60 ἀπ' ἀλλήλων ἡνίκα ἐπαιάνιζόν τε οἱ Ἕλληνες καὶ
ἤρχοντο ἀντίοι ἰέναι τοῖς πολεμίοις. καὶ ἅμα ἐφθέγ-
ξαντο πάντες οἷον τῷ 'Ενῡαλίῳ ἐλελίζουσι, καὶ πάντες
δὲ ἔθεον. λέγουσι δέ τινες ὡς καὶ ταῖς ἀσπίσι πρὸς
τὰ δόρατα ἐδούπησαν φόβον ποιοῦντες τοῖς ἵπποις.
65 πρὶν δὲ τόξευμα ἐξικνεῖσθαι ἐκκλίνουσιν οἱ βάρβαροι
καὶ φεύγουσι. καὶ ἐνταῦθα δὴ ἐδίωκον μὲν κατὰ κράτος οἱ Ἕλληνες, ἐβόων δὲ ἀλλήλοις μὴ θεῖν δρόμῳ,
ἀλλ' ἐν τάξει ἔπεσθαι. τὰ δ' ἅρματα ἐφέροντο τὰ
μὲν δι' αὐτῶν τῶν πολεμίων, τὰ δὲ καὶ διὰ τῶν 'Ελλή-
70 νων κενὰ ἡνιόχων. οἱ δ' ἐπεὶ προΐδοιεν, διίσταντο ·

---

56. Ζεὺς σωτὴρ καὶ νίκη: *Zeus
savior and victory*, the "watchword."

57. 'Αλλὰ δέχομαι: *Well, I accept it.*

58. εἰς τὴν αὑτοῦ χώρᾱν: *to his
own place.*

59. στάδια: see § 142.

δι-ειχέτην: impf. dual 3 pers.
of δι-έχω: *were separated.*

61. ἤρχοντο: from ἄρχομαι *begin.*

ἀντίοι: *to meet*; lit. *face to
face*; this adjective takes a dative.

62. οἷον: *what sort of shout,*
i.e. *the cry which.*

'Ενῡαλίῳ: *Enyalius*, a name of
Ares, god of war.

63. ταῖς ἀσπίσι: see § 141.

64. τοῖς ἵπποις: see § 53. *d.*

65. πρὶν . . . ἐξικνεῖσθαι: see
§ 524.

ἐκκλίνουσιν: historical present.
See note on p. 266, l. 4.

66. κατὰ κράτος: cp. ἀνὰ κράτος, § 443.

67. θεῖν δρόμῳ (§ 141). *to
charge on the run.*

68. τὰ μέν . . . τὰ δέ: § 99.

70. κενὰ ἡνιόχων: *empty of
charioteers.*

ἐπεὶ προΐδοιεν: *whenever they
saw them in front* (§ 417).

ἔστι δ' ὅστις καὶ κα⁻ελήφθη ὥσπερ ἐν ἱπποδρόμῳ
ἐκπλαγείς· καὶ οὐδὲν μέντοι οὐδὲ τοῦτον παθεῖν ἔφασαν, οὐδ' ἄλλος δὲ τῶν Ἑλλήνων ἐν ταύτῃ τῇ μάχῃ
ἔπαθεν οὐδεὶς οὐδέν, πλὴν ἐπὶ τῷ εὐωνύμῳ τοξευθῆναί
75 τις ἐλέγετο. Κῦρος δ' ὁρῶν τοὺς Ἕλληνας νῑκῶντας
τὸ καθ' αὑτοὺς καὶ διώκοντας, ἡδόμενος καὶ προσκυ-
νούμενος ἤδη ὑπὸ τῶν ἀμφ' αὐτόν, οὐδ' ὡς ἐξήχθη
διώκειν, ἀλλὰ συνεσπειραμένην ἔχων τὴν τῶν σὺν
ἑαυτῷ ἑξακοσίων ἱππέων τάξιν ἐπεμελεῖτο ὅ τι ποιή-
80 σει βασιλεύς. καὶ βασιλεὺς δὴ τότε μέσον ἔχων τῆ⸴
αὑτοῦ στρατιᾶς ὅμως ἔξω ἐγένετο τοῦ Κύρου εὐωνύμου κέρᾱτος. ἐπεὶ δ' οὐδεὶς ἐκ τοῦ ἀντίου αὐτῷ
ἐμάχετο οὐδὲ τοῖς αὐτοῦ τεταγμένοις ἔμπροσθεν, ἐπέ-
καμπτεν ὡς εἰς κύκλωσιν. ἔνθα δὴ Κῦρος δείσᾱς μὴ

---

71. **ἔστι δ' ὅστις**: *and a man,*
or *and somebody* ; lit. *there is who.*

72. **οὐδὲν** . . . **οὐδέ**: only one
of these negatives can be translated into English (§ 428).

οὐδέ: *not even.*

73. **οὐδ'** . . . **οὐδεὶς οὐδέν**: one
negative in English (§ 428).

74. **τοξευθῆναι**: see § 391.

75. **ὁρῶν**: *although he saw*
(§ 213. *c*).

76. **ἡδόμενος καὶ προσκυνούμε-
νος**: in the same construction as
ὁρῶν.

77. **οὐδ' ὥς**: *not even so, not
even under these circumstances.*

78. **διώκειν**: complementary infinitive.

συν-εσπειρᾱμένην : from συ-
σπειράομαι. The six hundred

horsemen were Cyrus's body-
guard.

79. **ἐπ-εμελεῖτο**: *watched to
see.*

80. **ἔχων**: *although he occupied*
(§ 213. *c*); the concessive force is
clearly indicated by the following
ὅμως *nevertheless.*

82. **κέρᾱτος**: for the construction see § 372.

ἐκ τοῦ ἀντίου: *from the opposing line.*

αὐτῷ: see § 317.

83. **τοῖς τεταγμένοις**: in the
same construction as αὐτῷ.

αὐτοῦ: to be taken with ἔμπροσθεν.

84. **ὡς εἰς κύκλωσιν**: *apparently for encircling* the army of
Cyrus, *i.e. for a flank march.*

85 ὄπισθεν γενόμενος κατακόψῃ τὸ Ἑλληνικὸν ἐλαύνει
ἀντίος · καὶ ἐμβαλὼν σὺν τοῖς ἑξακοσίοις νικᾷ τοὺς
πρὸ βασιλέως τεταγμένους καὶ εἰς φυγὴν ἔτρεψ:
τοὺς ἑξακισχῑλίους, καὶ ἀποκτεῖναι λέγεται αὐτὸς τῇ
ἑαυτοῦ χειρὶ Ἀρταγέρσην τὸν ἄρχοντα αὐτῶν. ὡς
90 δ' ἡ τροπὴ ἐγένετο, διασπείρονται καὶ οἱ Κύρου ἑξακόσιοι εἰς τὸ διώκειν ὁρμήσαντες, πλὴν πάνυ ὀλίγοι
ἀμφ' αὐτὸν κατελείφθησαν, σχεδὸν οἱ ὁμοτράπεζοι
καλούμενοι. σὺν τούτοις δὲ ὢν καθορᾷ βασιλέᾱ καὶ
τὸ ἀμφ' ἐκεῖνον στῖφος · καὶ εὐθὺς οὐκ ἠνέσχετο,
95 ἀλλ' εἰπὼν Τὸν ἄνδρα ὁρῶ ἵετο ἐπ' αὐτὸν καὶ παίει
κατὰ τὸ στέρνον καὶ τιτρώσκει διὰ τοῦ θώρᾱκος.
παίοντα δ' αὐτὸν ἀκοντίζει τις παλτῷ ὑπὸ τὸν ὀφθαλ-
μὸν βιαίως · καὶ ἐνταῦθα ἐμάχοντο καὶ βασιλεὺς καὶ
Κῦρος καὶ οἱ ἀμφ' αὐτοὺς ὑπὲρ ἑκατέρου. Κῦρος δὲ
100 αὐτός τε ἀπέθανε καὶ ὀκτὼ οἱ ἄριστοι τῶν περὶ αὐτὸν
ἔκειντο ἐπ' αὐτῷ. (i. 8. 1–27.)

---

85. κατα-κόψῃ : see § 438. a.

86. ἀντίος : to meet him. Cp.
p. 272, l. 61.

88. τοὺς ἑξακισχῑλίους : the
king's own body-guard.

89. ὡς : when.

91. εἰς τὸ διώκειν ὁρμήσαντες :
hastening to the pursuit.

92. σχεδόν : chiefly.

93. καλούμενοι : so-called.

94. ἠν-έσχετο : restrained himself (ἀν-έχω), remarkable for the
double augment.

95. Τὸν ἄνδρα ὁρῶ : direct
quotation.

παίει : supply αὐτόν, i.e. the
king.

97. ὑπὸ τὸν ὀφθαλμόν : the
accusative here follows ὑπό because
the verb ἀκοντίζει implies motion.

IV. *Discouragement of the soldiers after their generals had been treacherously removed by Tissaphernes.* (*Xenophon had not yet been elected general*)

ἐπεὶ δὲ οἱ στρατηγοὶ συνειλημμένοι ἦσαν, ἐν πολλῇ δὴ ἀπορίᾳ ἦσαν οἱ Ἕλληνες· καὶ γὰρ ἐπὶ ταῖς βασιλέως θύραις ἦσαν, κύκλῳ δὲ πάντῃ πολλὰ καὶ ἔθνη καὶ πόλεις πολέμιαι ἦσαν, ἀγορὰν δὲ οὐδεὶς ἔτι
5 παρέξειν ἔμελλεν, ἀπεῖχον δὲ τῆς Ἑλλάδος οὐ μεῖον ἢ μύρια στάδια, ἡγεμὼν δ' οὐδεὶς τῆς ὁδοῦ ἦν, ποταμοὶ δὲ διεῖργον ἀδιάβατοι ἐν μέσῳ τῆς οἴκαδε ὁδοῦ, προυδεδώκεσαν δὲ αὐτοὺς καὶ οἱ σὺν Κύρῳ ἀναβάντες βάρβαροι, μόνοι δὲ καταλελειμμένοι ἦσαν οὐδὲ ἱππέα
10 οὐδένα σύμμαχον ἔχοντες, ὥστε εὔδηλον ἦν ὅτι νικῶντες μὲν οὐδένα ἂν κατακάνοιεν, ἡττηθέντων δὲ αὐτῶν οὐδεὶς ἂν λειφθείη· ταῦτ' ἐννοούμενοι καὶ ἀθύμως

IV. 1. συν-ειλημμένοι ἦσαν: see συλλαμβάνω.

3. θύραις: *doors*, a Persian expression, somewhat like our *court*. The meaning here is, however, *in the heart of the king's country*.

κύκλῳ: *in a circle, surrounding* them (§ 141).

5. παρ-έξειν: regular construction with ἔμελλε (§ 156. 2) *was likely*.

τῆς Ἑλλάδος: genitive of separation (§ 201).

7. τῆς οἴκαδε (§ 70) ὁδοῦ: *the homeward way*.

8. προυδεδώκεσαν: pluperfect of προ-δίδωμι, contracted from

προεδεδώκεσαν. πρό and περί never suffer elision.

οἱ σὺν Κύρῳ ἀναβάντες βάρβαροι: the barbarian troops of Cyrus under the command of Ariaeus fled after the battle of Cunaxa and were no longer allied with the Greeks.

10. σύμμαχον: appositive to ἱππέα.

νῑκῶντες: conditional participle (§ 213. c), *if they should conquer*.

11. οὐδένα ἂν κατακάνοιεν: see § 266.

ἡττηθέντων αὐτῶν: genitive absolute (§ 401) expressing a condition.

12. ἀθύμως ἔχοντες: *being discouraged*.

ἔχοντες ὀλίγοι μὲν αὐτῶν εἰς τὴν ἑσπέραν σίτου ἐγεύσαντο, ὀλίγοι δὲ πῦρ ἀνέκαυσαν, ἐπὶ δὲ τὰ ὅπλα
15 πολλοὶ οὐκ ἦλθον ταύτην τὴν νύκτα, ἀνεπαύοντο δὲ
ὅπου ἐτύγχανεν ἕκαστος, οὐ δυνάμενοι καθεύδειν ὑπὸ
λύπης καὶ πόθου πατρίδων, γονέων, γυναικῶν, παίδων,
οὓς οὔποτ᾽ ἐνόμιζον ἔτι ὄψεσθαι.   (iii. 1. 2–3.)

V. *Under the command of Xenophon and Cheirisophus the sur-*
vivors of the "Ten Thousand" march on, until, from a
mountain in northern Armenia, they get a glimpse of the
Euxine (Black) Sea

ἐντεῦθεν ἦλθον πρὸς πόλιν μεγάλην καὶ εὐδαίμονα καὶ οἰκουμένην ἣ ἐκαλεῖτο Γυμνιάς. ἐκ ταύτης
τῆς χώρας ὁ ἄρχων τοῖς Ἕλλησιν ἡγεμόνα πέμπει,
ὅπως διὰ τῆς πολεμίας χώρας ἄγοι αὐτούς. ἐλθὼν
5 δ᾽ ἐκεῖνος λέγει ὅτι ἄξει αὐτοὺς πέντε ἡμερῶν εἰς
χωρίον ὅθεν ὄψονται θάλατταν. καὶ ἀφικνοῦνται ἐπὶ
τὸ ὄρος τῇ πέμπτῃ ἡμέρᾳ· ὄνομα δὲ τῷ ὄρει ἦν
Θήχης. ἐπεὶ δὲ οἱ πρῶτοι ἐγένοντο ἐπὶ τοῦ ὄρους,
κραυγὴ πολλὴ ἐγένετο. ἀκούσας δὲ ὁ Ξενοφῶν καὶ

---

13. **εἰς τὴν ἑσπέραν**: *into the*
evening, at evening.
σίτου: partitive genitive with
ἐγεύσαντο.
15. **ταύτην τὴν νύκτα**: see § 142.
16. **ὑπὸ λύπης**: *from grief.*
17. **πόθου πατρίδων κτλ.**: *and*
from desire of fatherlands, etc.
πατρίδων is called an "objective"
genitive, for it represents the object of the verbal idea contained
in the noun πόθος *desire.*

18. **ὄψεσθαι**: infinitive in indirect discourse (§ 110. *c*); see
ὁράω.

V. 4. **ὅπως . . . ἄγοι**: on the
purpose clause see § 268; the historical present **πέμπει** is a secondary tense, because it really
refers to past time.
5. **πέντε ἡμερῶν**: see § 155.
7. **τῇ πέμπτῃ ἡμέρᾳ**: see § 180.
τῷ ὄρει: see § 119.

10 οἱ ὀπισθοφύλακες ᾠήθησαν ἔμπροσθεν ἄλλους ἐπι-
τίθεσθαι πολεμίους· ἐπειδὴ δ᾽ ἡ βοὴ πλείων τε ἐγίγνετο καὶ ἐγγύτερον καὶ οἱ ἀεὶ ἐπιόντες ἔθεον δρόμῳ
ἐπὶ τοὺς ἀεὶ βοῶντας καὶ πολλῷ μείζων ἐγίγνετο ἡ
βοή, ἐδόκει δὴ μεῖζόν τι εἶναι τῷ Ξενοφῶντι, καὶ
15 ἀναβὰς ἐφ᾽ ἵππον καὶ Λύκιον καὶ τοὺς ἱππέας ἀνα-
λαβὼν ἐβοήθει· καὶ τάχα δὴ ἀκούουσι βοώντων τῶν
στρατιωτῶν Θάλαττα θάλαττα. ἔνθα δὴ ἔθεον πάντες καὶ οἱ ὀπισθοφύλακες, καὶ τὰ ὑποζύγια ἠλαύνετο
καὶ οἱ ἵπποι. ἐπεὶ δὲ ἀφίκοντο πάντες ἐπὶ τὸ ἄκρον,
20 ἐνταῦθα δὴ περιέβαλλον ἀλλήλους καὶ στρατηγοὺς
καὶ λοχαγοὺς δακρύοντες. καὶ ἐξαπίνης οἱ στρατιῶται φέρουσι λίθους καὶ ποιοῦσι κολωνὸν μέγαν. (iv.
7. 19–25.)

VI. *At the Euxine Sea the Greeks rest and celebrate their safe arrival with athletic games*

Καὶ ἦλθον ἐπὶ θάλατταν εἰς Τραπεζοῦντα πόλιν
Ἑλληνίδα οἰκουμένην ἐν τῷ Εὐξείνῳ Πόντῳ. ἐνταῦθα

---

10. **οἱ ὀπισθοφύλακες**: supply ἀκούσαντες.

ἄλλους πολεμίους: *other enemies*, for they knew from experience that they had enemies in the rear.

12. **ἀεί**: *continually, in succession*.

13. **πολλῷ** (§ 410) **μείζων**: *much louder*.

14. **ἐδόκει δὴ μεῖζόν τι εἶναι**: *it seemed to be something of more than ordinary importance*.

15. **Λύκιον**: *Lycius* was the commander of the cavalry.

16. **ἀκούουσι . . . τῶν στρατιωτῶν**: the genitive of the person is common after the verb of hearing.

17. **Θάλαττα θάλαττα**: the very words that were shouted.

20. **περι-έβαλλον**: *embraced*. On περί see p. 275, l. 8, προυδεδώκεσαν.

VI. 1. **Τραπεζοῦντα**: modern Trebizond.

ἔμειναν ἡμέρας ἀμφὶ τὰς τριάκοντα. ἀγορὰν δὲ παρεῖ-
χον τῷ στρατοπέδῳ Τραπεζούντιοι, καὶ ἐδέξαντό τε
5 τοὺς Ἕλληνας καὶ ξένια ἔδοσαν βοῦς καὶ ἄλφιτα καὶ
οἶνον. μετὰ δὲ τοῦτο τὴν θυσίᾶν ἣν εὔξαντο παρε-
σκευάζοντο· ἦλθον δ᾽ αὐτοῖς ἱκανοὶ βόες ἀποθῦσαι
τῷ Διὶ σωτήρια καὶ τῷ Ἡρακλεῖ ἡγεμόσυνα καὶ
τοῖς ἄλλοις θεοῖς ἃ εὔξαντο. ἐποίησαν δὲ καὶ ἀγῶνα
10 γυμνικὸν ἐν τῷ ὄρει ἔνθαπερ ἐσκήνουν. εἵλοντο δὲ
Δρακόντιον Σπαρτιάτην δρόμου τ᾽ ἐπιμεληθῆναι καὶ
τοῦ ἀγῶνος προστατῆσαι. ἐπειδὴ δὲ ἡ θυσίᾶ ἐγένετο, τὰ δέρματα παρέδοσαν τῷ Δρακοντίῳ, καὶ ἡγεῖσθαι ἐκέλευον ὅπου τὸν δρόμον πεποιηκὼς εἴη. ὁ δὲ
15 δείξᾶς οὗπερ ἑστηκότες ἐτύγχανον Οὗτος ὁ λόφος,
ἔφη, κάλλιστος τρέχειν ὅπου ἄν τις βούληται. Πῶς
οὖν, ἔφασαν, δυνήσονται παλαίειν ἐν σκληρῷ καὶ

---

3. ἀμφὶ τὰς τριάκοντα: see § 427.

5. ξένια: as guest gifts (gifts in
token of hospitality), appositive to
βοῦς, etc.

6. τὴν θυσίᾶν ἣν εὔξαντο: the
sacrifice which they had vowed.
The Greeks had vowed (iii. 2. 9),
at the proposal of Xenophon, to
make sacrifices to Zeus the Savior
as soon as they should arrive in a
friendly land; they had also vowed
to sacrifice to the other gods according to their ability.

7. ἱκανοὶ βόες ἀποθῦσαι: enough
oxen to sacrifice in payment (ἀπο-)
of their vow.

8. Διί: dative of Ζεύς (§ 606. 2).
σωτήρια: thank-offerings for
safety; ἡγεμόσυνα: thank-offerings
for good guidance; with both
words supply ἱερά: victims, offerings (lit. sacred things).

Ἡρακλεῖ: for declension see
§ 603.

11. ἐπιμεληθῆναι: expresses
purpose after εἵλοντο chose (§ 334).

13. τὰ δέρματα: these were to
serve as prizes for the victors in
the contests. Such prizes are
alluded to as early as Homer (Iliad
XXII. 159).

15. ἑστηκότες: see § 215.

16. τρέχειν: limits κάλλιστος:
fairest for running (§ 333).

17. ἐν σκληρῷ καὶ δασεῖ οὕτως: in
a place so rough and thickly wooded.

δασεῖ οὕτως; ὁ δ᾽ εἶπε, Μᾶλλόν τι ἀνιᾱ́σεται ὁ
καταπεσών. ἠγωνίζοντο δὲ παῖδες μὲν στάδιον τῶν
20 αἰχμαλώτων οἱ πλεῖστοι, δόλιχον δὲ Κρῆτες πλείους
ἢ ἐξήκοντα ἔθεον, πάλην δὲ καὶ πυγμὴν καὶ παγκρά-
τιον ἠγωνίζοντο · καὶ καλὴ θέᾱ ἐγένετο · πολλοὶ γὰρ
κατέβησαν καὶ ἅτε θεωμένων τῶν ἑταίρων πολλὴ
φιλονῑκίᾱ ἐγίγνετο.   (iv. 8. 22–27.)

---

18. **Μᾶλλόν τι κτλ.**: *all the more hurt will be the one that falls down.*

19. **ἠγωνίζοντο . . . . στάδιον**: the latter word is cognate accusative (§ 181), *contended [in] the stadium*, a race of six hundred Greek feet.

20. **δόλιχον**: *long foot-race*, cognate accusative with ἔθεον. This consisted of covering the length of the stadium several times (6, 12, 20, or 24).

21. **πάλην κτλ.**: cognate accusatives with ἠγωνίζοντο *contended in wrestling and boxing and the pancratium.* The last named was a very severe, rough-and-tumble fight, consisting partly of wrestling and partly of boxing.

23. **κατέβησαν**: *entered* the competition.

θεωμένων τῶν ἑταίρων: genitive absolute; the *causal* force is distinctly marked by the word ἅτε, which may be rendered *inasmuch as* or *since*.

SUMMARY OF FORMS

For the use of -ν movable see § 32.

Ā–DECLENSION, OR FIRST DECLENSION

592. FEMININE

		ἀρχή, ἡ, *rule*	χώρᾱ, ἡ, *country*	γέφῡρα, ἡ, *bridge*	θάλαττα, ἡ *sea*
Sing.	N.	ἀρχή, ἡ,	χώρᾱ, ἡ,	γέφῡρα, ἡ,	θάλαττα, ἡ
	G.	ἀρχῆs	χώρᾱs	γεφῡρᾱs	θαλάττηs
	D.	ἀρχῇ	χώρᾳ	γεφύρᾳ	θαλάττῃ
	A.	ἀρχήν	χώρᾱν	γέφῡραν	θάλατταν
	V.	ἀρχή	χώρᾱ	γέφῡρα	θάλαττα
Dual N. A. V.		ἀρχᾱ́	χώρᾱ	γεφύρᾱ	θαλάττᾱ
	G. D.	ἀρχαῖν	χώραιν	γεφύραιν	θαλάτταιν
Plur.	N.V.	ἀρχαί	χῶραι	γέφῡραι	θάλατται
	G.	ἀρχῶν	χωρῶν	γεφῡρῶν	θαλαττῶν
	D.	ἀρχαῖs	χώραιs	γεφύραιs	θαλάτταιs
	A.	ἀρχᾱ́s	χώρᾱs	γεφύρᾱs	θαλάττᾱs

593. MASCULINE

Sing.	N.	στρατιώτης, ὁ, *soldier*	νεᾱνίᾱς, ὁ, *young man*
	G.	στρατιώτου	νεᾱνίου
	D.	στρατιώτῃ	νεᾱνίᾳ
	A.	στρατιώτην	νεᾱνίᾱν
	V.	στρατιῶτα	νεᾱνίᾱ
Dual N. A. V.		στρατιώτᾱ	νεᾱνίᾱ
	G. D.	στρατιώταιν	νεᾱνίαιν
Plur.	N.V.	στρατιῶται	νεᾱνίαι
	G.	στρατιωτῶν	νεᾱνιῶν
	D.	στρατιώταιs	νεᾱνίαιs
	A.	στρατιώτᾱς	νεᾱνίᾱς

594. **CONTRACT NOUNS**

Sing. N.	(μνάᾱ)	μνᾶ, ἡ, *mina*	(γέᾱ)	γῆ, ἡ, *land*
G.	(μνάᾱς)	μνᾶς	(γέᾱς)	γῆς
D.	(μνάᾳ)	μνᾷ	(γέᾳ)	γῇ
A.	(μνάᾱν)	μνᾶν	(γέᾱν)	γῆν
V.	(μνάᾱ)	μνᾶ	(γέᾱ)	γῆ

Dual N. A. V.	(μνάᾱ)	μνᾶ
G. D.	(μνάαιν)	μναῖν

Plur. N. V.	(μνάαι)	μναῖ
G.	(μναῶν)	μνῶν
D.	(μνάαις)	μναῖς
A.	(μνάᾱς)	μνᾶς

O–DECLENSION, OR SECOND DECLENSION

595.

Sing. N.	ἄνθρωπος, ὁ, *man*	ὁδός, ἡ, *road*	πλοῖον, τό, *boat*
G.	ἀνθρώπου	ὁδοῦ	πλοίου
D.	ἀνθρώπῳ	ὁδῷ	πλοίῳ
A.	ἄνθρωπον	ὁδόν	πλοῖον
V.	ἄνθρωπε	ὁδέ	πλοῖον

Dual N. A. V.	ἀνθρώπω	ὁδώ	πλοίω
G. D.	ἀνθρώποιν	ὁδοῖν	πλοίοιν

Plur. N. V.	ἄνθρωποι	ὁδοί	πλοῖα
G.	ἀνθρώπων	ὁδῶν	πλοίων
D.	ἀνθρώποις	ὁδοῖς	πλοίοις
A.	ἀνθρώπους	ὁδούς	πλοῖα

596. **CONTRACT NOUN**

	SINGULAR		DUAL			PLURAL	
N.	(νόος) νοῦς, ὁ, *mind*	N. A. V.	(νόω) νώ	N. V.	(νόοι) νοῖ
G.	(νόου) νοῦ	G. D.	(νόοιν) νοῖν	G.	(νόων) νῶν
D.	(νόῳ) νῷ			D.	(νόοις) νοῖς
A.	(νόον) νοῦν.			A.	(νόους) νοῦς
V.	(νόε) νοῦ				

CONSONANT DECLENSION, OR THIRD DECLENSION

597.

Sing. N. V.	κῆρυξ, ὁ, *herald*	φάλαγξ, ἡ, *phalanx*	διῶρυξ, ἡ, *ditch*	κλώψ, ὁ, *thief*
G.	κήρῡκος	φάλαγγος	διώρυχος	κλωπός
D.	κήρῡκι	φάλαγγι	διώρυχι	κλωπί
A.	κήρῡκα	φάλαγγα	διώρυχα	κλῶπα
Dual N. A. V.	κήρῡκε	φάλαγγε	διώρυχε	κλῶπε
G. D.	κηρΰκοιν	φαλάγγοιν	διωρύχοιν	κλωποῖν
Plur. N. V.	κήρῡκες	φάλαγγες	διώρυχες	κλῶπες
G.	κηρΰκων	φαλάγγων	διωρύχων	κλωπῶν
D.	κήρῡξι	φάλαγξι	διώρυξι	κλωψί
A.	κήρῡκας	φάλαγγας	διώρυχας	κλῶπας

598.

Sing. N. V.	ἀσπίς, ἡ, *shield*	πούς, ὁ, *foot*	νύξ, ἡ, *night*	ἄρχων, ὁ, *ruler*
G.	ἀσπίδος	ποδός	νυκτός	ἄρχοντος
D.	ἀσπίδι	ποδί	νυκτί	ἄρχοντι
A.	ἀσπίδα	πόδα	νύκτα	ἄρχοντα
Dual N. A. V.	ἀσπίδε	πόδε	νύκτε	ἄρχοντε
G. D.	ἀσπίδοιν	ποδοῖν	νυκτοῖν	ἀρχόντοιν
Plur. N. V.	ἀσπίδες	πόδες	νύκτες	ἄρχοντες
G.	ἀσπίδων	ποδῶν	νυκτῶν	ἀρχόντων
D.	ἀσπίσι	ποσί	νυξί	ἄρχουσι
A.	ἀσπίδας	πόδας	νύκτας	ἄρχοντας

Sing. N. V.	χάρις, ἡ, *favor*	στράτευμα, τό, *army*
G.	χάριτος	στρατεύματος
D.	χάριτι	στρατεύματι
A.	χάριν	στράτευμα
Dual N. A. V.	χάριτε	στρατεύματε
G. D.	χαρίτοιν	στρατευμάτοιν
Plur. N. V.	χάριτες	στρατεύματα
G.	χαρίτων	στρατευμάτων
D.	χάρισι	στρατεύμασι
A.	χάριτας	στρατεύματα

599.

Sing. N. V.	ἀγών, ὁ, *contest*	ἡγεμών, ὁ, *guide*	μήν, ὁ, *month*	λιμήν, ὁ, *harbor*
G.	ἀγῶνος	ἡγεμόνος	μηνός	λιμένος
D.	ἀγῶνι	ἡγεμόνι	μηνί	λιμένι
A.	ἀγῶνα	ἡγεμόνα	μῆνα	λιμένα
Dual N. A. V.	ἀγῶνε	ἡγεμόνε	μῆνε	λιμένε
G. D.	ἀγώνοιν	ἡγεμόνοιν	μηνοῖν	λιμένοιν
Plur. N. V.	ἀγῶνες	ἡγεμόνες	μῆνες	λιμένες
G.	ἀγώνων	ἡγεμόνων	μηνῶν	λιμένων
D.	ἀγῶσι	ἡγεμόσι	μησί	λιμέσι
A.	ἀγῶνας	ἡγεμόνας	μῆνας	λιμένας

Sing. N.	γείτων, ὁ, *neighbor*	κρᾱτήρ, ὁ, *mixing-bowl*
G.	γείτονος	κρᾱτῆρος
D.	γείτονι	κρᾱτῆρι
A.	γείτονα	κρᾱτῆρα
V.	γεῖτον	κρᾱτήρ
Dual N. A. V.	γείτονε	κρᾱτῆρε
G. D.	γειτόνοιν	κρᾱτήροιν
Plur. N. V.	γείτονες	κρᾱτῆρες
G.	γειτόνων	κρᾱτήρων
D.	γείτοσι	κρᾱτῆρσι
A.	γείτονας	κρᾱτῆρας

600.

Sing. N.	πατήρ, ὁ, *father*	μήτηρ, ἡ, *mother*	θυγάτηρ, ἡ, *daughter*	ἀνήρ, ὁ, *man*
G.	πατρός	μητρός	θυγατρός	ἀνδρός
D.	πατρί	μητρί	θυγατρί	ἀνδρί
A.	πατέρα	μητέρα	θυγατέρα	ἄνδρα
V.	πάτερ	μῆτερ	θύγατερ	ἄνερ
Dual N. A. V.	πατέρε	μητέρε	θυγατέρε	ἄνδρε
G. D.	πατέροιν	μητέροιν	θυγατέροιν	ἀνδροῖν
Plur. N. V.	πατέρες	μητέρες	θυγατέρες	ἄνδρες
G.	πατέρων	μητέρων	θυγατέρων	ἀνδρῶν
D.	πατράσι	μητράσι	θυγατράσι	ἀνδράσι
A.	πατέρας	μητέρας	θυγατέρας	ἄνδρας

601.

Sing. N.	ὄρος,[1] τό, *mountain*			τριήρης,[1] ἡ, *trireme*	
G.	(ὄρε-ος)	ὄρους		(τριήρε-ος)	τριήρους
D.	(ὄρε-ϊ)	ὄρει		(τριήρε-ϊ)	τριήρει
A.		ὄρος		(τριήρε-α)	τριήρη
V.		ὄρος			τριήρες
Dual N. A. V.	(ὄρε-ε)	ὄρει		(τριήρε-ε)	τριήρει
G. D.	(ὀρέ-οιν)	ὀροῖν		(τριηρέ-οιν)	τριήροιν
Plur. N. V.	(ὄρε-α)	ὄρη		(τριήρε-ες)	τριήρεις
G.	(ὀρέ-ων)	ὀρέων or ὀρῶν		(τριηρέ-ων)	τριήρων
D.		ὄρεσι			τριήρεσι
A.	(ὄρε-α)	ὄρη			τριήρεις

Sing. N.	Σωκράτης,[1] ὁ, *Socrates*	
G.	(Σωκράτε-ος)	Σωκράτους
D.	(Σωκράτε-ϊ)	Σωκράτει
A.	(Σωκράτε-α)	Σωκράτη
V.	Σώκρατες	

602. κέρας, τό, *horn, wing* of an army, has two stems κερασ- and κερᾱτ- and a double declension :

	STEM κερᾱτ-	STEM κερασ-	
Sing. N. A.		κέρας,[1] τό, *horn, wing*	
G.	κέρᾱτ-ος	(κέρα-ος)	κέρως
D.	κέρᾱτ-ι	(κέρα-ϊ)	κέρᾳ
Dual N. A.	κέρᾱτ-ε	(κέρα-ε)	κέρᾱ
G. D.	κερᾱτ-οιν	(κερά-οιν)	κερῷν
Plur. N. A.	κέρᾱτ-α	(κέρα-α)	κέρᾱ
G.	κερᾱτ-ων		
D.	κέρᾱσι		

603.

Sing. N.	(Ἡρακλέης)	Ἡρακλῆς, ὁ, *Heracles*
G.	(Ἡρακλέε-ος)	Ἡρακλέους
D.	(Ἡρακλέε-ϊ)	Ἡρακλεῖ
A.	(Ἡρακλέε-α)	Ἡρακλέᾱ
V.	(Ἡράκλεες)	Ἡράκλεις

---

[1] The forms in parenthesis show the stem after σ has been dropped from the end (*e.g.* ὄρε-ος is for ὄρεσ-ος) and before contraction has taken place.

604.

Sing. N.	πόλις, ἡ, *city*	πῆχυς, ὁ, *cubit*	ἄστυ, τό, *town*	ἰχθύς, ὁ, *fish*
G.	πόλεως	πήχεως	ἄστεως	ἰχθύος
D.	(πόλε-ϊ) πόλει	(πήχε-ϊ) πήχει	(ἄστε-ϊ) ἄστει	ἰχθύϊ
A.	πόλιν	πῆχυν	ἄστυ	ἰχθύν
V.	πόλι	πῆχυ	ἄστυ	ἰχθύ
Dual N. A. V.	(πόλε-ε) πόλει	(πήχε-ε) πήχει	(ἄστε-ε) ἄστει	ἰχθύε
G. D.	πολέοιν	πηχέοιν	ἀστέοιν	ἰχθύοιν
Plur. N. V.	(πόλε-ες) πόλεις	(πήχε-ες) πήχεις	(ἄστε-α) ἄστη	ἰχθύες
G.	πόλεων	πήχεων	ἄστεων	ἰχθύων
D.	πόλεσι	πήχεσι	ἄστεσι	ἰχθύσι
A.	πόλεις	πήχεις	(ἄστε-α) ἄστη	ἰχθῦς

605.

Sing. N.	βασιλεύς, ὁ, *king*	βοῦς, ὁ, ἡ, *ox, cow*	ναῦς, ἡ, *ship*
G.	βασιλέως	βοός	νεώς
D.	βασιλεῖ	βοΐ	νηΐ
A.	βασιλέᾱ	βοῦν	ναῦν
V.	βασιλεῦ	βοῦ	ναῦ
Dual N. A. V.	βασιλῆ	βόε	νῆε
G. D.	βασιλέοιν	βοοῖν	νεοῖν
Plur. N. V.	(βασιλέ-ες) βασιλεῖς [1]	βόες	νῆες
G.	βασιλέων	βοῶν	νεῶν
D.	βασιλεῦσι	βουσί	ναυσί
A.	βασιλέᾱς	βοῦς	ναῦς

---

[1] Older -ῆς.

606.   IRREGULAR NOUNS

		1	2	3
Sing.	N.	γυνή, ἡ, *woman*	Ζεύς, ὁ, *Zeus*	χείρ, ἡ, *hand*
	G.	γυναικός	Διός	χειρός
	D.	γυναικί	Διί	χειρί
	A.	γυναῖκα	Δία	χεῖρα
	V.	γύναι	Ζεῦ	χείρ
Dual	N. A. V.	γυναῖκε		χεῖρε
	G. D.	γυναικοῖν		χεροῖν and χειροῖν
Plur.	N. V.	γυναῖκες		χεῖρες
	G.	γυναικῶν		χειρῶν
	D.	γυναιξί		χερσί
	A.	γυναῖκας		χεῖρας

		4	5	6	7
Sing.	N. A. V.	πῦρ, τό, *fire*	ὕδωρ, τό, *water*	δόρυ, τό, *spear*	γόνυ, τό, *knee*
	G.	πυρός	ὕδατος	δόρατος	γόνατος
	D.	πυρί	ὕδατι	δόρατι	γόνατι
Dual	N. A. V.			δόρατε	γόνατε
	G. D.			δοράτοιν	γονάτοιν
Plur.	N. A. V.	πυρά	ὕδατα	δόρατα	γόνατα
		watch fires			
	G.	πυρῶν	ὑδάτων	δοράτων	γονάτων
	D.	πυροῖς	ὕδασι	δόρασι	γόνασι

ADJECTIVES OF THE FIRST AND SECOND DECLENSIONS

607.   THREE ENDINGS

		ἀγαθός *good*			πολέμιος *hostile*		
		MASC.	FEM.	NEUT.	MASC.	FEM.	NEUT.
Sing.	N.	ἀγαθός	ἀγαθή	ἀγαθόν	πολέμιος	πολεμίᾱ	πολέμιον
	G.	ἀγαθοῦ	ἀγαθῆς	ἀγαθοῦ	πολεμίου	πολεμίᾱς	πολεμίου
	D.	ἀγαθῷ	ἀγαθῇ	ἀγαθῷ	πολεμίῳ	πολεμίᾳ	πολεμίῳ
	A.	ἀγαθόν	ἀγαθήν	ἀγαθόν	πολέμιον	πολεμίᾱν	πολέμιον
	V.	ἀγαθέ	ἀγαθή	ἀγαθόν	πολέμιε	πολεμίᾱ	πολέμιον

	MASC.	FEM.	NEUT.	MASC.	FEM.	NEUT.
Dual N. A. V.	ἀγαθώ	ἀγαθά	ἀγαθώ	πολεμίω	πολεμίᾱ	πολεμίω
G. D.	ἀγαθοῖν	ἀγαθαῖν	ἀγαθοῖν	πολεμίοιν	πολεμίαιν	πολεμίοιν
Plur. N. V.	ἀγαθοί	ἀγαθαί	ἀγαθά	πολέμιοι	πολέμιαι	πολέμια
G.	ἀγαθῶν	ἀγαθῶν	ἀγαθῶν	πολεμίων	πολεμίων	πολεμίων
D.	ἀγαθοῖς	ἀγαθαῖς	ἀγαθοῖς	πολεμίοις	πολεμίαις	πολεμίοις
A.	ἀγαθούς	ἀγαθάς	ἀγαθά	πολεμίους	πολεμίᾱς	πολέμια

608. TWO ENDINGS

	MASC. AND FEM.	NEUT.
Sing. N.	ἄπορος *impassable*	ἄπορον
G.		ἀπόρου
D.		ἀπόρῳ
A.		ἄπορον
V.	ἄπορε	ἄπορον
Dual N. A. V.		ἀπόρω
G. D.		ἀπόροιν
Plur. N. V.	ἄποροι	ἄπορα
G.		ἀπόρων
D.		ἀπόροις
A.	ἀπόρους	ἄπορα

CONTRACT ADJECTIVES OF THE FIRST AND SECOND DECLENSIONS

609. THREE ENDINGS

χρῡσοῦς *golden*

SINGULAR

	MASC.		FEM.		NEUT.	
N.	(χρύσεος)	χρῡσοῦς	(χρῡσέα)	χρῡσῆ	(χρύσεον)	χρῡσοῦν
G.	(χρῡσέου)	χρῡσοῦ	(χρῡσέᾱς)	χρῡσῆς	(χρῡσεον)	χρῡσου
D.	(χρῡσέῳ)	χρῡσῷ	(χρῡσέᾳ)	χρῡσῇ	(χρῡσέῳ)	χρῡσῷ
A.	(χρύσεον)	χρῡσοῦν	(χρῡσέᾱν)	χρῡσῆν	(χρύσεον)	χρῡσοῦν

DUAL

	MASC.		FEM.		NEUT.	
N. A.	(χρῡσέω)	χρῡσώ	(χρῡσέᾱ)	χρῡσᾱ	(χρῡσέω)	χρῡσώ
G. D.	(χρῡσέοιν)	χρῡσοῖν	(χρῡσέαιν)	χρῡσαῖν	(χρῡσέοιν)	χρῡσοῖν

PLURAL

N.	(χρύσεοι)	χρῡσοῖ	(χρύσεαι)	χρῡσαῖ	(χρύσεα)	χρῡσᾶ
G.	(χρυσέων)	χρῡσῶν	(χρῡσέων)	χρῡσῶν	(χρῡσέων)	χρῡσῶν
D.	(χρῡσέοις)	χρῡσοῖς	(χρῡσέαις)	χρῡσαῖς	(χρῡσέοις)	χρῡσοῖς
A.	(χρῡσέους)	χρῡσοῦς	(χρῡσέᾱς)	χρῡσᾶς	(χρύσεα)	χρῡσᾶ

ἀργυροῦς *silver*

SINGULAR

N.	(ἀργύρεος)	ἀργυροῦς	(ἀργυρέᾱ)	ἀργυρᾶ	(ἀργύρεον)	ἀργυροῦν
G.	(ἀργυρέου)	ἀργυροῦ	(ἀργυρέᾱς)	ἀργυρᾶς	(ἀργυρέου)	ἀργυροῦ
D.	(ἀργυρέῳ)	ἀργυρῷ	(ἀργυρέᾳ)	ἀργυρᾷ	(ἀργυρέῳ)	ἀργυρῷ
A.	(ἀργύρεον)	ἀργυροῦν	(ἀργυρέᾱν)	ἀργυρᾶν	(ἀργύρεον)	ἀργυροῦν

DUAL

N. A.	(ἀργυρέω)	ἀργυρώ	(ἀργυρέᾱ)	ἀργυρᾶ	(ἀργυρέω)	ἀργυρώ
G. D.	(ἀργυρέοιν)	ἀργυροῖν	(ἀργυρέαιν)	ἀργυραῖν	(ἀργυρέοιν)	ἀργυροῖν

PLURAL

N.	(ἀργύρεοι)	ἀργυροῖ	(ἀργύρεαι)	ἀργυραῖ	(ἀργύρεα)	ἀργυρᾶ
G.	(ἀργυρέων)	ἀργυρῶν	(ἀργυρέων)	ἀργυρῶν	(ἀργυρέων)	ἀργυρῶν
D.	(ἀργυρέοις)	ἀργυροῖς	(ἀργυρέαις)	ἀργυραῖς	(ἀργυρέοις)	ἀργυροῖς
A.	(ἀργυρέους)	ἀργυροῦς	(ἀργυρέᾱς)	ἀργυρᾶς	(ἀργύρεα)	ἀργυρᾶ

ἁπλοῦς *sincere*

SINGULAR

N.	(ἁπλόος)	ἁπλοῦς	(ἁπλέᾱ)	ἁπλῆ	(ἁπλόον)	ἁπλοῦν
G.	(ἁπλόου)	ἁπλοῦ	(ἁπλέᾱς)	ἁπλῆς	(ἁπλόου)	ἁπλοῦ
D.	(ἁπλόῳ)	ἁπλῷ	(ἁπλέᾳ)	ἁπλῇ	(ἁπλόῳ)	ἁπλῷ
A.	(ἁπλόον)	ἁπλοῦν	(ἁπλέᾱν)	ἁπλῆν	(ἁπλόον)	ἁπλοῦν

DUAL

N. A.	(ἁπλόω)	ἁπλώ	(ἁπλέᾱ)	ἁπλᾶ	(ἁπλόω)	ἁπλώ
G. D.	(ἁπλόοιν)	ἁπλοῖν	(ἁπλέαιν)	ἁπλαῖν	(ἁπλόοιν)	ἁπλοῖν

PLURAL

N.	(ἁπλόοι)	ἁπλοῖ	(ἁπλέαι)	ἁπλαῖ	(ἁπλόα)	ἁπλᾶ
G.	(ἁπλόων)	ἁπλῶν	(ἁπλέων)	ἁπλῶν	(ἁπλόων)	ἁπλῶν
D.	(ἁπλόοις)	ἁπλοῖς	(ἁπλέαις)	ἁπλαῖς	(ἁπλόοις)	ἁπλοῖς
A.	(ἁπλόους)	ἁπλοῦς	(ἁπλέᾱς)	ἁπλᾶς	(ἁπλόα)	ἁπλᾶ

610.   TWO ENDINGS

	MASC. AND FEM.	NEUT.
Sing. N.	εὔνους *well-disposed*	εὔνουν
G.	εὔνου	
D.	εὔνῳ	
A.	εὔνουν	
Plur. N.	εὔνοι	εὔνοα
G.	εὔνων	
D.	εὔνοις	
A.	εὔνους	εὔνοα

For uncontracted forms cp. νοῦς, § 596.

611. ADJECTIVES OF THE FIRST AND THIRD
                    DECLENSIONS

	MASC.	FEM.	NEUT.
Sing. N.	ἡδύς *sweet*	ἡδεῖα	ἡδύ
G.	ἡδέος	ἡδείᾱς	ἡδέος
D.	(ἡδέ-ϊ) ἡδεῖ	ἡδείᾳ	(ἡδέ-ϊ) ἡδεῖ
A.	ἡδύν	ἡδεῖαν	ἡδύ
V.	ἡδύ	ἡδεῖα	ἡδύ
Dual N. A. V.	(ἡδέ-ε) ἡδεῖ	ἡδείᾱ	(ἡδέ-ε) ἡδεῖ
G. D.	ἡδέοιν	ἡδείαιν	ἡδέοιν
Plur. N. V.	(ἡδέ-ες) ἡδεῖς	ἡδεῖαι	ἡδέα
G.	ἡδέων	ἡδειῶν	ἡδέων
D.	ἡδέσι	ἡδείαις	ἡδέσι
A.	ἡδεῖς	ἡδείᾱς	ἡδέα

ADJECTIVES OF THE THIRD DECLENSION

612.   STEMS IN -εσ

	MASC. AND FEM.	NEUT.
Sing. N.	ἀσφαλής[1] *safe*	ἀσφαλές
G.	(ἀσφαλέ-ος) ἀσφαλοῦς	
D.	(ἀσφαλέ-ϊ) ἀσφαλεῖ	
A.	(ἀσφαλέ-α) ἀσφαλῆ	ἀσφαλές
V.	ἀσφαλές	

---

[1] See footnote on p. 284.

	MASC. AND FEM.	NEUT.
Dual N. A. V.	(ἀσφαλέ-ε) **ἀσφαλεῖ**	
G. D.	(ἀσφαλέ-οιν) **ἀσφαλοῖν**	
Plur. N. V.	(ἀσφαλέ-ες) **ἀσφαλεῖς**	(ἀσφιλί-α) **ἀσφαλῆ**
G.	(ἀσφαλέ-ων) **ἀσφαλῶν**	
D.	**ἀσφαλέσι**	
A.	**ἀσφαλεῖς**	(ἀσφαλέ-α) **ἀσφαλῆ**

613.   STEMS IN -ν

	MASC. AND FEM.	NEUT.
Sing. N.	**εὐδαίμων** *fortunate*	**εὔδαιμον**
G.	**εὐδαίμονος**	
D.	**εὐδαίμονι**	
A.	**εὐδαίμονα**	**εὔδαιμον**
V.	**εὔδαιμον**	
Dual N. A. V.	**εὐδαίμονε**	
G. D.	**εὐδαιμόνοιν**	
Plur. N. V.	**εὐδαίμονες**	**εὐδαίμονα**
G.	**εὐδαιμόνων**	
D.	**εὐδαίμοσι**	
A.	**εὐδαίμονας**	**εὐδαίμονα**

614.   COMPARATIVES IN -ων

	MASC. AND FEM.	NEUT.
Sing. N.	**ἡδίων** *sweeter*	**ἥδῑον**
G.	**ἡδίονος**	
D.	**ἡδίονι**	
A.	**ἡδίονα** or **ἡδίω**	**ἥδῑον**
V.	**ἥδῑον**	
Dual N. A. V.	**ἡδίονε**	
G. D.	**ἡδῑόνοιν**	
Plur. N. V.	**ἡδίονες** or **ἡδίους**	**ἡδῑονα** or **ἡδίω**
G.	**ἡδῑόνων**	
D.	**ἡδίοσι**	
A.	**ἡδίονας** or **ἡδίους**	**ἡδίονα** or **ἡδίω**

615. STEMS IN -ντ

		MASC.	FEM.	NEUT.
Sing.	N. V.	πᾶς *all*	πᾶσα	πᾶν
	G.	παντός	πάσης	παντός
	D.	παντί	πάσῃ	παντί
	A.	πάντα	πᾶσαν	πᾶν
Plur.	N. V.	πάντες	πᾶσαι	πάντα
	G.	πάντων	πασῶν	πάντων
	D.	πᾶσι	πάσαις	πᾶσι
	A.	πάντας	πάσᾱς	πάντα

PARTICIPLES

616.

		MASC.	FEM.	NEUT.
1. Sing.	N. V.	ὤν *being*	οὖσα	ὄν
	G.	ὄντος	οὔσης	ὄντος
	D.	ὄντι	οὔσῃ	ὄντι
	A.	ὄντα	οὖσαν	ὄν
Dual	N. A. V.	ὄντε	οὔσᾱ	ὄντε
	G. D.	ὄντοιν	οὔσαιν	ὄντοιν
Plur.	N. V.	ὄντες	οὖσαι	ὄντα
	G.	ὄντων	οὐσῶν	ὄντων
	D.	οὖσι	οὔσαις	οὖσι
	A.	ὄντας	οὔσᾱς	ὄντα

a. Second aorist active participles are declined like ὤν, as λιπών, λιποῦσα, λιπόν, *having left.*

		MASC.	FEM.	NEUT.
2. Sing.	N. V.	λύων *loosing*	λύουσα	λῦον
	G.	λύοντος	λῡούσης	λύοντος
	D.	λύοντι	λῡούσῃ	λύοντι
	A.	λύοντα	λύουσαν	λῦον
Dual	N. A. V.	λύοντε	λῡούσᾱ	λύοντε
	G. D.	λῡόντοιν	λῡούσαιν	λῡόντοιν
Plur.	N. V.	λύοντες	λύουσαι	λύοντα
	G.	λῡόντων	λῡουσῶν	λῡόντων
	D.	λύουσι	λῡούσαις	λύουσι
	A.	λύοντας	λῡούσᾱς	λύοντα

a. Participles of more than two syllables, like κωλῦ́ων *hindering*, are inflected

κωλῦ́ων, κωλῦ́ουσα, κωλῦ̂ον (observe the accent), etc.

617.

	MASC.	FEM.	NEUT.
Sing. N. V.	ἱστᾱ́ς *setting*	ἱστᾶσα	ἱστάν
G.	ἱστάντος	ἱστᾱ́σης	ἱστάντος
D.	ἱστάντι	ἱστᾱ́σῃ	ἱστάντι
A.	ἱστάντα	ἱστᾶσαν	ἱστάν
Dual N. A. V.	ἱστάντε	ἱστᾱ́σᾱ	ἱστάντε
G. D.	ἱστάντοιν	ἱστᾱ́σαιν	ἱστάντοιν
Plur. N. V.	ἱστάντες	ἱστᾶσαι	ἱστάντα
G.	ἱστάντων	ἱστᾱσῶν	ἱστάντων
D.	ἱστᾶσι	ἱστᾱ́σαις	ἱστᾶσι
A.	ἱστάντας	ἱστᾱ́σᾱς	ἱστάντα

618.

	MASC.	FEM.	NEUT.
Sing. N. V.	λῡ́σᾱς *having loosed*	λῡ́σᾱσα	λῦσαν
G.	λῡ́σαντος	λῡσᾱ́σης	λῡ́σαντος
D.	λῡ́σαντι	λῡσᾱ́σῃ	λῡ́σαντι
A.	λῡ́σαντα	λῡ́σᾱσαν	λῦσαν
Dual N. A. V.	λῡ́σαντε	λῡσᾱ́σᾱ	λῡ́σαντε
G. D.	λῡσάντοιν	λῡσᾱ́σαιν	λῡσάντοιν
Plur. N. V.	λῡ́σαντες	λῡ́σᾱσαι	λῡ́σαντα
G.	λῡσάντων	λῡσᾱσῶν	λῡσάντων
D.	λῡ́σᾱσι	λῡσᾱ́σαις	λῡ́σᾱσι
A.	λῡ́σαντας	λῡσᾱ́σᾱς	λῡ́σαντα

a. Participles of more than two syllables, like ἀκούσᾱς *having heard*, are inflected

ἀκούσᾱς, ἀκούσᾱσα, ἀκοῦσαν (observe the accent), etc.

619.

	MASC.	FEM.	NEUT.
Sing. N. V.	δεικνῡ́ς *showing*	δεικνῦσα	δεικνύν
G.	δεικνύντος	δεικνῡ́σης	δεικνύντος
D.	δεικνύντι	δεικνῡ́σῃ	δεικνύντι
A.	δεικνύντα	δεικνῦσαν	δεικνύν

	MASC.	FEM.	NEUT.
Dual N. A. V.	δεικνύντε	δεικνῦσᾱ	δεικνύντε
G. D.	δεικνύντοιν	δεικνύσαιν	δεικνύντοιν
Plur. N. V.	δεικνύντες	δεικνῦσαι	δεικνύντα
G.	δεικνύντων	δεικνῦσῶν	δεικνύντων
D.	δεικνῦσι	δεικνύσαις	δεικνῦσι
A.	δεικνύντας	δεικνύσᾱς	δεικνύντα

620.

	MASC.	FEM.	NEUT.
Sing. N. V.	τιθείς *placing*	τιθεῖσα	τιθέν
G.	τιθέντος	τιθείσης	τιθέντος
D.	τιθέντι	τιθείσῃ	τιθέντι
A.	τιθέντα	τιθεῖσαν	τιθέν
Dual N. A. V.	τιθέντε	τιθείσᾱ	τιθέντε
G. D.	τιθέντοιν	τιθείσαιν	τιθέντοιν
Plur. N. V.	τιθέντες	τιθεῖσαι	τιθέντα
G.	τιθέντων	τιθεισῶν	τιθέντων
D.	τιθεῖσι	τιθείσαις	τιθεῖσι
A.	τιθέντας	τιθείσᾱς	τιθέντα

a. Similarly are declined aorist passive participles:

λυθείς *having been loosed,* λυθεῖσα. λυθέν, etc.

621.

	MASC.	FEM.	NEUT.
Sing. N. V.	διδούς *giving*	διδοῦσα	διδόν
G.	διδόντος	διδούσης	διδόντος
D.	διδόντι	διδούσῃ	διδόντι
A.	διδόντα	διδοῦσαν	διδόν
Dual N. A. V.	διδόντε	διδούσᾱ	διδόντε
G. D.	διδόντοιν	διδούσαιν	διδόντοιν
Plur. N. V.	διδόντες	διδοῦσαι	διδόντα
G.	διδόντων	διδουσῶν	διδόντων
D.	διδοῦσι	διδούσαις	διδοῦσι
A.	διδόντας	διδούσᾱς	διδόντα

622.

	MASC.		FEM.	
Sing. N. V.	(τῑμάων)	τῑμῶν *honoring*	(τῑμάουσα)	τῑμῶσα
G.	(τῑμάοντος)	τῑμῶντος	(τῑμαούσης)	τῑμώσης
D.	(τῑμάοντι)	τῑμῶντι	(τῑμαούσῃ)	τῑμώσῃ
A.	(τῑμάοντα)	τῑμῶντα	(τῑμάουσαν)	τῑμῶσαν

NEUT.

N.V.	(τῑμάον)	τῑμῶν
G.	(τῑμάοντος)	τῑμῶντος
D.	(τῑμάοντι)	τῑμῶντι
A.	(τῑμάον)	τῑμῶν

	MASC.		FEM.	
Dual N. A. V.	(τῑμάοντε)	τῑμῶντε	(τῑμαούσᾱ)	τῑμώσᾱ
G. D.	(τῑμαόντοιν)	τῑμώντοιν	(τῑμαούσαιν)	τῑμώσαιν

NEUT.

N. A. V.	(τῑμάοντε)	τῑμῶντε
G. D.	(τῑμαόντοιν)	τῑμώντοιν

	MASC.		FEM.	
Plur. N. V.	(τῑμάοντες)	τῑμῶντες	(τῑμάουσαι)	τῑμῶσαι
G.	(τῑμαόντων)	τῑμώντων	(τῑμαουσῶν)	τῑμωσῶν
D.	(τῑμάουσι)	τῑμῶσι	(τῑμαούσαις)	τῑμώσαις
A.	(τῑμάοντας)	τῑμῶντας	(τῑμαούσᾱς)	τῑμώσᾱς

NEUT.

N.V.	(τῑμάοντα)	τῑμῶντα
G.	(τῑμαόντων)	τῑμώντων
D.	(τῑμάουσι)	τῑμῶσι
A.	(τῑμάοντα)	τῑμῶντα

	MASC.		FEM.	
Sing. N. V.	(ποιέων)	ποιῶν *making*	(ποιέουσα)	ποιοῦσα
G.	(ποιέοντος)	ποιοῦντος	(ποιεούσης)	ποιούσης
D.	(ποιέοντι)	ποιοῦντι	(ποιεούσῃ)	ποιούσῃ
A.	(ποιέοντα)	ποιοῦντα	(ποιέουσαν)	ποιοῦσαν

NEUT.

N.V.	(ποιέον)	ποιοῦν
G.	(ποιέοντος)	ποιοῦντος
D.	(ποιέοντι)	ποιοῦντι
A.	(ποιέον)	ποιοῦν

	MASC.		FEM.	
Dual N. A. V.	(ποιέοντε)	ποιοῦντε	(ποιεούσᾱ)	ποιούσᾱ
G. D.	(ποιεόντοιν)	ποιούντοιν	(ποιεούσαιν)	ποιούσαιν

NEUT.

N. A. V.	(ποιέοντε)	ποιοῦντε
G. D.	(ποιεόντοιν)	ποιούντοιν

	MASC.		FEM.	
Plur. N. V.	(ποιέοντες)	ποιοῦντες	(ποιέουσαι)	ποιοῦσαι.
G.	(ποιεόντων)	ποιούντων	(ποιεουσῶν)	ποιουσῶν
D.	(ποιέουσι)	ποιοῦσι	(ποιεούσαις)	ποιούσαις
A.	(ποιέοντας)	ποιοῦντας	(ποιεούσᾱς)	ποιούσᾱς

NEUT.

N. V.	(ποιέοντα)	ποιοῦντα
G.	(ποιεόντων)	ποιούντων
D.	(ποιέουσι)	ποιοῦσι
A.	(ποιέοντα)	ποιοῦντα

a. δηλόων *showing*, which contracts to

δηλῶν, δηλοῦσα, δηλοῦν,

is declined like ποιῶν, ποιοῦσα, ποιοῦν.

PERFECT ACTIVE PARTICIPLES

623. λελυκώς *having loosed* (λελυκοτ-)

	MASC.	FEM.	NEUT.
Sing. N. V.	λελυκώς	λελυκυῖα	λελυκός
G.	λελυκότος	λελυκυίᾱς	λελυκότος
D.	λελυκότι	λελυκυίᾳ	λελυκότι
A.	λελυκότα	λελυκυῖαν	λελυκός
Dual N. A. V.	λελυκότε	λελυκυίᾱ	λελυκότε
G. D.	λελυκότοιν	λελυκυίαιν	λελυκότοιν
Plur. N. V.	λελυκότες	λελυκυῖαι	λελυκότα
G.	λελυκότων	λελυκυιῶν	λελυκότων
D.	λελυκόσι	λελυκυίαις	λελυκόσι
A.	λελυκότας	λελυκυίᾱς	λελυκότα

624. ἑστώς *standing* (ἑστωτ-)

	MASC.	FEM.	NEUT.
Sing. N. V.	ἑστώς	ἑστῶσα	ἑστός
G.	ἑστῶτος	ἑστώσης	ἑστῶτος
D.	ἑστῶτι	ἑστώσῃ	ἑστῶτι
A.	ἑστῶτα	ἑστῶσαν	ἑστός

	Masc.	Fem.	Neut.
Dual N. A. V.	ἑστῶτε	ἑστώσᾱ	ἑστῶτε
G. D.	ἑστώτοιν	ἑστώσαιν	ἑστώτοιν
Plur. N. V.	ἑστῶτες	ἑστῶσαι	ἑστῶτα
G.	ἑστώτων	ἑστωσῶν	ἑστώτων
D.	ἑστῶσι	ἑστώσαις	ἑστῶσι
A.	ἑστῶτας	ἑστώσᾱς	ἑστῶτα

a. ἑστώς is contracted from ἑσταώς; the neuter ἑστός is irregular.

625. IRREGULAR ADJECTIVES

	μέγας *great*			πολύς *much*		
	Masc.	Fem.	Neut.	Masc.	Fem.	Neut.
Sing. N.	μέγας	μεγάλη	μέγα	πολύς	πολλή	πολύ
G.	μεγάλου	μεγάλης	μεγάλου	πολλοῦ	πολλῆς	πολλοῦ
D.	μεγάλῳ	μεγάλῃ	μεγάλῳ	πολλῷ	πολλῇ	πολλῷ
A.	μέγαν	μεγάλην	μέγα	πολύν	πολλήν	πολύ
Plur. N.	μεγάλοι	μεγάλαι	μεγάλα	πολλοί	πολλαί	πολλά
G.	μεγάλων	μεγάλων	μεγάλων	πολλῶν	πολλῶν	πολλῶν
D.	μεγάλοις	μεγάλαις	μεγάλοις	πολλοῖς	πολλαῖς	πολλοῖς
A.	μεγάλους	μεγάλᾱς	μεγάλα	πολλούς	πολλᾱς	πολλά

626. NUMERALS

	εἷς *one*			δύο *two*
	Masc.	Fem.	Neut.	Masc., Fem., Neut.
N.	εἷς	μία	ἕν	N. A. δύο
G.	ἑνός	μιᾶς	ἑνός	G. D. δυοῖν
D.	ἑνί	μιᾷ	ἑνί	
A.	ἕνα	μίαν	ἕν	

	τρεῖς *three*		τέτταρες *four*	
	Masc. and Fem.	Neut.	Masc. and Fem.	Neut.
N.	τρεῖς	τρία	τέτταρες	τέτταρα
G.	τριῶν		τεττάρων	
D.	τρισί		τέτταρσι	
A.	τρεῖς	τρία	τέτταρας	τέτταρα

627.

	MASC.	FEM.	NEUT.
Sing. N.	οὐδείς *nobody*	οὐδεμία	οὐδέν *nothing*
G.	οὐδενός	οὐδεμιᾶς	οὐδενός
D.	οὐδενί	οὐδεμιᾷ	οὐδενί
A.	οὐδένα	οὐδεμίαν	οὐδέν

Masc. Plur. N. οὐδένες, G. οὐδένων, D. οὐδέσι, A. οὐδένας

PRONOUNS

628. PERSONAL

	FIRST PERSON	SECOND PERSON	THIRD PERSON *Indirect Reflexive*
Sing. N.	ἐγώ *I*	σύ *thou*	
G.	ἐμοῦ, μου	σοῦ, σου	[οὗ], [οὑ]
D.	ἐμοί, μοι	σοί, σοι	οἷ, οἱ, *to himself*
A.	ἐμέ, με	σέ, σε	[ἕ], [ἑ]
Dual N. A.	νώ	σφώ	
G. D.	νῷν	σφῷν	
Plur. N.	ἡμεῖς *we*	ὑμεῖς *you*	σφεῖς
G.	ἡμῶν	ὑμῶν	σφῶν
D.	ἡμῖν	ὑμῖν	σφίσι
A.	ἡμᾶς	ὑμᾶς	σφᾶς

629. αὐτός *self, same, him* (in oblique cases), etc.

	MASC.	FEM.	NEUT.
Sing. N.	αὐτός	αὐτή	αὐτό
G.	αὐτοῦ	αὐτῆς	αὐτοῦ
D.	αὐτῷ	αὐτῇ	αὐτῷ
A.	αὐτόν	αὐτήν	αὐτό
Dual N. A.	αὐτώ	αὐτά	αὐτώ
G. D.	αὐτοῖν	αὐταῖν	αὐτοῖν
Plur. N.	αὐτοί	αὐταί	αὐτά
G.	αὐτῶν	αὐτῶν	αὐτῶν
D.	αὐτοῖς	αὐταῖς	αὐτοῖς
A.	αὐτούς	αὐτάς	αὐτά

ἄλλος, ἄλλη, ἄλλο, *another, other*, is declined like αὐτός

630.　　　　　　　　REFLEXIVE

ἐμαυτοῦ of myself

	SINGULAR		PLURAL	
	MASC.	FEM.	MASC.	FEM.
G.	ἐμαυτοῦ	ἐμαυτῆς	ἡμῶν αὐτῶν	
D.	ἐμαυτῷ	ἐμαυτῇ	ἡμῖν αὐτοῖς	ἡμῖν αὐταῖς
A.	ἐμαυτόν	ἐμαυτήν	ἡμᾶς αὐτούς	ἡμᾶς αὐτάς

σεαυτοῦ of yourself

	MASC.	FEM.	MASC.	FEM.
G.	σεαυτοῦ or σαυτοῦ	σεαυτῆς or σαυτῆς	ὑμῶν αὐτῶν	
D.	σεαυτῷ or σαυτῷ	σεαυτῇ or σαυτῇ	ὑμῖν αὐτοῖς	ὑμῖν αὐταῖς
A.	σεαυτόν or σαυτόν	σεαυτήν or σαυτήν	ὑμᾶς αὐτούς	ὑμᾶς αὐτάς

ἑαυτοῦ of himself

	MASC.	FEM.	NEUT.	MASC.	FEM.	NEUT.
G.	ἑαυτοῦ	ἑαυτῆς	ἑαυτοῦ	ἑαυτῶν	ἑαυτῶν	ἑαυτῶν
D.	ἑαυτῷ	ἑαυτῇ	ἑαυτῷ	ἑαυτοῖς	ἑαυταῖς	ἑαυτοῖς
A.	ἑαυτόν	ἑαυτήν	ἑαυτό	ἑαυτούς	ἑαυτάς	ἑαυτά

or, contracted,

G.	αὑτοῦ	αὑτῆς	αὑτοῦ	αὑτῶν	αὑτῶν	αὑτῶν
D.	αὑτῷ	αὑτῇ	αὑτῷ	αὑτοῖς	αὑταῖς	αὑτοῖς
A.	αὑτόν	αὑτήν	αὑτό	αὑτούς	αὑτάς	αὑτά

Plural also :　σφῶν αὐτῶν
　　　　　　　σφίσιν αὐτοῖς, αἷς
　　　　　　　σφᾶς αὐτούς, ἅς

631.　　　　　　　　RECIPROCAL

ἀλλήλοιν of one another

	DUAL			PLURAL		
	MASC.	FEM.	NEUT.	MASC.	FEM.	NEUT.
G.	ἀλλήλοιν	ἀλλήλαιν	ἀλλήλοιν	ἀλλήλων	ἀλλήλων	ἀλλήλων
D.	ἀλλήλοιν	ἀλλήλαιν	ἀλλήλοιν	ἀλλήλοις	ἀλλήλαις	ἀλλήλοις
A.	ἀλλήλω	ἀλλήλᾱ	ἀλλήλω	ἀλλήλους	ἀλλήλᾱς	ἄλληλα

632.

DEFINITE ARTICLE

	MASC.	FEM.	NEUT.
Sing. N.	ὁ *the*	ἡ	τό
G.	τοῦ	τῆς	τοῦ
D.	τῷ	τῇ	τῷ
A.	τόν	τήν	τό
Dual N. A.	τώ	τώ	τώ
G. D.	τοῖν	τοῖν	τοῖν
Plur. N.	οἱ	αἱ	τά
G.	τῶν	τῶν	τῶν
D.	τοῖς	ταῖς	τοῖς
A.	τούς	τάς	τά

633.

DEMONSTRATIVE

	MASC.	FEM.	NEUT.	MASC.	FEM.	NEUT.
Sing. N.	ὅδε *this*	ἥδε	τόδε	οὗτος *this*	αὕτη	τοῦτο
G.	τοῦδε	τῆσδε	τοῦδε	τούτου	ταύτης	τούτου
D.	τῷδε	τῇδε	τῷδε	τούτῳ	ταύτῃ	τούτῳ
A.	τόνδε	τήνδε	τόδε	τοῦτον	ταύτην	τοῦτο
Dual N. A.	τώδε	τώδε	τώδε	τούτω	τούτω	τούτω
G. D.	τοῖνδε	τοῖνδε	τοῖνδε	τούτοιν	τούτοιν	τούτοιν
Plur. N.	οἵδε	αἵδε	τάδε	οὗτοι	αὗται	ταῦτα
G.	τῶνδε	τῶνδε	τῶνδε	τούτων	τούτων	τούτων
D.	τοῖσδε	ταῖσδε	τοῖσδε	τούτοις	ταύταις	τούτοις
A.	τούσδε	τάσδε	τάδε	τούτους	ταύτᾱς	ταῦτα

	MASC.	FEM.	NEUT.
Sing. N.	ἐκεῖνος *that*	ἐκείνη	ἐκεῖνο
G.	ἐκείνου	ἐκείνης	ἐκείνου
D.	ἐκείνῳ	ἐκείνῃ	ἐκείνῳ
A.	ἐκεῖνον	ἐκείνην	ἐκεῖνο
Dual N. A.	ἐκείνω	ἐκείνω	ἐκείνω
G. D.	ἐκείνοιν	ἐκείνοιν	ἐκείνοιν
Plur. N.	ἐκεῖνοι	ἐκεῖναι	ἐκεῖνα
G.	ἐκείνων	ἐκείνων	ἐκείνων
D.	ἐκείνοις	ἐκείναις	ἐκείνοις
A.	ἐκείνους	ἐκείνᾱς	ἐκεῖνα

634. INTERROGATIVE   635. INDEFINITE

	Masc. and Fem.	Neut.	Masc. and Fem.	Neut.
Sing. N.	τίς *who?*	τί *what?*	τις *anybody*	τι *anything*
G.	τίνος, τοῦ		τινός, του	
D.	τίνι, τῷ		τινί, τῳ	
A.	τίνα	τί	τινά	τι
Dual N. A.	τίνε		τινέ	
G. D.	τίνοιν		τινοῖν	
Plur. N.	τίνες	τίνα	τινές	τινά
G.	τίνων		τινῶν	
D.	τίσι		τισί	
A.	τίνας	τίνα	τινάς	τινά

636. RELATIVE

	SINGULAR				DUAL				PLURAL	
	Masc.	Fem.	Neut.		Masc.	Fem.	Neut.		Masc. Fem.	Neut.
N.	ὅς	ἥ	ὅ	N. A.	ὥ	ὥ	ὥ	N.	οἵ αἵ	ἅ
G.	οὗ	ἧς	οὗ	G. D.	οἷν	οἷν	οἷν	G.	ὧν ὧν	ὧν
D.	ᾧ	ᾗ	ᾧ					D.	οἷς αἷς	οἷς
A.	ὅν	ἥν	ὅ					A.	οὕς ἅς	ἅ

637. INDEFINITE RELATIVE

	MASC.	FEM.	NEUT.
Sing. N.	ὅστις	ἥτις	ὅ τι or ὅ,τι
G.	οὗτινος, ὅτου	ἧστινος	οὗτινος, ὅτου
D.	ᾧτινι, ὅτῳ	ᾗτινι	ᾧτινι, ὅτῳ
A.	ὅντινα	ἥντινα	ὅ τι or ὅ,τι
Dual N. A.	ὥτινε	ὥτινε	ὥτινε
G. D.	οἷντινοιν	οἷντινοιν	οἷντινοιν
Plur. N.	οἵτινες	αἵτινες	ἅτινα
G.	ὧντινων, ὅτων	ὧντινων	ὧντινων, ὅτων
D.	οἷστισι, ὅτοις	αἷστισι	οἷστισι, ὅτοις
A.	οὕστινας	ἅστινας	ἅτινα

638.

	Direct or indirect interrogatives:	Indirect interrogatives or indefinite relatives:	The definite relative meaning
PRONOUNS	τίς *who ?*	ὅστις	*who* is ὅς
	ποῖος { *of what sort ?* / *what sort of ?*	ὁποῖος	*of what sort* is οἷος
	πόσος { *how great ?* / *how much ?* / *how many ?*	ὁπόσος	*as great as* / *as much as* } is ὅσος / *as many as*
ADVERBS	πότε *when ?*	ὁπότε	*when* is ὅτε
	ποῦ *where ?*	ὅπου	*where* is οὗ or ἔνθα
	πῶς *how ?*	ὅπως	*how, as,* is ὡς or ὥσπερ

VERBS

639. ### PERSONAL ENDINGS

INDICATIVE, SUBJUNCTIVE, AND OPTATIVE

	ACTIVE		MIDDLE	
	Primary Tenses	*Secondary Tenses*	*Primary Tenses*	*Secondary Tenses*
Sing. 1.	-μι	-ν	-μαι	-μην
2.	-ς	-ς	-σαι	-σο
3.	-σι	——	-ται	-το
Dual 2.	-τον	-τον	-σθον	-σθον
3.	-τον	-την	-σθον	-σθην
Plur. 1.	-μεν	-μεν	-μεθα	-μεθα
2.	-τε	-τε	-σθε	-σθε
3.	-νσι	-ν, -σαν	-νται	-ντο

IMPERATIVE

	ACTIVE				MIDDLE		
	Sing.	*Dual*	*Plur.*		*Sing.*	*Dual*	*Plur.*
2.	-θι	-τον	-τε		-σο	-σθον	-σθε
3.	-τω	-των	-ντων		-σθω	-σθων	-σθων

INFINITIVE ENDINGS

ACTIVE	MIDDLE
εν (contracted with thematic vowel to -ειν) and -ναι	-σθαι

640. VOWEL STEMS: UNCONTRACTED.

1. ACTIVE

			PRES.	IMPF.	FUT.
Indic.	Sing.	1.	λύω	ἔλῡον	λύσω
		2.	λύεις	ἔλῡες	λύσεις
		3.	λύει	ἔλῡε	λύσει
	Dual	2.	λύετον	ἐλύετον	λύσετον
		3.	λύετον	ἐλῡέτην	λύσετον
	Plur.	1.	λύομεν	ἐλύομεν	λύσομεν
		2.	λύετε	ἐλύετε	λύσετε
		3.	λύουσι	ἔλῡον	λύσουσι
Subjv.	Sing.	1.	λύω		
		2.	λύῃς		
		3.	λύῃ		
	Dual	2.	λύητον		
		3.	λύητον		
	Plur.	1.	λύωμεν		
		2.	λύητε		
		3.	λύωσι		
Opt.	Sing.	1.	λύοιμι		λύσοιμι
		2.	λύοις		λύσοις
		3.	λύοι		λύσοι
	Dual	2.	λύοιτον		λύσοιτον
		3.	λῡοίτην		λῡσοίτην
	Plur.	1.	λύοιμεν		λύσοιμεν
		2.	λύοιτε		λύσοιτε
		3.	λύοιεν		λύσοιεν
Imv.	Sing.	2.	λῦε		
		3.	λῡέτω		
	Dual	2.	λύετον		
		3.	λῡέτων		
	Plur.	2.	λύετε		
		3.	λῡόντων		
Inf.			λύειν		λύσειν
Partic.			λύων, λύουσα, λῦον (§ 616. 2)		λύσων, λύσουσα, λῦσον (cp. § 616. 2)

INFLECTION OF λΰ-ω *I loose*

VOICE

			1 AOR.	1 PF.	1 PLUP.
Indic.	Sing.	1.	ἔλῡσα	λέλυκα	ἐλελύκη
		2.	ἔλῡσας	λέλυκας	ἐλελύκης
		3.	ἔλῡσε	λέλυκε	ἐλελύκει(ν)
	Dual	2.	ἐλΰσατον	λελύκατον	ἐλελύκετον
		3.	ἐλῡσάτην	λελύκατον	ἐλελυκέτην
	Plur.	1.	ἐλΰσαμεν	λελύκαμεν	ἐλελύκεμεν
		2.	ἐλΰσατε	λελύκατε	ἐλελύκετε
		3.	ἔλῡσαν	λελύκᾱσι	ἐλελύκεσαν
Subjv.	Sing.	1.	λΰσω	[λελύκω (§ 436)	
		2.	λΰσῃς	λελύκῃς	
		3.	λΰσῃ	λελύκῃ	
	Dual	2.	λΰσητον	λελύκητον	
		3.	λΰσητον	λελύκητον	
	Plur.	1.	λΰσωμεν	λελύκωμεν	
		2.	λΰσητε	λελύκητε	
		3.	λΰσωσι	λελύκωσι]	
Opt.	Sing.	1.	λΰσαιμι	[λελύκοιμι (§ 436)	
		2.	λΰσαις, λΰσειας (§ 254)	λελύκοις	
		3.	λΰσαι, λΰσειε	λελύκοι	
	Dual	2.	λΰσαιτον	λελύκοιτον	
		3.	λῡσαίτην	λελυκοίτην	
	Plur.	1.	λΰσαιμεν	λελύκοιμεν	
		2.	λΰσαιτε	λελύκοιτε	
		3.	λΰσαιεν, λΰσειαν (§ 254)	λελύκοιεν]	
Imv.	Sing.	2.	λῦσον	(§ 437)	
		3.	λῡσάτω		
	Dual	2.	λΰσατον		
		3.	λῡσάτων		
	Plur.	2.	λΰσατε		
		3.	λῡσάντων		
Inf.			λῦσαι	λελυκέναι	
Partic.			λΰσᾱς, λΰσᾱσα, λῦσαν (§ 618)	λελυκώς, λελυκυῖα, λελυκός (§ 623)	

2. MIDDLE

		PRES.	IMPF.	FUT.
Indic.	Sing. 1.	λύομαι	ἐλυόμην	λύσομαι
	2.	λύῃ, λύει	ἐλύου	λύσῃ, λύσει
	3.	λύεται	ἐλύετο	λύσεται
	Dual 2.	λύεσθον	ἐλύεσθον	λύσεσθον
	3.	λύεσθον	ἐλυέσθην	λύσεσθον
	Plur. 1.	λυόμεθα	ἐλυόμεθα	λυσόμεθα
	2.	λύεσθε	ἐλύεσθε	λύσεσθε
	3.	λύονται	ἐλύοντο	λύσονται
Subjv.	Sing. 1.	λύωμαι		
	2.	λύῃ		
	3.	λύηται		
	Dual 2.	λύησθον		
	3.	λύησθον		
	Plur. 1.	λυώμεθα		
	2.	λύησθε		
	3.	λύωνται		
Opt.	Sing. 1.	λυοίμην		λυσοίμην
	2.	λύοιο		λύσοιο
	3.	λύοιτο		λύσοιτο
	Dual 2.	λύοισθον		λύσοισθον
	3.	λυοίσθην		λυσοίσθην
	Plur. 1.	λυοίμεθα		λυσοίμεθα
	2.	λύοισθε		λύσοισθε
	3.	λύοιντο		λύσοιντο
Imv.	Sing. 2.	λύου		
	3.	λυέσθω		
	Dual 2.	λύεσθον		
	3.	λυέσθων		
	Plur. 2.	λύεσθε		
	3.	λυέσθων		
Inf.		λύεσθαι		λύσεσθαι
Partic.		λυόμενος, λυομένη, λυόμενον		λυσόμενος, -η, -ον

VOICE

			1 AOR.	PF.	PLUP.
Indic.	Sing.	1.	ἐλῡσάμην	λέλυμαι	ἐλελύμην
		2.	ἐλύσω	λέλυσαι	ἐλέλυσο
		3.	ἐλύσατο	λέλυται	ἐλέλυτο
	Dual	2.	ἐλύσασθον	λέλυσθον	ἐλέλυσθον
		3.	ἐλῡσάσθην	λέλυσθον	ἐλελύσθην
	Plur.	1.	ἐλῡσάμεθα	λελύμεθα	ἐλελύμεθα
		2.	ἐλύσασθε	λέλυσθε	ἐλέλυσθε
		3.	ἐλύσαντο	λέλυνται	ἐλέλυντο
Subjv.	Sing.	1.	λύσωμαι	λελυμένος ὦ	
		2.	λύσῃ	λελυμένος ᾖς	
		3.	λύσηται	λελυμένος ᾖ	
	Dual	2.	λύσησθον	λελυμένω ἦτον	
		3.	λύσησθον	λελυμένω ἦτον	
	Plur.	1.	λῡσώμεθα	λελυμένοι ὦμεν	
		2.	λύσησθε	λελυμένοι ἦτε	
		3.	λύσωνται	λελυμένοι ὦσι	
Opt.	Sing.	1.	λῡσαίμην	λελυμένος εἴην	
		2.	λύσαιο	λελυμένος εἴης	
		3.	λύσαιτο	λελυμένος εἴη	
	Dual	2.	λύσαισθον	λελυμένω εἴητον or εἶτον	
		3.	λῡσαίσθην	λελυμένω εἰήτην or εἴτην	
	Plur.	1.	λῡσαίμεθα	λελυμένοι εἴημεν or εἶμεν	
		2.	λύσαισθε	λελυμένοι εἴητε or εἶτε	
		3.	λύσαιντο	λελυμένοι εἴησαν or εἶεν	
Imv.	Sing.	2.	λῦσαι	λέλυσο	
		3.	λῡσάσθω	λελύσθω	
	Dual	2.	λύσασθον	λέλυσθον	
		3.	λῡσάσθων	λελύσθων	
	Plur.	2.	λύσασθε	λέλυσθε	
		3.	λῡσάσθων	λελύσθων	
Inf.			λύσασθαι	λελύσθαι	
Partic.			λῡσάμενος, -η, -ον	λελυμένος, -η, -ον	

3. PASSIVE VOICE

			FUT. PF.	1 AOR.	1 FUT.
Indic.	Sing.	1.	λελύσομαι	ἐλύθην	λυθήσομαι
		2.	λελύσῃ, λελύσει	ἐλύθης	λυθήσῃ, λυθήσε
		3.	λελύσεται	ἐλύθη	λυθήσεται
	Dual	2.	λελύσεσθον	ἐλύθητον	λυθήσεσθον
		3.	λελύσεσθον	ἐλυθήτην	λυθήσεσθον
	Plur.	1.	λελῡσόμεθα	ἐλύθημεν	λυθησόμεθα
		2.	λελύσεσθε	ἐλύθητε	λυθήσεσθε
		3.	λελύσονται	ἐλύθησαν	λυθήσονται
Subjv.	Sing.	1.		λυθῶ	
		2.		λυθῇς	
		3.		λυθῇ	
	Dual	2.		λυθῆτον	
		3.		λυθῆτον	
	Plur.	1.		λυθῶμεν	
		2.		λυθῆτε	
		3.		λυθῶσι	
Opt.	Sing.	1.	λελῡσοίμην	λυθείην	λυθησοίμην
		2.	λελύσοιο	λυθείης	λυθήσοιο
		3.	λελύσοιτο	λυθείη	λυθήσοιτο
	Dual	2.	λελύσοισθον	λυθεῖτον or λυθείητον	λυθήσοισθον
		3.	λελῡσοίσθην	λυθείτην or λυθειήτην	λυθησοίσθην
	Plur.	1.	λελῡσοίμεθα	λυθεῖμεν or λυθείημεν	λυθησοίμεθα
		2.	λελύσοισθε	λυθεῖτε or λυθείητε	λυθήσοισθε
		3.	λελύσοιντο	λυθεῖεν or λυθείησαν	λυθήσοιντο
Imv.	Sing.	2.		λύθητι	
		3.		λυθήτω	
	Dual	2.		λύθητον	
		3.		λυθήτων	
	Plur.	2.		λύθητε	
		3.		λυθέντων	
Inf.			λελύσεσθαι	λυθῆναι	λυθήσεσθαι
Partic.			λελῡσόμενος, -η, -ον	λυθείς, λυθεῖσα, λυθέν (§ 620. *a*)	λυθησόμενος, -η, -ον

641. As examples of the second aorist and second perfect systems (§§ 83, 445, 485), the second aorist (active and middle) and the second perfect and pluperfect of λείπω *leave* are here given.

			2 AOR. ACT.	2 AOR. MID.	2 PF.	2 PLUP.
Indic.	Sing.	1.	ἔλιπον	ἐλιπόμην	λέλοιπα	ἐλελοίπη
		2.	ἔλιπες	ἐλίπου	λέλοιπας	ἐλελοίπης
		3.	ἔλιπε	ἐλίπετο	λέλοιπε	ἐλελοίπει(ν)
	Dual	2.	ἐλίπετον	ἐλίπεσθον	λελοίπατον	ἐλελοίπετον
		3.	ἐλιπέτην	ἐλιπέσθην	λελοίπατον	ἐλελοιπέτην
	Plur.	1.	ἐλίπομεν	ἐλιπόμεθα	λελοίπαμεν	ἐλελοίπεμεν
		2.	ἐλίπετε	ἐλίπεσθε	λελοίπατε	ἐλελοίπετε
		3.	ἔλιπον	ἐλίποντο	λελοίπᾱσι	ἐλελοίπεσαν
Subjv.	Sing.	1.	λίπω	λίπωμαι	[λελοίπω (§ 446)	
		2.	λίπῃς	λίπῃ	λελοίπῃς	
		3.	λίπῃ	λίπηται	λελοίπῃ	
	Dual	2.	λίπητον	λίπησθον	λελοίπητον	
		3.	λίπητον	λίπησθον	λελοίπητον	
	Plur.	1.	λίπωμεν	λιπώμεθα	λελοίπωμεν	
		2.	λίπητε	λίπησθε	λελοίπητε	
		3.	λίπωσι	λίπωνται	λελοίπωσι]	
Opt.	Sing.	1.	λίποιμι	λιποίμην	[λελοίποιμι (§ 446)	
		2.	λίποις	λίποιο	λελοίποις	
		3.	λίποι	λίποιτο	λελοίποι	
	Dual	2.	λίποιτον	λίποισθον	λελοίποιτον	
		3.	λιποίτην	λιποίσθην	λελοιποίτην	
	Plur.	1.	λίποιμεν	λιποίμεθα	λελοίποιμεν	
		2.	λίποιτε	λίποισθε	λελοίποιτε	
		3.	λίποιεν	λίποιντο	λελοίποιεν]	
Imv.	Sing.	2.	λίπε	λιποῦ		
		3.	λιπέτω	λιπέσθω		
	Dual	2.	λίπετον	λίπεσθον		
		3.	λιπέτων	λιπέσθων		
	Plur.	2.	λίπετε	λίπεσθε		
		3.	λιπόντων	λιπέσθων		

	2 AOR. ACT.	2 AOR. MID.	2 PF.
Inf.	λιπεῖν	λιπέσθαι	λελοιπέναι
Partic.	λιπών, λιποῦσα,	λιπόμενος,	λελοιπώς, -υῖα, -ός (cp
	λιπόν (§ 616. 1. *a*)	-η, -ον	§ 623)

642. As an example of the second passive system, the second aorist passive and the second future passive of βλάπτω *hurt* are here given.

			2 AOR. PASS.	2 FUT. PASS.
Indic.	Sing.	1.	ἐβλάβην	βλαβήσομαι
		2.	ἐβλάβης	βλαβήσῃ or -σει
		3.	ἐβλάβη	βλαβήσεται
	Dual	2.	ἐβλάβητον	βλαβήσεσθον
		3.	ἐβλαβήτην	βλαβήσεσθον
	Plur.	1.	ἐβλάβημεν	βλαβησόμεθα
		2.	ἐβλάβητε	βλαβήσεσθε
		3.	ἐβλάβησαν	βλαβήσονται
Subjv.	Sing.	1.	βλαβῶ	
		2.	βλαβῇς	
		3.	βλαβῇ	
	Dual	2.	βλαβῆτον	
		3.	βλαβῆτον	
	Plur.	1.	βλαβῶμεν	
		2.	βλαβῆτε	
		3.	βλαβῶσι	
Opt.	Sing.	1.	βλαβείην	βλαβησοίμην
		2.	βλαβείης	βλαβήσοιο
		3.	βλαβείη	βλαβήσοιτο
	Dual	2.	βλαβεῖτον or βλαβείητον	βλαβήσοισθον
		3.	βλαβείτην or βλαβειήτην	βλαβησοίσθην
	Plur.	1.	βλαβεῖμεν or βλαβείημεν	βλαβησοίμεθα
		2.	βλαβεῖτε or βλαβείητε	βλαβήσοισθε
		3.	βλαβεῖεν or βλαβείησαν	βλαβήσοιντο

			2 Aor. Pass.	2 Fut. Pass.
Imv.	Sing.	2.	βλάβηθι	
		3.	βλαβήτω	
	Dual	2.	βλάβητον	
		3.	βλαβήτων	
	Plur.	2.	βλάβητε .	
		3.	βλαβέντων	
Inf.			βλαβῆναι	βλαβήσεσθαι
Partic.			βλαβείς, βλαβεῖσα, βλαβέν	βλαβησόμενος, -η,
			(§ 620. *a*)	-ον

CONTRACT VERBS

643. Verbs in -άω, -έω, -όω are contracted only in the present and imperfect. For the principles of contraction, see §§ 504, 505, 507, 516, 528. τῖμάω (τῖμα-) *honor*, ποιέω (ποιε-) *make*, and δηλόω (δηλο-) *manifest* are inflected as follows in the present and imperfect of the active, middle, and passive.

ACTIVE
Present Indicative
SINGULAR

1.	(τῖμάω)	τῖμῶ	(ποιέω)	ποιῶ	(δηλόω)	δηλῶ
2.	(τῖμάεις)	τῖμᾷς	(ποιέεις)	ποιεῖς	(δηλόεις)	δηλοῖς
3.	(τῖμάει)	τῖμᾷ	(ποιέει)	ποιεῖ	(δηλόει)	δηλοῖ

DUAL

| 2. | (τῖμάετον) | τῖμᾶτον | (ποιέετον) | ποιεῖτον | (δηλόετον) | δηλοῦτον |
| 3 | (τῖμάετον) | τῖμᾶτον | (ποιέετον) | ποιεῖτον | (δηλόετον) | δηλοῦτον |

PLURAL

1	(τῖμάομεν)	τῖμῶμεν	(ποιέομεν)	ποιοῦμεν	(δηλόομεν)	δηλοῦμεν
2.	(τῖμάετε)	τῖμᾶτε	(ποιέετε)	ποιεῖτε	(δηλόετε)	δηλοῦτε
3.	(τῖμάουσι)	τῖμῶσι	(ποιέουσι)	ποιοῦσι	(δηλόουσι)	δηλοῦσι

Imperfect
SINGULAR

1.	(ἐτίμαον)	ἐτίμων	(ἐποίεον)	ἐποίουν	(ἐδήλοον)	ἐδήλουν
2.	(ἐτίμαες)	ἐτίμᾱς	(ἐποίεες)	ἐποίεις	(ἐδήλοες)	ἐδήλους
3.	(ἐτίμαε)	ἐτίμᾱ	(ἐποίεε)	ἐποίει	(ἐδήλοε)	ἐδήλου

DUAL

2. (ἐτῑμάετον)   ἐτῑμᾶτον   (ἐποιέετον)   ἐποιεῖτον   (ἐδηλόετον)   ἐδηλοῦτο|
3. (ἐτῑμαέτην)   ἐτῑμάτην   (ἐποιεέτην)   ἐποιείτην   (ἐδηλοέτην)   ἐδηλούτη|

PLURAL

1. (ἐτῑμάομεν)   ἐτῑμῶμεν   (ἐποιέομεν)   ἐποιοῦμεν   (ἐδηλόομεν)   ἐδηλοῦμε|
2. (ἐτῑμάετε)   ἐτῑμᾶτε   (ἐποιέετε)   ἐποιεῖτε   (ἐδηλόετε)   ἐδηλοῦτε
3. (ἐτῑμαον)   ἐτῑμων   (ἐποίεον)   ἐποίουν   (ἐδήλοον)   ἐδήλουν

Present Subjunctive

SINGULAR

1. (τῑμάω)   τῑμῶ   (ποιέω)   ποιῶ   (δηλόω)   δηλῶ
2. (τῑμάῃς)   τῑμᾷς   (ποιέῃς)   ποιῇς   (δηλόῃς)   δηλοῖς
3. (τῑμάῃ)   τῑμᾷ   (ποιέῃ)   ποιῇ   (δηλόῃ)   δηλοῖ

DUAL

2. (τῑμάητον)   τῑμᾶτον   (ποιέητον)   ποιῆτον   (δηλόητον)   δηλῶτον
3. (τῑμάητον)   τῑμᾶτον   (ποιέητον)   ποιῆτον   (δηλόητον)   δηλῶτον

PLURAL

1. (τῑμάωμεν)   τῑμῶμεν   (ποιέωμεν)   ποιῶμεν   (δηλόωμεν)   δηλῶμεν
2. (τῑμάητε)   τῑμᾶτε   (ποιέητε)   ποιῆτε   (δηλόητε)   δηλῶτε
3. (τῑμάωσι)   τῑμῶσι   (ποιέωσι)   ποιῶσι   (δηλόωσι)   δηλῶσι

Present Optative

SINGULAR

1. (τῑμαοίην)   τῑμῴην   (ποιεοίην)   ποιοίην   (δηλοοίην)   δηλοίην
2. (τῑμαοίης)   τῑμῴης   (ποιεοίης)   ποιοίης   (δηλοοίης)   δηλοίης
3. (τῑμαοίη)   τῑμῴη   (ποιεοίη)   ποιοίη   (δηλοοίη)   δηλοίη

DUAL

2. (τῑμαοίητον) [τῑμῴητον (ποιεοίητον) [ποιοίητον (δηλοοίητον) [δηλοίητο|
3. (τῑμαοιΐτην) τῑμῴτην] (ποιεοιήτην) ποιοιήτην] (δηλοοιήτην) δηλοιήτη|

PLURAL

1. (τῑμαοίημεν) [τῑμῴημεν (ποιεοίημεν) [ποιοίημεν (δηλοοίημεν) [δηλοίημε|
2. (τῑμαοίητε)   τῑμῴητε   (ποιεοίητε) ποιοίητε   (δηλοοίητε)   δηλοίητε
3. (τῑμαοίησαν) τῑμῴησαν](ποιεοίησαν) ποιοίησαν] (δηλοοίησαν) δηλοίησα|

or [1]   or [1]   or [1]

---

[1] The forms with the mood sign ιη are commonly found in the singular; t
forms with the mood sign ι (without η), in the dual and plural.

SINGULAR

(τῑμάοιμι)	[τῑμῷμι	(ποιέοιμι)	[ποιοῖμι	(δηλόοιμι)	[δηλοῖμι
(τῑμάοις)	τῑμῷς	(ποιέοις)	ποιοῖς	(δηλόοις)	δηλοῖς
(τῑμάοι)	τῑμῷ]	(ποιέοι)	ποιοῖ]	(δηλόοι)	δηλοῖ]

DUAL

(τῑμάοιτον)	τῑμῷτον	(ποιέοιτον)	ποιοῖτον	(δηλόοιτον)	δηλοῖτον
(τῑμαοίτην)	τῑμῴτην	(ποιεοίτην)	ποιοίτην	(δηλοοίτην)	δηλοίτην

PLURAL

(τῑμάοιμεν)	τῑμῷμεν	(ποιέοιμεν)	ποιοῖμεν	(δηλόοιμεν)	δηλοῖμεν
(τῑμάοιτε)	τῑμῷτε	(ποιέοιτε)	ποιοῖτε	(δηλόοιτε)	δηλοῖτε
(τῑμάοιεν)	τῑμῷεν	(ποιέοιεν)	ποιοῖεν	(δηλόοιεν)	δηλοῖεν

Present Imperative

SINGULAR

(τίμαε)	τίμᾱ	(ποίεε)	ποίει	(δήλοε)	δήλου
(τῑμαέτω)	τῑμάτω	(ποιεέτω)	ποιείτω	(δηλοέτω)	δηλούτω

DUAL

(τῑμάετον)	τῑμᾶτον	(ποιέετον)	ποιεῖτον	(δηλόετον)	δηλοῦτον
(τῑμαέτων)	τῑμάτων	(ποιεέτων)	ποιείτων	(δηλοέτων)	δηλούτων

PLURAL

(τῑμάετε)	τῑμᾶτε	(ποιέετε)	ποιεῖτε	(δηλόετε)	δηλοῦτε
(τῑμαόντων)	τῑμώντων	(ποιεόντων)	ποιούντων	(δηλοόντων)	δηλούντων

Present Infinitive

(τῑμάειν)	τῑμᾶν [1]	(ποιέειν)	ποιεῖν [1]	(δηλόειν)	δηλοῦν [1]

Present Participle (see § 622 and *a*)

(τῑμάων)	τῑμῶν	(ποιέων)	ποιῶν	(δηλόων)	δηλῶν

MIDDLE AND PASSIVE

Present Indicative

SINGULAR

(τῑμάομαι)	τῑμῶμαι	(ποιέομαι)	ποιοῦμαι	(δηλόομαι)	δηλοῦμαι
(τῑμάῃ or τῑμάει)	τῑμᾷ	(ποιέῃ or ποιέει)	ποιῇ or ποιεῖ	(δηλόῃ or δηλόει)	δηλοῖ
(τῑμάεται)	τῑμᾶται	(ποιέεται)	ποιεῖται	(δηλόεται)	δηλοῦται

---

[1] As the infinitive ending -ειν is a contraction of the thematic vowel ε and εν
p. § 639), τῑμᾶν really represents τῑμα-ε-εν; ποιεῖν, ποιε-ε-εν; and δηλοῦν,
λο-ε-εν.

DUAL

2. (τῑμάεσθον) τῑμᾶσθον (ποιέεσθον) ποιεῖσθον (δηλόεσθον) δηλοῦσθον
3. (τῑμάεσθον) τῑμᾶσθον (ποιέεσθον) ποιεῖσθον (δηλόεσθον) δηλοῦσθον

PLURAL

1. (τῑμαόμεθα) τῑμώμεθα (ποιεόμεθα) ποιούμεθα (δηλοόμεθα) δηλούμεθα
2. (τῑμάεσθε) τῑμᾶσθε (ποιέεσθε) ποιεῖσθε (δηλόεσθε) δηλοῦσθε
3. (τῑμάονται) τῑμῶνται (ποιέονται) ποιοῦνται (δηλόονται) δηλοῦνται

Imperfect

SINGULAR

1. (ἐτῑμαόμην) ἐτῑμώμην (ἐποιεόμην) ἐποιούμην (ἐδηλοόμην) ἐδηλούμην
2. (ἐτῑμάου) ἐτῑμῶ (ἐποιέου) ἐποιοῦ (ἐδηλόου) ἐδηλοῦ
3. (ἐτῑμάετο) ἐτῑμᾶτο (ἐποιέετο) ἐποιεῖτο (ἐδηλόετο) ἐδηλοῦτο

DUAL

2. (ἐτῑμάεσθον) ἐτῑμᾶσθον (ἐποιέεσθον) ἐποιεῖσθον (ἐδηλόεσθον) ἐδηλοῦσθον
3. (ἐτῑμαέσθην) ἐτῑμάσθην (ἐποιεέσθην) ἐποιείσθην (ἐδηλοέσθην) ἐδηλούσθην

PLURAL

1. (ἐτῑμαόμεθα) ἐτῑμώμεθα (ἐποιεόμεθα) ἐποιούμεθα (ἐδηλοόμεθα) ἐδηλούμεθα
2. (ἐτῑμάεσθε) ἐτῑμᾶσθε (ἐποιέεσθε) ἐποιεῖσθε (ἐδηλόεσθε) ἐδηλοῦσθε
3. (ἐτῑμάοντο) ἐτῑμῶντο (ἐποιέοντο) ἐποιοῦντο (ἐδηλόοντο) ἐδηλοῦντο

Present Subjunctive

SINGULAR

1. (τῑμάωμαι) τῑμῶμαι (ποιέωμαι) ποιῶμαι (δηλόωμαι) δηλῶμαι
2. (τῑμάῃ) τῑμᾷ (ποιέῃ) ποιῇ (δηλόῃ) δηλοῖ
3 (τῑμάηται) τῑμᾶται (ποιέηται) ποιῆται (δηλόηται) δηλῶται

DUAL

2. (τῑμάησθον) τῑμᾶσθον (ποιέησθον) ποιῆσθον (δηλόησθον) δηλῶσθον
3. (τῑμάησθον) τῑμᾶσθον (ποιέησθον) ποιῆσθον (δηλόησθον) δηλῶσθον

PLURAL

1. (τῑμαώμεθα) τῑμώμεθα (ποιεώμεθα) ποιώμεθα (δηλοώμεθα) δηλώμεθα
2. (τῑμάησθε) τῑμᾶσθε (ποιέησθε) ποιῆσθε (δηλόησθε) δηλῶσθε
3. (τῑμάωνται) τῑμῶνται (ποιέωνται) ποιῶνται (δηλόωνται) δηλῶνται

Present Optative

SINGULAR

1. (τῑμαοίμην) τῑμῴμην (ποιεοίμην) ποιοίμην (δηλοοίμην) δηλοίμην
2. (τῑμάοιο) τῑμῷο (ποιέοιο) ποιοῖο (δηλόοιο) δηλοῖο
3. (τῑμάοιτο) τῑμῷτο (ποιέοιτο) ποιοῖτο (δηλόοιτο) δηλοῖτο

DUAL

(τῑμάοισθον)	τῑμῷσθον	(ποιέοισθον)	ποιοῖσθον	(δηλόοισθον)	δηλοῖσθον
(τῑμαοίσθην)	τῑμῴσθην	(ποιεοίσθην)	ποιοίσθην	(δηλοοίσθην)	δηλοίσθην

PLURAL

(τῑμαοίμεθα)	τῑμῴμεθα	(ποιεοίμεθα)	ποιοίμεθα	(δηλοοίμεθα)	δηλοίμεθⱥ
(τῑμάοισθε)	τῑμῷσθε	(ποιέοισθε)	ποιοῖσθε	(δηλόοισθε)	δηλοῖσθε
(τῑμάοιντο)	τῑμῷντο	(ποιέοιντο)	ποιοῖντο	(δηλόοιντο)	δηλοῖντο

Present Imperative

SINGULAR

(τῑμάου)	τῑμῶ	(ποιέου)	ποιοῦ	(δηλόου)	δηλοῦ
(τῑμαέσθω)	τῑμάσθω	(ποιεέσθω)	ποιείσθω	(δηλοέσθω)	δηλούσθω

DUAL

(τῑμάεσθον)	τῑμᾶσθον	(ποιέεσθον)	ποιεῖσθον	(δηλόεσθον)	δηλοῦσθον
(τῑμαέσθων)	τῑμάσθων	(ποιεέσθων)	ποιείσθων	(δηλοέσθων)	δηλούσθων

PLURAL

(τῑμάεσθε)	τῑμᾶσθε	(ποιέεσθε)	ποιεῖσθε	(δηλόεσθε)	δηλοῦσθε
(τῑμαέσθων)	τῑμάσθων	(ποιεέσθων)	ποιείσθων	(δηλοέσθων)	δηλούσθων

Present Infinitive

(τῑμάεσθαι)	τῑμᾶσθαι	(ποιέεσθαι)	ποιεῖσθαι	(δηλόεσθαι)	δηλοῦσθαι

Present Participle

(τῑμαόμενος)	τῑμώμενος	(ποιεόμενος)	ποιούμενος	(δηλοόμενος)	δηλούμενος

644. Liquid Verbs: future active and middle of φαίνω *show*.

Indicative

		FUTURE ACTIVE		FUTURE MIDDLE	
Sing.	1.	(φανέω)	φανῶ	(φανέομαι)	φανοῦμαι
	2.	(φανέεις)	φανεῖς	(φανέῃ or -έει)	φανῇ or -εῖ
	3.	(φανέει)	φανεῖ	(φανέεται)	φανεῖται
Dual	2.	(φανέετον)	φανεῖτον	(φανέεσθον)	φανεῖσθον
	3.	(φανέετον)	φανεῖτον	(φανέεσθον)	φανεῖσθον
Plur.	1.	(φανέομεν)	φανοῦμεν	(φανεόμεθα)	φανούμεθα
	2.	(φανέετε)	φανεῖτε	(φανέεσθε)	φανεῖσθε
	3.	(φανέουσι)	φανοῦσι	(φανέονται)	φανοῦνται

Optative

Sing.	1.	(φανεοίην)	φανοίην	(φανεοίμην)	φανοίμην
	2.	(φανεοίης)	φανοίης	(φανέοιο)	φανοῖο
	3.	(φανεοίη)	φανοίη	(φανέοιτο)	φανοῖτο
Dual	2.	(φανέοιτον)	φανοῖτον	(φανέοισθον)	φανοῖσθον
	3.	(φανεοίτην)	φανοίτην	(φανεοίσθην)	φανοίσθην
Plur.	1.	(φανέοιμεν)	φανοῖμεν	(φανεοίμεθα)	φανοίμεθα
	2.	(φανέοιτε)	φανοῖτε	(φανέοισθε)	φανοῖσθε
	3.	(φανέοιεν)	φανοῖεν	(φανέοιντο)	φανοῖντο

or

Sing.	1.	(φανέοιμι)	[φανοῖμι
	2.	(φανέοις)	φανοῖς
	3.	(φανέοι)	φανοῖ]

Infinitive

(φανέειν)   φανεῖν   (φανέεσθαι)   φανεῖσθαι

Participle

(φανέων, φανέουσα,   φανών, φανοῦσα,   (φανεόμενος,   φανούμενος,
   φανέον)   φανοῦν (cp.   -η, -ον)   -η, -ον
   § 622)

645. Liquid Verbs: first aorist active and middle of φαίνω *show*.

Indicative

		1 AORIST ACTIVE	1 AORIST MIDDLE
Sing.	1.	ἔφηνα	ἐφηνάμην
	2.	ἔφηνας	ἐφήνω
	3.	ἔφηνε	ἐφήνατο
Dual	2.	ἐφήνατον	ἐφήνασθον
	3.	ἐφηνάτην	ἐφηνάσθην
Plur.	1.	ἐφήναμεν	ἐφή άμεθα
	2.	ἐφήνατε	ἐφήνασθε
	3.	ἔφηναν	ἐφήναντο

Subjunctive

Sing.	1.	φήνω	φήνωμαι
	2.	φήνῃς	φήνῃ
	3.	φήνῃ	φήνηται

	1 Aorist Active	1 Aorist Middle
Dual 2.	φήνητον	φήνησθον
3.	φήνητον	φήνησθον
Plur. 1.	φήνωμεν	φηνώμεθα
2.	φήνητε	φήνησθε
3.	φήνωσι	φήνωνται

Optative

Sing. 1.	φήναιμι	φηναίμην
2.	φήναις or φήνειας (cp. § 254)	φήναιο
3.	φήναι or φήνειε	φήναιτο
Dual 2.	φήναιτον	φήναισθον
3.	φηναίτην	φηναίσθην
Plur. 1.	φήναιμεν	φηναίμεθα
2.	φήναιτε	φήναισθε
3.	φήναιεν or φήνειαν (cp. § 254)	φήναιντο

Imperative

Sing. 2.	φῆνον	φῆναι
3.	φηνάτω	φηνάσθω
Dual 2.	φήνατον	φήνασθον
3.	φηνάτων	φηνάσθων
Plur. 2.	φήνατε	φήνασθε
3.	φηνάντων	φηνάσθων

Infinitive

φῆναι	φήνασθαι

Participle

φήνᾱς, -ᾱσα, φῆναν (cp. § 618)	φηνάμενος, -η, -ον

CONJUGATION OF MI-VERBS

646. Root class. — Inflection of τίθημι *place*, ἵστημι *set*, δίδωμι *give*, in the present, imperfect, and second aorist tenses; and of ἐπριάμην *I bought*.

ACTIVE
Present Indicative

Sing. 1.	τί-θη-μι	ἵ-στη-μι	δί-δω-μι
2.	τί-θη-s	ἵ-στη-s	δί-δω-s
3.	τί-θη-σι	ἵ-στη-σι	δί-δω-σι

Dual 2.	τί-θε-τον	ἵ-στα-τον	δί-δο-τον
3.	τί-θε-τον	ἵ-στα-τον	δί-δο-τον
Plur. 1.	τί-θε-μεν	ἵ-στα-μεν	δί-δο-μεν
2.	τί-θε-τε	ἵ-στα-τε	δί-δο-τε
3.	τι-θέ-ᾱσι	ἱ-στᾶσι	δι-δό-ᾱσι

Imperfect

Sing. 1.	ἐ-τί-θη-ν	ἵ-στη-ν	ἐ-δί-δουν (§ 570)
2.	ἐ-τί-θεις (§ 559)	ἵ-στη-s	ἐ-δί-δους
3.	ἐ-τί-θει	ἵ-στη	ἐ-δί-δου
Dual 2.	ἐ-τί-θε-τον	ἵ-στα-τον	ἐ-δί-δο-τον
3.	ἐ-τι-θέ-την	ἱ-στά-την	ἐ-δι-δό-την
Plur. 1.	ἐ-τί-θε-μεν	ἵ-στα-μεν	ἐ-δί-δο-μεν
2.	ἐ-τί-θε-τε	ἵ-στα-τε	ἐ-δί-δο-τε
3.	ἐ-τί-θε-σαν	ἵ-στα-σαν	ἐ-δί-δο-σαν

Present Subjunctive

Sing. 1.	τι-θῶ	ἱ-στῶ	δι-δῶ
2.	τι-θῇ-s	ἱ-στῇ-s	δι-δῷ-s
3.	τι-θῇ	ἱ-στῇ	δι-δῷ
Dual 2.	τι-θῆ-τον	ἱ-στῆ-τον	δι-δῶ-τον
3.	τι-θῆ-τον	ἱ-στῆ-τον	δι-δῶ-τον
Plur. 1.	τι-θῶ-μεν	ἱ-στῶ-μεν	δι-δῶ-μεν
2.	τι-θῆ-τε	ἱ-στῆ-τε	δι-δῶ-τε
3.	τι-θῶ-σι	ἱ-στῶ-σι	δι-δῶ-σι

Present Optative

Sing. 1.	τι-θείη-ν	ἱ-σταίη-ν	δι-δοίη-ν
2.	τι-θείη-s	ἱ-σταίη-s	δι-δοίη-s
3.	τι-θείη	ἱ-σταίη	δι-δοίη
Dual 2.	τι-θεῖ-τον	ἱ-σταῖ-τον	δι-δοῖ-τον
3.	τι-θεί-την	ἱ-σταί-την	δι-δοί-την
Plur. 1.	τι-θεῖ-μεν	ἱ-σταῖ-μεν	δι-δοῖ-μεν
2.	τι-θεῖ-τε	ἱ-σταῖ-τε	δι-δοῖ-τε
3.	τι-θεῖε-ν	ἱ-σταῖε-ν	δι-δοῖε-ν
	or [1]	or [1]	or [1]

---

[1] In the dual and plural the forms without η are commonly found.

Dual 2. [τι-θείη-τον]   [ἱ-σταίη-τον]   [δι-δοίη-τον]
     3. [τι-θειή-την]   [ἱ-σταιή-την]   [δι-δοιή-την]

Plur. 1. [τι-θείη-μεν]   [ἱ-σταίη-μεν]   [δι-δοίη-μεν]
      2. [τι-θείη-τε]   [ἱ-σταίη-τε]   [δι-δοίη-τε]
      3. [τι-θείη-σαν]   [ἱ-σταίη-σαν]   [δι-δοίη-σαν]

Present Imperative

Sing. 2. τί-θει (§ 559)   ἵ-στη (§ 551)   δί-δου (§ 570)
      3. τι-θέ-τω   ἱ-στά-τω   δι-δό-τω

Dual 2. τί-θε-τον   ἵ-στα-τον   δί-δο-τον
     3. τι-θέ-των   ἱ-στά-των   δι-δό-των

Plur. 2. τί-θε-τε   ἵ-στα-τε   δί-δο-τε
      3. τι-θέ-ντων   ἱ-στά-ντων   δι-δό-ντων

Present Infinitive

τι-θέ-ναι   ἱ-στά-ναι   δι-δό-ναι

Present Participle

τι-θείς, -εῖσα, -έν   ἱ-στάς, -ᾶσα, -άν   δι-δούς, -οῦσα, -όν
(§ 620)   (§ 617)   (§ 621)

MIDDLE AND PASSIVE
Present Indicative

Sing. 1. τί-θε-μαι   ἵ-στα-μαι   δί-δο-μαι
      2. τί-θε-σαι   ἵ-στα-σαι   δί-δο-σαι
      3. τί-θε-ται   ἵ-στα-ται   δί-δο-ται

Dual 2. τί-θε-σθον   ἵ-στα-σθον   δί-δο-σθον
     3. τί-θε-σθον   ἵ-στα-σθον   δί-δο-σθον

Plur. 1. τι-θέ-μεθα   ἱ-στά-μεθα   δι-δό-μεθα
      2. τί-θε-σθε   ἵ-στα-σθε   δί-δο-σθε
      3. τί-θε-νται   ἵ-στα-νται   δί-δο-νται

Imperfect

Sing. 1. ἐ-τι-θέ-μην   ἱ-στά-μην   ἐ-δι-δό-μην
      2. ἐ-τί-θε-σο   ἵ-στα-σο   ἐ-δί-δο-σο
      3. ἐ-τί-θε-το   ἵ-στα-το   ἐ-δί-δο-το

Dual 2. ἐ-τί-θε-σθον   ἵ-στα-σθον   ἐ-δί-δο-σθον
     3. ἐ-τι-θέ-σθην   ἱ-στά-σθην   ἐ-δι-δό-σθην

Plur. 1.	ἐ-τι-θέ-μεθα	ἱ-στά-μεθα	ἐ-δι-δό-μεθα
2.	ἐ-τί-θε-σθε	ἵ-στα-σθε	ἐ-δί-δο-σθε
3.	ἐ-τί-θε-ντο	ἵ-στα-ντο	ἐ-δί-δο-ντο

Present Subjunctive

Sing. 1.	τι-θῶ-μαι	ἱ-στῶ-μαι	δι-δῶ-μαι
2.	τι-θῇ	ἱ-στῇ	δι-δῷ
3.	τι-θῆ-ται	ἱ-στῆ-ται	δι-δῶ-ται
Dual 2.	τι-θῆ-σθον	ἱ-στῆ-σθον	δι-δῶ-σθον
3.	τι-θῆ-σθον	ἱ-στῆ-σθον	δι-δῶ-σθον
Plur. 1.	τι-θώ-μεθα	ἱ-στώ-μεθα	δι-δώ-μεθα
2.	τι-θῆ-σθε	ἱ-στῆ-σθε	δι-δῶ-σθε
3.	τι-θῶ-νται	ἱ-στῶ-νται	δι-δῶ-νται

Present Optative

Sing. 1.	τι-θεί-μην	ἱ-σταί-μην	δι-δοί-μην
2.	τι-θεῖ-ο	ἱ-σταῖ-ο	δι-δοῖ-ο
3.	τι-θεῖ-το	ἱ-σταῖ-το	δι-δοῖ-το
Dual 2.	τι-θεῖ-σθον	ἱ-σταῖ-σθον	δι-δοῖ-σθον
3.	τι-θεί-σθην	ἱ-σταί-σθην	δι-δοί-σθην
Plur. 1.	τι-θεί-μεθα	ἱ-σταί-μεθα	δι-δοί-μεθα
2.	τι-θεῖ-σθε	ἱ-σταῖ-σθε	δι-δοῖ-σθε
3.	τι-θεῖ-ντο	ἱ-σταῖ-ντο	δι-δοῖ-ντο

or [1]

Sing. 1.	τι-θοί-μην
2.	τι-θοῖ-ο
3.	τι-θοῖ-το
Dual 2.	τι-θοῖ-σθον
3.	τι-θοί-σθην
Plur. 1.	τι-θοί-μεθα
2.	τι-θοῖ-σθε
3.	τι-θοῖ-ντο

Present Imperative

Sing. 2.	τί-θε-σο	ἵ-στα-σο	δί-δο-σο
3.	τι-θέ-σθω	ἱ-στά-σθω	δι-δό-σθω

---

[1] Cp. ποιοίμην (§ 643).

Dual 2. τί-θε-σθον   ἵ-στα-σθον   δί-δο-σθον
    3. τι-θέ-σθων   ἱ-στά-σθων   δι-δό-σθων

Plur. 2. τί-θε-σθε   ἵ-στα-σθε   δί-δο-σθε
    3. τι-θέ-σθων   ἱ-στά-σθων   δι-δό-σθων

Present Infinitive

τί-θε-σθαι   ἵ-στα-σθαι   δί-δο-σθαι

Present Participle

τι-θέ-μενος   ἱ-στά-μενος   δι-δό-μενος

SECOND AORIST

Indicative

	ACTIVE	MIDDLE	ACTIVE	MIDDLE	ACTIVE	MIDDLE
Sing. 1.	(ἔθηκα)	ἐ-θέμην	ἔ-στη-ν [1]	ἐπριάμην [2]	(ἔδωκα)	ἐ-δό-μην
2.	(ἔθηκας)	ἔ-θου	ἔ-στη-ς	ἐπρίω	(ἔδωκας)	ἔ-δου
3.	(ἔθηκε)	ἔ-θε-το	ἔ-στη	ἐπρίατο	(ἔδωκε)	ἔ-δο-το
Dual 2.	ἔ-θε-τον	ἔ-θε-σθον	ἔ-στη-τον	ἐ-πρία-σθον	ἔ-δο-τον	ἔ-δο-σθον
3.	ἐ-θέ-την	ἐ-θέ-σθην	ἐ-στή-την	ἐ-πριά-σθην	ἐ-δό-την	ἐ-δό-σθην
Plur. 1.	ἔ-θε-μεν	ἐ-θέ-μεθα	ἔ-στη-μεν	ἐ-πριά-μεθα	ἔ-δο-μεν	ἐ-δό-μεθα
2.	ἔ-θε-τε	ἔ-θε-σθε	ἔ-στη-τε	ἐ-πρία-σθε	ἔ-δο-τε	ἔ-δο-σθε
3.	ἔ-θε-σαν	ἔ-θε-ντο	ἔ-στη-σαν	ἐ-πρία-ντο	ἔ-δο-σαν	ἔ-δο-ντο

Subjunctive

	ACTIVE	MIDDLE	ACTIVE	MIDDLE	ACTIVE	MIDDLE
Sing. 1.	θῶ	θῶ-μαι	στῶ	πρίω-μαι	δῶ	δῶ-μαι
2.	θῇ-ς	θῇ	στῇ-ς	πρίῃ	δῷ-ς	δῷ
3.	θῇ	θῆ-ται	στῇ	πρίη-ται	δῷ	δῶ-ται
Dual 2.	θῆ-τον	θῆ-σθον	στῆ-τον	πρίη-σθον	δῶ-τον	δῶ-σθον
3.	θῆ-τον	θῆ-σθον	στῆ-τον	πρίη-σθον	δῶ-τον	δῶ-σθον
Plur. 1.	θῶ-μεν	θώ-μεθα	στῶ-μεν	πριώ-μεθα	δῶ-μεν	δώ-μεθα
2.	θῆ-τε	θῆ-σθε	στῆ-τε	πρίη-σθε	δῶ-τε	δῶ-σθε
3.	θῶ-σι	θῶ-νται	στῶ-σι	πρίω-νται	δῶ-σι	δῶ-νται

Optative

	ACTIVE	MIDDLE	ACTIVE	MIDDLE	ACTIVE	MIDDLE
Sing. 1.	θείη-ν	θεί-μην	σταίη-ν	πριαί-μην	δοίη-ν	δοί-μην
2.	θείη-ς	θεῖ-ο	σταίη-ς	πρίαι-ο	δοίη-ς	δοῖ-ο
3.	θείη	θεῖ-το [3]	σταίη	πρίαι-το	δοίη	δοῖ-το

---

[1] stood.   [2] bought, § 550.   [3] Or θοῖτο.

Dual	2.	θεῖ-τον	θεῖ-σθον	σταῖ-τον	πρίαι-σθον	δοῖ-τον	δοῖ-σθον
	3.	θεί-την	θεί-σθην	σταί-την	πριαί-σθην	δοί-την	δοί-σθην
Plur.	1.	θεῖ-μεν	θεί-μεθα	σταῖ-μεν	πριαί-μεθα	δοῖ-μεν	δοί-μεθα
	2.	θεῖ-τε	θεῖ-σθε	σταῖ-τε	πρίαι-σθε	δοῖ-τε	δοῖ-σθε
	3.	θεῖε-ν	θεῖ-ντο	σταῖε-ν	πρίαι-ντο	δοῖε-ν	δοῖ-ντο
		or	or	or		or	
Dual	2.	[θείη-τον]		[σταίη-τον]		[δοίη-τον]	
	3.	[θειή-την]		[σταιή-την]		[δοιή-την]	
Plur.	1.	[θείη-μεν]	θοίμεθα	[σταίη-μεν]		[δοίη-μεν]	
	2.	[θείη-τε]	θοῖσθε	[σταίη-τε]		[δοίη-τε]	
	3.	[θείη-σαν]	θοῖντο	[σταίη-σαν]		[δοίη-σαν]	

Imperative

Sing.	2.	θέ-ς	θοῦ	στῆ-θι	πρίω	δό-ς	δοῦ
	3.	θέ-τω	θέ-σθω	στή-τω	πριά-σθω	δό-τω	δό-σθω
Dual	2.	θέ-τον	θέ-σθον	στῆ-τον	πρία-σθον	δό-τον	δό-σθον
	3.	θέ-των	θέ-σθων	στή-των	πριά-σθων	δό-των	δό-σθων
Plur.	2.	θέ-τε	θέ-σθε	στῆ-τε	πρία-σθε	δό-τε	δό-σθε
	3.	θέ-ντων	θέ-σθων	στά-ντων	πριά-σθων	δό-ντων	δό-σθων

Infinitive

| | θεῖ-ναι | θέ-σθαι | στῆ-ναι | πρία-σθαι | δοῦ-ναι | δό-σθαι |

Participle

	θείς,	θέ-μενος,	στάς,	πριά-μενος,	δούς,	δό-μενος,
	θεῖσα,	-η, -ον	στᾶσα,	-η, -ον	δοῦσα,	-η, -ον
	θέν [1]		στάν [2]		δόν [3]	

SECOND PERFECT OF MI-VERBS

647. A few verbs of the μι-class have a second perfect
and pluperfect. Only the dual and plural occur in the indicative; for the singular, the first perfect and pluperfect
are used. The second perfect and pluperfect of ἵστημι
are inflected as follows:

---

[1] Cp. § 620.   [2] Cp. § 617.   [3] Cp. § 621.

SECOND PERFECT

	INDIC.	SUBJV.	OPT. (poetic)	IMV. (poetic)
Sing. 1.	(ἔστηκα) *stand*	ἑστῶ	ἑσταίη-ν	
2.	(ἔστηκας)	ἑστῇ-s	ἑσταίη-s	ἔστα-θι
3.	(ἔστηκε)	ἑστῇ	ἑσταίη	ἑστά-τω
Dual 2.	ἔστα-τον	ἑστῆ-τον	ἑσταίη-τον or -αῖτον	ἔστα-τον
3.	ἔστα-τον	ἑστῆ-τον	ἑσταιή-την or -αίτην	ἑστά-των
Plur. 1.	ἔστα-μεν	ἑστῶ-μεν	ἑσταίη-μεν or -αῖμεν	
2.	ἔστα-τε	ἑστῆ-τε	ἑσταίη-τε or -αῖτε	ἔστα-τε
3.	ἑστᾶσι	ἑστῶ-σι	ἑσταίη-σαν or -αῖεν	ἑστά-ντων

Infinitive ἑστά-ναι   *Participle* ἑστώ-s, ἑστῶσα, ἑστός (§ 624)

SECOND PLUPERFECT

Sing. 1.	(εἱστήκη) *stood*	Dual 2.	ἔστα-τον	Plur. 1.	ἔστα-μεν
2.	(εἱστήκης)	3.	ἑστά-την	2.	ἔστα-τε
3.	(εἱστήκει)			3.	ἔστα-σαν

648. **-νῡμι class.** — Inflection of the present system of δείκνῡμι *show* and of second aorist ἔδῦν *entered*.

Indicative

	ACTIVE		MIDDLE AND PASSIVE		ACTIVE
	Present	*Imperfect*	*Present*	*Imperfect*	*2 Aorist*
Sing. 1.	δείκ-νῡ-μι	ἐ-δείκ-νῡ-ν	δείκ-νυ-μαι	ἐ-δεικ-νύ-μην	ἔ-δῦ-ν
2.	δείκ-νῡ-s	ἐ-δείκ-νῡ-s	δείκ-νυ-σαι	ἐ-δείκ-νυ-σο	ἔ-δῦ-s
3.	δείκ-νῡ-σι	ἐ-δείκ-νῡ	δείκ-νυ-ται	ἐ-δείκ-νυ-το	ἔ-δῦ
Dual 2.	δείκ-νυ-τον	ἐ-δείκ-νυ-τον	δείκ-νυ-σθον	ἐ-δείκ-νυ-σθον	ἔ-δῦ-τον
3.	δείκ-νυ-τον	ἐ-δείκ-νύ-την	δείκ-νυ-σθον	ἐ-δεικ-νύ-σθην	ἐ-δύ-την
Plur. 1.	δείκ-νυ-μεν	ἐ-δείκ-νυ-μεν	δείκ-νύ-μεθα	ἐ-δεικ-νύ-μεθα	ἔ-δῦ-μεν
2.	δείκ-νυ-τε	ἐ-δείκ-νυ-τε	δείκ-νυ-σθε	ἐ-δείκ-νυ-σθε	ἔ-δῦ-τε
3.	δεικ-νύ-ᾱσι	ἐ-δείκ-νυ-σαν	δείκ-νυ-νται	ἐ-δείκ-νυ-ντο	ἔ-δῦ-σαν

Subjunctive

Sing. 1.	δεικνύω	δεικνύωμαι	δύω
2.	δεικνύῃς	δεικνύῃ	δύῃς
3.	δεικνύῃ	δεικνύηται	δύῃ
Dual 2.	δεικνύητον	δεικνύησθον	δύητον
3.	δεικνύητον	δεικνύησθον	δύητον

Plur.	1.	δεικνύωμεν	δεικνυώμεθα	δύωμεν
	2.	δεικνύητε	δεικνύησθε	δύητε
	3.	δεικνύωσι	δεικνύωνται	δύωσι

Optative

Sing.	1.	δεικνύοιμι	δεικνυοίμην
	2.	δεικνύοις	δεικνύοιο
	3.	δεικνύοι	δεικνύοιτο
Dual	2.	δεικνύοιτον	δεικνύοισθον
	3.	δεικνυοίτην	δεικνυοίσθην
Plur.	1.	δεικνύοιμεν	δεικνυοίμεθα
	2.	δεικνύοιτε	δεικνύοισθε
	3.	δεικνύοιεν	δεικνύοιντο

Imperative

Sing.	2.	δείκ-νῡ (§ 579)	δείκ-νυ-σο	δῦ-θι
	3.	δεικ-νύ-τω	δεικ-νύ-σθω	δύ-τω
Dual	2.	δείκ-νυ-τον	δείκ-νυ-σθον	δῦ-τον
	3.	δεικ-νύ-των	δεικ-νύ-σθων	δύ-των
Plur.	2.	δείκ-νυ-τε	δείκ-νυ-σθε	δῦ-τε
	3.	δεικ-νύ-ντων	δεικ-νύ-σθων	δύ-ντων

Infinitive

δεικ-νύ-ναι	δείκ-νυ-σθαι	δῦ-ναι

Participle

δεικ-νῡ́ς, -ῦσα, -ύν	δεικ-νύ-μενος, -η, -ον	δῡ́ς, δῦσα, δύν
(§ 619)		(cp. § 619)

649. ἵημι (ἑ-, ἡ-) *send* is inflected nearly like τίθημι (§ 646). The inflection of the present and second aorist systems is as follows:

		ACTIVE			MIDDLE (PASSIVE)		MIDDLE
		Indicative				*Indicative*	
		PRES.	IMPF.	2 AOR.	PRES.	IMPF.	2 AOR.
Sing.	1.	ἵημι	ἵην	(ἧκα)	ἵεμαι	ἱέμην	— εἵμην
	2.	ἵης, ἱεῖς	ἵεις	(ἧκας)	ἵεσαι	ἵεσο	— εἷσο
	3.	ἵησι	ἵει	(ἧκε)	ἵεται	ἵετο	— εἷτο

Dual 2.	ἵετον	ἵετον	— εἶτον	ἵεσθον	ἵεσθον	— εἶσθον
3.	ἵετον	τέτην	— εἴτην	ἵεσθον	τέσθην	— εἴσθην
Plur. 1.	ἵεμεν	ἵεμεν	— εἶμεν	ἱέμεθα	ἱέμεθα	— εἵμεθα
2.	ἵετε	ἵετε	— εἶτε	ἵεσθε	ἵεσθε	— εἶσθε
3.	ἱᾶσι	ἵεσαν	— εἶσαν	ἵενται	ἵεντο	— εἶντο

Subjunctive

Sing. 1.	ἱῶ	— ὧ	ἱῶμαι	— ὧμαι
2.	ἱῇς	— ᾗς	ἱῇ	— ᾗ
3.	ἱῇ	— ᾗ	ἱῆται	— ῆται
Dual 2.	ἱῆτον	— ῆτον	ἱῆσθον	— ῆσθον
3.	ἱῆτον	— ῆτον	ἱῆσθον	— ῆσθον
Plur. 1.	ἱῶμεν	— ὧμεν	ἱώμεθα	— ὥμεθα
2.	ἱῆτε	— ῆτε	ἱῆσθε	— ῆσθε
3.	ἱῶσι	— ὧσι	ἱῶνται	— ὧνται

Optative

Sing. 1.	ἱείην	— εἴην	ἱείμην	— εἵμην
2.	ἱείης	— εἴης	ἱεῖο	— εἶο
3.	ἱείη	— εἴη	ἱεῖτο	— εἶτο (— οἶτο)
Dual 2.	ἱεῖτον or ἱείητον	— εἶτον or εἴητον	ἱεῖσθον	— εἶσθον
3.	ἱείτην or ἱειήτην	— εἴτην or εἰήτην	ἱείσθην	— εἴσθην
Plur. 1.	ἱεῖμεν or ἱείημεν	— εἶμεν or εἴημεν	ἱείμεθα	— εἵμεθα (— οἵμεθα)
2.	ἱεῖτε or ἱείητε	— εἶτε or εἴητε	ἱεῖσθε	— εἶσθε (— οἶσθε)
3.	ἱεῖεν or ἱείησαν	— εἶεν or εἴησαν	ἱεῖντο	— εἶντο (— οἶντο)

Imperative

Sing. 2.	ἵει	— ἕς	ἵεσο	— οὗ
3.	ἱέτω	— ἕτω	ἱέσθω	— ἔσθω
Dual 2.	ἵετον	— ἕτον	ἵεσθον	— ἔσθον
3.	ἱέτων	— ἕτων	ἱέσθων	— ἔσθων
Plur. 2.	ἵετε	— ἕτε	ἵεσθε	— ἔσθε
3.	ἱέντων	— ἕντων	ἱέσθων	— ἔσθων

Infinitive

ἰέναι — εἶναι ἵεσθαι — ἔσθαι

Participle

ἰείς, ἰεῖσα, — εἴς, — εἶσα, ἱέμενος — ἔμενος
ἰέν (cp. § 620) — ἕν (cp. § 620)

Future: — ἥσω in prose only in composition; — ἥσομαι.
First Aorist: ἧκα in prose usually in composition, — ἡκάμην; both only in the indicative.
Perfect Active: — εἶκα only in composition.
Perfect Middle (Passive): — εἶμαι, — εἴμην (pluperfect); — εἴσθω, — εἶσθαι, — εἱμένος only in composition.
Aorist Passive: — εἴθην, — ἑθῶ, — ἑθῆναι, — ἑθείς; only in composition.
Future Passive: — ἑθήσομαι only in composition.
Verbal Adjectives: — ἑτός, — ἑτέος; only in composition.

650. εἰμί (ἐσ-; cp. Lat. *es-se*) *I am* is inflected as follows:

		PRESENT			IMPERFECT
	INDIC.	SUBJV.	OPT.	IMV.	INDIC.
Sing. 1.	εἰμί	ὦ	εἴην		ἦ or ἦν
2.	εἶ	ᾖς	εἴης	ἴσθι	ἦσθα
3.	ἐστί	ᾖ	εἴη	ἔστω	ἦν
Dual 2.	ἐστόν	ἦτον	εἴητον or εἶτον	ἔστον	ἦστον
3.	ἐστόν	ἦτον	εἰήτην or εἴτην	ἔστων	ἦστην
Plur. 1.	ἐσμέν	ὦμεν	εἴημεν or εἶμεν		ἦμεν
2.	ἐστέ	ἦτε	εἴητε or εἶτε	ἔστε	ἦτε or ἦστε (rare)
3.	εἰσί	ὦσι	εἴησαν or εἶεν	ἔστων	ἦσαν

Inf.: εἶναι. Partic.: ὤν, οὖσα, ὄν, gen. ὄντος, οὔσης, ὄντος, etc.

FUTURE (with middle forms)

ἔσομαι, ἔσῃ (or ἔσει), ἔσται, ἔσεσθον, ἔσεσθον, ἐσόμεθα, ἔσεσθε, ἔσονται, opt. ἐσοίμην, inf. ἔσεσθαι, partic. ἐσόμενος, -η, -ον

a. In the imperative 3 pl. ὄντων and ἔστωσαν also occur.

b. All the forms of the present indicative except εἶ are enclitic.

c. In composition ὤν retains its accent, as παρών, παροῦσα, παρόντος, etc.; and so ἔσται, as παρέσται.

651. εἶμι (ἰ-, εἰ-; cp. Lat. *ī-re*) *go* has only the present system.

| | PRESENT | | | | IMPERFECT |
	INDIC.	SUBJV.	OPT.	IMV.	INDIC.
Sing. 1.	εἶμι	ἴω	ἴοιμι or ἰοίην		ᾖα or ᾔειν
2.	εἶ	ἴῃς	ἴοις	ἴθι	ᾔεισθα or ᾔεις
3.	εἶσι	ἴῃ	ἴοι	ἴτω	ᾔειν or ᾔει
Dual 2.	ἴτον	ἴητον	ἴοιτον	ἴτον	ᾖτον
3.	ἴτον	ἴητον	ἰοίτην	ἴτων	ᾔτην
Plur. 1.	ἴμεν	ἴωμεν	ἴοιμεν		ᾖμεν
2.	ἴτε	ἴητε	ἴοιτε	ἴτε	ᾖτε
3.	ἴᾱσι	ἴωσι	ἴοιεν	ἰόντων	ᾖσαν or ᾔεσαν

Inf.: ἰέναι. Partic.: ἰών, ἰοῦσα, ἰόν, gen. ἰόντος, ἰούσης, ἰόντος, etc.
Verbal Adjectives: ἰτός, ἰτέος, ἰτητέος.

a. The imperative 3 pl. ἴτωσαν occurs rarely.

b. The participle ἰών is accented like a second aorist. The accent of the simple form of participle and infinitive is kept in composition, as ἀπιών, ἀπιοῦσα, ἀπιέναι. Otherwise the compounds have recessive accent so far as the rules allow: ἄπειμι, ἄπεισι, but ἀπῇα, ἀπῇμεν.

652. φημί (φα-, φη-, cp. Lat. *fā-rī*) *say, say yes,* or *assent* is inflected in the present as follows:

| | PRESENT | | | | IMPERFECT |
	INDIC.	SUBJV.	OPT.	IMV.	INDIC.
Sing. 1.	φημί	φῶ	φαίην		ἔφην
2	φής	φῇς	φαίης	φαθί or φάθι	ἔφησθα or ἔφης
3.	φησί	φῇ	φαίη	φάτω	ἔφη
Dual 2.	φατόν	φῆτον	not found	φάτον	ἔφατον
3.	φατόν	φῆτον	not found	φάτων	ἐφάτην
Plur. 1.	φαμέν	φῶμεν	φαῖμεν or φαίημεν		ἔφαμεν
2.	φατέ	φῆτε	φαίητε	φάτε	ἔφατε
3.	φᾱσί	φῶσι	φαῖεν or φαίησαν	φάντων	ἔφασαν

Inf.: **φάναι.** Partic.: poet. **φάς, φᾶσα, φάν** (Attic prose **φάσκων**).
Verbal Adjectives : **φατός** (poet.), **φατέος**.
Future : **φήσω, φήσειν, φήσων.**
First Aorist : **ἔφησα, φήσω, φήσαιμι, ——, φῆσαι, φήσᾱς.**
Pf. Pass. Imv. : **πεφάσθω** *let it be said.*

a. All the forms of the present indicative except **φής**
are enclitic.

653. In place of **ἦμαι** *sit* we find usually **κάθ-ημαι** in
Attic prose and comedy. **κάθημαι** sometimes is perfect
in meaning (*I have sat, I have been seated*). The **σ** of the
verb stem does not appear except before **-το.**

		PRESENT			IMPERFECT
	INDIC.	SUBJV.	OPT.	IMV.	INDIC.
Sing. 1.	κάθημαι	καθῶμαι	καθοίμην		ἐκαθήμην or καθήμην
2.	κάθησαι	καθῇ	καθοῖο	κάθησο	ἐκάθησο	καθῆσο
3.	κάθηται	καθῆται	καθοῖτο	καθήσθω	ἐκάθητο	καθῆστο[1]
Dual 2.	κάθησθον	καθῆσθον	καθοῖσθον	κάθησθον	ἐκάθησθον	καθῆσθον
3.	κάθησθον	καθῆσθον	καθοίσθην	καθήσθων	ἐκαθήσθην	καθήσθην
Plur. 1.	καθήμεθα	καθώμεθα	καθοίμεθα		ἐκαθήμεθα	καθήμεθα
2.	κάθησθε	καθῆσθε	καθοῖσθε	κάθησθε	ἐκάθησθε	καθῆσθε
3.	κάθηνται	καθῶνται	καθοῖντο	καθήσθων	ἐκάθηντο	καθῆντο

Inf.: **καθῆσθαι.** Partic.: **καθήμενος.**

a. In the imperfect **ἐκαθήμην** is used about as often as
καθήμην.

654. **κεῖμαι** (**κει-**) *lie, am laid,* regularly used in the
present and imperfect instead of the perfect and pluperfect
passive of **τίθημι** *place.*

		PRESENT			IMPERFECT
	INDIC.	SUBJV.	OPT.	IMV.	INDIC.
Sing. 1.	κεῖμαι				ἐκείμην
2.	κεῖσαι			κεῖσο	ἔκεισο
3.	κεῖται	κέηται	κέοιτο	κείσθω	ἔκειτο

[1] Or **καθῆτο.**

	INDIC.	SUBJV.	OPT.	IMV.	INDIC.
Dual 2.	κεῖσθον			κεῖσθον	ἔκεισθον
3.	κείσθον			κείσθων	ἐκείσθην
Plur. 1.	κείμεθα				ἐκείμεθα
2.	κεῖσθε	(δια)κέησθε		κεῖσθε	ἔκεισθε
3.	κεῖνται	(κατα)κέωνται	(προσ)κέοιντο	κείσθων	ἔκειντο

Inf.: κεῖσθαι. Partic.: κείμενος.

Future: κείσομαι, κείσῃ or κείσει, κείσεται, etc.

a. In the subjunctive and optative κει- becomes κε before a vowel.

b. Compounds have recessive accent only in present indicative and imperative: κατάκειμαι, κατάκεισο, but κατακεῖσθαι.

655. οἶδα (ἰδ, εἰδ-ε, οἰδ-; cp. Lat. *videō) know* is a perfect with the meaning of a present, and formed without reduplication. The second perfect and second pluperfect are inflected as follows:

			2 PERFECT			2 PLUPERFECT
	INDIC.	SUBJV.	OPT.		IMV.	INDIC.
Sing. 1.	οἶδα	εἰδῶ	εἰδείην			ᾔδη or ᾔδειν
2.	οἶσθα	εἰδῇς	εἰδείης		ἴσθι	ᾔδησθα ᾔδεις
3.	οἶδε	εἰδῇ	εἰδείη		ἴστω	ᾔδει(ν)
Dual 2.	ἴστον	εἰδῆτον	εἰδεῖτον		ἴστον	ᾖστον
3.	ἴστον	εἰδῆτον	εἰδείτην		ἴστων	ᾔστην
Plur. 1.	ἴσμεν	εἰδῶμεν	εἰδεῖμεν or εἰδείημεν			ᾖσμεν ᾔδεμεν
2.	ἴστε	εἰδῆτε	εἰδεῖτε	εἰδείητε	ἴστε	ᾖστε ᾔδετε
3.	ἴσᾱσι	εἰδῶσι	εἰδεῖεν	εἰδείησαν ἴστων		ᾖσαν ᾔδεσαν

Inf.: εἰδέναι. Partic.: εἰδώς, εἰδυῖα, εἰδός.

Verbal Adjective: ἰστέος. Future: εἴσομαι.

Compound: σύνοιδα *am conscious of.*

SUMMARY OF SYNTAX

USES OF THE CASES

656. Nominative:
    1. Subject (§ 53. *a*).
    2. Predicate nominative (§ 53. *k*).

657. Vocative:
    Person addressed (cp. § 64, *O brave captain*).

658. Accusative:
    1. DIRECT OBJECT (§ 53. *b*).
    2. COGNATE (§§ 181, 356).
    3. Adverbial (§ 284).
    4. Specification (§ 279).
    5. Extent of time or space (§ 142).
    6. Limit of motion, always with a preposition (cp. § 53. *e*).
    7. Two accusatives after verbs of *making* and *appointing; asking* and *depriving* (§§ 510, 511).
    8. Subject of infinitive (§ 53. *g*).
    9. Absolute (§ 566).

659. Genitive:

True genitive.
    1. "OF" RELATIONS, including
    2. Subjective and Objective (§ 53. *f*).
    3. Possession (§§ 53. *f*, 72).
    4. Measure (§ 278).
    5. Material (cp. § 502. II. 16).
    6. Value (§ 402).
    7. PARTITIVE (§ 179).
    8. Time *within which* (§ 155).
    9. After adverbs of place (§ 372).

10. SEPARATION (§ 201).
11. Comparison (§ 355).

12. Absolute (§ 401).
13. With ὑπό to express agent (§ 390).
14. In the predicate (§ 229).

660. Dative:

True dative.

1. "TO" OR "FOR" RELATIONS, including
2. Indirect object, etc. (§ 53. c).
3. Interest (advantage or disadvantage) (§ 53. d).
4. Possession (§ 119).
5. Agent with perfect passive (§ 458) and verbals in -τέος (§ 478).

6. LOCATIVE: Time when (§ 180).
   Place where (after prepositions, ἐν, etc.).
7. INSTRUMENTAL, including
8. Means and Manner, etc. (§ 141).
9. Degree of difference (§ 410).
10. Respect (§ 322).
11. Cause (§ 403).
12. Association (§ 317).

13. Dative with adjectives (§ 111).
14. After verbs compounded with certain prepositions (§ 136).

USES OF THE MOODS

For constructions that take the negative μή instead of οὐ see μή in the general VOCABULARY.

661. Indicative, — in addition to independent statements and ordinary relative clauses, note especially:

1. ἐπεί and ἐπειδή *when* with imperfect or *after*
   with aorist indicative (§ 167); ὅτε *when* commonly with the imperfect, of past time.

2. ἐπεί and ὅτι causal *since* with various tenses of
   indicative (§ 310).

3. ἕως, ἔστε, and μέχρι, *while, so long as, until,*
   with present or past indicative (§§ 522. 1,
   548. I. 2).

4. πρίν *until,* after a negative clause, with aorist
   indicative (§ 523. 1).

5. εἰ *if* with various tenses of indicative in *real*
   conditions (§ 106).

6. εἰ *if* with imperfect or aorist indicative in contrary to fact (*unreal*) conditions — much
   less frequent (§ 545).

7. εἰ *if* with future indicative in *warning future*
   conditions (§ 242).

8. ὥστε *so that* with various tenses of indicative
   to express result (§ 147).

   [Cp. ὥστε with infinitive (§ 147).]

9. ὅπως with future indicative after verbs signifying *to strive for, to care for,* or *to effect*
   (§ 535).

662. Subjunctive:

1. Introduced by ἐάν (ἄν, ἤν) in protasis of more
   vivid future (§ 241) or present general condition (§§ 398, 399).

2. Introduced by relative (ὅς, ὅστις) or temporal
   word (ἐπεί, ὅτε, ἕως, etc.) in protasis (§§ 248,
   400, 522. 2, 523. 2).

   NOTE. — ἄν always accompanies the subjunctive in
   protasis. ὅτε + ἄν = ὅταν; ὁπότε + ἄν = ὁπόταν; ἐπεί
   + ἄν = ἐπάν or ἐπήν; ἐπειδή + ἄν = ἐπειδάν.

most subjs are fut. few are present.

3. Introduced by ἵνα, ὅπως, or ὡς, *in order that*, after primary tenses and sometimes after secondary tenses (§§ 243, 535. *a*).

4. Introduced by μή *lest* or μὴ οὐ *lest not* after verbs of *fearing* in primary tenses and some times in secondary tenses (§ 438).

5. Hortatory, in first person (§ 244).

6. Deliberative, in first person (§ 564).

7. Prohibitory, in second person of aorist tense with μή (§ 309. 2).

663. Optative:

1. In future wishes (§ 584).

[Wishes that cannot be realized (in present or past time) are expressed by the imperfect or aorist indicative introduced by εἴθε or εἰ γάρ (§ 585); they may also be expressed by using ὤφελον *I ought, etc.*, with the infinitive (§ 586).]

2. In indirect discourse after a secondary tense of the verb of *saying*, representing an indicative or subjunctive of the *same tense* in the direct discourse (§ 260).

[But the indicative or the mood of the direct quotation may be retained (§ 260).]

3. In indirect questions (§§ 345, 565).

[But the indicative or the mood of the direct question may be retained (§ 345).]

4. With ἄν in the potential use (§ 266). ἄν can never stand first in its clause.

5. Introduced by εἰ *if* in protasis of the less vivid future condition (§ 267) or past general condition (*iterative* optative), § 416.

6. Introduced by a relative (ὅς, ὅστις) or temporal

word (ὅτε, etc.) in protasis of a condition, particularly of the past general (*iterative* optative), § 417.

7. Introduced by ἵνα, ὅπως, or ὡς, *in order that*, after secondary tenses (§§ 268, 535. *a*).

8. Introduced by μή *lest* or μὴ οὐ *lest not* after verbs of *fearing* in secondary tenses (§ 438. *a*).

664. Imperative:

1. In commands.

2. In prohibitions: μή and the *present* imperative (§ 309. 1).

[The *aorist* subjunctive with μή is also used (§ 309. 2).]

665. Infinitive:

1. In indirect discourse after ἔφη *he said*, ἐνόμισε *he thought*, and similar verbs, when the infinitive represents an indicative or optative of the *same tense* in the direct discourse (§§ 110, 156. 1); if ἄν was used with the optative (or indicative) of direct discourse, it is retained with the infinitive of indirect discourse (§§ 277, 546).

2. After verbs of *promising*, *hoping*, and *swearing*: the future infinitive; negative, if required, μή (§ 519).

3. With δοκεῖ *he seems* and λέγεται *he is said* in the "personal" use (§§ 391, 512).

4. As subject of verbs meaning *is*, *is possible*, etc.; with δεῖ *it is necessary*, δοκεῖ *it seems best*, etc. (§§ 223, 512. *a*).

5. With ἀνάγκη *it is necessary*, ὥρᾱ *it is time*, etc. (§ 230).

6. With verbs like δύναμαι *be able*, κελεύω *command*, βούλομαι *wish*, ἐθέλω *wish* (§ 98).

7. With the article τό, τοῦ, τῷ as a neuter substantive in various constructions; especially common is διὰ τό with the infinitive: *on account of the fact that*, etc. (§ 500).

8. With ὥστε *so as* indicating a result (§ 147).
   [Cp. ὥστε with the indicative (§ 147).]

9. With adjectives of *ability* and *fitness*, like ἱκανός *able* (§ 333).

10. With πρίν *before* after an affirmative clause (§ 524).
    [After a negative clause πρίν usually means *until* and has the construction of other temporal words (§ 523).]

11. Rarely expressing purpose (after verbs signifying *to give* or *to appoint*).
    The negative with the infinitive is μή except in indirect discourse, when οὐ is regularly used.

USES OF THE PARTICIPLE

666. 1. As an attributive adjective (§ 211).

2. With or without the article to represent a relative clause: οἱ βουλόμενοι *those that desire* (§ 212).

3. To represent a temporal, causal, concessive, or conditional clause (§ 213).

4. Common is ἔχων or λαβών *with* agreeing with the subject (§ 213. *b*).

5. To indicate purpose: the *future* participle with or without ὡς is used (§§ 331, 332).

6. In the genitive absolute construction (§ 401).

7. In the accusative absolute construction (§ 566).

8. With verbs of *perception* whether of the mind or of the senses (§ 440): ὁρῶ *see*, ἀκούω *hear*, etc., ὁρῶ αὐτὸν ἰόντα *I see him coming*.

9. In the construction of indirect discourse (§§ 441, 449, 520).

   [For such a participle a clause with ὅτι may be used (§ 442).]

10. With τυγχάνω *happen*, λανθάνω *escape notice*, and οἴχομαι *be gone* (cp. §§ 215, 318, 443).

11. With verbs of *beginning, ceasing*, etc. (§ 439).

    The negative with the participle is οὐ; but the conditional participle takes μή.

667. PURPOSE IS COMMONLY EXPRESSED

1. By ἵνα, ὅπως, or ὡς, *in order that*, with the subjunctive. After a secondary tense the optative is commonly used (§§ 243, 268). Negative: μή.

2. By the future participle (§§ 331, 332).

668.   FORMS OF CONDITIONAL SENTENCES

Simple or Real (§ 106)

PROTASIS	APODOSIS
Present. εἰ with pres. indic.:	any form of verb:
εἰ ταῦτα λέγει,	ἀληθῆ λέγει
if he says this,	he speaks the truth.
Past. εἰ with past tense of indic.:	any form of verb:
εἰ ταῦτα ἔλεξεν,	ἀληθῆ ἔλεξεν
if he said this,	he spoke the truth.

Contrary to Fact or Unreal (§ 545)

Present. εἰ with impf. indic.:	impf. indic. with ἄν:
εἰ ταῦτα ἔλεγεν,	οὐκ ἂν ἀληθῆ ἔλεγεν
if he were (now) saying this,	he would not be speaking the truth.

Past. εἰ with aor. indic.:   aor. indic. with ἄν:

   εἰ ταῦτα ἔλεξεν,   οὐκ ἂν ἀληθῆ ἔλεξεν
   if he had said this (then),   he would not have spoken
                                               the truth.

General (§§ 399, 416)

Present. ἐάν with subjv.:   pres. indic.:

   ἐάν τι λέγῃ (or λέξῃ),   ἀληθῆ λέγει
   if [ever] he says anything,   he speaks the truth.

Past. εἰ with opt.:   impf. indic.:

   εἴ τι λέγοι (or λέξειεν),   ἀληθῆ ἔλεγεν
   if he [ever] said anything,   he spoke the truth.

More Vivid Future (§ 241)

ἐάν with subjv.:   fut. indic. or equiv.:

   ἐὰν ταῦτα λέγῃς (or λέξῃς),   ἀληθῆ λέξεις
   if you say (*or* shall say) this,   you will speak the truth.

Less Vivid Future (§ 267)

εἰ with opt.:   opt. with ἄν:

   εἰ ταῦτα λέγοις (or λέξειας),   ἀληθῆ ἂν λέγοις (or λέξειας)
   if you should say this,   you would speak the truth.

Warning Future (§ 242)

εἰ with fut. indic.:   fut. indic. or equiv.:

   εἰ ταῦτα λέξεις,   κακὸς φανεῖ
   if you say this,   you will appear base.

INDIRECT DISCOURSE

USES OF COMMON VERBS THAT TAKE THE CONSTRUCTION OF INDIRECT DISCOURSE

669.   I. A FINITE MOOD with ὅτι or ὡς follows λέγω
(active) *say*, εἶπον *said*, ἀποκρίνομαι *reply*, and

often those verbs with which the participle in indirect discourse is also regular. Such verbs are mentioned below in 3.

2. AN INFINITIVE follows φημί *say*, λέγεται (passive) *is said*, νομίζω *think*, οἴομαι *think*, ὑπισχνέομαι *promise*, ἀκούω *hear*, and other verbs meaning *to think* or *to agree*.

3. A PARTICIPLE follows ὁράω *see*, αἰσθάνομαι *perceive*, ἀκούω *hear*, οἶδα *know*, δῆλός εἰμι *be evident*, ἀγγέλλω *announce*, and other verbs of similar meaning. But see 1 above.

   a. Observe that ἀκούω *hear* belongs in all three of the preceding classes.

   b. When εἶπε means *he bade*, *he commanded*, *he proposed*, an infinitive *not* in indirect discourse follows, as after κελεύω *command*. The other verbs of *saying* may be similarly used.

   c. With the infinitive ἐπίσταμαι means *know how* (instead of *know that*), μανθάνω *learn how* (instead of *learn that*).

USES OF THE ADVERB ἄν

670.   1. In protases, always with subjunctive: ἐάν (εἰ + ἄν), ὃς ἄν, ἐπειδάν (ἐπειδή + ἄν), etc.

2. In apodoses, (*a*) with the optative in less vivid future conditions, (*b*) with the imperfect or aorist indicative in contrary to fact conditions.

3. With the optative in the potential use (§ 266).

4. With the infinitive of indirect discourse when the infinitive with ἄν represents an optative with ἄν, § 277 (or past tense of the indicative with ἄν, § 546), of the direct discourse.

A FEW IMPORTANT LISTS

671. SOME VERBS WHOSE MEANING DISTINCTLY
CHANGES IN THE MIDDLE VOICE

ACTIVE	MIDDLE
αἱρέω *take*	*choose*
ἐπιτίθημι *put upon*	*attack* (with dat.)
ἔχω *have, hold*	*come next*
	cling to (with gen.)
λύω *release*	*ransom*
παύω *stop* (another)	*cease* (intr.)
πείθω *persuade* (with acc.)	*obey* (with dat.)
συμβουλεύω *advise* (with dat.)	*consult* (with dat.)
φαίνω *show*	*appear*
φοβέω *frighten*	*fear*
φυλάττω *guard*	*guard against*

672. SOME VERBS WHOSE PASSIVE IS EXPRESSED
BY A DIFFERENT VERB

αἱρέω *take*	ἁλίσκομαι *be taken*
[but αἱρέομαι (mid.) *choose*	αἱρέομαι (pass.) *be chosen*]
ἀποκτείνω *kill*	ἀποθνῄσκω *be killed*
νῑκάω *conquer*	ἡττάομαι *be conquered*
τέθηκα *have put* or *placed*	κεῖμαι *have been placed*
εὖ (or καλῶς) τινα ποιέω *do* *somebody a kindness*	εὖ ὑπό τινος πάσχω *be done* *a kindness by somebody*

673. SOME VERBS WHOSE AORISTS ARE PASSIVE IN
FORM, BUT NOT IN MEANING (DEPONENTS PASSIVE)

	Aorist Passive
βούλομαι *wish*	ἐβουλήθην *I wished*
δέομαι *ask, beg*	ἐδεήθην *I begged*
δύναμαι *be able*	ἐδυνήθην *I was able*
ἐπιμελέομαι *take care*	ἐπεμελήθην *I took care*
οἴομαι *think*	ᾠήθην *I thought*
πορεύομαι *proceed*	ἐπορεύθην *I proceeded*
φοβέομαι *fear*	ἐφοβήθην *I feared*

674. SOME VERBS WHOSE IMPERFECT INDICATIVE
APPEARS IRREGULAR IN AUGMENT

Present	Imperfect
ἐάω *permit*	εἴων (*i.e.* εἴαον)
ἕπομαι *follow*	εἱπόμην
ἔχω *have*	εἶχον
ὁράω *see*	ἑώρων (*i.e.* ἑώραον)

675. Distinguish among

αἰτέω *ask* a favor *of* somebody, *ask somebody for*
something (with two accusatives).

ἀξιόω *ask* as a right, *demand* (with infinitive).

δέομαι *want* or *ask* a person (in the genitive) to do
something (infinitive).

ἐρωτάω
2 aor. ἠρόμην { *ask* a question, *inquire;* may be followed by accusative of person
and indirect question.

ABBREVIATIONS

A. or acc.	= accusative.	interr.	= interrogative.
abl.	= ablative.	intr.	= intransitive.
abs.	= absolute.	irreg.	= irregular.
act.	= active.	κτλ.	= καὶ τὰ λοιπά = *etc.*
adj.	= adjective.	Lat.	= Latin.
adv.	= adverb.	lit.	= literal, literally.
aor.	= aorist.	masc.	= masculine.
art.	= article.	mid.	= middle.
comp.	= comparative.	N. or nom.	= nominative.
conj.	= conjunction.	neg.	= negative.
const.	= construction.	neut.	= neuter.
cp.	= compare.	obj.	= object.
D. or dat.	= dative.	opt.	= optative.
def.	= definite.	p., pp.	= page, pages.
dem.	= demonstrative.	part. gen.	= partitive genitive.
dep.	= deponent.	partic.	= participle.
dim.	= diminutive.	pass.	= passive.
dir.	= direct.	pers.	= person.
disc.	= discourse.	pf.	= perfect.
e.g.	= *for example.*	pl. or plur.	= plural.
Eng.	= English.	plup.	= pluperfect.
equiv.	= equivalent.	poss. gen.	= possessive genitive.
etc.	= *and so forth.*	pred.	= predicate.
fem.	= feminine.	prep.	= preposition.
Fig.	= Figure.	pres.	= present.
fut.	= future.	priv.	= privative.
G. or gen.	= genitive.	pron.	= pronoun.
i.e.	= *that is.*	rel.	= relative.
impers.	= impersonal.	sing.	= singular.
impf.	= imperfect.	subj.	= subject.
imv.	= imperative.	subjv.	= subjunctive.
indecl.	= indeclinable.	subst.	= substantive.
indef.	= indefinite.	sup.	= superlative.
indic.	= indicative.	trans.	= transitive.
indir.	= indirect.	V. or voc.	= vocative.
inf.	= infinitive.	vocab.	= vocabulary.
interj.	= interjection.	§	= section.

ENGLISH–GREEK VOCABULARY

For numerals not included in the following list see § 421.

A

abandon: ἀπολείπω, ἐκλείπω, καταλείπω.

able: δυνατός, ή, όν; ἱκανός, ή, όν; οἷός τε, οἵα τε, οἷόν τε.

able, be: δύναμαι.

about: ἀμφί with acc. (round about, near); περί with gen. (concerning); περί with dat. (near); περί with acc. (around, in relation to).

about (with numerals): ὡς.

about, be: μέλλω.

above: ὑπέρ with gen.

Abrocomas: Ἀβροκόμᾱς, ᾱ, ὁ.

accept: δέχομαι.

accompany: συμπορεύομαι.

accomplish: πράττω, διαπράττομαι.

according to: κατά with acc.

accordingly: δή, οὖν.

accuse falsely: διαβάλλω.

Achaean: Ἀχαιός, οῦ, ὁ.

across: πέρᾱν.

addition to, in: πρός with dat.

admirable: θαυμαστός, ή, όν.

admire: θαυμάζω.

advise: συμβουλεύω.

afoot: πεζός, ή, όν.

afraid, be: φοβέομαι.

after (conj.): ἐπεί, ἐπειδή.

after (prep.): μετά with acc.

again: πάλιν, ἔτι.

against: ἀντί in composition; ἐπί with acc.; κατά with acc.; πρός with acc.

agree: συντίθεμαι.

agreement: σύνθημα, ατος, τό.

all: ὅλος, η, ον (entire); πᾶς, πᾶσα, πᾶν.

all together: ἅπᾱς, ᾱσα, ᾱν; σύμπᾱς, ᾱσα, αν.

allow: ἐάω.

ally: σύμμαχος, ου, ὁ.

alone: μόνος, η, ον.

along: κατά with acc.

already: ἤδη.

also: καί.

altogether: πάνυ.

always: ἀεί.

ambassador: πρεσβευτής, οῦ, ὁ; pl. πρέσβεις, εων, οἱ.

ancient: ἀρχαῖος, ᾱ, ον.

and: καί.

and in fact: γάρ; καὶ γάρ.

and not: οὐδέ, μηδέ.

announce: ἀγγέλλω.

annoyance: ὄχλος, ου, ὁ.

another: ἄλλος, η, ο.

another place, in: ἄλλῃ.

another, one: ἀλλήλοιν.

answer: ἀποκρίνομαι.

any, anybody, anything: τις, τι.

anywhere: πῃ, που.

apart, apart from: χωρίς.

apart, be: διέχω.

appear: φαίνομαι.

approach (noun): ἔφοδος, ου, ἡ.

approach (verb): ἔπειμι.

Ariaeus: Ἀριαῖος, ου, ὁ.

arise (take place): γίγνομαι.
Aristippus: Ἀρίστιππος, ου, ὁ.
arms (of war): ὅπλα, ων, τά.
army: στράτευμα, ατος, τό; στρατιά, ᾶς, ἡ.
around (see 'about'): περί with dat.; περί with acc.
arrange: τάττω.
arrangement: τάξις, εως, ἡ.
arrest: συλλαμβάνω.
arrive: ἀφικνέομαι.
arrow: τόξευμα, ατος, τό.
Artapates: Ἀρταπάτης, ου, ὁ.
Artaxerxes: Ἀρταξέρξης, ου, ὁ.
as, as if: ὡς, ὥσπερ.
as (of comparison): ὡς, ὥσπερ.
as (with sup.): ὅτι, ὡς.
as many as, as much as: ὅσος, η, ον; ὁπόσος, η, ον.
as often as: ὁπότε.
as (= such as): οἷος, ᾱ, ον.
ask about: πυνθάνομαι.
ask (a favor): αἰτέω, δέομαι.
ask (a question): ἐρωτάω, 2 aor. ἠρόμην.
ask (as a right): ἀξιόω.
ask for: αἰτέω.
ass: ὄνος, ου, ὁ.
assemble: ἀθροίζω (trans.), συνέρχομαι.
assembly: ἐκκλησίᾱ, ᾶς, ἡ.
at: ἐπί with dat.
at any rate: μήν, οὖν.
Athenian: Ἀθηναῖος, ᾱ, ον.
attack: ἐπιτίθεμαι, ἐπίκειμαι.
attempt: πειράομαι.
attend: πάρειμι.
avoid: φεύγω.
away, be: ἀπέχω.
away from: ἀπό.

B

Babylon: Βαβυλών, ῶνος, ἡ.
back: πάλιν.

bad: κακός, ή, όν.
badly: κακῶς.
barbarian (adj.): βαρβαρικός, ή, όν
barbarian (noun): βάρβαρος, ου, ὁ.
bare: ψῑλός, ή, όν.
battle: μάχη, ης, ἡ.
be: γίγνομαι, εἰμί.
beast, wild: θηρίον, ου, τό.
beast (of burden): ὑποζύγιον, ου, τό
bear: φέρω.
beautiful: καλός, ή, όν.
beautifully: καλῶς.
because of: διά with acc.; ὑπό with gen.
become: γίγνομαι.
before (adv.): πρόσθεν, πρόσθεν . . . πρίν, τὸ πρόσθεν, ἔμπροσθεν.
before (conj.): πρίν.
before (prep.): πρό.
beg: αἰτέω, δέομαι.
begin: ἄρχω, ἄρχομαι.
beginning: ἀρχή, ῆς, ἡ.
behold: θεάομαι, ὁράω.
behooves, it: χρή.
believe: ἡγέομαι.
beneath: ὑπό with dat.
beside: παρά or πρός with dat.
besides: ἔτι.
best (adj.): ἄριστος, η, ον; βέλτιστος, η, ον; κράτιστος, η, ον.
best (adv.): ἄριστα, etc.
better (adj.): ἀμείνων, ον; βελτίων, ον; κρείττων, ον.
better (adv.): ἄμεινον, etc.; μᾶλλον.
between: μεταξύ with gen.; ἐν μέσῳ.
bewilder: ἐκπλήττω.
beyond: ὑπέρ with acc.
bid: κελεύω.
big: μέγας, μεγάλη, μέγα.
bird: ὄρνῑς, ῑθος, ὁ and ἡ.
birth: γένος, ους, τό.
Boeotian: Βοιώτιος, ᾱ, ον.
born, be: γίγνομαι.
both . . . and: τε . . . καί; καί . . . καί.

bother: ὄχλος, ου, ὁ.
bow: τόξον, ου, τό.
bowman: τοξότης, ου, ὁ.
boy: παῖς, παιδός, ὁ.
brave: ἀγαθός, ή, όν.
bravery: ἀρετή, ῆς, ἡ.
breadth: εὖρος, ους, τό.
break: λύω.
break through: διακόπτω.
breastplate: θώραξ, ᾱκος, ὁ.
bridge: γέφῡρα, ᾱς, ἡ.
brilliancy: λαμπρότης, ητος, ἡ.
bring about: διαπράττομαι.
bring into harbor: κατάγω.
brother: ἀδελφός, οῦ, ὁ.
burn: καίω or κάω.
business: πρᾶγμα, ατος, τό.
but: ἀλλά, δέ (postpositive).
buy: ἀγοράζω (bought also ἐπριάμην).
by: διά with acc. (by means of);
   κατά with acc. (as in 'by land');
   ὑπό with gen. (of the agent); παρά
   with dat. (by the side of).
by far: πολύ.
by no means: ἥκιστα.

C

call: καλέω.
call together: συγκαλέω.
camp (noun): στρατόπεδον, ου, τό.
camp (verb): σκηνόω; see 'encamp.'
canal: διῶρυξ, υχος, ἡ.
captain: λοχᾱγός, οῦ, ὁ.
capture: αἱρέω, (pass.) ἁλίσκομαι.
Carduchi: Καρδοῦχοι, ων, οἱ.
care for, take care of: ἐπιμελέομαι.
carriage: ἅμαξα, ης, ἡ.
carry: φέρω.
catch (by hunting): θηρεύω.
cattle: πρόβατον, ου, τό.
cavalry: ἱππεῖς, οἱ.
cavalry, consisting of: ἱππικός, ή, όν.
cease (intr.): παύομαι.
cease (= make cease): παύω, ἀνα-
   παύω.

Celaenae: Κελαιναί, ῶν, αἱ.
certain, a: τις, τι.
certainly: γε, μήν.
Chalus: Χάλος, ου, ὁ.
chance (verb): τυγχάνω.
chance upon: ἐντυγχάνω, ἐπιτυγχάνω.
character: τρόπος, ου, ὁ.
chariot: ἅρμα, ατος, τό.
chastise: κολάζω.
cheat: ἐξαπατάω.
Cheirisophus: Χειρίσοφος, ου, ὁ.
child: παῖς, παιδός, ὁ and ἡ; τέκνον,
   ου, τό.
choose: αἱρέομαι.
Cilicia: Κιλικίᾱ, ᾱς, ἡ.
Cilician woman: Κίλισσα, ης, ἡ.
circumstances: πράγματα, ων, τά.
citadel: ἀκρόπολις, εως, ἡ.
city: πόλις, εως, ἡ.
claim (as one's right): ἀξιόω.
clear: δῆλος, η, ον; φανερός, ά, όν.
Clearchus: Κλέαρχος, ου, ὁ.
closely set (=closely planted): πυκνός,
   ή, όν.
collect: ἀθροίζω, συλλέγω, συνάγω.
column (military): τάξις, εως, ἡ.
come: ἔρχομαι, ἀφικνέομαι; have
   come: ἥκω.
come! ἄγε (interj.).
come down (= reach down): καθήκω.
come forth: ἐξέρχομαι.
come in: εἰσέρχομαι.
come on: ἔπειμι.
come to: παραγίγνομαι, προσέρχομαι,
   προσήκω.
come together: συνέρχομαι.
come up: προσέρχομαι.
come upon: καταλαμβάνω.
come upon by chance: ἐντυγχάνω,
   ἐπιτυγχάνω.
command (= rule): ἄρχω.
command (= order): ἐπιτάττω, κελεύω, παραγγέλλω (εἶπον).
commander: ἄρχων, οντος, ὁ; ἡγεμών,
   όνος, ὁ.

common : κοινός, ή, όν.

compact, make a : συντίθεμαι.

company (of soldiers): λόχος, ου, ὁ.

compel : ἀναγκάζω.

concerning : περί with gen.; ἀμφί with gen.

confine : κατακλείω.

conquer : νῑκάω, (pass.) ἡττάομαι.

consider: σκέπτομαι.

contend: ἀγωνίζομαι.

contest: ἀγών, ῶνος, ὁ.

continually : ἀεί.

contrary to : παρά with acc.

converse : διαλέγομαι.

corpse : νεκρός, οῦ, ὁ.

country : χώρᾱ, ᾱς, ἡ.

cow : βούς, βοός, ἡ.

cowardly : κακός, ή, όν.

Cretan : Κρής, Κρητός, ὁ.

crisis : καιρός, οῦ, ὁ.

cross : διαβαίνω.

crossed, able to be : διαβατός, ή, όν; necessary to be : διαβατέος, ᾱ, ον.

crowd : ὄχλος, ου, ὁ; πλῆθος, ους, τό.

cubit : πῆχυς, εως, ὁ.

custom : νόμος, ου, ὁ.

cut down : κατακόπτω.

cut off : ἀπολαμβάνω, ἀποκόπτω.

cut through (in pieces): διακόπτω.

Cyrus : Κῦρος, ου, ὁ.

D

danger : κίνδῡνος, ου, ὁ.

danger, incur : κινδῡνεύω.

daric : δᾱρεικός, οῦ, ὁ.

Darius : Δᾱρεῖος, ου, ὁ.

darkness : σκότος, ους, τό, and σκότος, ου, ὁ.

daughter : θυγάτηρ, θυγατρός, ἡ.

day : ἡμέρᾱ, ᾱς, ἡ.

day's journey : σταθμός, οῦ, ὁ.

death, put to : ἀποκτείνω.

deceive utterly : ἐξαπατάω.

decide : κρίνω.

declare : φημί.

deed : ἔργον, ου, τό; πρᾶγμα, ατος, τό.

deem worthy : ἀξιόω.

deep : βαθύς, εῖα, ύ.

delay : μέλλω.

deliberate : βουλεύομαι.

demand : ἀξιόω.

deny : οὔ φημι.

deprive : ἀφαιρέομαι.

descend : καταβαίνω.

descent : κατάβασις, εως, ἡ.

descry : καθοράω.

desert (verb): ἀπολείπω.

deserted : ἔρημος, η, ον, or ἔρημος, ον.

deserts (justice) : δίκη, ης, ἡ.

desire : δέομαι, ἐθέλω, ἐπιθῡμέω. See 'wish.'

despondency : ἀθῡμίᾱ, ᾱς, ἡ.

destroy : ἀπόλλῡμι, λύω.

devise : βουλεύω.

die : ἀποθνῄσκω, τελευτάω.

die off : ἀποθνῄσκω.

difficult : χαλεπός, ή, όν.

difficulty : ἀπορίᾱ, ᾱς, ἡ; πρᾶγμα, ατος, τό.

direct : ἐπιτάττω, παραγγέλλω.

direct the mind : προσέχω τὸν νοῦν.

discouragement : ἀθῡμίᾱ, ᾱς, ἡ.

dismiss : ἀποπέμπω, ἀφίημι.

distant, be : ἀπέχω.

distinguish oneself : ἐπιδείκνυμαι.

distribute : διαδίδωμι.

ditch : τάφρος, ου, ἡ.

division (military) : τάξις, εως, ἡ.

do : ποιέω, πράττω.

down along : κατά with acc.

down from : κατά with gen.

down over : κατά with acc.

draw near : προσελαύνω.

draw up : τάττω.

drink (noun): ποτόν, οῦ, τό.

drive : ἐλαύνω.

drive in : εἰσελαύνω.

drive out : ἐξελαύνω.

drive past : παρελαύνω.

drive up : προσελαύνω.

E

each : ἕκαστος, η, ον.

eagerly : προθύμως.

earlier than : πρόσθεν . . . πρίν.

earth : γῆ, γῆς, ἡ.

easy : ῥᾴδιος, ᾱ, ον.

effect : πρᾱ́ττω, διαπρᾱ́ττομαι.

either . . . or : ἤ . . . ἤ.

elder : πρεσβύτερος, ᾱ, ον.

elsewhere : ἄλλῃ.

embarrassment : ἀπορίᾱ, ᾱς, ἡ.

empire : ἀρχή, ῆς, ἡ.

empty : κενός, ή, όν.

encamp : στρατοπεδεύω and -ομαι;
see ' camp.'

encounter : ἐντυγχάνω, ἐπιτυγχάνω.

end (noun): τέλος, ους, τό.

end (verb): τελευτάω; put an end to :
παύω.

enemy : οἱ πολέμιοι; personal enemy :
ἐχθρός, οῦ, ὁ.

enlist : λαμβάνω.

enter : δύω, δύνω, εἰσέρχομαι.

entire : ὅλος, η, ον; πᾶς, πᾶσα, πᾶν;
see ' all.'

equip : παρασκευάζω.

escape : ἀποφεύγω.

escape notice : λανθάνω.

Euphrates : Εὐφρᾱ́της, ου, ὁ.

ever : ποτέ.

ever yet : πώποτε.

every : πᾶς, πᾶσα, πᾶν; see ' each.'

evident : δῆλος, η, ον; φανερός, ά, όν.

evident, make : δηλόω.

exceedingly : ἰσχῡρῶς.

excellence : ἀρετή, ῆς, ἡ.

exercise : γυμνάζω.

exile : φυγάς, άδος, ὁ.

expedition : στόλος, ου, ὁ; στρατείᾱ,
ᾱς, ἡ.

expedition, make an : στρατεύω.

extend : καθήκω.

extensive : πολύς, πολλή, πολύ.

extreme : ἔσχατος, η, ον.

F

face about : ἀναστρέφομαι.

fact, and in : γάρ, καὶ γάρ.

fail : ἐκλείπω.

faithful : πιστός, ή, όν.

family : γένος, ους, τό.

father : πατήρ, πατρός, ὁ.

fatherland : πατρίς, ίδος, ἡ.

favor : χάρις, ιτος, ἡ.

favor, show : χαρίζομαι.

fear (noun): φόβος, ου, ὁ.

fear (verb): δέδοικα, φοβέομαι.

fearful : δεινός, ή, όν; φοβερός, ά, όν.

fearfully : φοβερῶς.

feed : τρέφω.

few : ὀλίγος, η, ον.

field, take the : στρατεύομαι; take the
field with : συστρατεύομαι.

fight (noun): μάχη, ης, ἡ.

fight (verb): μάχομαι.

finally : τέλος.

find : εὑρίσκω, καταλαμβάνω.

find by chance : ἐντυγχάνω, ἐπιτυγχάνω.

finish : τελευτάω.

fire : πῦρ, πυρός, τό.

first : πρῶτος, η, ον.

fish : ἰχθῡ́ς, ύος, ὁ.

fitness : ἀρετή, ῆς, ἡ.

flee, flee from : φεύγω; flee away :
ἀποφεύγω.

flight : φυγή, ῆς, ἡ.

flight, put to : τρέπω εἰς φυγήν.

fodder : χῑλός, οῦ, ὁ.

follow : ἕπομαι.

following (adj.): ὑστεραῖος, ᾱ, ον.

follows, as : ὧδε.

food : σῑτίον, ου, τό; σῖτος, ου, ὁ.

foot : πούς, ποδός, ὁ; on foot : πεζός,
ή, όν.

for (conj.): γάρ.

for (prep.): ἐπί with dat.; περί with
gen.

for (= instead of) : ἀντί with gen.

force (*noun*): δύναμις, εως, ἡ.
force (*verb*): ἀναγκάζω.
fordable: διαβατός, ή, όν.
forearm: πῆχυς, εως, ὁ.
foreign: βαρβαρικός, ή, όν.
foreigner: βάρβαρος, ου, ὁ.
former: πρότερος, ᾱ, ον; πρόσθεν (*adv*. as *adj*.).
formerly: τὸ ἀρχαῖον, τὸ πρόσθεν.
fortress: τεῖχος, ους, τό.
fortunate: εὐδαίμων, ον.
forward: εἰς τὸ πρόσθεν.
fresh: νέος, ᾱ, ον.
friend: φίλος, ου, ὁ.
friendly: φίλος, η, ον.
friendship: φιλίᾱ, ᾶς, ἡ.
frighten: φοβέω.
frightful: δεινός, ή, όν; φοβερός, ά, όν.
from: ἀπό (away from); ἐκ (out from); παρά and πρός (from the side of); ὑπό (because of).
front, in: ἔμπροσθεν.
fugitive: φυγάς, άδος, ὁ.
full: μεστός, ή, όν; πλήρης, ες.
furnish: παρέχω.
future, in the: τὸ λοιπόν.

G

games (= contest of games): ἀγών, ῶνος, ὁ.
garrison: φυλακή, ῆς, ἡ.
gate: πύλη, ης, ἡ.
gather together: ἀθροίζω, συλλέγω.
gathering: ἀγών, ῶνος, ὁ.
gaze at: θεάομαι.
general (*adj*.): κοινός, ή, όν.
general (*noun*): στρατηγός, οῦ, ὁ.
gift: δῶρον, ου, τό.
girl: παῖς, παιδός, ἡ.
give: δίδωμι.
give over: παραδίδωμι.
gladly: ἡδέως.
go: εἶμι, ἔρχομαι, πορεύομαι.
go across: διαβαίνω.

go away (or back): ἄπειμι, ἀπέρχομαι.
go by: παρέρχομαι.
go down: καταβαίνω.
go forth: ἔξειμι, ἐξέρχομαι.
go forward: προέρχομαι.
go on: ἔπειμι.
go out: ἔξειμι, ἐξέρχομαι.
go past: παρέρχομαι.
go through: διέρχομαι.
go to: προσέρχομαι.
go together: συνέρχομαι.
go up (inland): ἀναβαίνω.
god: θεός, οῦ, ὁ.
goddess: θεός, οῦ, ἡ.
gold (*adj*.), golden: χρῡσοῦς, ῆ, οῦν.
gold (*noun*): χρῡσίον, ου, τό.
gone, be (*or* have gone): οἴχομαι.
good: ἀγαθός, ή, όν.
grace: χάρις, ιτος, ἡ.
grain: σῑτίον, ου, τό; σῖτος, ου, ὁ.
grant (as a favor): χαρίζομαι.
grass: χῑλός, οῦ, ὁ.
gratify: χαρίζομαι.
gratitude: χάρις, ιτος, ἡ.
great: μέγας, μεγάλη, μέγα.
great (= how great, as great as): ὅσος, η, ον; ὁπόσος, η, ον.
greave: κνημίς, ῖδος, ἡ.
Greece: Ἑλλάς, άδος, ἡ.
Greek (*adj*.): Ἑλληνικός, ή, όν.
Greek (*noun*): Ἕλλην, ηνος, ὁ.
Greek force: Ἑλληνικόν, οῦ, τό.
groundless: κενός, ή, όν.
guard (*noun*): φύλαξ, ακος, ὁ; (=garrison) φυλακή, ῆς, ἡ.
guard (*verb*): φυλάττω.
guest-friend: ξένος, ου, ὁ.
guide (*noun*): ἡγεμών, όνος, ὁ.
guide (*verb*): ἡγέομαι.

H

half (*adj*.): ἥμισυς, εια, υ.
half (*noun*): τὸ ἥμισυν.
halt: τίθεμαι τὰ ὅπλα.
halting place: σταθμός, οῦ, ὁ.

hand: χείρ, χειρός, ή.

hand, be at: παραγίγνομαι, πάρειμι.

handsome: καλός, ή, όν.

happen: γίγνομαι, τυγχάνω.

happen upon: ἐντυγχάνω, ἐπιτυγχάνω.

harbor: λιμήν, ένος, ό.

hard: χαλεπός, ή, όν.

harm: βλάπτω.

harsh: χαλεπός, ή, όν.

harshly: ἰσχῡρῶς.

hasten: ἵεμαι, σπεύδω.

have: ἔχω.

he (in 'and he,' 'but he'): ὁ δέ.

head: κεφαλή, ῆς, ή.

hear, hear of: ἀκούω.

height: ἄκρον, ου, τό.

Hellas: Ἑλλάς, άδος, ή.

Hellenic: Ἑλληνικός, ή, όν.

helper: ὑπηρέτης, ου, ό.

herald: κῆρυξ, ῡκος, ό.

here: αὐτοῦ (= here on the spot), ἐνταῦθα, ἐνθάδε.

higher (adv.): ἀνωτέρω.

highest (adv.): ἀνωτάτω.

highest point of: ἄκρος, ᾱ, ον.

hill: λόφος, ου, ό.

himself: ἑαυτοῦ.

hinder: κωλύω.

hold: ἔχω.

holy: ἱερός, ά, όν.

home (= homeward): οἴκαδε.

honor (noun): τῑμή, ῆς, ή.

honor (verb): τῑμάω.

honorable: καλός, ή, όν.

honorably: καλῶς.

hoplite: ὁπλίτης, ου, ό.

horse: ἵππος, ου, ό.

horse, consisting of: ἱππικός, ή, όν.

horseman: ἱππεύς, έως, ό.

host: πλῆθος, ους, τό.

hostile: ἐχθρός, ά, όν; πολέμιος, ᾱ, ον; πολεμικός, ή, όν.

hour: ὥρᾱ, ᾱς, ή.

house: οἰκίᾱ, ᾱς, ή.

how (interr.): πῶς.

how (rel.): ὅπως, ὅπῃ.

how great, how much (how many): ὅσος, η, ον; ὁπόσος, η, ον.

however: μέντοι.

hundred: ἑκατόν.

hunt: θηρεύω.

hurl: βάλλω, ἵημι.

hurt: βλάπτω.

husband: ἀνήρ, ἀνδρός, ό.

I

I: ἐγώ.

if: εἰ; ἐάν or ἄν or ἤν with subjv.

impassable: ἄβατος, ον; ἀδιάβατος, ον; ἄπορος, ον.

impossible: ἀδύνατος, ον.

in: ἐν.

in company with: μετά with gen.

in front of: πρό.

in sight of: πρός with gen.

inclose: κατακλείω.

indeed: δή.

infantry: οἱ πεζοί.

inferior, be: ἡττάομαι.

inflict (e.g. punishment): ἐπιτίθημι.

injure: ἀδικέω, βλάπτω.

inland: ἄνω.

inquire: πυνθάνομαι; see also 'ask.'

instead of: ἀντί.

intend: μέλλω.

interpreter: ἑρμηνεύς, έως, ό.

into: εἰς.

into the midst of: μετά with acc.

invisible: ἀφανής, ές.

invite: καλέω.

Ionian: Ἰωνικός, ή, όν.

J

javelin: παλτόν, οῦ, τό.

judge: κρίνω.

judgment: γνώμη, ης, ή.

just: δίκαιος, ᾱ, ον.

just as: ὥσπερ.

justice: δίκη, ης, ή.

justly: δικαίως.

K

kill : ἀποκτείνω.
kindle : καίω or κάω.
king : βασιλεύς, έως, ὁ.
king, be : βασιλεύω.
kingdom : βασιλεία, ᾱς, ἡ.
kinglike : βασιλικός, ή, όν.
kinship : γένος, ους, τό.
knee : γόνυ, γόνατος, τό.
know : γιγνώσκω, οἶδα.
knowledge, without the knowledge of :
   λάθρᾳ.

L

labor : κάμνω.
Lacedaemon : Λακεδαίμων, ονος, ἡ.
Lacedaemonian : Λακεδαιμόνιος, ᾱ, ον.
land : γῆ, γῆς, ἡ; χώρᾱ, ᾱς, ἡ.
large : μέγας, μεγάλη, μέγα; πολύς,
   πολλή, πολύ.
last : ἔσχατος, η, ον.
later (adj.): ὕστερος, ᾱ, ον; ὑστεραῖος,
   ᾱ, ον.
latest : ὕστατος, η, ον.
law : νόμος, ου, ὁ.
lead : ἄγω, ἡγέομαι.
lead away (or lead back): ἀπάγω.
lead down : κατάγω.
lead in : εἰσάγω.
lead out : ἐξάγω.
lead together : συνάγω.
lead up : ἀνάγω.
leader : ἡγεμών, όνος, ὁ.
learn : γιγνώσκω, μανθάνω.
learn about : πυνθάνομαι.
least, at : γε.
least of all : ἥκιστα.
leave : λείπω.
leave behind : ἀπολείπω, καταλείπω.
leave off (or leave out): ἐκλείπω.
left, what is : λοιπός, ή, όν.
lest : μή.
lest not : μὴ οὐ.
let : ἐάω.
letter : ἐπιστολή, ῆς, ἡ.

libation : σπονδή, ῆς, ἡ.
lie (recline) : κεῖμαι.
lie down : κατάκειμαι.
lie upon : ἐπίκειμαι.
light (verb) : καίω or κάω.
light-armed : ψῑλός, ή, όν.
light-armed warrior : γυμνής, ῆτος, ὁ.
like : ὥσπερ.
line (military): τάξις, εως, ἡ.
listen : ἀκούω.
little : ὀλίγος, η, ον.
live : ζάω.
long : μακρός, ά, όν.
longer (adv.) : ἔτι.
look : βλέπω.
look down on : καθοράω.
look on : θεάομαι.
loose : λύω.
lose : ἀπόλλῡμι.
Lydia : Λῡδίᾱ, ᾱς, ἡ.
Lydian : Λῡδιος, ᾱ, ον.

M

magnanimity : ἀρετή, ῆς, ἡ.
make : ποιέω.
man : ἀνήρ, ἀνδρός, ὁ; ἄνθρωπος, ου, ὁ.
manage : διαπράττομαι.
manner : τρόπος, ου, ὁ.
many : πολύς, πολλή, πολύ (in pl.).
many (how many, as many as): ὅσος,
   η, ον; ὁπόσος, η, ον.
march : ἐλαύνω.
march in : εἰσελαύνω.
march out : ἐξελαύνω.
market, market-place : ἀγορά, ᾶς, ἡ.
marshal : τάττω.
master : δεσπότης, ου, ὁ.
matter : πρᾶγμα, ατος, τό.
means, by no : ἥκιστα.
Medes : Μῆδοι, ων, οἱ.
Menon : Μένων, ωνος, ὁ.
messenger : ἄγγελος, ου, ὁ.
method : τρόπος, ου, ὁ.
middle (middle of): μέσος, η, ον.

midnight : μέσαι νύκτες.

midst, in the : ἐν μέσῳ.

might : κράτος, ους, τό.

mina : μνᾶ, ᾶς, ἡ.

mind : νοῦς, οῦ, ὁ.

Mithradates : Μιθραδάτης, ου, ὁ.

mixing bowl : κρᾱτήρ, ῆρος, ὁ.

money : ἀργύριον, ου, τό; χρήματα, ων, τά.

month : μήν, μηνός, ὁ.

monthly : κατὰ μῆνα.

more (adv.) : μᾶλλον.

most (adv.) : μάλιστα.

mother : μήτηρ, μητρός, ἡ.

mountain : ὄρος, ους, τό.

much (adj.) : πολύς, πολλή, πολύ.

much (adv.) : πολύ.

much (how much, as much as) : ὅσος, η, ον; ὁπόσος, η, ον.

multitude : πλῆθος, ους, τό.

must, one : χρή; see 'necessary.'

my : ἐμός, ή, όν.

myself : ἐμαυτοῦ, ῆς.

N

name : ὄνομα, ατος, τό.

narrow : στενός, ή, όν.

near : ἐγγύς; πρός with dat.; περί with acc.

necessary (adj.) : ἐπιτήδειος, ᾱ, ον.

necessary, it is : δεῖ, χρή, ἀνάγκη (ἐστί).

necessity : ἀνάγκη, ης, ἡ.

need : δέομαι; there is need : δεῖ, χρή.

neighbor : γείτων, ονος, ὁ.

neither . . . nor : οὔτε (μήτε) . . . οὔτε (μήτε).

never : οὔποτε, μήποτε.

never yet : οὔπω.

new : νέος, ᾱ, ον.

next : ὑστεραῖος, ᾱ, ον; (adv.), ἔπειτα.

night : νίξ, νυκτός, ἡ.

night, by : νύκτωρ.

noble : καλός, ή, όν.

noble-mindedness : ἀρετή, ῆς, ἡ.

nobly : καλῶς.

noise : θόρυβος, ου, ὁ.

no longer, no more : οὐκέτι.

no one : οὐδείς, μηδείς.

nobody : οὐδείς, μηδείς.

nor : οὐδέ, μηδέ.

not : οὐ, μή.

not even : οὐδέ, μηδέ.

not yet : οὔπω.

nothing : οὐδέν, μηδέν.

now (inferential) : δή.

now (temporal) : ἤδη, νῦν.

O

O : ὦ.

oath : ὅρκος, ου, ὁ.

oath, take : ὄμνῡμι.

obey : πείθομαι.

observe : καθοράω, σκέπτομαι.

occupy : καταλαμβάνω.

occupy beforehand : προκαταλαμβάνω

off : ἀπό.

offer : δίδωμι (pres. and impf.).

offer (= sacrifice) : θύω, θύομαι.

often : πολλάκις; as often as : ὁπότε, ὅτε.

old : ἀρχαῖος, ᾱ, ον; of old (adv.) : τὸ ἀρχαῖον.

older : πρεσβύτερος, ᾱ, ον.

on : ἐπί with gen. or dat.

on account of : διά with acc.

on behalf of : ὑπέρ with gen.

once (upon a time) : ποτέ.

once, at : εὐθύς.

one another : ἀλλήλοιν.

one, the : ὁ μέν; see Lesson VI.

only (adj.) : μόνος, η, ον.

opinion : γνώμη, ης, ἡ.

opportunity : καιρός, οῦ, ὁ.

opposite : κατά with acc.

or : ἤ.

order (noun) : τάξις, εως, ἡ.

order (verb) : κελεύω (= command), τάττω (= marshal).

Orontas : Ὀρόντᾱς, ᾱ, ὁ.

other: ἄλλος, η, ον.

other (others), the; ὁ δέ, οἱ δέ; see Lesson VI.

otherwise: ἄλλως.

our: ἡμέτερος, ᾱ, ον.

out of: ἐκ.

outcry: κραυγή, ῆς, ἡ.

outside: ἔξω.

over: ὑπέρ with gen. or acc.

overtake: καταλαμβάνω.

ox: βοῦς, βοός, ὁ.

P

pack up: συσκευάζω.

palace: βασίλεια, ων, τά.

parasang: παρασάγγης, ου, ὁ.

Parysatis: Παρύσατις, ιδος, ἡ.

Pasion: Πᾱσίων, ωνος, ὁ.

pass: ἔκβασις, εως, ἡ; πάροδος, ου, ἡ.

pass (passing over): ὑπερβολή, ῆς, ἡ.

pass along (a watchword): διαδίδωμι.

passable: διαβατός, ή, όν.

passage: πάροδος, ου, ἡ.

pay: μισθός, οῦ, ὁ.

peace: εἰρήνη, ης, ἡ.

pelt: βάλλω.

peltast: πελταστής, οῦ, ὁ.

perceive: αἰσθάνομαι, πυνθάνομαι.

perish: ἀποθνῄσκω, ἀπόλλυμαι.

permit: ἐάω.

permitted, it is: ἔξεστι.

Persian (adj.): Περσικός, ή, όν.

Persian (noun): Πέρσης, ου, ὁ.

persuade: πείθω.

pertain to: προσήκω.

phalanx: φάλαγξ, αγγος, ἡ.

Phrygia: Φρυγίᾱ, ᾱς, ἡ.

Pisidians: Πῑσίδαι, ῶν, οἱ.

place (noun): τόπος, ου, ὁ; χωρίον, ου, τό.

place, in the same: αὐτοῦ.

place (verb): ἵστημι.

place, take: γίγνομαι.

place, take one's: καθίσταμαι.

place together: συντίθημι.

place upon: ἐπιτίθημι.

plain (adj.): δῆλος, η, ον; φανερός, ά, όν.

plain (noun): πεδίον, ου, τό.

plan (noun): γνώμη, ης, ἡ.

plan (verb): βουλεύομαι.

plan with: συμβουλεύω.

pleased, be: ἥδομαι.

pledges: δεξιαί, ῶν, αἱ; πιστά, ῶν, τά.

plethrum: πλέθρον, ου, τό.

plot (noun): ἐπιβουλή, ῆς, ἡ.

plot against: ἐπιβουλεύω.

plunder: ἁρπάζω; plunder utterly: διαρπάζω.

point out: δείκνῡμι, δεικνύω (and ἐπιδείκνῡμι).

possessions: χρήματα, ων, τά.

possible, it is: ἔξεστιν, ἔστιν, οἷόν τέ ἐστιν.

post, take one's: τίθεμαι τὰ ὅπλα.

power (in the power of): ἐπί with [dat.

prepare: παρασκευάζω.

prepared: ἕτοιμος, η, ον, or ἕτοιμος, ον.

present, be: παραγίγνομαι, πάρειμι.

primitive: ἀρχαῖος, ᾱ, ον.

proceed: πορεύομαι, προέρχομαι.

proceed with: συμπορεύομαι.

promise: ὑπισχνέομαι.

proposed: εἶπον.

proposition: γνώμη, ης, ἡ.

prosperous: εὐδαίμων, ον.

provide: παρέχω.

province: ἀρχή, ῆς, ἡ.

provisions: ἐπιτήδεια, ων, τά.

provisions, get: ἐπισῑτίζομαι.

Proxenus: Πρόξενος, ου, ὁ.

punish: κολάζω.

punishment, inflict . . . on: δίκην ἐπιτίθημι.

punishment, suffer: δίκην δίδωμι.

pursue: διώκω.

put: τίθημι.

put together: συντίθημι.

put upon: ἐπιτίθημι.

Q

quick : ταχύς, εῖα, ύ.
quickly : ταχέως, τάχα, ταχύ.

R

rally : ἀναστρέφομαι.
rapidly : see ' quickly.'
rather : μᾶλλον.
ravine : χαράδρᾱ, ᾱς, ἡ.
reach down : καθήκω.
reach to : προσήκω.
readily : προθύμως.
ready : ἕτοιμος, η, ον, or ἕτοιμος, ον.
ready, make : συσκευάζω.
ready, make oneself : παρασκευάζομαι.
rear : τρέφω.
receive : δέχομαι, λαμβάνω; of pay:
    λαμβάνω, φέρω.
related : προσήκων.
remain : μένω.
remaining : λοιπός, ή, όν.
remember : μέμνημαι.
remind : μιμνῄσκω.
reply : ἀποκρίνομαι.
report : ἀγγέλλω, ἀπαγγέλλω.
rest : ἀναπαύομαι.
rest of : λοιπός, ή, όν; the rest of : ὁ
    ἄλλος, etc.
restore : κατάγω.
return : ἄπειμι.
ride : ἐλαύνω.
ride in : εἰσελαύνω.
ride past : παρελαύνω.
ride up : προσελαύνω.
right (hand) : δεξιᾱ́, ᾶς, ἡ.
right measure, time, place : καιρός,
    οῦ, ὁ.
right (= on the right hand) : δεξιός,
    ᾱ́, όν.
risk, run a : κινδῡνεύω.
river : ποταμός, οῦ, ὁ.
road : ὁδός, οῦ, ἡ.
road by : πάροδος, ον, ἡ.
road up : ἄνοδος, ον, ἡ.

rob : ἀφαιρέομαι.
royal : βασίλειος, ον; βασιλικός, ή, όν.
rule (noun) : ἀρχή, ῆς, ἡ.
rule (verb) : ἄρχω; rule as king : βα-
    σιλεύω.
ruler : ἄρχων, οντος, ὁ.
run (noun) : δρόμος, ου, ὁ.
run (verb) : τρέχω, θέω.
run away (by stealth) : ἀποδιδρᾱ́σκω.

S

sack : διαρπάζω.
sacred : ἱερός, ᾱ́, όν.
sacrifice : θύω, θύομαι.
safe : ἀσφαλής, ές.
safely : ἀσφαλῶς.
safety : σωτηρίᾱ, ᾱς, ἡ.
safety, in : ἐν ἀσφαλεῖ.
sail : πλέω.
sail away : ἀποπλέω.
sailing, sailing weather : πλοῦς, οῦ, ὁ.
same : ὁ αὐτός.
same time, at the : ἅμα.
Sardis : Σάρδεις, εων, αἱ.
satisfaction, give : δίκην δίδωμι.
satrap : σατράπης, ου, ὁ.
save : σῴζω.
save from (= bring safely back) :
    ἀποσῴζω.
say : λέγω, φημί.
sea : θάλαττα, ης, ἡ.
season : ὥρᾱ, ᾱς, ἡ.
secretly : λάθρᾳ.
secure : ἀσφαλής, ές.
see : θεάομαι, ὁράω.
seem : δοκέω; seem best : δοκέω.
seize : αἱρέω, ἁρπάζω, καταλαμβάνω,
    συλλαμβάνω.
seize beforehand : προκαταλαμβάνω.
self : αὐτός.
send : πέμπω, ἵημι.
send after : μεταπέμπομαι.
send ahead : προπέμπω.
send away : ἀποπέμπω.
send down : καταπέμπω.

send forward : προπέμπω.

send off : ἀποπέμπω.

send with : συμπέμπω.

sent after : μετάπεμπτος, ον.

sentinel : φύλαξ, ακος, ὁ.

separate : κρίνω.

separated, be : διέχω.

servant : ὑπηρέτης, ου, ὁ.

serve in war : στρατεύομαι; serve in war with : συστρατεύομαι.

set : ἵστημι, τίθημι; of the sun : δύω, δύνω.

severe : χαλεπός, ή, όν.

shameful : αἰσχρός, ά, όν.

sheep : πρόβατον, ου, τό.

shield : ἀσπίς, ίδος, ἡ.

shoot : τοξεύω.

short : βραχύς, εῖα, ύ.

show : δείκνῡμι, δεικνύω (and ἐπιδείκνῡμι), δηλόω, φαίνω.

shun : φεύγω.

shut (= shut up) : κατακλείω.

side, on the other : πέρᾱν.

sight, out of : ἀφανής, ές.

silver (adj.) : ἀργυροῦς, ᾶ, οῦν.

silver (noun) : ἀργύριον, ου, τό.

simple : ἁπλοῦς, ἡ, οῦν.

since : ἐπεί, ἐπειδή, ὁπότε.

sincere : ἁπλοῦς, ἡ, οῦν.

skillful : δεινός, ή, όν.

slander : διαβάλλω.

slave : ἀνδράποδον, ου, τό.

slay : ἀποκτείνω; (pass.) ἀποθνήσκω.

sling : σφενδόνη, ης, ἡ.

small : μῑκρός, ά, όν.

smite : παίω.

snow : χιών, όνος, ἡ.

so as : ὥστε.

so great : τοσοῦτος, τοσαύτη, τοσοῦτο.

so long as : ἔστε, ἕως.

so many (much) : τοσοῦτος, τοσαύτη, τοσοῦτο.

so that : ὥστε.

Socrates : Σωκράτης, ους, ὁ.

soldier : στρατιώτης, ου, ὁ.

some : οἱ μέν.   See Lesson VI.

some, somebody, something : τις, τι.

somewhere : που.

Sophaenetus : Σοφαίνετος, ου, ὁ.

source : πηγαί, ῶν, αἱ.

Spartan : Λακεδαιμόνιος, ᾱ, ον.

spear : δόρυ, δόρατος, τό; λόγχη, ης, ἡ.

speech : λόγος, ου, ὁ.

splendor : λαμπρότης, ητος, ἡ.

spread (of a report) : διέρχομαι.

spring : πηγή, ῆς, ἡ.

stadium : στάδιον, ου, τό.

stage : σταθμός, οῦ, ὁ.

stand : ἵστημι (intr. tenses).

stand up : ἀνίσταμαι.

start up : ἀνίστημι.

station : καθίστημι.

steal : κλέπτω.

steep : ὄρθιος, ᾱ, ον.

still : ἔτι.

stone : λίθος, ου, ὁ.

stop, make to : παύω.

straightway : εὐθύς, ἤδη.

strange : θαυμαστός, ή, όν.

strength : δύναμις, εως, ἡ; κράτος, ους, τό.

strike : παίω.

strong : δυνατός, ή, όν; ἰσχῡρός, ά, όν.

stronghold : χωρίον, ου, τό.

strongly : ἰσχῡρῶς.

struggle : ἀγωνίζομαι.

such : τοιοῦτος, τοιαύτη, τοιοῦτο.

such as : τοιοῦτος οἷος.

suffer : πάσχω.

sufficient : ἱκανός, ή, όν.

suitable : ἐπιτήδειος, ᾱ, ον.

summon : καλέω, μεταπέμπομαι.

summoned : μετάπεμπτος, ον.

sun : ἤλιος, ου, ὁ.

supplies : ἐπιτήδεια, ων, τά.

supply : παρέχω.

support : τρέφω.

supporter : ὑπηρέτης, ου, ὁ.

suppose : οἴομαι.

sure, to be : μήν.

surely: **γε.**
surpass: **νῑκάω.**
surprised, be: **θαυμάζω.**
surrender: **παραδίδωμι.**
suspicion: **ὑποψίᾱ, ᾱς, ἡ.**
swear: **ὄμνῡμι.**
sweet: **ἡδύς, εῖα, ύ.**
swift: **ταχύς, εῖα, ύ.**
swiftly: **ταχέως, ταχύ.**
Syennesis: **Συέννεσις, ιος, ὁ.**
Syria: **Συρίᾱ, ᾱς, ἡ.**

T

take (= seize): **αἱρέω, λαμβάνω.**
take away for oneself: **ἀφαιρέομαι.**
take back: **ἀπολαμβάνω.**
take off: **ἀπολαμβάνω.**
take together: **συλλαμβάνω.**
talent: **τάλαντον, ου, τό.**
Tarsus: **Ταρσοί, ῶν, οἱ.**
tax: **δασμός, οῦ, ὁ.**
teach: **διδάσκω.**
tear to pieces: **διαρπάζω.**
tent: **σκηνή, ῆς, ἡ.**
terrible: **δεινός, ή, όν; φοβερός, ά, όν.**
terrify utterly: **ἐκπλήττω.**
than: **ἤ.**
thankful, feel: **χάριν ἔχω.**
that (*conj.*): **ὅτι;** (= in order that) **ἵνα, ὅπως, ὡς.**
that (*dem. pron.*): **ἐκεῖνος, ἐκείνη, ἐκεῖνο.**
that (*rel. pron.*): **ὅς, ἥ, ὅ.**
the: **ὁ, ἡ, τό.**
then (inferential): **τοίνυν.**
then (temporal): **τότε, εῖτα, ἔπειτα, ἔνθα, ἐντεῦθεν.**
thence: **ἐντεῦθεν.**
there: **ἐνταῦθα, ἔνθα, αὐτοῦ.**
thereafter: **τὸ λοιπόν.**
therefore: **οὖν, τοίνυν, τοιγαροῦν, ὥστε.**
thereupon: **εῖτα, ἔπειτα.**

thick: **παχύς, εῖα, ύ.**
thickly grown (wooded): **δασύς, εῖα, ύ.**
thief: **κλώψ, κλωπός, ὁ.**
think: **ἡγέομαι, νομίζω, οἴομαι, δοκέω.**
this: **ὅδε, ἥδε, τόδε; οὗτος, αὕτη, τοῦτο.**
Thracian: **Θρᾷξ, Θρᾳκός, ὁ.**
throng: **ὄχλος, ου, ὁ; πλῆθος, ους, τό.**
through: **διά** with gen.
throw: **βάλλω.**
thus: **οὕτω, οὕτως, ὧδε.**
Tigris: **Τίγρης, ητος, ὁ.**
timbers: **ξύλα, ων, τά.**
time: **χρόνος, ου, ὁ.**
time, at any, at some: **ποτέ.**
time, at that: see 'then.'
time (= in the time of): **ἐπί** with gen.
time, fit or proper: **ὥρᾱ, ᾱς, ἡ.**
time, right, proper: **καιρός, οῦ, ὁ.**
Tissaphernes: **Τισσαφέρνης, ους, ὁ.**
to: **εἰς** (= into); **ἐπί** with acc.; **παρά** with acc.; **πρός** with acc.; **ὡς** with acc. (of persons).
together with: **ἅμα.**
top of: **ἄκρος, ᾱ, ον.**
toward: **πρός** with gen. or acc.
town: **ἄστυ, εως, τό.**
tree: **δένδρον, ου, τό.**
trench: **διῶρυξ, υχος, ἡ.**
tribute: **δασμός, οῦ, ὁ.**
trireme: **τριήρης, ους, ἡ.**
trouble: **πρᾱγματα, ων, τά.**
truce: **σπονδαί, ῶν, αἱ.**
true: **ἀληθής, ές.**
trumpet: **σάλπιγξ, ιγγος, ἡ.**
trust: **πέποιθα.**
truth, in: **δή, μήν.**
try: **πειράομαι.**
turn (*noun*): **τρόπος, ου, ὁ.**
turn (*verb*): **στρέφω, τρέπω.**
turn about or back: **ἀναστρέφω** and **-ομαι.**
turn out (= happen): **γίγνομαι.**

U

under : ὑπό with dat. or acc.; (from under) ὑπό with gen.
understand : ἐπίσταμαι.
understanding : γνώμη, ης, ἡ.
undertake : ὑπισχνέομαι.
unguarded : ἀφύλακτος, ον.
unjust : ἄδικος, ον.
unprepared : ἀπαράσκευος, ον.
unprotected : ψιλός, ή, όν.
until : ἔστε, ἕως, μέχρι, πρίν.
unwilling : ἄκων, ουσα, ον.
up (adv.): ἄνω.
up (prep.), up along, up through : ἀνά.
upon : ἐπί with dat. or acc.
urge on : σπεύδω.
urged : εἶπον.
use : χράομαι.
useful : χρήσιμος, η, ον, or χρήσιμος, ον.

V

vain : κενός, ή, όν.
very : μάλα, πάνυ; ὡς with sup.
victory : νίκη, ης, ἡ.
view : σκέπτομαι.
village : κώμη, ης, ἡ.
village chief : κωμάρχης, ου, ὁ.
virtue : ἀρετή, ῆς, ἡ.
visible : φανερός, ά, όν.
voice : φωνή, ῆς, ἡ.
voyage : πλοῦς, οῦ, ὁ.
vulnerable : τρωτός, ή, όν.

W

wage war : πολεμέω.
wagon : ἅμαξα, ης, ἡ.
wait for : μένω.
wall : τεῖχος, ους, τό.
want : δέομαι.

war : πόλεμος, ου, ὁ; make war on, wage war : πολεμέω.
warlike : πολεμικός, ή, όν.
watch fires : πυρά, ῶν, τά.
watchword : σύνθημα, ατος, τό.
water : ὕδωρ, ὕδατος, τό.
way : ὁδός, οῦ, ἡ.
way down : κατάβασις, εως, ἡ.
way to : ἔφοδος, ου, ἡ.
way up : ἄνοδος, ου, ἡ.
way, in what (interr.): πῶς.
way, in what (rel.): ὅπῃ, ὅπως.
weary, am : κάμνω.
well (adv.): εὖ.
well! (in address): ἀλλά.
well-disposed : εὔνους, ουν.
what sort (of): οἷος, ᾱ, ον; ὁποῖος, ᾱ, ον.
whatever : ὅ τι.
wheel about : στρέφω.
when : ὅτε, ἐπεί, ἐπειδή; (with subjv.) ὅταν, ἐπειδάν; (= whenever) ὁπότε, ὅτε.
whence : ἔνθεν, ὅθεν.
where (interr. = whither): ποῖ.
where (rel.): ἔνθα; (= whence) ἔνθεν; (= whither) ὅποι.
where, wherever : ὅπῃ, ὅπου.
whether : εἰ.
whether . . . or : πότερον (πότερα) . . . ἤ.
which : ὅς, ἥ, ὅ; ὅστις, ἥτις, ὅ τι.
which, the very one : ὅσπερ, ἥπερ, ὅπερ.
while : ἔστε, ἕως.
whither (interr.): ποῖ.
whither (= whithersoever): ὅποι.
who, which, what (interr.): τίς, τί.
who (rel.): ὅς, ἥ, ὅ; ὅστις, ἥτις, ὅ τι.
whoever (or whichever): ὅστις, ἥτις, ὅ τι.
whole : ὅλος, η, ον; πᾶς, πᾶσα, πᾶν; ἅπᾱς, ᾱσα, ᾱν; σύμπᾱς, ᾱσα, αν.
wholly : πάνυ.
why (interr.): τί.
width : εὖρος, ους, τό.

wife: γυνή, γυναικός, ἡ.

wine: οἶνος, ου, ὁ.

wish: βούλομαι, ἐθέλω. See ' desire.'

with: μετά with gen.; σύν.

with the aid of: σύν.

within: εἴσω, ἔνδον.

without: ἄνευ, (outside) ἔξω.

woman: γυνή, γυναικός, ἡ.

wonder (= wonder at): θαυμάζω.

wonderful: θαυμαστός, ή, όν.

wood: ξύλον, ου, τό; (hewn or split) ξύλα, ων, τά.

word: λόγος, ου, ὁ.

work: ἔργον, ου, τό.

worse (*adj.*): κακίων, ον; χείρων, ον.

worse (*adv.*): κάκῑον, χεῖρον.

worthy: ἄξιος, ᾱ, ον.

wound: τιτρώσκω.

write: γράφω.

wrong, do, be in the: ἀδικέω.

X

Xenias: Ξενίᾱς, ου, ὁ.

Xenophon: Ξενοφῶν, ῶντος, ὁ.

Y

yearn: ἐπιθῡμέω.

yet: ἔτι (temporal), μέντοι (adversative).

young: νέος, ᾱ, ον.

young man: νεᾱνίσκος, ου, ὁ.

you: σύ.

your (sing.): σός, σή, σόν.

your (pl.): ὑμέτερος, ᾱ, ον.

yourself: σεαυτοῦ, ῆς.

Z

zealously: προθῡμως.

GREEK–ENGLISH VOCABULARY

AND INDEX TO THE LESSONS

The Roman numerals indicate the number of the special vocabulary in which a word occurs. References to sections are made by Arabic numerals. If no references are placed under a word, it occurs for the first time in the SELECTIONS FROM THE ANABASIS (pp. 263–279).

For the principal parts of compound verbs see the simple verbs. In the few instances where compounds occur without the simple verbs, the principal parts are given under the compounds. If, in place of an active form, a middle form occurs in the principal parts, the middle form is understood to be used in the active sense. Thus ἀκούω *I hear*, ἀκούσομαι *I shall hear*.

If a part is omitted from its proper place, the indication is that the part does not occur, at least in Attic Greek.

A

ἀ- or ἀν- before vowels, a negative prefix called *alpha privative*, equivalent to Lat. *in-* and Eng. *un-*.

ἄ-βατος, ον (ἀ- priv. and theme βα-, cp. δια-βαίνω): *not to be trodden on, impassable.* Cp. ἀ-διά-βατος. § 476. XXIX.

'Aβροκόμᾱς, ᾱ (Doric gen., for ου), ὁ: *Abrocomas*, a satrap of Phoenicia and Syria. XXXI.

ἀγαθός, ή, όν: *good, brave.* §§ 64, 116. Comp. ἀμείνων, βελτῑ́ων, κρείττων; sup. ἄριστος, βέλτιστος, κράτιστος; § 360. I. III.

ἀγγέλλω (for ἀγγελ + yω, theme ἀγγελ-), ἀγγελῶ, ἤγγειλα, ἤγγελκα, ἤγγελμαι, ἠγγέλθην: *announce, report*, with ὅτι or partic. in indir. disc. § 669. 3. Cp. ἄγγελος. LV.

ἄγγελος, ου, ὁ: *messenger.* XLV.

ἄγε, imv. of ἄγω used as an interjection: *come!* ἄγε (or ἄγετε) δή: *come now!* XXIX.

ἀγορά, ᾶς, ἡ: *market-place, market.* IX.

ἀγοράζω (theme ἀγοραδ-), ἀγοράσω, ἠγόρασα, ἠγόρακα, ἠγόρασμαι, ἠγοράσθην: *buy.* Cp. ἀγορά. XV.

ἄγω, ἄξω (§ 153), ἤγαγον (§§ 87, 239, 258), ἦχα (§ 445), ἦγμαι (§ 466. *a*), ἤχθην (§ 387. I): *lead, bring; carry, convey*; MID. sometimes *marry* (§ 324). § 487. I.

ἀγών, ῶνος, ὁ: *gathering, contest, games.* § 220. XX.

ἀγωνίζομαι (theme ἀγωνιδ-), ἀγωνιοῦμαι (§ 543); ἠγωνισάμην, ἠγώνισμαι: *contend* as in games, *struggle.* Cp. ἀγών. LV.

ἀδελφός, οῦ, ὁ: *brother*. The voc. sing. with irreg. accent is ἄδελφε. VIII.

ἀ-διά-βατος, ον (ἀ- priv. and διαβαίνω): *not to be crossed, impassable*. § 476. VII.

ἀδικέω (ἄδικος), ἀδικήσω, ἠδίκησα, ἠδίκηκα, ἠδίκημαι, ἠδικήθην: *do wrong to, injure, be in the wrong*. LV.

ἄ-δικος, ον (ἀ- priv. and δίκη, cp. δίκαιος): *unjust*. XLVI.

ἀ-δύνατος, ον (ἀ- priv. and δύναμαι): *impossible*. LX.

ἀεί, adv.: *always, continually, in succession*. XLII.

Ἀθηναῖος, ᾱ, ον: *Athenian*. XXI.

ἀθροίζω (theme ἀθροιδ-), ἀθροίσω, ἤθροισα, ἤθροικα, ἤθροισμαι, ἠθροίσθην): *gather together, collect, assemble* (trans.); MID. *gather* (intr.), *muster*, with εἰς and acc. XXVII, XXX.

ἀθῡμία, ᾱς, ἡ: *discouragement, despondency*. LIV.

ἀθύμως (adv. of ἄθῡμος *out of heart, discouraged*): *dejectedly*. ἀθύμως ἔχειν: *be discouraged*.

Αἰγύπτιος, ᾱ, ον (Αἴγυπτος *Egypt*): *Egyptian*.

αἱρέω, αἱρήσω, εἷλον, ᾕρηκα, ᾕρημαι, ᾑρέθην: *take, capture, seize;* MID. *choose*. LI (cp. XXVI and XXXII).

αἰσθάνομαι (theme αἰσθ-, pres. tense suffix αν%), αἰσθήσομαι (with lengthened theme), ᾐσθόμην, ᾔσθημαι: *perceive*. §§ 441, 442. XXXVIII.

αἰσχρός, ά, όν: *shameful, disgraceful*. Comp. αἰσχίων, sup. αἴσχιστος, § 352. b. XXXV.

αἰτέω, αἰτήσω, ᾔτησα, ᾔτηκα, ᾔτημαι, ᾐτήθην: *ask a favor, beg, ask for* something *from* somebody (two accs.); MID. *ask* for oneself. LI.

αἰχμ-άλωτος, ον (αἰχμή *spear-point* and ἁλίσκομαι): *captured by the spear;* οἱ αἰχμάλωτοι: *the captives*.

ἀκοντίζω, ἀκοντιῶ, etc.: *hit* with a javelin.

ἀκούσᾱς, 1 aor. act. partic. of ἀκούω: *having heard*. Declined in § 209.

ἀκούω, ἀκούσομαι, ἤκουσα, ἀκήκοα (§ 447), ἠκούσθην (σ is irregularly inserted): *hear, hear of, listen,* with object in gen. or acc., or with gen. of person and acc. of thing; may be followed by ὅτι clause (§ 262), or by inf. (§ 262. a), or by partic. (§ 442. a). XVII.

ἀκρό-πολις, εως, ἡ: high part of a city, *citadel*. XXXII.

ἄκρος, ᾱ, ον: *top of, highest point of;* τὸ ἄκρον (subst.): *the height*. Cp. Lat. *acus, acūtus, aciēs*. XXXII.

ἄκων, ουσα, ον (for declension cp. κωλύων, § 206): *unwilling*. Used like a partic. in the gen. abs. const. XL.

ἀληθεύω (ἀληθής), ἀληθεύσω, ἠλήθευσα: *speak the truth*.

ἀληθής, ές: *true*. Comp. ἀληθέστερος, sup. ἀληθέστατος, § 351. d. XXXIV.

ἀληθινός, ή, όν (ἀληθής): *true, worthy of the name, trusty*.

ἀλ-ίσκομαι (themes ἀλ- and ἁλο-), ἁλώσομαι, ἑάλων or ἥλων, ἑάλωκα or ἥλωκα: *be taken, be captured*. Used as pass. of αἱρέω. §§ 573. a, 574, 575. LVIII.

ἀλλά (ἄλλος), conj.: *otherwise, but;* sometimes in an address, *well !* V.

ἄλλη, adv. (dat. fem. of ἄλλος, with ὁδῷ or χώρᾳ understood): *elsewhere, in another place* or *direction*. XLVII.

ἀλλήλοιν, αιν, οιν, reciprocal pron.: *of one another*. § 377. XXXVIII.

ἄλλος, η, ο: *other, another; besides;* preceded by article, *the other, the rest of*. § 124. X.

ἄλλως (adv. of ἄλλος): *otherwise.*
ἄλλως ἔχειν: see ἔχω. LIV.

ἄλφιτα, ων, τά: *barley meal.*

ἅμα, adv.: *at the same time, together
with,* with dat. ἅμα τῇ ἡμέρᾳ: *at
the same time with the day, at daybreak.* ἅμα ἡλίῳ δύνοντι: *at sunset*
(§ 591). XIII.

ἅμαξα, ης, ἡ: *carriage, wagon.* § 140,
XI.

ἀμείνων: comp. of ἀγαθός.

Ἀμπρακιώτης, ου, ὁ: *an Ambracian,*
a citizen of Ambracia in Epīrus.

ἀμφί, prep.: with GEN. *concerning,
about* (but in prose περί is generally used in this sense); with ACC.
about. οἱ ἀμφὶ Κῦρον: *Cyrus and
his men* (lit. *those* [the men] *about
Cyrus*). οἱ ἀμφ' αὐτόν: *those about
him.* XVII.

ἄν: modal adv. See §§ 249, 266. *a*,
267, 276, 277, 530. *a*, 531, 545, 546.
ἄν (εἰ + ἄν) = ἐάν: *if,* conj. with subjv.
§§ 241, 249, 399. XXII.

ἀνά, prep. with acc. only: *up, up along,
up through.* (In composition also
back.) ἀνὰ κράτος: *to the limit of
strength, at full speed.* XXVI.

ἀνα-βαίνω: *go up; go inland* ('up'
from the coast); *mount* one's horse.
XXVI.

ἀναγκάζω (theme ἀναγκαδ-, cp.
ἀνάγκη), ἀναγκάσω, ἠνάγκασα,
ἠνάγκακα, ἠνάγκασμαι, ἠναγκά-
σθην: *compel, force.* LVI.

ἀνάγκη, ης, ἡ: *necessity;* with or
without ἐστί(ν): *it is necessary*
(§ 230). XXI.

ἀν-άγω (ἀνά + ἄγω): *lead up;* lead
'up' from the coast; MID. *put to
sea* (§ 502). XXXIX.

ἀνα-κάω: *light, kindle.*

ἀνα-λαμβάνω: *take up, take along.*

ἀνα-παύω: *make cease;* MID. *rest.*
LIX.

ἀνα-στρέφω: *turn back, turn about*
(intr.); PASS. in mid. sense, *turn
about, face about, rally.* XLI.

ἀνα-ταράττω: *stir up;* pf. pass. partic.
ἀνα-τεταραγμένον: *confused.*

ἀνδράποδον, ου, τό (ἀνήρ and πούς):
slave taken in war. LVII.

ἄνευ, prep. with gen. only: *without.*
LVI.

ἀν-έχω, impf. ἠν-εῖχον and 2 aor. ἠν-
έσχον with double augment: *hold
up;* MID. *hold oneself up, endure;
restrain oneself.*

ἀνήρ, ἀνδρός, ὁ: *man; husband.*
ὦ ἄνδρες στρατιῶται (or Ἕλληνες): *fellow soldiers* (or *Greeks*).
Cp. Lat. *vir.* § 321. XXXI.

ἄνθρωπος, ου, ὁ: *man.* Cp. Lat.
homō. § 56. III.

ἀνιάω, ἀνιάσω, ἠνίāσα, ἠνιάθην: *vex;*
fut. mid. as pass. ἀνιάσομαι: *shall
be grieved* or *hurt.*

ἀν-ίστημι: *make stand up, start up;*
(intr.) *stand up.* For intr. tenses
see § 555. LVI.

ἄν-οδος, ου, ἡ (ἀνά + ὁδός): *road up,
way up.* XXXIX.

ἀντί, prep. with gen. only: *instead
of, for;* in comp.: *against.*
LVI.

ἀντίος, ā, ον: *face to face, opposite,
against,* with dat. ἐκ τοῦ ἀντίου:
*from the opposite side, from the
opposing line.*

ἄνω, adv. (cp. ἀνά): *up;* up from the
sea, *inland, into the interior.* Comp.
ἀνωτέρω (*higher*), sup. ἀνωτάτω
(*highest*), § 369. I. XXXVII.

ἄξιος, ā, ον: *worthy, worth.* With
gen., § 402. Comp. ἀξιώτερος, sup.
ἀξιώτατος, § 351. *b.* XXXV.

ἀξιόω (ἄξιος), ἀξιώσω, ἠξίωσα, ἠξίωκα,
ἠξίωμαι, ἠξιώθην: *deem worthy;
claim* as one's right, *demand, ask.*
LIII.

ἀπ-αγγέλλω: *bring back a message, report.* LV.

ἀπ-άγω: *lead away, lead back.* LIV.

ἀ-παράσκευος, ον (ἀ- priv. and παρα-σκευάζω): *unprepared.* XXXVII.

ἅ-πᾱς, ᾱσα, ᾱν (πᾶς): *all together, all.* The prefix ἀ- signifies *together*; cp. ἅμα. XXVIII.

ἄπ-ειμι (εἶμι): *go away; go back, return.* LX.

ἀπ-ελαύνω: *drive off, ride off.*

ἀπ-έρχομαι, fut. supplied by ἄπ-ειμι, ἀπ-ῆλθον, ἀπ-ελήλυθα: *go away, go back.* Cp. Vocab. XIX.

ἀπ-έχω: *be distant, be away,* with gen. of person or place and acc. of extent of space. XVIII.

ἀπ-ῆλθον: *I* or *they went away;* see ἀπ-έρχομαι. XIX.

ἁπλοῦς, ῆ, οῦν: *simple, sincere.* § 609. L.

ἀπό, prep. with gen. only: *off, from, away from.* Cp. Lat. *ab.* X.

ἀπο-βλέπω: *look away* or *off.*

ἀπο-γιγνώσκω: *abandon the idea of,* with gen.

ἀπο-διδρᾱ́σκω (δι-δρᾱ́-σκω, δρᾱ́σομαι, ἔδρᾱν, δέδρᾱκα): *run away* by stealth; *run away from* (with acc.). § 553. LVI.

ἀπο-δίδωμι: *give back, pay.*

ἀπο-θνῄσκω (θνῄσκω *die,* θανοῦμαι, ἔθανον, τέθνηκα *be dead*): *die off, die, perish, be slain, be killed.* X.

ἀπο-θύω: *sacrifice* what is due on account of a vow.

ἀπο-κόπτω: *cut off.* XLI.

ἀπο-κρίνομαι (mid. of ἀπο-κρίνω, see κρίνω): *give one's decision, answer, reply.* With ὅτι clause, § 669. 1. LV.

ἀπο-κτείνω (κτείνω for κτεν-γω, theme κτεν-, *kill,* κτενῶ, ἔκτεινα, ἔκτονα): *put to death, slay, kill.* The pass. is supplied by ἀπο-θνῄσκω. LV.

ἀπο-λαμβάνω: *take* or *receive back; take off, cut off* (§ 444. I. 12). XXXIII.

ἀπο-λείπω: *leave behind, desert, abandon.* XLII.

ἀπ-όλλῡμι (ὄλλῡμι for ὀλ-νυ-μι, themes ὀλ-, ὀλε-, *destroy,* ὀλῶ, ὤλεσα, ὀλώλεκα [§ 447] and 2 pf. ὄλωλα, ὠλόμην): *destroy* utterly, *lose;* MID. and 2 pf. act., *perish, be lost.* LIX.

ἀπο-πέμπω: *send off* or *away, dismiss.* X.

ἀπο-πλέω: *sail off* or *away.* LI.

ἀπορίᾱ, ᾱς, ἡ (cp. ἄ-πορος, πορεύομαι): lack of way out, *embarrassment, difficulty.* XLVII.

ἄπορος, ον: *impassable; needy, without resources* (§ 232). § 118. III.

ἀπο-σπάω, -σπάσω, -έσπασα, -έσπακα, -έσπασμαι, -εσπάσθην: *draw away.*

ἀπο-σῴζω: *save from* something, *bring safely back.* LVIII.

ἀπο-φεύγω: *flee away, escape.* XII.

ἄρα, post-positive particle: *then* (inferential).

ἀργύριον, ου, τό: *silver, money.* L.

ἀργυροῦς, ᾶ, οῦν (cp. ἀργύριον): *of silver, silver.* § 609. L.

ἀρετή, ῆς, ἡ (cp. ἄρ-ιστος): *fitness, excellence, bravery; virtue, noble-mindedness, magnanimity.* XXXVII.

Ἀριαῖος, ου, ὁ: *Ariaeus,* a Persian nobleman. οἱ μετὰ Ἀριαίου: *Ariaeus and his men* (§ 557). XXV.

Ἀρίστιππος, ου, ὁ: *Aristippus,* a Thessalian general of mercenary soldiers. XIX.

ἄριστος: see ἀγαθός.

ἅρμα, ατος, τό: *chariot* for use in battle. See p. 252, Fig. 22. LVI.

ἁρπάζω (theme ἁρπαδ-), ἁρπάσω
(§ 153) and ἁρπάσομαι (dep.),
ἥρπασα (§ 164), ἥρπακα (§ 432.
e, f), ἥρπασμαι (§ 467. a), ἡρπάσθην (§ 387. 2): seize, make booty
of, plunder. § 487. I.

Ἀρταγέρσης, ου, ὁ: Artagerses, commander of the Persian king's body-
guard of six thousand.

Ἀρταξέρξης, ου, ὁ: Artaxerxes; in
this book, Artaxerxes II, king of
Persia is meant, the son of Darius
and Parysatis, and brother of Cyrus.
XIV.

Ἀρταπάτης, ου, ὁ: Artapates, a
friend of Cyrus. XXXV.

ἀρχαῖος, ᾱ, ον (ἀρχή): primitive, of
old, old, ancient. τὸ ἀρχαῖον (adv.
acc.): of old, formerly. XXVII.

ἀρχή, ῆς, ἡ: beginning, rule, province,
empire. § 93. VI.

ἄρχω (cp. ἀρχή), ἄρξω, ἦρξα (§ 164),
ἦργμαι, ἤρχθην: begin, rule, command, with gen.; MID. begin, with
gen. or inf. VIII, XXXIV.

ἄρχων, οντος, ὁ: ruler, commander.
Really the pres. masc. partic. of
ἄρχω. §§ 195, 199, 200. XVIII.

ἀσπίς, ίδος, ἡ: shield. See p. 97,
Fig. 10. §§ 195, 196. XVIII.

ἄστυ, εως, τό: town. § 282. XXVII.

ἀσφαλής, ές: secure, safe (§ 275).
ἐν ἀσφαλεῖ: in safety. Comp.
ἀσφαλέστερος, sup. ἀσφαλέστατος,
§ 351. d. XXVI, XXXV.

ἀσφαλῶς, adv. (ἀσφαλής): securely,
safely. Comp. ἀσφαλέστερον, sup.
ἀσφαλέστατα, §§ 366, 368.
XXXVII.

ἅτε, adv. (neut. pl. of ὅσ-τε): as,
since, accompanying causal partic.

αὑτῆς: see αὑτοῦ.

αὐτός, ή, ό, as intensive pron.: self,
very; when preceded by article,
same; in gen., dat., and acc., used

as pron. of third pers.: him, her, it,
them. §§ 122, 123, 127, 307, 308.
X.

αὐτοῦ (cp. αὐτός), adv.: in the very
place, here, there. LIX.

αὑτοῦ, ῆς, οῦ (contracted from ἑαυτοῦ), reflexive pron. of third pers.:
of himself, herself, etc. §§ 376. 3,
379. XXXVIII.

ἀφ-αιρέομαι (mid. of αἱρέω): take
away for oneself, deprive, rob
somebody of something (two accs.).
LI.

ἀφανής, ές: invisible, out of sight.
XXVI.

ἀφ-ίημι: let go away, dismiss. LVII.

ἀφ-ικ-νέ-ομαι (theme ἱκ-; νε- appears
only in pres. system), ἀφ-ίξομαι,
ἀφ-ῑκόμην, ἀφ-ῖγμαι, dep. mid.:
arrive, come. LI.

ἀ-φύλακτος, ον (ἀ- priv. and φυλάττω), unguarded; off one's guard.
§ 476. IV.

Ἀχαιός, οῦ, ὁ: an Achaean, inhabitant of Achaea. XXVI.

B

Βαβυλών, ῶνος, ἡ: Babylon. XXXII.

βαθύς, εῖα, ύ: deep. XLVIII.

βαίνω (themes βα- or βη-, βαν-),
βήσομαι, ἔβην (§ 553), βέβηκα
(§ 432. a): go. See ἀνα-βαίνω,
δια-βαίνω, etc.

βάλλω (for βαλ + yω, themes βαλ-,
βλη-), βαλῶ, ἔβαλον, βέβληκα, βέβλημαι, ἐβλήθην: throw, hurl, pelt.
Often with acc. of pers. and dat. of
means. LVII.

βαρβαρικός, ή, όν (βάρβαρος): foreign, barbarian, not Greek. τὸ
βαρβαρικόν: the barbarian force.
LVIII.

βαρβαρικῶς: in a foreign tongue, in
the Persian language.

βάρβαρος, ου, ὁ : *foreigner, barbarian.*
VIII.

βασιλεία, ᾱς, ἡ (βασιλεύω) : *kingdom.*
LVI.

βασίλειος, ον (βασιλεύς) : *of a king,
royal.* τὰ βασίλεια (neut. pl.
subst.): the royal buildings, *the
palace.* XIX.

βασιλεύς, έως, ὁ, *king.* §§ 290, 292.
XXVIII.

βασιλεύω (βασιλεύς), βασιλεύσω,
ἐβασίλευσα : *be king, rule as king.*
XIX.

βασιλικός, ή, όν (βασιλεύς, βασίλειος) : *kinglike, fit to be king;
royal.* XXXV.

βέλτιστος : see ἀγαθός.

βελτίων, ῑον : see ἀγαθός.

βιαίως, adv. : *with might, violently.*

βίος, ου, ὁ : *living, subsistence, livelihood.* Bio-logy (λόγος).

βλάπτω (theme βλαβ-), βλάψω,
ἔβλαψα, βέβλαφα, βέβλαμμαι,
ἐβλάφθην, 2 aor. pass. ἐβλάβην :
hurt, harm. §§ 408; 414, 484, 487,
642. XLI.

βλέπω, βλέψομαι, ἔβλεψα : *look.*
XXIX.

βοάω, βοήσομαι, ἐβόησα : *cry out,
shout.*

βοή, ῆς, ἡ : *outcry, shouting.*

βοη-θέω, βοηθήσω, ἐβοήθησα, βεβοή-
θηκα, βεβοήθημαι : run to the rescue
at an outcry, *run to assist, assist.*

Βοιώτιος, ᾱ, ον : *Boeotian,* an inhabitant of Boeotia. XIV.

βουλεύω, βουλεύσω, ἐβούλευσα, βεβού-
λευκα, βεβούλευμαι, ἐβουλεύθην :
plan, devise; the simple verb is
commonly dep. mid. βουλεύομαι :
*take counsel with oneself, plan,
deliberate.* Cp. ἐπι-βουλεύω and
συμ-βουλεύω. XXXII.

βούλομαι, βουλήσομαι (with lengthened theme), βεβούλημαι, ἐβουλή-

θην (§ 389), dep. pass. : *wish.*
XXX.

βοῦς, βοός, ὁ, ἡ : *ox, cow.* Cp. Lat.
bōs. § 290. XXVIII.

βραδέως : *slowly.*

βραχύς, εῖα, ύ : *short.* Comp. βραχύ
τερος, sup. βραχύτατος, § 351. c.
βραχύτερα : *a shorter distance*
(§ 460). XXXV.

Γ

γάρ, postpositive conj. : *for, and in
fact;* sometimes *why !* VIII.

γε, enclitic particle, regularly following
the emphatic word : *certainly, surely,
at least,* etc. LIV.

γείτων, ονος, ὁ : *neighbor.* § 220. XX.

γένος, ους, τό : *kinship, family, birth.*
Lat. *genus, gēns.* XXXI.

γερρο-φόρος, ον, ὁ (γέρρον *wicker
shield* and φέρω) : one who carries a wicker shield, *wicker-shield
bearer.*

γεύω, γεύσω, ἔγευσα, γέγευμαι : *give a
taste of;* MID. *taste,* with gen.

γέφῡρα, ᾱς, ἡ : *bridge.* § 140. XI.

γῆ, ῆς, ἡ : *earth, land.* § 594. L.

γίγνομαι (for γι-γεν-ο-μαι, reduplicated pres. from theme γεν-), γενήσομαι (theme γεν-η-), ἐγενόμην,
γέγονα (§ 445), γεγένημαι (§ 456) :
*become, be born, be, get; happen,
arise, take place, turn out.* XXXII.

γιγνώσκω (reduplicated pres. from
theme γνο-, with pres. suffix σκ%),
γνώσομαι, ἔγνων, ἔγνωκα, ἔγνωσμαι,
ἐγνώσθην : *learn, know, judge,* with
ὅτι or partic. or inf. in indir. disc.
Cp. Lat. (g)nōscō, ī-gnōtus. §§ 573.
b, 574, 575. LV.

γνώμη, ης, ἡ (γνῶ-ναι) : *opinion, judgment; plan, proposition; understanding.* XXIX.

γονεύς, έως, ὁ (γίγνομαι) : *parent.*

γόνυ, γόνατος, τό: *knee.* Lat. *genū.*
§ 336. 6. XXXIII.

γράφω, γράψω, ἔγραψα, γέγραφα, γέ-
γραμμαι (§ 465. *a*), ἐγράφην: *write.*
§§ 409, 415. XXIV.

γυμνάζω (theme γυμναδ-), γυμνάσω,
ἐγύμνασα, γεγύμνακα, γεγύμνασμαι,
ἐγυμνάσθην: *exercise.* Cp. γυμνής.
XLII.

γυμνής, ῆτος, ὁ: *light-armed warrior,*
javelin hurler, bowman, or slinger.
XXI.

Γυμνιάς, άδος, ἡ: *Gymnias,* a city in
Armenia.

γυμνικός, ή, όν: *gymnastic, athletic.*

γυνή, γυναικός, ἡ: *woman, wife.*
§ 336. 1. XXXIII.

Δ

δακρύω, δακρύσω, ἐδάκρῡσα: *weep.*

δᾱρεικός, οῦ, ὁ: *daric,* a Persian gold
coin, worth about $5.40. XXII.

Δᾱρεῖος, ον, ὁ: *Darius.* The person
indicated in this book is Darius II,
king of Persia, father of Artaxerxes
II and Cyrus the Younger. XVIII.

δασμός, οῦ, ὁ: *tribute, tax.* XXVII.

δασύς, εῖα, ύ: *thickly grown, thickly
wooded,* with dat. (instrumental).
Cp. Lat. *dēnsus.* XXVIII.

δέ, postpositive conj.: *and, but,* weaker
than ἀλλά. V.

δέδια, 2 pf. of μι-formation, same in
meaning as δέδοικα: *fear;* partic.
δεδιώς: *fearing* (§ 568).

δέδοικα, pf. with pres. meaning (from
δείδω): *fear;* 1 aor. ἔδεισα. Cp.
δεινός. XLIV.

δέῃ, subjv. of δεῖ, impers. verb: *it is
necessary.* XXIII.

δεῖ (contracted from δέει), fut. δεήσει,
aor. ἐδέησε, impers. verb: *it is necessary.* §§ 223, 479. XX.

δείδω (pres. not found in prose), aor.

ἔδεισα, 2 pf. δέδοικα and (μι-form)
δέδια: *fear;* the pf. forms have pres.
meaning. See δέδοικα.

δείκ-νῡμι (and δεικ-νύω, theme δεικ-),
δείξω, ἔδειξα, δέδειχα, δέδειγμαι, ἐδείχθην: *show, point out.* §§ 579, 580,
581, 619, 648. LIX.

δεικνύς, pres. act. partic. of δείκνῡμι:
showing. Declined in § 619.

δείλη, ης, ἡ: *afternoon,* early or
late.

δεινός, ή, όν: *fearful, terrible, frightful; skillful.* τὸ δεινόν (subst.):
danger. XLII.

δείσᾱς: see δείδω.

δέκα, indecl.: *ten.* Lat. *decem.* XI.

δένδρον, ου, τό: *tree.* Dat. pl. δένδροις
and δένδρεσι (from nom. τὸ δένδρος).
XXVIII.

δεξιός, ά, όν: *right, on the right hand*
or *side.* δεξιά, ᾶς, ἡ (supply χείρ):
the right hand, as a *pledge.* τὰ
δεξιὰ τοῦ κέρᾱτος: *the right (of
the) wing.* Lat. *dexter.* LVIII.

δέοι, opt. of δεῖ: *it is necessary* (Vocab.
XX). XXXVII.

δέομαι, δεήσομαι, δεδέημαι, ἐδεήθην
(cp. § 389), dep. pass.: *want, need;
desire, ask, beg.* Often with gen. or
with gen. of pers. and inf. Cp. δεῖ.
LIX.

δέρμα, ατος, τό: *hide, skin.* Dermato-
logy, epi-dermis.

δεσπότης, ου, ὁ: *master.* Voc. δέ-
σποτα. XLVIII.

δεύτερος, ᾱ, ον: *second.* (τὸ) δεύτερον: *for the second time.*

δέχομαι, δέξομαι, ἐδεξάμην, δέδεγμαι,
ἐδέχθην: *receive, accept.* XXXII.

δή: postpositive particle, emphasizing
the preceding word. δή is difficult
to render adequately, but is sometimes translated by *now, then,
accordingly, very, in truth, indeed.*
XXI.

δῆλος, η, ον: *plain, clear, evident.*
See § 449 and *a.* XV.

δηλόω (δῆλος), δηλώσω, ἐδήλωσα,
δεδήλωκα, δεδήλωμαι, ἐδηλώθην:
show, make evident. §§ 529, 622.
a, 643. LIII.

δηλῶν, pres. act. partic. of δηλόω:
showing. Declined in § 622. *a.*

διά, prep.: with GEN. *through;* with
ACC. *on account of, by means of.* XI.

δια-βαίνω: *go across, cross.* XI.

δια-βάλλω: *accuse falsely, slander.*
LVIII.

δια-βατέος, ᾱ, ον (verbal adj. of δια-
βαίνω, theme βα-): *necessary to be
crossed.* § 477. I. XLVIII.

δια-βατός, ή, όν (verbal adj. of δια-
βαίνω, theme βα-): *able to be
crossed, fordable* (of a river). Cp.
ἀ-διά-βατος. § 475. XLVIII.

δια-βήσομαι: fut. of δια-βαίνω (Vocab.
XI). XXXII.

δια-δίδωμι: *give from hand to hand,
distribute.* LVIII.

δια-κόπτω: *cut through, cut in pieces,
break through.* XLI.

διᾱκόσιοι, αι, α: *two hundred.* § 421.

δια-λέγομαι (cp. λέγω *say*), δια-
λέξομαι, irreg. pf. δι-είλεγμαι,
δι-ελέχθην (§ 389), dep. pass.:
converse, with dat. (§ 317). XXX.

δια-λείπω: *leave an interval, be distant.*

δια-πρᾱ́ττομαι (cp. πρᾱ́ττω), δια-
πρᾱ́ξομαι, δι-επρᾱξάμην, δια-
πέπρᾱγμαι: *carry through to the
end, bring about, accomplish, effect*
(for oneself); *manage* that, with
acc. and inf. or ὅπως clause (§ 535.
a). XXXIV.

δι-αρπάζω: *tear in pieces, plunder
utterly* or *thoroughly, sack.* XIV.

δια-σπείρω (σπείρω *sow,* σπερῶ,
ἔσπειρα, ἔσπαρμαι, ἐσπάρην): *scatter;* MID. (of soldiers) *scatter.*

διδά-σκω (theme διδαχ-), διδάξω, ἐδίδαξα, δεδίδαχα, δεδίδαγμαι, ἐδιδά-
χθην: *teach.* LX.

διδούς, pres. act. partic. of δίδωμι:
giving. Declined in § 621.

δίδωμι, δώσω, ἔδωκα and ἔδοτον. δέδωκα, δέδομαι, ἐδόθην: *give,* sometimes *offer* (in pres. and impf.).
δίκην διδόναι: *give satisfaction,
suffer punishment.* Cp. δῶρον.
Lat. *dō, dōnum.* §§ 570, 571, 572,
621, 646. LVIII.

δι-είργω (εἴργω *shut out,* εἴρξω, εἶρξα,
εἴργμαι, εἴρχθην): *separate, shut off.*

δι-έρχομαι: *go through, travel, spread*
with λόγος (*report*) as subj. See
δι-ῆλθον.

δι-έχω: *be apart, be separated.* XVII.

δι-ῆλθον, 2 aor.: *I* or *they went through,
traveled; spread* with λόγος (*word*
or *report*) as subject. See δι-έρχομαι.
XXIV.

Διί: see Ζεύς.

δι-ίστημι: *set apart;* intr. tenses,
stand apart, open ranks.

δίκαιος, ᾱ, ον (δίκη): *just.* Comp. δι-
καιότερος, sup. δικαιότατος, § 351.*a.*
XXV, XXXV.

δικαίως, adv. (δίκαιος): *justly.* Comp.
δικαιότερον, sup. δικαιότατα, §§ 366,
368. XXV, XXXVII.

δίκη, ης, ἡ: *justice, deserts.* δίκην
ἐπι-τιθέναι: *inflict punishment* on
somebody (dat.). δίκην διδόναι:
give satisfaction, suffer punishment
(§ 576). IX.

δισ-χῑ́λιοι, αι, α: *two thousand.* § 421.

διωκτέος, ᾱ, ον (verbal adj. of διώκω):
necessary to be pursued. § 477. 2.
XLVIII.

διώκω, διώξω or διώξομαι, ἐδίωξα, δε-
δίωχα, δεδίωγμαι, ἐδιώχθην: *pursue.*
XVII.

διῶρυξ, υχος, ἡ: *trench, canal.* § 187.
XVII.

δοκέω (theme δοκ-, but δοκε- in pres. system), δόξω, ἔδοξα, δέδογμαι, ἐδό-χθην: *seem, be reputed; seem best; think.* § 512. LI.

δόλιχος, ου, ὁ: *long foot-race,* from six to twenty-four times the length of the stadium. δόλιχον θεῖν: *run the long race.*

δόρυ, δόρατος, τό: *spear* of a Greek hoplite. See p. 152, Fig. 19. § 336. 5. XXXIII.

δουπέω, ἐδούπησα: *strike* heavily, *clash,* with dat. (of instrument) and πρός with acc.

Δρακόντιος, ου, ὁ: *Dracontius,* a soldier from Sparta.

δρεπανη-φόρος, ον: *scythe-bearing,* epithet of two-wheeled Asiatic chariots, which carried, for use on the battle field, scythes fixed to the axles and pointed obliquely downward. See p. 270, Fig. 25.

δρόμος, ου, ὁ (cp. ἔδραμον): a *run; race course* (§ 514). δρόμῳ: *on the run.* θεῖν δρόμῳ: *run with speed, run fast, charge on the run.* See p. 79, Fig. 6. XII.

δύνα-μαι, δυνήσομαι, δεδύνημαι, ἐδυ-νήθην (or ἠδυνήθην), dep. pass.: *be able.* Cp. δύναμις. LVI.

δύναμις, εως, ἡ: *force, strength.* XXVII.

δυνατός, ή, όν (δύναμαι): *able, strong; possible.* Cp. § 333. XXXIV.

δύ/ω: see δύω.

δύο, gen. and dat. δυοῖν, but generally used indeclinably: *two.* Lat. *duo.* § 423. XV.

δύ-ω (and δύνω), δύσω, ἔδῡσα (trans.), ἔδῡν (intr.), δέδῡκα, δέδυμαι, ἐδύθην: *enter, set* (used of the sun). §§ 580, 582, 648. LIX.

δώ-δεκα (δύο + δέκα), indecl.: *twelve.* XXXI.

δῶρον, ου, τό: *gift.* Cp. Lat. *dōnum.* XLIII.

E

ἐάν = εἰ + ἄν, conj. with subjv.: *if.* §§ 241, 399. XXII.

ἑαυτοῦ, ῆς, οῦ, reflexive pron. of third pers.: *of himself, herself,* etc. §§ 376. 3, 379. XXXVIII.

ἐάω, ἐάσω, εἴᾱσα, εἴᾱκα, εἴᾱμαι, εἰάθην: *permit, allow, let.* The augment is irreg. §§ 515. *a,* 518. *a.* LII.

ἐγγύς, adv.: *near,* with gen. Comp. ἐγγύτερον or ἐγγυτέρω, sup. ἐγγύ-τατα or ἐγγυτάτω, § 369. 2. XXXVII.

ἐγώ, ἐμοῦ or μου: *I.* Lat. *ego.* §§ 304, 306, 308. XXIX.

ἔδεισα: see δέδοικα. XI.

ἔδραμον: see τρέχω. XI.

ἐθέλω, ἐθελήσω (with lengthened theme). ἠθέλησα, ἠθέληκα: *wish, desire.* VI.

ἔθνος, ους, τό: *nation, tribe.* Ethnology.

εἰ, proclitic conj.: *if.* εἰ μή: *if not, except* (§ 557). εἴ τι: *whatsoever* (§ 232). §§ 106, 242, 267, 416, 545. After an interr. verb or equivalent: *whether,* introducing an indirect question. §§ 343. *a,* 363. VII, XXXIV.

εἰ γάρ: used in wishes; see §§ 584, 585.

εἶδον, 2 aor.: *I* or *they saw.* Subjv. ἴδω, opt. ἴδοιμι, imv. ἰδέ (§ 301. *a*), inf. ἰδεῖν, partic. ἰδών. See ὁράω. XIX.

εἰδῶ, εἰδώς: see οἶδα.

εἴθε: used in wishes; see §§ 584, 585.

εἴκοσι(ν), indecl.: *twenty.* XXVI.

εἴληφα: see λαμβάνω.

εἱλόμην, 2 aor. mid. of εἷλον: *I took for myself, I chose.* Subjv. ἕλωμαι, opt. ἑλοίμην, imv. ἑλοῦ, inf. ἑλέ-σθαι, partic. ἑλόμενος. See αἱρέω. XXXII.

εἶλον, 2 aor.: *I* or *they took, seized.*
Subjv. ἕλω, opt. ἕλοιμι, imv. ἕλε,
inf. ἑλεῖν, partic. ἑλών. See αἱρέω.
XXVI.

εἶ-μι, impf. ᾖα: *go, shall go;* pres.
serving as fut. of ἔρχομαι. § 651.
LX.

εἰμί, impf. ἦ or ἦν, fut. ἔσομαι: *am,
be.* §§ 101, 102, etc., 650. VII.

εἶναι: see εἰμί. VII.

εἶπον, 2 aor.: *I* or *they said.* Subjv.
εἴπω, opt. εἴποιμι, imv. εἰπέ (§ 301.*a*),
inf. εἰπεῖν, partic. εἰπών. With ὅτι
that and finite verb, § 262. In the
sense of *commanded, proposed, urged,*
εἶπον is followed by the inf.; cp. § 98.
XXIV, XXXII.

εἴρηκα, pf.: *I have said, I have mentioned.* § 448. Supplies missing
pf. act. of λέγω *say.* XLV.

εἰρήνη, ης, ἡ: *peace.* LVII.

εἷς, μία, ἕν, gen. ἑνός, μιᾶς, ἑνός: *one.*
§ 422. XLIII.

εἰς, proclitic prep. with acc. only: *into,
to; for;* with numerals, *to the number of, about* (§ 219). εἰς τὴν ἑσπέραν: *into the evening, at evening.* V.

εἰσ-άγω: *lead in.* XXXV.

εἰσ-ελαύνω: *drive in, ride* or *march
in,* with εἰς and acc. XXXVIII.

εἰσ-ῆλθον, 2 aor. of εἰσ-έρχομαι: *I* or
they came in, entered. XXI.

εἴσω, adv.: *within,* with gen. XLVI.

εἶτα, adv.: *then, thereupon.* X.

εἶχον (§ 80): see ἔχω.

ἐκ, before a vowel ἐξ, proclitic prep.
with gen. only: *out from, from.* V.

ἕκαστος, η, ον: *each;* used in predicate position to modify a noun with
the article; used also without the
article. XXII.

ἑκάτερος, ᾱ, ον: *each.*

ἑκατέρωθεν: *from both sides, on both
sides.*

ἑκατέρωσε: *in both directions.*

ἑκατόν, indecl.: *hundred.* XV.

ἔκ-βασις, εως, ἡ (ἐκ-βαίνω): *passage
out, mountain pass.* L.

ἐκεῖ, adv.: *there.*

ἐκεῖνος, η, ο: *that, that one, that man;
he, him,* etc. §§ 174, 175. *a*, 176,
307. XV.

ἐκκλησίᾱ, ᾶς, ἡ (ἐκ-καλέω *summon
forth*): *assembly.* XXXVIII.

ἐκ-κλίνω (κλίνω *bend,* κλινῶ, ἔκλῑνα,
κέκλιμαι, ἐκλίθην and ἐκλίνην):
bend out of line, *turn* in flight.

ἐκ-λείπω: *leave out, abandon;* (intr.)
leave off, fail. LVIII.

ἐκ-πλέω: *sail forth, sail off.*

ἐκ-πλήττω (πλήττω, theme πληγ-
or πλαγ-, *strike,* πλήξω, ἔπληξα,
πέπληγα, πέπληγμαι, ἐπλήγην, but
in comp. -επλάγην): *strike out* of
one's wits, *terrify utterly, bewilder.*
§ 466. *a.* XLI.

ἐλαύνω (theme ἐλα-; the pres. is for
ἐλα-νυ-ω), ἐλῶ (§ 544. *a*), ἤλασα
(§ 165), ἐλήλακα (§ 447), ἐλήλα-
μαι, ἠλάθην: *drive, ride, march.*
XV.

ἐλάχιστος: see ὀλίγος.

ἐλελίζω, ἠλέλιξα (ἐλελεῦ a war cry):
shout ἐλελεῦ, *raise the war cry, cry
out.*

ἐλήλακα: see ἐλαύνω.

ἐλήλυθα: see ἔρχομαι.

ἐλθέ: imv. of ἦλθον (ἔρχομαι), § 301.*a.*

ἔλθω: subjv. of ἦλθον (ἔρχομαι).
XXII.

Ἑλλάς, άδος, ἡ: *Hellas,* the name
given by the Hellēnes to their own
country. From the Romans they received the appellation *Greeks* (Lat.
Graecī), and their land was called
Greece (Lat. *Graecia*). XVIII.

Ἕλλην, ηνος, ὁ: *a Greek.* XX.

Ἑλληνικός, ή, όν (Ἕλλην): *Hellenic,
Greek.* τὸ Ἑλληνικόν (neut. subst.):
the Greek force. XXVII, XXXIX.

Ἑλληνικῶς, adv.: in the Greek tongue, *in Greek.*

Ἑλληνίς, ίδος ("Ελλην), fem. adj.: *Greek.*

ἐμαυτοῦ, ῆς, reflexive pron. of first pers.: *of myself,* etc. §§ 376. 1, 379. XXXVIII.

ἐμ-βάλλω: *attack.*

ἐμός, ή, όν (cp. ἐμοῦ, gen. of ἐγώ): *my, mine.* § 126. X.

ἔμ-προσθεν, adv. (ἐν + πρόσθεν): *in front, before,* sometimes with gen. XLVII.

ἐν, proclitic prep. with dat. only: *in; among.* II.

ἐνδέκατος, η, ον (ἔν-δεκα *eleven*): *eleventh.*

ἔνδον, adv.: *within.* οἱ ἔνδον: *those within.* XLI.

ἐν-δύω: *put on.* § 588.

ἕνεκα, prep. with gen. only: *for the sake of.* Usually after its noun.

ἔνθα, rel. adv.: *where;* dem.: *there;* of time, ἔνθα δή: *then indeed.* XLIV.

ἔνθα-περ (strengthened ἔνθα): *just where, where;* the word *very* may be used with the antecedent to translate -περ.

ἔνθεν, rel. adv.: *whence, from which, where.* XXIV.

ἔνιοι, αι, α (from ἔνι [*i.e.* ἔν-εστι] + οἵ): *some.* XLV.

ἐν-νοέω: *have in mind.*

ἐνταῦθα, adv.: *there, thither.* VI.

ἐντεῦθεν, adv.: *thence;* of time, *then.* XI.

ἐν-τυγχάνω: *chance upon, happen upon, come upon by chance, encounter,* with dat. XLVII.

Ἐνυάλιος, ου, ὁ: *Enyalius,* a name of Ares, the Greek god of war.

ἕξ: indecl.: *six.* Lat. *sex.* § 421.

ἔξ: see ἐκ.

ἐξ-άγω: *lead out, induce* (§ 394). X.

ἑξακισ-χίλιοι, αι, α: *six thousand.* § 421.

ἑξακόσιοι, αι, α (ἕξ): *six hundred.* § 421.

ἐξ-απατάω (ἀπατάω *deceive,* ἀπατήσω, ἠπάτησα, ἠπάτηκα, ἠπάτημαι, ἠπατήθην): *utterly deceive, cheat.* LIV.

ἐξαπίνης, adv.: *suddenly.*

ἔξ-ειμι (εἶμι): *go out, go forth.* LX.

ἐξ-ελαύνω: *drive out; march out* or *forth.* XI.

ἐξ-έρχομαι, fut. ἔξ-ειμι (εἶμι), 2 aor. ἐξ-ῆλθον, 2 pf. ἐξ-ελήλυθα: *go forth.* Cp. XXV.

ἔξ-εστι(ν), 3 sing. of ἔξ-ειμι (εἰμί): *it is possible* or *permitted* (§ 223). ἐξ-όν: *it being possible* (§ 566). XX.

ἑξήκοντα (ἕξ), indecl.: *sixty.* § 421.

ἐξ-ῆλθον, 2 aor.: *I* or *they went forth.* XXV.

ἐξ-ήχθη: see ἐξ-άγω.

ἐξ-ικνέομαι (cp. ἀφ-ικνέομαι): *reach, reach* the mark.

ἐξ-όν: see ἔξεστι(ν).

ἐξ-οπλίζω: *arm fully;* MID. *fully arm oneself.*

ἔξω, adv.: *without, outside,* sometimes with gen. οἱ ἔξω: *those without.* XLI.

ἔξω: see ἔχω.

ἐπάν (ἐπεί + ἄν), conj. with subjv.: *when* (§ 248. 2. *a*); *whenever* (§ 400).

ἐπεί, temporal conj.: *when, after* (§ 167); *whenever* (§ 417); causal conj.: *since* (§ 310). XIV, XXIX.

ἐπειδάν (ἐπειδή + ἄν), conj. with subjv.: *when, after* (§ 248. 2. *a*); *whenever* (§ 400). ἐπειδὰν τάχιστα: *as soon as* (§ 533). XXIII.

ἐπειδή (ἐπεί and δή), temporal conj.: *when, after* (§ 167); causal conj.: *since* (§ 310). ἐπειδὴ τάχιστα: *as soon as.* XIV.

ἔπ-ειμι (εἶμι): *go* or *come on, approach.*
LX.

ἐπεί-περ (strengthened ἐπεί), causal
conj.: *since indeed* (§ 310). XXIX.

ἔπειτα, adv.: *thereupon, then, next.*
XXXVI.

ἐπήν (ἐπεί + ἄν), conj. with subjv.:
when (§ 248. 2. *a*); *whenever*
(§ 400).

ἐπί, prep.: with GEN. *on, in the time
of;* with DAT. *on, upon, at, in the
power of, for;* with ACC. *against*
(often with idea of hostility), *to,
upon; after,* i.e. *to get* (§§ 405,
451). ἐπὶ τούτοις: *upon this,
thereupon* (§ 347). ἐπὶ πολύ: *for
a long distance* (§ 557). VIII.

ἐπι-βουλεύω: *plot against,* with dat.
X.

ἐπι-βουλή, ῆς, ἡ: *plot* (against). Cp.
ἐπι-βουλεύω. XXXVIII.

ἐπι-δείκνῡμι: *show, point out;* MID. in
sense of act., and also *distinguish
oneself.* LIX.

ἐπι-θῡμέω, ἐπι-θῡμήσω, ἐπ-εθύμησα:
have one's heart set on, *yearn, desire,* with inf. or gen. LII.

ἐπι-κάμπτω (κάμπτω *bend,* κάμψω,
ἔκαμψα, κέκαμμαι, ἐκάμφθην): *bend
to, wheel.*

ἐπί-κειμαι: *lie upon, attack,* with dat.
LIX.

ἐπι-μελέομαι, ἐπι-μελήσομαι, ἐπι-
μεμέλημαι, ἐπ-εμελήθην, dep. pass.:
take care of, care for, with gen. or
object clause; *give heed, observe,
watch to see.* LIV.

ἐπ-ιόντες: see ἔπ-ειμι (εἶμι).

ἐπι-σῑτίζομαι (theme σῑτιδ-), -σῑτιοῦ-
μαι, -εσῑτισάμην: *get provisions* for
oneself. Cp. σῖτος. LV.

ἐπί-σταμαι, ἐπιστήσομαι, ἠπιστήθην:
understand. LVI.

ἐπι-στήσᾱς: see ἐφ-ίστημι.

ἐπιστολή, ῆς, ἡ: *letter.* VIII.

ἐπι-τάττω: *enjoin* something (acc.)
on somebody (dat.), *direct, command.* XLVII.

ἐπιτήδειος, ᾱ, ον: *suitable, necessary.*
τὰ ἐπιτήδεια (neut. pl. subst.):
provisions, supplies. XIII.

ἐπι-τίθημι: *put* or *place upon; put* or
inflict punishment (δίκην) *on* somebody (τινί); MID. *set oneself upon,
attack,* with dat. LVII.

ἐπι-τυγχάνω: *chance upon, happen
upon, find,* with dat. XXXV.

ἕπομαι (for σέπομαι), ἕψομαι, 2 aor.
ἑσπόμην, impf. with irreg. augment
εἱπόμην: *follow,* with dat. (§ 317).
Cp. Lat. *sequor.* XLII.

ἐπριάμην, 2 aor.: *I bought.* No pres.
from this verb. §§ 550, 646.
LVI.

ἑπτά, indecl.: *seven.* Lat. *septem.*
§ 421.

ἔργον, ου, τό: *work, deed, under-
taking.* § 49. II.

ἔρημος, η, ον, or ἔρημος, ον: *deserted.*
σταθμοὶ ἔρημοι: *marches through
the desert.* LIII.

ἑρμηνεύς, έως, ὁ: *interpreter.* XXX.

ἔρυμα, ατος, τό: *defense, protection.*

ἔρχομαι, fut. supplied by εἶμι (§ 651),
2 aor. ἦλθον (Vocab. XVIII), 2 pf.
ἐλήλυθα (§ 447): *come, go.* For
the *simple* ἐλήλυθα, ἥκω is commonly used. XXX.

ἐρωτάω, ἐρωτήσω, ἠρώτησα, ἠρώτηκα,
ἠρώτημαι, ἠρωτήθην: *ask* a question, *inquire.* Cp. ἠρόμην (§ 346),
which is often used for ἠρώτησα
LII.

ἔσεσθαι: see ἔσομαι, fut. of εἰμί.

ἔσομαι: see εἰμί.

ἑσπέρᾱ, ᾱς, ἡ: *evening.* Lat. *vesper.*

ἔστε, temporal conj.: *while, so long as,
until.* §§ 521, 522. LII.

ἔστι(ν): *it is possible.* See εἰμί.
§ 102. VII.

ἔστω: 3 sing. imv. of εἰμί.

ἑστώς, pf. act. partic. of ἵστημι: *standing*. Declined in § 624.

ἔσχατος, η, ον: *last, extreme*. § 361. *a*. XXXVI.

ἔσχον (§ 88): see ἔχω.

ἑταῖρος, ου, ὁ: *companion*.

ἕτερος, ᾱ, ον: the *other ;* pl. subst. *others.* Hetero-dox (δόξα *opinion*).

ἔτι, adv.: *still, yet, besides, longer, again*. XX.

ἕτοιμος, η, ον, or ἕτοιμος, ον: *ready, prepared*. XXXVIII.

εὖ (adv. of ἀγαθός): *well*. Comp. ἄμεινον, etc., sup. ἄριστα, etc., § 369. 3. εὖ πάσχειν: *be treated kindly* (§ 537). XXXVII.

εὐ-δαίμων, ον (δαίμων *divinity*): having a good divinity, *fortunate, prosperous*. § 222. Comp. εὐδαιμονέστερος, sup. εὐδαιμονέστατος, § 351. *e.* XX.

εὔ-δηλος, ον: *perfectly clear, very clear*.

εὐθύς, adv.: *straightway, at once*. XIII.

εὔ-νους, ουν: *well disposed*. §§ 499, 610. L.

εὔ-ξεινος, ον (ξεῖνος *stranger*): *hospitable*. ὁ Εὔξεινος Πόντος: *the Euxine* or *Black Sea*.

εὑρίσκω, εὑρήσω, ηὗρον, ηὕρηκα, ηὕρημαι, ηὑρέθην: *find*. For 2 aor. act. imv. εὑρέ see § 301. *a*. XLIV.

εὖρος, ους, τό: *breadth, width*. XXVI.

Εὐφρᾱτης, ου, ὁ: *Euphrātes*, a great river in western Asia. XV.

εὔχομαι, εὔξομαι, εὐξάμην or ηὐξάμην, εὖγμαι or ηὖγμαι: *pray, vow*.

εὐ-ώνυμος, ον (εὖ and ὄνομα): of good name or omen; *left* as opposed to right. The Greeks avoided the use of the regular word for *left*, ἀριστερός, because in their regard the left

was the side of evil omens; and they regularly referred to the left by the euphemistic word εὐώνυμος. ἐπὶ τοῦ εὐωνύμου and ἐπὶ τῷ εὐωνύμῳ: *on the left wing*.

ἔφασαν: *they said ;* see φημί. VIII.

ἔφη: *he said ;* see φημί. VIII.

ἐφ-ίστημι: *halt, rein in* one's horse.

ἔφοδος, ου, ἡ (ἐπί + ὁδός): *way to, approach*. XLI.

ἐχθρός, ά, όν: *hostile*. ἐχθρός (subst.), οὗ, ὁ: personal *enemy*. To be distinguished from πολέμιος and οἱ πολέμιοι *the enemy* in war. Comp. ἐχθίων, sup. ἔχθιστος, § 352. *b*. XXXI.

ἔχω, ἕξω (§ 153) or σχήσω (§ 154), ἔσχον (§ 88), ἔσχηκα, ἔσχημαι, impf. εἶχον (§ 80): *have, hold, occupy ; restrain* (§ 335); *consider* (§ 365); *be able*, with inf.; MID. *be next, come next*, with gen. ἀθύμως ἔχειν: *be discouraged ;* ἄλλως ἔχειν: *be otherwise ;* κακῶς ἔχειν: *be bad ;* καλῶς ἔχειν: *be good, be well ;* οὕτως ἔχειν: *be thus* or *so* (§ 536); ἔχων: *with* (§ 213. *b*). § 487. I.

ἕως, temporal conj.: *while, so long as, until*. §§ 521, 522. LII.

Z

ζάω, ζήσω: *live*. In contract forms ζάω has η for ᾱ (§ 517). LII.

Ζεύς, Διός, ὁ: *Zeus*, the most exalted of the gods, and honored by all Greeks. For declension see § 606. 2.

H

ἤ, conj.: *or ; than* (after comparative idea); ἤ . . . ἤ: *either . . . or*. XXVIII.

ἡ, fem. art., proclitic in nom. sing. and nom. pl. αἱ (§ 20): *the;* see ὁ.
ἡ δέ: *and she, but she,* indicating a change of subject from the preceding sentence. ἡ may mean *she,* but only with μέν and δέ. §§ 93, 632. VI.

ἥ, fem. rel. pron.: *who, which;* see ὅς.

ἤγαγον (§ 87): see ἄγω.

ἡγεμόσυνα, ων, τά (ἡγεμών), adj. with ἱερά understood: *thank-offerings for good guidance.*

ἡγεμών, όνος, ὁ (ἡγέομαι): *leader, guide, commander.* § 220. XX.

ἡγέομαι, ἡγήσομαι, ἡγησάμην, ἥγημαι, dep. mid.: *lead, guide,* with gen. or dat.; *think, believe.* LI.

ἦγον (§ 82): see ἄγω.

ἡδέως, adv. (ἡδύς): *gladly.* Comp. ἥδῑον, sup. ἥδιστα, §§ 366, 368. XXXVII.

ἤδη, adv.: *now, already, straightway.* XXXIII.

ἥδομαι (theme ἡδ-): *be pleased;* ἡσθήσομαι (fut. pass.): *shall be pleased;* ἥσθην (aor. pass.): *was pleased;* with supplementary partic. (§ 439) or dat. of cause (§ 403). Cp. ἡδύς. XLIV.

ἡδύς, εῖα, ύ: *sweet.* § 288. Comp. ἡδίων (§ 354), sup. ἥδιστος (§ 352. *a*). Cp. Lat. *suāvis.* XXVIII.

ἥκιστα, adv. (sup. of κακός, ἥττων): *least of all, by no means* (§ 360. 2). XXXVI.

ἥκω, ἥξω: *come, have come;* pres. with pf. meaning. X.

ἦλθον, 2 aor. of ἔρχομαι: *I* or *they came* or *went.* XVIII.

ἥλιος, ου, ὁ: *sun.* LIX.

ἡμεῖς, ἡμῶν: *we;* see ἐγώ *I* (§ 304).

ἡμελημένως, adv.: *carelessly.*

ἡμέρᾱ, ᾱς, ἡ: *day.* XIII.

ἡμέτερος, ᾱ, ον (ἡμεῖς): *our, ours.* § 126. X.

ἥμισυς, εια, υ: *half.* τὸ ἥμισυ (with στρατεύματος): *the half.* ἥμισυς takes the gender and the number of its part. gen. Cp. Lat. *sēmi-,* Eng. hemi-. XXVIII.

ἤν (εἰ + ἄν) = ἐάν: *if,* conj. with subjv. §§ 241, 399. XXII.

ἦν, 3 sing. impf. of εἰμί: *he (she* or *it) was; it was possible.* III, VII.

ἡνίκα, temporal conj.: *when.*

ἡνί-οχος, ου, ὁ (ἡνία *reins* and ἔχω): *one who holds the reins, charioteer.*

Ἡρακλῆς, έους, ὁ: *Heracles,* son of Zeus and Alcmene, famed for his deeds of might. He was invoked as a guide of travelers. § 603.

ἡρόμην, 2 aor.: *I asked* (a question) or *inquired;* subjv. ἔρωμαι, opt. ἐροίμην, imv. ἐροῦ, inf. ἐρέσθαι, partic. ἐρόμενος. The pres. and other tenses are supplied by ἐρωτάω, which see. XXXIV.

ἦσαν, 3 pl. impf. of εἰμί: *they were.* III.

ἡττάομαι (ἥττων), ἡττήσομαι, ἥττημαι, ἡττήθην: *be inferior, be conquered;* used as pass. of νῑκάω. LIV.

ἥττων: comp. of κακός. § 360. 2.

Θ

θ': see τε.

θάλαττα, ης, ἡ: *sea.* § 140. XI.

θαυμάζω (theme θαυμαδ-), θαυμάσομαι, ἐθαύμασα, τεθαύμακα, ἐθαυμάσθην: *wonder, be surprised; wonder at, admire,* with acc. XIV.

θαυμαστός, ή, όν (verbal adj. of θαυμάζω): *admirable, wonderful, strange.* XLVIII.

θέᾱ, ᾱς, ἡ: *sight, spectacle.*

θεάομαι (θέᾱ), θεᾱ́σομαι, ἐθεᾱσάμην, τεθέᾱμαι: *look on, gaze at, see.* LII.

θεός, οὗ, ὁ: *god;* ἡ: *goddess.* The voc. case is the same as the nom. VII.

θέω, θεύσομαι: *run.* See also δρόμος. LI.

θηρεύω, θηρεύσω, ἐθήρευσα, τεθήρευκα, τεθήρευμαι, ἐθηρεύθην: *hunt, catch* (by hunting). Cp. θηρίον. XLII.

θηρίον, ου, τό: *wild beast.* XLII.

Θήχης, ους, ὁ: *Thēches,* the mountain south of Trapezus from which the survivors of the Ten Thousand first saw the Euxine Sea.

θνῄσκω: see ἀπο-θνῄσκω. The pf. τέθνηκα (§ 432. *b, d*) *be dead, be slain,* commonly occurs without a prefix.

θόρυβος, ου, ὁ: *noise.* LX.

Θρᾷξ, Θρᾳκός, ὁ: a *Thracian, Thracian.* XVII.

θυγάτηρ, τρός, ἡ: *daughter.* § 321. XXXI.

θύρα, ᾱς, ἡ: *door.*

θυσίᾱ, ᾱς, ἡ (θύω): a *sacrifice.*

θύω, θύσω, ἔθῡσα, τέθυκα (§ 432. *b*), τέθυμαι, ἐτύθην (§ 487): *sacrifice, offer* to a god; MID. *sacrifice, offer* for oneself or from one's own resources. XXIII, XXXIV.

θώρᾱξ, ᾱκος, ὁ: *breastplate.* See p. 86, Fig. 7. XVII.

I

ἰδέ (§ 301. *a*), ἰδεῖν, ἴδοιμι: see εἶδον and ὁράω.

ἱδρόω, ἵδρωσα: *sweat.*

ἴδω, ἰδών: see εἶδον and ὁράω.

ἰέναι: pres. inf. of εἶμι.

ἱερός, ά, όν: *sacred, holy.* τὰ ἱερά: *the victims,* then *the omens from the victims* sacrificed (the usual or ordinary offering). XLV.

ἵημι, ἥσω, ἧκα and εἷτον, εἷκα, εἷμαι, εἵθην: *send, hurl* (with something, in dat.); MID. *hurl oneself, hasten.* §§ 561, 562, 563, 649. LVII.

ἱκανός, ή, όν: *sufficient, enough, able.* § 333. XXXII.

ἵνα, conj. expressing purpose: *in order that, that.* § 243. XXII.

ἰόντος: see ἰών and εἶμι.

ἱππεύς, έως, ὁ (ἵππος): *horseman;* pl. *cavalry.* XXVIII.

ἱππικός, ή, όν (ἵππος): *of horse, of cavalry.* LVI.

ἱππόδρομος, ου, ὁ (ἵππος and δραμεῖν): *race track.* Hippodrome.

ἵππος, ου, ὁ: *horse.* § 48. ἐφ᾽ ἵππου: *on horseback,* with verb meaning *ride* (§ 232). ἀφ᾽ ἵππου: *on horseback,* with verb meaning *hunt* (§ 420). II.

ἴσμεν: see οἶδα.

ἴσος, η, ον: *equal.* ἐν ἴσῳ: *in even step, in step.* Iso-thermal (θερμός *hot*).

ἱστάς, pres. act. partic. of ἵστημι: *setting.* Declined in § 617.

ἴστε: see οἶδα.

ἵστημι, στήσω, ἔστησα and ἔστην, ἔστηκα and ἔστατον, ἐστάθην: *set, place, make stand, halt;* intr. tenses: *stand, stand still, stop* (see § 555). Cp. Lat. *stō.* §§ 551, 552, 617, 624, 646, 647. LVI.

ἰσχυρός, ά, όν: *strong.* Comp. ἰσχῡρότερος, sup. ἰσχῡρότατος, § 351. *a.* XXXV.

ἰσχῡρῶς, adv. (ἰσχυρός): *strongly, exceedingly, harshly.* Comp. ἰσχῡρότερον, sup. ἰσχῡρότατα, §§ 366, 368. XXXVII.

ἰχθῡς, ύος, ὁ: *fish.* § 283. XXVII.

ἴχνος, ους, τό: *track, footprint.*

ἰών: pres. partic. of εἶμι.

Ἰωνικός, ή, όν (Ἰωνίᾱ): *of Ionia, Ionian.* XXVII.

K

καθ-εύδω, καθευδήσω, impf. ἐκάθευδον and καθῦδον: *sleep.*

καθ-ήκω: *come down, reach down, extend.* XXVI.

κάθ-ημαι: *sit;* pres. partic. καθήμενος: *seated.* § 653.

καθ-ίστημι: *set* or *place down, station;* intr. tenses: *be placed, stationed,* or *established; station oneself, take one's place.* For intr. tenses cp. ἵστημι, § 555. LVI.

καθ-οράω: *look down on, descry, observe.* Cp. 2 aor. κατ-εῖδον.

καί, conj.: *and, also, even.* καί . . . καί: *both . . . and.* καί . . . δέ: *and also,* 'also' being represented by καί. καὶ γάρ: *and in fact;* or *for also, for even;* sometimes may be rendered *yes, for.* III, XV.

καιρός, οῦ, ὁ: the right measure, *right time, right place; proper time; opportunity, crisis.* XLIV.

καίω: see κᾱ́ω.

κακίων: comp. of κακός (§ 360. 2).

κακός, ή, όν: *bad, cowardly.* Comp. κακίων, χείρων, ἥττων; sup. κάκιστος, χείριστος, ἥκιστα (adv.); § 360. 2. VI, XXXVI.

κακῶς, adv. (κακός): *badly, ill.* Comp. κάκιον, etc., *worse,* sup. κάκιστα, etc., § 368. Cp. the adj. κακός, § 360. 2. κακῶς ἔχειν: see ἔχω. κακῶς ποιεῖν: see ποιεῖν. XXXVII.

καλέω, καλῶ (fut. for καλέσω, § 544), ἐκάλεσα, κέκληκα, κέκλημαι, ἐκλήθην: *call, summon, invite; call, name.* LV.

καλός, ή, όν: *beautiful, handsome, noble, honorable*(§ 232. I. 14), *fair, favorable.* Comp. καλλίων, sup. κάλλιστος, § 360. 3. VI, XXXVI. :αλῶς, adv. (καλός): *beautifully, nobly, honorably.* Comp. κάλ-

λῑον, sup. κάλλιστα (§ 368) *most successfully* (§ 394). καλῶς ἔχειν: see ἔχω. XXII, XXXVII.

κάμ-νω (theme καμ-), καμοῦμαι, ἔκαμον (2 aor.), κέκμηκα: *labor, be weary.* LX.

κᾱ́ν: by crasis (§ 30) for καὶ ἄν (= καὶ ἐάν).

Καρδοῦχοι, ων, οἱ: the *Carduchi,* a mountain people on the left bank of the Tigris. XXIV.

κατά, prep.: with GEN. *down from;* with ACC. *down over, down along, along, opposite, against, by* in a local sense; *according to, by* in a distributive sense, as κατὰ μῆνα: *by the month, monthly;* κατὰ ἔθνη: *by nations, nation by nation.* κατὰ θάλατταν: *by sea.* κατὰ μέσον: *along* or *opposite the middle, at the middle.* κατὰ τὸ στέρνον: *on the breast.* τὸ καθ᾽ αὑτούς: *the division opposite themselves.* κατὰ κράτος: *with might and main.* XX.

κατα-βαίνω: *go down, descend; enter* games. Cp. ἀνα-βαίνω. XXXIV.

κατά-βασις, εως, ἡ (κατα-βαίνω): *descent, way down* a mountain side; the *descent* from the interior to the sea. XLVII.

κατ-άγω: *lead down; bring* a ship (especially a captured one) *into harbor; restore* exiles. XLII.

κατα-θεάομαι: *gaze down, survey.*

κατα-καίνω (καίνω kill, κανῶ, ἔκανον, κέκονα): *kill.*

κατά-κειμαι: *lie down.* LIX.

κατα-κλείω: *shut up, confine, inclose.* XLVI.

κατα-κόπτω: *cut down.* XLI.

κατα-λαμβάνω: *seize, occupy, overtake, come upon, find,* with acc. XXXII.

κατα-λείπω: *leave behind, leave, abandon.* XXVI.

κατα-λελειμμένοι: see κατα-λείπω.

κατα-λύω: *unloose; unyoke, halt* (intr.).

κατα-πέμπω: *send down*, especially to the sea. XXXIX.

κατα-πηδάω (πηδάω *leap*, πηδήσομαι, ἐπήδησα, πεπήδηκα): *jump down.*

κατα-πίπτω (πίπτω *fall*, πεσοῦμαι, ἔπεσον, πέπτωκα): *fall down.*

κατα-φανής, ές (φαίνω): *in sight, visible.*

κατ-εῖδον, 2 aor.: *I* or *they looked down on, descried, observed.* Cp. καθ-οράω. XXIV.

κάω or καίω, καύσω, ἔκαυσα, κέκαυκα, κέκαυμαι, ἐκαύθην: *burn, light, kindle.* XXI.

κεῖμαι, κείσομαι: *lie; lie outstretched,* as the dead on the battlefield. This verb is used as the pass. of the pf. tenses of τίθημι, in the meaning *be placed, be set.* With τὰ ὅπλα κεῖται cp. the act. θέσθαι τὰ ὅπλα. § 654. LIX.

Κελαιναί, ῶν, αἱ: *Celaenae,* a city in Phrygia. XXXIII.

κελεύω, κελεύσω, ἐκέλευσα, κεκέλευκα, κεκέλευσμαι, ἐκελεύσθην (σ is irregularly inserted in the last two parts): *command, bid, order.* VI.

κενός, ή, όν: *empty; vain, groundless.* XXV.

κέρας, κέρᾱτος or κέρως, τό: *horn; wing* of an army. See § 602 for declension.

κερδαλέος, ᾱ, ον (κέρδος): *profitable.* Comp. κερδαλεώτερος.

κέρδος, ους, τό: *gain, profit, pay.*

κεφαλή, ῆς, ἡ: *head.* Cp. Lat. *caput.* LVI.

κῆρυξ, ῡκος, ὁ: *herald.* § 187. XVII.

Κιλικίᾱ, ᾱς, ἡ: *Cilicia.* XI.

Κίλιξ, ικος, ὁ: *Cilician,* a native of Cilicia. XLI.

Κίλισσα, ης, ἡ: *Cilician woman.* XI.

κινδῡνεύω, κινδῡνεύσω, ἐκινδύνευσα, κεκινδύνευκα, κεκινδύνευμαι, ἐκινδῡνεύθην: *incur danger, run a risk.* XIX.

κίνδῡνος, ου, ὁ: *danger.* κίνδῡνός ἐστι(ν): *there is danger.* Cp. κινδῡνεύω. XL.

Κλέαρχος, ου, ὁ: *Clearchus,* a Lacedaemonian general in the service of Cyrus. V.

κλείω, κλείσω, ἔκλεισα, κέκλεικα, κέκλειμαι, ἐκλείσθην (σ is irregularly inserted): *shut.* XLVI.

κλέπτω (themes κλεπ-, κλαπ-, κλοπ-), κλέψω, ἔκλεψα, κέκλοφα, κέκλεμμαι, ἐκλάπην: *steal.* Cp. κλώψ. XVIII.

κλώψ, κλωπός, ὁ: *thief.* § 187. XVII.

κνημίς, ῖδος, ἡ: *greave.* See p. 101, Fig. 11. XVIII.

κοινός, ή, όν: *common, in common, general.* LIX.

κολάζω (theme κολαδ-), κολάσω, ἐκόλασα, κεκόλασμαι, ἐκολάσθην: *chastise, punish.* XXXVII.

κολωνός, οῦ, ὁ: *hill, mound* of stones. Cp. Lat. *culmen, collis.*

κονιορτός, οῦ, ὁ (κόνις *dust,* and ὄρνῡμι *rouse*): *a rising of dust.*

κόπτω (theme κοπ-), κόψω, ἔκοψα, κέκοφα, κέκομμαι, ἐκόπην: *cut.* §§ 409, 473. XLI.

κράνος, ους, τό: *helmet.* See p. 156, Fig. 20. Cranium.

κρᾱτήρ, ῆρος, ὁ: *mixing bowl.* Lat. *crātēra.* See p. 109, Fig. 12. § 220. XX.

κράτιστος, η, ον: *best;* sup. of ἀγαθός.

κράτος, ους, τό: *strength, might;* ἀνὰ κράτος: to the limit of strength, *at full speed;* κατὰ κράτος: *with might and main.* XLIV.

κραυγή, ῆς, ἡ: *outcry.* LX.

Κρής, Κρητός, ὁ: *Cretan,* a native of Crete. XLVI.

κρίνω (for κριν + yω, theme κριν-),
κρινῶ, ἔκρῑνα, κέκρικα, κέκριμαι,
ἐκρίθην: *separate, judge, decide.*
Cp. Lat. *cernō.* LV.

κτάομαι, κτήσομαι, ἐκτησάμην, κέ-
κτημαι, ἐκτήθην: *acquire;* in pf.
possess, gain.

κύκλος, ου, ὁ: *circle;* κύκλῳ: *in a
circle, around.* Cycle.

κυκλόω, κυκλώσω, ἐκύκλωσα, κεκύ-
κλωμαι, ἐκυκλώθην: *encircle, sur-
round.*

κύκλωσις, εως, ἡ (κυκλόω): *an encircling, flank march.*

Κῦρος, ου, ὁ: *Cyrus.* The person
indicated by the name in this book
is *Cyrus the Younger,* son of Darius
and Parysatis. IV.

κωλύω, κωλύσω, ἐκώλῡσα, κεκώλῡκα,
κεκώλῡμαι, ἐκωλύθην: *hinder.*
§ 206. VII.

κωλύων, pres. act. partic. of κωλύω:
hinaering. Declined in § 206.

κωμ-άρχης, ου, ὁ (κώμη and ἄρχω):
ruler or *head man of a village,
village chief.* XLVI.

κώμη, ης, ἡ: *village.* § 96. VI.

Λ

λαβέ: 2 aor. act. imv. of λαμβάνω.
§ 301. *a.*

λάβω: see λαμβάνω.

λάθρᾳ, adv.: *secretly;* with gen.: *without the knowledge of.* XXVIII.

Λακεδαιμόνιος, ᾱ, ον (Λακεδαίμων):
Lacedaemonian, Spartan. XVIII.

Λακεδαίμων, ονος, ἡ: *Lacedaemon* or
Lacedaemonia. XXVII.

λαμβάνω (themes λαβ-, ληβ-, § 218),
λήψομαι, ἔλαβον, εἴληφα (§ 448),
εἴλημμαι (§ 465. *a*), ἐλήφθην
(§ 387. I): *take, receive, enlist*
(soldiers, § 324); λαβών: *with*
(§ 213. *b*). § 487. V.

λαμπρότης, ητος, ἡ: *splendor, brilliancy.* XIX.

λανθάνω (themes λαθ-, ληθ-, cp. § 218),
λήσω, ἔλαθον, λέληθα, λέλησμαι:
lie hid, escape notice of; with supplementary partic. in const. like
τυγχάνω (§ 215); thus ἔλαθεν ἐλθών: *he went secretly,* lit. *he escaped
notice going.* XLIV.

λέγω, λέξω, ἔλεξα, pf. act. supplied by
εἴρηκα, λέλεγμαι (but δι-εί-λεγμαι),
ἐλέχθην: *say,* followed by ὅτι or ὡς
that and a finite verb (§§ 260, 261).
In pass. followed by inf., § 391.
XXIV.

λείπω (themes λειπ-, λοιπ-, λιπ-),
λείψω (§ 153), ἔλιπον (§ 85), λέλοιπα (§ 445), λέλειμμαι (§§ 462. I,
465), ἐλείφθην (§ 387. I): *leave.*
§§ 85, etc., 483, 487, 641. I.

λελυκώς, pf. act. partic. of λύω: *having loosed.* Declined in § 435.

λευκο-θώρᾱξ, ᾱκος, ὁ, adj.: *with white
corslet.*

λευκός, ή, όν: *white.*

λήψομαι (theme ληβ-): fut. of λαμβάνω (Vocab. V). XXXII.

λίθος, ου, ὁ: *stone.* LVII.

λιμήν, ένος, ὁ: *harbor.* § 220. XX.

λιπών, 2 aor. act. partic. of λείπω:
having left. Declined in § 208.

λόγος, ου, ὁ: *word, speech, report*
(§ 263), *account* (§ 533). VIII.

λόγχη, ης, ἡ: *spear point, spear.*
See p. 30, Fig. 2; p. 256, Fig. 23.
LVIII.

λοιπός, ή, όν (λείπ-ω): *left, rest of,
remaining;* τὸ λοιπόν (adv. acc.
§ 284): *thereafter, in the future.*
XXVII.

λόφος, ου, ὁ: *hill.* XI.

λοχᾱγός, οῦ, ὁ (λόχος and ἄγω): *captain.* IV.

λόχος, ου, ὁ: *company* of soldiers.
II.

Λυδία, ᾱς, ἡ: *Lydia,* a district of western Asia Minor, of which Sardis was the chief city. XXXIX.

Λύδιος, ᾱ, ον (Λυδία): *Lydian.* LVI.

λυθείς, aor. pass. partic. of λύω: *having been loosed.* Declined in § 388.

Λύκιος, ου, ὁ: *Lycius,* commander of the cavalry organized by the Ten Thousand during their retreat.

λύπη, ης, ἡ: *grief.*

λύσᾱς, 1 aor. act. partic. of λύω: *having loosed.* For declension cp. § 209. *b.*

λύσων, fut. act. partic. of λύω: *about to loose.* For declension cp. § 207.

λύω, λύσω, ἔλῡσα, λέλυκα, λέλυμαι, ἐλύθην: *loose, break, destroy;* MID. *ransom.* §§ 45, etc., 482, 487, 640. I.

λύων, pres. act. partic. of λύω: *loosing.* For declension cp. §§ 206. *a,* 616. 2.

M

μακρός, ά, όν: *long.* Comp. μακρότερος, sup. μακρότατος, § 351. *a.* XXXV.

μάλα, adv.: *very.* Comp. μᾶλλον *more,* sup. μάλιστα *most.* §§ 369. 4, 370. XXXVII.

μᾶλλον, comp. adv.: *more, better, rather.* See μάλα. § 370. XXII.

μανθάνω (themes μαθ-, μαθη-, cp. τυγχάνω, § 218), μαθήσομαι, ἔμαθον, μεμάθηκα: *learn.* May be followed by ὅτι clause (§ 262), or in sense of *learn how* by inf. (§ 457). See also § 457. *a.* XXIV.

μάντις, εως, ὁ: *soothsayer.*

μάχη, ης, ἡ: *battle, fight.* § 93. VI.

μάχομαι (cp. μάχη), μαχοῦμαι (for μαχέσομαι, § 544), ἐμαχεσάμην (with lengthened theme), μεμάχη-

μαι: *fight,* with dat. (§ 317), or πρός *against* and acc. XXXVII.

μέγας, μεγάλη, μέγα: *great, large* loud (of a noise). Comp. μείζων, sup. μέγιστος (§ 360. 4). § 337. 1. XXXIII.

μέγιστος, η, ον: see μέγας.

μείζων, μεῖζον: see μέγας.

μεῖον, adv. (cp. μῑκρός): *less.*

μείων, ον: *smaller, fewer* (in pl.); comp. of μῑκρός.

μελανίᾱ, ᾱς, ἡ (μέλᾱς *black*): *blackness.*

μέλει, μελήσει, ἐμέλησε, μεμέληκε, impers.: *it is a care,* with dat. of person and ὅπως clause.

μέλλω, μελλήσω, ἐμέλλησα: *be about, intend,* with fut., pres., or aor. inf.; *delay.* § 156. 2. XIII.

μέμνημαι (pf. with pres. meaning), μεμνήσομαι (§ 473), ἐμνήσθην: *remember.* For const. see § 457 and *a.* May take obj. in gen. The pres. act. is μιμνήσκω *remind,* which form is made up of the reduplication μι- plus the theme μνη- (long form of μνα-) plus the pres. suffix ισκ⅖; fut. μνήσω, 1 aor. ἔμνησα. XLVI.

μέν, postpositive particle, used with a word or clause that is contrasted with a following word (in another clause) or a second clause. The second word or clause often has δέ, which is sometimes replaced by another conjunction. μέν sometimes means *on the one hand;* but more often it is to be omitted in translation. ὁ μέν . . . ὁ δέ: *the one . . . the other;* οἱ μέν . . . οἱ δέ: *some . . . others.* See δέ. VI.

μέντοι, postpositive particle: *however, yet.* XV.

μένω (themes μεν-, μενη-), μενῶ, ἔμεινα, μεμένηκα: *remain, wait for.* Cp. Lat. *maneō.* §§ 541, 542. LV

Μένων, ωνος, ὁ: *Menon*, a Thessalian general in the service of Cyrus. XXV.

μέσος, η, ον: *middle, middle of* (§ 192); (τὸ) μέσον: *the middle, the midst* (§ 219); ἐν μέσῳ: *in the midst, between,* with gen.; μέσον ἡμέρᾱς: *midday.* XVII.

μεστός, ή, όν: *full,* with gen. VI.

μετά, prep.: with GEN. *with, in company with;* with ACC. *into the midst of, after.* XV.

μεταξύ, adv.: *between,* with gen. IX.

μετα-πέμπομαι (mid. of μετα-πέμπω *send for*), -πέμψομαι, -επεμψάμην, -πέπεμμαι: *send after* to come to oneself; *summon.* XXX.

μετά-πεμπτος, ον (verbal adj. of μετα-πέμπομαι): *sent after, summoned.* XLVIII.

μέχρι, temporal conj.: *until.* §§ 521, 522. LII.

μή, (1) neg. adv.: *not;* with inf. (§§ 98, 519. *b*), in protases (§§ 106. *b*, 216, etc.), purpose clauses (§§ 243, 268), object clauses (§ 535), prohibitions (§ 309), wishes (§§ 584, 585), with hortatory subjv. (§ 244), and deliberative subjv. (§ 564). (2) conj.: *lest,* after verbs of *fearing;* μή οὐ: *lest not* (§ 438). VI, XLIV.

μη-δέ: *and not, nor, not even.* Used like μή. Cp. οὐδέ. XLIII.

μηδ-είς, μηδε-μία, μηδ-έν (μηδέ + εἷς): *nobody, no one, no, nothing.* Used like μή. § 426. *a.* XLIII.

Μῆδοι, ων, οἱ: the *Medes.* LIX.

μήν, μηνός, ὁ: *month.* Lat. *mēnsis.* § 220. XX.

μήν, postpositive adv.: *in truth, certainly;* γε μήν: *to be sure, at any rate.* LIX.

μή-ποτε: *never.* Used like μή *not.* LIV.

μή-τε . . . μή-τε: *neither . . . nor.* Used like μή. Cp. οὔτε . . . οὔτε. XLIII.

μήτηρ, μητρός, ἡ: *mother.* Lat. *māter.* § 321. XXXI.

Μιθραδάτης, ου, ὁ: *Mithradātes.* XLIV.

μῑκρός, ά, όν: *small.* Comp. μῑκρότερος, sup. μῑκρότατος, § 360. 5. Comp. also μείων, μεῖον: *fewer* (in pl.). XXXVI.

μισθός, οῦ, ὁ: *pay.* XX.

μισθοφορά, ᾶς, ἡ (μισθός and φέρω): *receipt of wages, pay.*

μνᾶ, ᾶς, ἡ: *mina*, one sixtieth of a talent, *i.e.* about $18. § 594. L.

μόνος, η, ον: *alone, only.* XLVII.

μύριοι, αι, α: *ten thousand.* § 421.

N

ναῦς, νεώς, ἡ: *ship.* § 605.

νεᾱνίᾱς, ου, ὁ: *young man.* § 593.

νεᾱνίσκος, ου, ὁ: *young man.* XXI.

νεκρός, οῦ, ὁ: *dead body, corpse.* Cp. Lat. *necō.* LIX.

νέος, ᾱ, ον: *new, fresh, young.* Comp. νεώτερος, sup. νεώτατος. Cp. Lat. *novus.* XXXV.

νεφέλη, ης, ἡ: *cloud.*

νῑκάω (νίκη), νῑκήσω, ἐνίκησα, νενίκηκα, νενίκημαι, ἐνῑκήθην: *conquer, surpass.* The pass. is often expressed by ἡττάομαι. LII.

νίκη, ης, ἡ: *victory.* XI.

νομίζω (theme νομιδ-), νομιῶ (§ 543), ἐνόμισα, νενόμικα, νενόμισμαι, ἐνομίσθην: *think, consider.* With inf. § 110. VIII.

νόμος, ου, ὁ: *custom, law.* XXXIX.

νοῦς, οῦ, ὁ: *mind.* § 596. L.

νύκτωρ, adv. (cp. νύξ): *by night.* XXXIII.

νῦν, adv.: *now* (of time). Lat. *nunc.* XX.

νύξ, νυκτός, ἡ: *night;* μέσαι νύκτες: *midnight* (middle watches of the night). Lat. *nox.* §§ 195, 196, 198. XVIII.

Ξ

Ξενίας, ου, ὁ: *Xenias,* an Arcadian general in the service of Cyrus. XII.

ξένιος, ᾱ, ον (ξένος): *hospitable, relating to hospitality;* ξένια, neut. pl. subst.: *gifts in token of hospitality, guest-gifts.*

ξένος, ου, ὁ: *guest-friend.* XIX.

Ξενοφῶν, ῶντος, ὁ: *Xenophon,* the author of the *Anabasis.* See pp. 264, 265. LIV.

ξύλινος, η, ον (ξύλον): *made of wood, wooden.*

ξύλον, ου, τό: *wood;* pl. of hewn or split *wood; timbers.* XXIV.

O

ὁ, ἡ, τό, gen. τοῦ, τῆς, τοῦ, def. art.: *the.* The forms of the definite article are often used for possessive pronouns of the first, second, or third person, either singular or plural, as suggested by the context, *i.e. my, your, his, her, our, their.* In this VOCABULARY, placed after a noun, ὁ, ἡ, and τό indicate its gender. ὁ δέ: *and he, but he;* ἡ δέ: *and she, but she,* indicating a change of subject from the preceding sentence. ὁ may mean *he,* and ἡ *she,* but only with μέν (which see) and δέ. §§ 48, 49, 67–70, 89, 93, 143, 281 (footnote 1), 307, 427, 632. II, VI.

ὅδε, ἥδε, τόδε, dem. pron.: *this,* often with reference to what is to follow; τάδε: *these things* as follows (§ 175). §§ 173, 176, 307. XV.

ὁδός, οῦ, ἡ: *way, road.* § 115. IX.

ὅθεν, rel. adv.: *whence, from which place, from what source.* LI.

οἶδα (2 pf. with pres. meaning), ᾔδη (2 plup.) or ᾔδειν, εἴσομαι (fut.): *know.* § 655. With partic. or ὅτι clause, § 669. LX.

οἴκαδε, adv. (cp. οἰκία): *homeward, home.* XXII.

οἰκέω (cp. οἰκίᾱ), οἰκήσω, ᾤκησα, ᾤκηκα, ᾤκημαι, ᾠκήθην: *dwell, inhabit;* πόλις οἰκουμένη: *an inhabited city.* The pass. partic. may sometimes be translated *be situated.*

οἰκίᾱ, ᾱς, ἡ: *house.* XIII.

οἶμαι: see οἴομαι.

οἶνος, ου, ὁ: *wine.* § 60. III.

οἴομαι (often οἶμαι), οἰήσομαι (with lengthened theme), ᾠήθην (§ 389), dep. pass.: *think, suppose.* XXXVIII.

οἷος, ᾱ, ον, rel. pron.: *of what sort, what sort of, (such) as;* οἷός τε: *able;* οἷόν τ' ἐστίν: *it is possible.* Lat. *quālis.* LIV.

οἴσω: see φέρω.

οἴχομαι, οἰχήσομαι (with lengthened theme): *be gone, have gone* (pres. with pf. meaning). Often with supplementary partic.; cp. § 215. XXX.

ὀκτα-κόσιοι, αι, α: *eight hundred,* § 421.

ὀκτώ, indecl.: *eight.* Lat. *octō.* XXXIX.

ὀλίγος, η, ον: *little, few.* Comp. ἐλάττων, sup. ἐλάχιστος, § 360. 6. XXXVI.

ὅλος, η, ον: *whole, entire, all.* XVII.

ὁμαλῶς: *evenly, with even step.*

ὄμ-νῡ-μι (and ὀμ-νύω, themes ὀμ-, ὀμο-), ὀμοῦμαι, ὤμοσα, ὀμώμοκα (§ 447), ὀμώμο(σ)μαι, ὠμό(σ)θην: *swear, promise with an oath, take oath.* LIX.

ὁμο-τράπεζος, ον: sitting *at the same table*. As subst. masc. *table companion*.

ὅμως, adv.: *nevertheless*.

ὄνομα, ατος, τό: *name*. XXXVII.

ὄνος, ου, ὁ: *ass*. Lat. *asinus*. LVI.

ὅπῃ, rel. adv.: *where, wherever; how, in what way*. Cp. πῃ. XL.

ὄπισθεν, adv.: *behind*.

ὀπισθο-φύλαξ, ακος, ὁ: *one who guards the rear ;* οἱ ὀπισθοφύλακες: *the rear guard*.

ὁπλίζω, ὥπλισα, ὥπλισμαι, ὡπλίσθην (ὅπλον): *arm ;* MID. *arm oneself*.

ὁπλίτης, ου, ὁ (ὅπλον): a heavy-armed soldier, *hoplite*. See p. 139, Fig. 18. XII.

ὅπλον, ου, τό: *implement;* commonly pl. ὅπλα, τά: *arms* of war. See p. 28, Fig. 1; p. 139, Fig. 18. II.

ὅποι, rel. adv.: *whithersoever, whither, where*. § 343. XXIII.

ὁποῖος, ᾱ, ον, indef. rel. pron. and indir. interr.: *of what sort, what sort of*. XLVII.

ὁπόσος, η, ον, indef. rel. pron. and indir. interr.: *as many as, how great*, (pl.) *how many*. Cp. ὅσος. XLII.

ὁπότε, rel. adv.: *when, whenever, as often as; since*. Cp. ὅτε. XLII.

ὅπου, rel. adv.: *wherever, where*. § 343. XXIII.

ὅπως, (1) conj.: *in order that, that*, with purpose clause (§§ 243, 268); *how*, with object clause (§ 535). (2) rel. adv.: *how, in what way*. XXII, XXXIX, LIV.

ὁράω (impf. ἑώρων), ὄψομαι, εἶδον, ἑώρᾱκα or ἑόρᾱκα, ἑώρᾱμαι or ὦμμαι, ὤφθην: *see, behold*. With acc. and partic. (rarely with ὅτι clause). §§ 440, 441, 520. LII.

ὄρθιος, ᾱ, ον: *steep*. IX.

ὅρκος, ου, ὁ: *oath*. IX.

ὁρμάω, ὁρμήσω, ὥρμησα, ὥρμηκα,

ὥρμημαι, ὡρμήθην: *start, hasten.* MID. *set out*.

ὄρνῑς, ῑθος, ὁ and ἡ: *bird*. Acc. sing. both ὄρνῑν (§ 197) and ὄρνῑθα. XVIII.

Ὀρόντᾱς, ᾱ (Doric .gen., for ου), ὁ: *Orontas*, a Persian. XXXI.

ὄρος, ους, τό: *mountain*. § 272. XXVI.

ὅς, ἥ, ὅ, rel. pron.: ` *who, which, that*. §§ 125, 135, 285. X.

ὅσος, η, ον, rel. pron.: *as great as, as much as, as many as, all that, as* (*many*); *how great, how much, how many;* ὅσον, adv. acc.: *as far as;* with numerals, *about* (§ 444). XXXVII.

ὅσ-περ, ἥ-περ, ὅ-περ (strengthened ὅς): *the very one which, the very thing which*. XXIX.

ὅστις, ἥτις, ὅ τι (or ὅ,τι): indef. rel. pron.: *whoever* or *whichever, whatever; who, which, what;* often with conditional force, *if anybody* (= εἴ τις), *if anything* (= εἴ τι); ἔστιν ὅστις: there is who, *somebody*. §§ 228, 343. XXI.

ὅταν = ὅτε + ἄν (§ 248. 2. *a*), conj. with subjv.: *when, whenever* (§ 400). XXIX.

ὅτε, rel. adv.: *when, at the time when*, commonly with impf. indic.; *whenever*, with opt. (§ 417). XVIII.

ὅτι, conj.: *that*, introducing a quotation (§ 260); *because, since* (§ 310). As adv., like ὡς, strengthens a superlative. Thus ὅτι ἀπαρασκευότατος: *as unprepared as possible*. XXIV, XXXVII.

ὅ τι or ὅ,τι: neut. of ὅστις.

ὅτου: see ὅστις.

ὅτῳ: see ὅστις.

οὗ, dat. οἷ, pl. σφεῖς, indirect reflexive of the third person: *of himself, to himself*, etc. § 378 and *a*. XXXVIII.

οὐ, proclitic neg. adv.: *not;* before a vowel with smooth breathing, written οὐκ; before a rough breathing, οὐχ. At the end of a sentence, οὔ. VI. οὐ, οὐκ, οὐχ, used in interrogative sentence: *not;* expects the answer *yes.* Cp. Lat. *nōnne.* VII.

οὐδέ (οὐ + δέ): *nor, not even;* Lat. *nē . . . quidem.* § 428. VIII.

οὐδ-είς, οὐδε-μία, οὐδ-έν (οὐδέ + εἷς): *nobody, no one, no, nothing.* § 426. οὐδέν: *in no respect, not at all* (cp. § 284). XLIII.

οὐκ-έτι, adv.: *no longer, no more.* XVII.

οὖν, postpositive particle: *therefore, accordingly, at any rate.* XIV.

οὗ-περ (strengthened οὗ): *just where, the very place where.*

οὔ-ποτε, adv.: *never.* XXV.

οὔ-πω, adv.: *not yet, never yet.* XXXV.

οὔτε . . . οὔτε (οὐ + τε): *neither . . . nor.* VIII.

οὗτος, αὕτη, τοῦτο, dem. pron.: *this, this man, he,* etc.; ταῦτα: *these things, this* (§ 177); ἐκ τούτου: *thereupon* (§ 588). §§ 171, 172, 175, 176, 307. XV.

οὕτω(s), adv. (οὗτος): *thus, in this way* (usually with reference to what goes before), *so;* οὕτως ἔχειν: see ἔχω. XXXVII.

ὀφθαλμός, οῦ, ὁ: *eye.* Ophthalmia.

ὄχλος, ου, ὁ: *crowd, throng; annoyance, bother.* XXXV.

ὄψεσθαι: see ὁράω.

Π

παγ-κράτιον, ου, τό (πᾶς and κράτος): *the pancratium,* an athletic contest composed of both boxing and wrestling.

πάθω: 2 aor. subjv. of πάσχω.

παιᾱνίζω, ἐπαιάνισα: *sing the paean* or war song.

παῖς, παιδός, ὁ and ἡ: *child, boy, girl;* ἐκ παίδων: *from boyhood* (§ 203). The gen. (and dat.) dual is exceptionally accented παίδοιν, and the gen. pl. παίδων. The voc. sing. is παῖ. XVIII.

παίω, παίσω, ἔπαισα, πέπαικα, ἐπαίσθην (σ is irregularly inserted): *strike, smite.* XII.

παλαίω(πάλη),ἐπάλαισα,ἐπαλαίσθην (σ is irregularly inserted): *wrestle.*

πάλη, ης, ἡ: *wrestling.*

πάλιν, adv.: *back, again.* X.

παλτόν, οῦ, τό: *javelin,* used by barbarians; the Greek hoplite's spear was called δόρυ. V.

πάντῃ, adv. (cp. πᾶς): *on all sides.*

πάνυ, adv. (cp. πᾶς): *wholly, altogether, very.* XXXIX.

παρά, prep.: with GEN. *from* the side of; with DAT. *by* the side of, after verbs of rest; with ACC. *to* the side of, after verbs of motion; *along; contrary to.* IX.

παρ-αγγέλλω: *give directions to, direct, command,* with dat. of pers. or acc. of pers. and inf. LV.

παρα-γίγνομαι: *come (to), be at hand, be present.* Cp. πάρ-ειμι. XXXII.

παρα-δίδωμι: *give over, surrender; pass along* (a watch word: σύνθημα). LVIII.

παραμηρίδιον, ου, τό: *protection for the thigh;* pl. *thigh pieces, cuisses.*

παρασάγγης, ου, ὁ: *parasang,* a Persian measure of distance, about 3.3 English miles. Cp. our *league* (3 miles). XV.

παρα-σκευάζω (σκευάζω, theme σκευαδ-, *prepare,* σκευάσω, ἐσκεύασα, ἐσκεύασμαι, ἐσκευάσθην): *prepare, equip;* MID. *make oneself ready, prepare oneself;* also *prepare* for oneself. §§ 315. I, II, 467. a. XXX.

πάρ-ειμι (εἰμί) : *be by, be at hand, be present; attend,* with dat. X.

παρ-ελαύνω : *drive past, drive by, march past, ride past.* XI.

παρ-έρχομαι, 2 aor. παρ-ῆλθον : *go by, go past.* XLII.

παρ-έχω : *hold beside, furnish, provide, supply; cause* (§§ 405, 502). XIII.

πάροδος, ου, ἡ (παρά + ὁδός) : *road by* or *past, passage, pass.* IX.

Παρύσατις, ιδος, ἡ : Parysatis, wife of Darius II, king of Persia, and mother of Artaxerxes II and Cyrus the Younger. XXXI.

πᾶς, πᾶσα, πᾶν : *every* (in sing.), *all, whole.* §§ 289, 293. XXVIII.

Πᾱσίων, ωνος, ὁ : *Pasion,* a Greek general (from Megara) employed by Cyrus. XLIII.

πάσχω (themes παθ-, πενθ-, πονθ-), πείσομαι (for πενθ-σομαι), ἔπαθον, πέπονθα (§ 445) : *suffer;* πάσχω τι (§ 181); *suffer something,* euphemism for *be hurt* or *be killed;* κακῶς πάσχειν : *to be injured;* εὖ πάσχειν : *to be treated kindly* (§ 537). XXII.

Πατηγύᾱς, ᾱ (Doric gen., for Attic ου), ὁ : *Pategyas,* a Persian companion of Cyrus.

πατήρ, πατρός, ὁ : *father.* Lat. *pater.* § 321. XXXI.

πατρίς, ίδος, ἡ (cp. πατήρ) : *fatherland.* XXIX.

παύω, παύσω, ἔπαυσα, πέπαυκα, πέπαυμαι, ἐπαύθην : *make to stop, stop* (trans.), *put an end to;* MID. *stop oneself, cease.* § 439. XXVI, XXXII.

παχύς, εῖα, ύ : *thick* in diameter. XXVIII.

πεδίον, ου, τό : *plain.* § 49. II.

πεζός, ἡ, όν : *afoot, on foot;* οἱ πεζοί : *the infantry.* VII.

πείθω, πείσω, ἔπεισα (§ 164), πέπεικα

(§ 432. *f*) and πέποιθα (§ 445 and *a*), πέπεισμαι (§ 467), ἐπείσθην (§ 387. 2) : *persuade;* MID. and PASS. *obey,* with dat. § 487. I, XXXIX.

πειράομαι, πειράσομαι, ἐπειρᾱσάμην, πεπείρᾱμαι, and ἐπειράθην : *try, attempt.* § 518. *a.* LII.

πείσομαι : either (1) fut. of πάσχω, *suffer* (Vocab. XXII) or (2) fut. mid. of πείθω (Vocab. I) in mid. meaning *obey* (with dat.). XXXII.

πειστέον (verbal adj. of πείθομαι), impers. : *one must obey,* with dat. § 477. 2. XLVIII.

πελάζω, πελάσω and πελῶ, ἐπέλασα, ἐπελάσθην : *approach.*

πελταστής, οῦ, ὁ : a light-armed soldier, *peltast.* See. p. 67, Fig. 4; . p. 117, Fig. 14. § 146. XII.

πέμπτος, η, ον (πέντε) : *fifth.*

πέμπω (themes πεμπ-, πομπ-), πέμψω (§ 153), ἔπεμψα (§ 164), πέπομφα (§§ 445, 488), πέπεμμαι (§ 465. *b*), ἐπέμφθην (§ 387. 1) : *send.* § 487. I.

πεντακόσιοι, αι, α (πέντε) : *five hundred.* XIX.

πέντε, indecl. : *five.* XIII.

πεντε-καί-δεκα, indecl. : *five and ten, fifteen.* XXVII.

πέρᾱν, adv. : *across, on the other side,* with gen.; ἐν τῷ πέρᾱν : *on the other side* or *bank.* XXIII.

περί (like πρό, never suffers elision of the final vowel), prep. : with GEN. *about, concerning, for,* as a prize; with DAT. (not common in prose) *around, about;* with ACC. *around, about, near, in relation to.* XI.

περι-βάλλω : *throw around, throw one's arms around, embrace.*

Πέρσης, ου, ὁ : a *Persian.* Voc. Πέρσα. XXIV.

Περσικός, ή, όν (Πέρσης) : *Persian.* XXIV.

πῃ, enclitic adv.: *anywhere.* XVII.

πηγή, ῆς, ἡ: *spring* of water; generally pl.: *source.* XXXII.

πῆχυς, εως, ὁ: *forearm, cubit,* 1½ Greek feet. § 282. XXVII.

Πίγρης, ητος, ὁ: *Pigres,* interpreter of Cyrus.

πίπτω (themes πετ-, πτ-, and πτω-), πεσοῦμαι (for πετέομαι), ἔπεσον (for ἔπετον), πέπτωκα: *fall.* See κατα-πίπτω.

Πισίδαι, ῶν, οἱ: *Pisidians,* natives of Pisidia. XII.

πιστός, ή, όν (cp. πείθω): *trustworthy, faithful;* πιστά, ῶν, τά, neut. pl. subst.: *pledges.* Comp. πιστότερος, sup. πιστότατος, § 351. *a.* VIII.

πλέθρον, ου, τό: *plethrum,* 100 Greek feet. XXVII.

πλεῖστος: see πολύς.

πλείων: see πολύς.

πλέω, πλεύσομαι (also πλευσοῦμαι, contracted from πλευ-σέ-ο-μαι), ἔπλευσα, πέπλευκα, πέπλευσμαι (σ is irregularly inserted): *sail.* § 508. LI.

πλῆθος, ους, τό: *crowd, throng, host, multitude.* LIII.

πλήθω (cp. πλῆθος): *be full;* ἀμφὶ ἀγορὰν πλήθουσαν: *about the time of full market, i.e.* the middle of the forenoon.

πλήν, adv. and conj.: *except, except that;* prep. with gen.: *except.*

πλήρης, ες: *full.* Cp. Lat. *plē-nus.* XXVII.

πλησίον, adv.: *near.*

πλοῖον, ου, τό (πλέω): *boat.* See p. 36, Fig. 3. § 60. III.

πλοῦς, οῦ, ὁ (cp. πλέω): *voyage; a sailing, sailing weather.* L.

ποδ-ήρης, ες: *reaching to the feet.*

πόθος, ου, ὁ: *desire,* with gen.

ποῖ, interr. adv.: *whither, where?* LVII.

ποιέω, ποιήσω, ἐποίησα, πεποίηκα, πεποίημαι, ἐποιήθην: *do, make.* The mid. is translated like the act., but implies *in* or *for one's own interest;* κακῶς ποιεῖν: *do harm to, injure,* with acc. (§ 537). §§ 509, 622, 643. LI.

ποιητέος, ᾱ, ον (verbal adj. of ποιέω, with ἐστί or εἰσί expressed or understood): *necessary to be done, must be done.* LIV.

ποιῶν, pres. act. partic. of ποιέω: *making.* Declined in § 622.

πολεμέω (πόλεμος), πολεμήσω, ἐπολέμησα, πεπολέμηκα, πεπολέμημαι, ἐπολεμήθην: *wage war, make war on,* with dat. (§ 317), or πρός and acc. LII.

πολεμικός, ή, όν (πόλεμος): *suited to war, warlike; hostile.* LI.

πολέμιος, ᾱ, ον (πόλεμος): *of war, hostile;* οἱ πολέμιοι (subst. adj.): *the enemy.* Comp. πολεμιώτερος (§ 540. I. 11). § 117. IX.

πόλεμος, ου, ὁ: *war.* XXXVII.

πόλις, εως, ἡ: *city.* § 282. XXVII.

πολλάκις, adv. (πολύς): *often.* XLII.

πολύ, adv. (cp. πολύς): *much, by far.* § 410. *a.* XXXVII.

πολύς, πολλή, πολύ: *much, many; extensive, large; loud* (of noise), § 337. 2; οἱ πολλοί: *the many, the most;* τὸ πολὺ τοῦ στρατεύματος: *the most of the army;* ἐπὶ πολύ: *over* or *for a long distance.* Comp. πλείων or πλέων, sup. πλεῖστος, § 360. 7. πλεῖστοι: *very many* (§ 533); οἱ πλεῖστοι: *the most.* XXXIII, XXXVI.

πόντος, ου, ὁ: *sea;* ὁ Εὔξεινος Πόντος: *the Euxine* or *Black Sea.*

πορεία, ᾱς, ἡ: *journey.*

πορεύομαι, πορεύσομαι, πεπόρευμαι, ἐπορεύθην (§ 389), dep. pass.: *go, proceed, travel.* Cp. ἄπορος. XXX.

πορευτέος, ᾱ, ον (verbal adj. of πορεύομαι) : necessary *to be passed over, to be traversed;* neut. impers. *one must proceed.* § 477. 2. XLVIII.

ποταμός, οῦ, ὁ : *river.* § 56. III.

ποτέ, enclitic adv. of time : *ever, at any time, at some time, once* on a time. L.

πότερον (πότερα) . . . ἤ, introducing a double question, direct or indirect : *whether . . . or.* § 362. XXXVI.

ποτόν, οῦ, τό : *drink.* XLVII.

που, indef. adv., enclitic : *somewhere, anywhere.* XLVII.

πούς, ποδός, ὁ : *foot.* Also the Greek unit of length. Lat. *pēs.* §§ 195, 196, 198. XVIII.

πρᾶγμα, ατος, τό (πράττω) : something done, *business, deed, matter, difficulty;* pl. sometimes *circumstances,* often *trouble.* XXII.

πράττω (theme πρᾱγ-, § 218), πρᾱ́ξω, ἔπρᾱξα, πέπρᾱγα and πέπρᾱχα, πέπρᾱγμαι (§ 466. *a*), ἐπρᾱ́χθην (§ 387. 1) : *accomplish, effect, do; fare* (§§ 375, 538). XIX.

πρέσβεις, εων, οἱ : *ambassadors.* The nom. sing. is πρεσβευτής, οῦ, ὁ. XXVII.

[πρέσβυς, poetic], comp. πρεσβύτερος *older,* sup. πρεσβύτατος *oldest,* § 351. *c.* Cp. pl. πρέσβεις. XXXV.

πρίασθαι : see ἐπριάμην.

πρίν, temporal conj. : *before, until;* πρόσθεν (Vocab. XXVI) . . . πρίν = Lat. *prius . . . quam: earlier than, before.* §§ 523, 524. LII.

πρό (like περί, never suffers elision of the final vowel), prep. with gen. only : *before, in front of.* Lat. *prō.* XVII.

πρόβατον, ου, τό : *cattle, sheep.* XXXV.

προ-δίδωμι : *betray.*

πρό-ειμι (εἶμι) : *go forward, advance.*

προ-έρχομαι, 2 aor. προ-ῆλθον, 2 pf. προ-ελήλυθα (§ 447) : *go before, go forward, proceed.* XLV.

προθύμως (adv. of πρόθυμος *ready, eager*) : *readily, eagerly, zealously.* Comp. προθυμότερον, sup. προθυμότατα. XXXVII.

προ-θύω : *sacrifice before;* MID. *offer a preliminary sacrifice* to ascertain something for one's own interest.

προ-ίδοιεν : 2 aor. opt. of προ-οράω.

προ-κατα-λαμβάνω : *seize* or *occupy beforehand.* XLVII.

Πρόξενος, ου, ὁ : *Proxenus,* a Theban general employed by Cyrus. XIV.

προ-οράω, 2 aor. προ-εῖδον : *see in front* of oneself, *see approaching.*

προ-πέμπω : *send forward* or *ahead.* XXX.

πρός, prep. : with GEN. *from the side of, from, toward;* πρὸς (τῶν) θεῶν : *before the gods, in the sight of the gods;* with DAT. *near, beside, in addition to;* with ACC. *to, toward, against; with reference to* (§ 335). II, XXIX.

προσ-αναλίσκω (ἀναλίσκω *spend,* ἀνᾱλώσω, ἀνήλωσα, ἀνήλωκα, ἀνήλωμαι, ἀνηλώθην) : *spend besides, spend in addition.*

πρόσ-ειμι (εἶμι) : *come on, advance.*

προσ-ελαύνω : *drive up, ride up, draw near.* XX.

προσ-έρχομαι : *go to, come to, come up,* sometimes with dat. of pers. or with εἰς and acc. XXXVI.

προσ-έχω, with τὸν νοῦν : *direct the mind to,* with dat. L.

προσ-ήκω : *come to, reach to, pertain to;* pres. partic. *related,* with dat. XXXI.

πρόσθεν, adv. (cp. πρός): *forward*
(of space): *before, former* (of
time); ἡ πρόσθεν (§ 70) νύξ: *the
night before;* ὁ πρόσθεν λόγος: *the
previous account* (§ 533). XXVI.
τὸ πρόσθεν (adv. acc.): *before,
formerly;* εἰς τὸ πρόσθεν: *to the
front* (§ 319). XXXVII.

προσ-κυνέω, προσ-κυνήσω, προσ-εκύ-
νησα: *do homage to, salute.*

προ-στατέω, προ-εστάτησα: *stand
before, manage,* with gen.

πρότερος, ᾱ, ον: *former, earlier*
(§ 361). XXXVI.

προυδεδώκεσαν: contracted from προεδεδώκεσαν, plup. of προ-δίδωμι.

προ-φαίνω: *show forth;* MID. *appear.*

πρῶτος, η, ον: *first* (§ 361); οἱ πρῶτοι: *the van* (§ 375); adv. πρῶτον:
first (§ 284). XXIII.

πυγμή, ῆς, ἡ: *boxing.*

πυκνός, ή, όν: *closely set, closely standing, closely planted.* XXVIII.

πύλη, ης, ἡ: *gate.* XLVI.

πυνθάνομαι (themes πευθ-, πυθ-,
cp. § 218), πεύσομαι, ἐπυθόμην,
πέπυσμαι: *inquire, ask; learn,
perceive.* §§ 441, 442. XXXIX.

πῦρ, πυρός, τό: *fire;* πυρά, τά:
watch fires. § 336. 3. XXXIII.

πώ-ποτε, adv. of time: *ever yet, ever.*
LI.

πῶς, interr. adv.: *how, in what way?*
LI.

Ρ

ῥᾴδιος, ᾱ, ον: *easy.* Comp. ῥᾴων,
sup. ῥᾷστος, § 360. 8. XXXII.

Σ

σάλπιγξ, γγος, ἡ: *trumpet.* See
p. 90, Fig. 8. XVII.

Σάρδεις, εων, αἱ: *Sardis,* a city in
Lydia. XXVII.

σατράπης, ου, ὁ: *satrap,* Persian

name for a provincial governor appointed by the king. XXIV.

σαυτοῦ, ῆς (contracted from σεαυτοῦ,
ῆς), reflexive pron. of second person:
of yourself, etc. §§ 376. 2, 379.
XXXVIII.

σεαυτοῦ, ῆς, reflexive pron. of second
person: *of yourself,* etc. §§ 376. 2,
379. XXXVIII.

Σιλᾱνός, οῦ, ὁ: *Silānus,* a soothsayer.

σῑτίον, ον, τό (dim. of σῖτος): *grain,
food.* XLVII.

σῖτος, ον, ὁ: *grain, food;* in the pl.
the declension irregularly changes
to neut. σῖτα, τά. IV.

σκεπτέον (verbal adj. of σκέπτομαι),
impers.: *it must be considered, one
must consider,* with ὅπως clause
(§ 535). § 477. 2. XLVIII.

σκέπτομαι, σκέψομαι, ἐσκεψάμην,
ἔσκεμμαι, dep. mid.: *view, observe,
consider.* The pres. and impf. are
rare in Attic. XXXIV.

σκηνή, ῆς, ἡ: *tent.* VI.

σκηνόω (σκηνή), ἐσκήνωσα, (κατ-)
ἐσκήνωκα: *stay in a tent, camp.*
LIII.

σκληρός, ά, όν: *hard, rough;* ἐν
σκληρῷ: *in a rough place.*

σκότος, ους, τό: *darkness.* Also ὁ
σκότος, gen. ου. XXVIII.

σός, σή, σόν (cp. σοῦ, gen. of σύ):
thy, your (sing.), *yours.* § 126. X.

Σοφαίνετος, ου, ὁ: *Sophaenetus,* a
Greek general, from Stymphālus
in Arcadia, employed by Cyrus.
XLIII.

σπάνις, εως, ἡ: *scarcity, want,* with
gen.

Σπαρτιάτης, ου, ὁ (Σπάρτη *Sparta*):
a Spartan.

σπεύδω (theme σπευδ-), σπεύσω,
ἔσπευσα: *urge on, hasten.* XLII.

σπονδή, ῆς, ἡ: *libation;* pl. *truce.* IX.

σπουδή, ῆς, ἡ (σπεύδω): *haste.*

στάδιον, ου, τό : *staaium* (race course) : then a measure of distance, *stade*, 600 Greek feet. Pl. both στάδιοι, οἱ, and στάδια, τά. See p. 95, Fig. 9. XVII.

σταθμός, οῦ, ὁ: *day's journey, stage; halting place* (first meaning, but less common). XI.

στενός, ή, όν: *narrow.* IX.

στέρνον, ου, τό: *breast.*

στῖφος, ους, τό: *crowd.*

στόλος, ου, ὁ: *expedition.* IX.

στρατεία, ᾱς, ἡ (στρατεύω): *expedition.* LI.

στράτευμα, ατος, τό (cp. στρατιά): *army.* §§ 195, 199. XVIII.

στρατεύω, στρατεύσω, ἐστράτευσα, ἐστράτευκα (§ 432. c), ἐστράτευμαι: *make an expedition;* dep. MID. *take the field, serve in war.* Cp. στράτευ-μα, etc. XXXI.

στρατηγός, οῦ, ὁ: *general.* III.

στρατιά, ᾶς, ἡ: *army.* § 114. IX.

στρατιώτης, ου, ὁ (στρατιά, etc.): *soldier.* § 146. XII.

στρατοπεδεύω (στρατόπεδον) and dep. mid. στρατοπεδεύομαι, ἐστρατοπεδευσάμην, ἐστρατοπέδευμαι (§ 456): *encamp.* XL.

στρατό-πεδον, ου, τό: *camp.* Cp. στράτευμα. XXIX.

στρέφω (themes στρεφ-, στραφ-), στρέψω, ἔστρεψα, ἔστραμμαι (§ 490), ἐστράφην (§ 489): *turn; wheel about.* §§ 409, 487. XLI.

σύ, σοῦ: *you* (sing.), §§ 304, 306, 308. XXIX.

συγ-καλέω (σύν + καλέω): *call together.* LV.

Συέννεσις, ιος (non-Attic gen.), ὁ: *Syennesis,* king of Cilicia. XXXVIII.

συλ-λαμβάνω: *take together, seize, arrest.* Cp. Lat. *comprehendō.* § 465. *a.* X.

συλ-λέγω, συλ-λέξω, συν-έλεξα, συν-είλοχα (§ 448), συν-είλεγμαι, συν-ελέχθην and συν-ελέγην (§ 409): *gather together, collect.* This -λέγω is a different verb from λέγω *say.* §§ 415, 487. XIV.

συμ-βουλεύω (σύν + βουλεύω): *plan with, advise,* with dat.; MID. *consult* (§ 514), with dat. XIV.

σύμ-μαχος, ον, ὁ (μάχη): *fellow-fighter, ally.* XXVIII.

σύμ-πᾱς, ᾶσα, αν (σύν + πᾶς): *all together, all, whole.* XLIII.

συμ-πέμπω (σύν + πέμπω): *send a person* (in acc.) *with a person* (in dat.). X.

συμ-πορεύομαι: *proceed with, accompany.* XXXVII.

σύν, prep. with dat. only: *with, with the aid of.* III.

συν-άγω: *lead together, collect.* XII.

συν-αντάω, συνήντησα: *meet.*

συν-ειλημμένος: see συλ-λαμβάνω.

συν-είλοχα: see συλ-λέγω.

συν-έλαβον: see συλ-λαμβάνω.

συν-έρχομαι, 2 aor. συν-ῆλθον: *go or come together, assemble.* XLIII.

σύνθημα, ατος, τό (συν-τίθημι): *agreement; watchword.* XXIX.

συν-τάττω: *draw up together, form in line;* MID. *form in line* (intr.).

συν-τίθημι: *place* or *set together;* MID. place oneself in agreement with somebody, *agree* with somebody (dat.), *make a compact.* May be followed by inf. of indir. disc. LVII.

Συρίᾱ, ᾱς, ἡ: *Syria.* XIX.

συ-σκευάζω (σύν + σκευάζω, theme σκευαδ-, *prepare,* σκευάσω, ἐσκεύασα, ἐσκεύασμαι, ἐσκευάσθην): *make ready* (by getting things together, συν-), *pack up,* with acc ; MID. *pack up* one's own baggage, *pack up.* XXXIV.

συ-σπειράομαι, συν-εσπείραμαι, συν-εσπειράθην : *be coiled up together, be drawn up in close array.*

συ-στρατεύω (σύν + στρατεύω), usually dep. MID. συ-στρατεύομαι : *take the field with, serve in war with,* with dat. XXXI.

συχνός, ή, όν : *considerable, much.*

σφάγιον, ου, τό : victim for a propitiatory sacrifice; τὰ σφάγια : *the omens from the propitiatory sacrifices* (a special offering).

σφενδόνη, ης, ἡ : *sling.* See p. 112, Fig. 13. XXI.

σχεδόν, adv.: *nearly; chiefly.*

σῴζω (themes σῳδ- and σω-), σώσω, ἔσωσα, σέσωκα, σέσω(σ)μαι, ἐσώθην: *save;* MID. *save oneself.* XXX.

Σωκράτης, ους, ὁ : *Socrates,* (1) the Achaean, a general employed by Cyrus; to be distinguished from (2) the famous philosopher of Athens. § 273. XXVI.

σωτήρ, ῆρος, ὁ (σῴζω) : *savior.*

σωτηρίᾱ, ᾱς, ἡ (σωτήρ) : *safety.* XX.

σωτήριος, ᾱ, ον (σωτήρ) : *bringing safety, salutary.* Neut. pl. σωτήρια (supply ἱερά) : *thank-offerings for safety.*

T

τ᾽ : see τε.

τὰ μέν . . . τὰ δέ (cp. ὁ, ἡ, τό) : *some . . . others.*

τάλαντον, ου, τό : *talent,* an amount of money = about $1080. XXIII.

τάξις, εως, ἡ (τάττω) : *order, arrangement;* military *line, column, division;* ἐν τάξει : *in line.* XXXVIII.

τάραχος, ου, ὁ (ταράττω *stir up*) : *disturbance, confusion.*

Ταρσοί, ῶν, οἱ : *Tarsus,* the chief city of Cilicia. XXXIII.

τάττω (theme ταγ-, cp. § 182, NOTE), τάξω, ἔταξα, τέταχα, τέταγμαι (§ 466), ἐτάχθην : *arrange, draw up, marshal* troops. XXXVIII.

ταῦτα : neut. pl. of οὗτος.

τάφρος, ου, ἡ : *ditch.* IX.

τάχα or ταχέως, adv.: *swiftly, quickly, rapidly* = ταχύ. Comp. θᾶττον, sup. τάχιστα, § 368. ὡς (or ὅτι) τάχιστα : *as quickly as possible* (§ 373); ἐπειδή (or ἐπειδὰν) τάχιστα : *as soon as* (§ 533). XXV.

τάχιστος : see ταχύς.

ταχύ, adv.: *quickly,* § 367. XXII.

ταχύς, εῖα, ύ : *swift, quick.* Comp. θᾶττων, sup. τάχιστος, § 352. *a.* τὴν ταχίστην [ὁδόν] : *by the quickest way* (§ 356). XXXV.

τε, enclitic conj.: *and;* τε . . . καί : *both . . . and.* VII.

τέθνηκα (§ 432. *b, d*) : see θνῄσκω and ἀπο-θνῄσκω. XLIV.

τεῖχος, ους, τό : *wall; fortress* XXVI.

τέκνον, ου, τό : *child.* XLII.

τελευτάω (τελευτή *end*), τελευτήσω, ἐτελεύτησα, τετελεύτηκα, ἐτελευτήθην: *end, finish, die.* LIII.

τέλος, ους, τό : *end.* As adv. acc.: *finally* (§ 284). XXVII.

τετρακισχίλιοι, αι, α : *four thousand.* § 421.

τέτταρες, α : *four.* §§ 421, 425.

Τίγρης, ητος, ὁ : *Tigris,* a great river of western Asia. L.

τιθείς, pres. act. ʃartic. of τίθημι: *placing.* Declined in § 620.

τίθημι, θήσω, ἔθηκα and ἔθετον, τέθηκα, ἐτέθην: *put, set.* The pf. pass. is supplied by κεῖμαι. τίθεσθαι τὰ ὅπλα : *set down one's arms, rest one's arms* on the ground; therefore (1) *take a military position, take one's post;* (2) *halt.* §§ 559, 560, 620, 646. LVII.

τῑμάω (τῑμή), τῑμήσω, ἐτίμησα, τετίμηκα, τετίμημαι, ἐτῑμήθην : *honor*.
§§ 518, 622, 643. LII.

τῑμή, ῆς, ἡ : *honor*. XXXIX.

τῑμῶν, pres. act. partic. of τῑμάω :
honoring. Declined in § 622.

τίς, τί, interr. pron.: *who ? which ?
what ? τί: what ?* often as adv:
why ? (§ 284). §§ 226, 343. XXI.

τις, τι, enclitic indef. pron.: *any, some,
anybody, somebody, anything, something; a certain.* § 227. XXI.

Τισσαφέρνης, ους, ὁ : *Tissaphernes*, a
Persian satrap. § 273. *b*. XXVI.

τιτρώσκω (theme τρω-, reduplicated
in pres. τι-τρω, and with the pres.
suffix σκ%), τρώσω, ἔτρωσα, τέτρωμαι, ἐτρώθην : *wound*. XLVI.

τό : see ὁ; τὸ καθ' αὑτούς: *the division opposite themselves* (§ 526).
II.

τοι-γαρ-οῦν, strong particle of inference : *therefore*. XXXIX.

τοίνυν, inferential particle, post-positive : *therefore, then*. LIII.

τοιοῦτος, τοιαύτη, τοιοῦτο (declined
like οὗτος, § 171), dem. pron.: *of
such a sort, such,* often understood
or expressed as antecedent of οἷος.
τοιοῦτος οἷος: *such as.* The neut.
is also τοιοῦτον as well as τοιοῦτο.
Cp. Lat. *tālis.* LIV.

τόξευμα, ατος, τό (τοξεύω) : *arrow*.
XVIII.

τοξεύω, τοξεύσομαι, ἐτόξευσα, τετόξευμαι, ἐτοξεύθην : *shoot* with bow (τόξον) and arrow. XLVI.

τόξον, ου, τό : *bow*. XXXIII.

τοξότης, ου, ὁ (τόξον) : *bowman*.
See p. 68, Fig. 5. § 146. XII.

τόπος, ου, ὁ : *place*. L.

τοσοῦτος, τοσαύτη, τοσοῦτο (declined like οὗτος, § 171), dem.
pron.: *so much, so great, so many;*
often followed by correlative word

like ὅσος *as.* The neut. is also
τοσοῦτον as well as τοσοῦτο. Cp.
Lat. *tantus.* XLV.

τότε, adv. of time : *then, at that time.*
XXIV.

Τραπεζούντιος, ᾱ, ον (Τραπεζοῦς) :
Trapezuntian. Subst. nom. pl. *the
Trapezuntians.*

Τραπεζοῦς, οῦντος, ἡ : *Trapezus*, a
Greek city on the Euxine Sea,
modern Trebizond.

τρεῖς, τρία : *three.* §§ 421, 424. Cp.
Lat. *trēs.*

τρέπω (themes τροπ-, τρεπ-, τραπ-),
τρέψω, ἔτρεψα and ἔτραπον, τέ-
τροφα and τέτραφα, τέτραμμαι
(§ 490), ἐτρέφθην and ἐτράπην
(§§ 409, 489): *turn;* τρέπω εἰς
φυγήν: *put to flight.* There are
two aorists in the mid. voice also :
ἐτρεψάμην and ἐτραπόμην. XIV.

τρέφω (themes τροφ-, τρεφ-, τραφ-,
for θροφ-, etc.), θρέψω, ἔθρεψα, τέ-
τροφα, τέθραμμαι (§ 490), ἐτράφην
(§ 409) : *feed, support, rear.* XLI.

τρέχω, fut. δραμοῦμαι, 2 aor. ἔδραμον
(XI), pf. δεδράμηκα, mid. δεδράμη-
μαι : *run.* XXIII.

τριάκοντα, indecl. (τρεῖς) : *thirty.*
§ 421.

τριᾱκόσιοι, αι, α: *three hundred.*
§ 421.

τριήρης, ους, ἡ : *trireme.* See p. 125,
Fig. 15; p. 132, Fig. 16. § 274.
XXVI.

τρισ-χίλιοι, αι, α : *three thousand.*
§ 421.

τρίτος, η, ον (τρεῖς) : *third;* τῇ
τρίτῃ [ἡμέρᾳ] : *on the third day.*

τροπή, ῆς, ἡ (τρέπω) : *rout.*

τρόπος, ου, ὁ (τρέπω) : *turn, manner,
method, character.* LI.

τρω-τός, ή, όν (verbal adj. of τιτρώσκω) : *able to be wounded, vulnerable.* XLVIII.

τυγχάνω (themes τευχ-, τυχ-, τυχη-,
§ 218), τεύξομαι, ἔτυχον, τετύχηκα:
hit, with gen.; *happen, chance*, with
supplementary partic. XIX.

Υ

ὕδωρ, ὕδατος, τό: *water; rain*. § 336.
4. XXXIII.

ὑμεῖς: *you* (pl.), see σύ, § 304.

ὑμέτερος, ᾱ, ον (ὑμεῖς): *your* (pl.),
yours. § 126. X.

ὑπ-άρχω: begin, *support, serve*, with dat.

ὑπέρ, prep.: with GEN. *over, above;*
on behalf of; with ACC. *over, beyond.*
XXIX.

ὑπερβολή, ῆς, ἡ (ὑπερ-βάλλω *hurl over,*
pass over): passing over, *pass*. XLIV.

ὑπηρέτης, ου, ὁ: *servant, helper, sup-*
porter. XXXIX.

ὑπ-ισχνέομαι (ἴσχω, strong form of
ἔχω, with pres. suffix νε-), ὑπο-
σχήσομαι, ὑπ-εσχόμην, ὑπ-έσχη-
μαι: *undertake, promise*, with inf.
§ 519. LII.

ὑπό, prep.: with GEN. *from under,*
by (with pass. verb, § 390); *because*
of, from; with DAT. *under, beneath*
(with verbs of rest); with ACC. *under*
(with verbs of motion). XXXIX.

ὑπο-ζύγιον, ου, τό (ζυγόν *yoke*): something *under the yoke, beast of bur-*
den. XLVIII.

ὑπο-χωρέω (χωρέω *give place, with-*
draw, χωρήσω, ἐχώρησα, κεχώ-
ρηκα, κεχώρημαι, ἐχωρήθην): *re-*
treat.

ὑποψία, ᾱς, ἡ: *suspicion*. XXIV.

ὑστεραῖος, ᾱ, ον: *later, following;*
τῇ ὑστεραίᾳ (supply ἡμέρᾳ): *on the*
following day (§ 180); εἰς τὴν ὑστεραίᾱν (ἡμέρᾱν): *on the morrow, on*
the following day (§ 568). XV.

ὕστερος, ᾱ, ον: *later* (§ 361); ὕστερον, adv. acc.: *later*. XXXVI.

Φ

φαίνω (for φαν + yω, theme φαν-),
φανῶ, ἔφηνα, πέφηνα (*have ap-*
peared), πέφασμαι, ἐφάνθην (*was*
shown) and ἐφάνην (*appeared*):
bring to light, show; MID. and
PASS. usually *appear*. In mid. and
pass. the verb may take a supplementary partic. like δῆλός ἐστι(ν)
(§ 449). §§ 541, 542, 644, 645.
LV.

φάλαγξ, αγγος, ἡ: *line of battle,*
phalanx. § 187. XVII.

φανερός, ά, όν: *visible, clear, evident.*
§ 449. XLV.

φᾱσί(ν): *they say:* see φημί. VIII.

φέρω (themes φερ-, οἰ-, ἐνεκ-, ἐνεγκ-),
οἴσω, ἤνεγκα or ἤνεγκον, ἐνήνοχα,
ἐνήνεγμαι, ἠνέχθην: *bear, carry;*
carry away, receive (as pay). Cp.
Lat. *ferō*. LX.

φεύγω (themes φευγ-, φυγ-), φεύξο-
μαι or φευξοῦμαι (for φευξέομαι),
ἔφυγον, πέφευγα (§ 445): *flee, flee*
from, avoid, shun. Lat. *fugiō*. V.

φη-μί (theme φα-), φήσω, ἔφησα:
say, declare; οὔ φημι: *deny, say*
. . . *not* (§ 156. I. *a*). With inf.
§§ 110, 652. Cp. Lat. *fārī*. LX.

φησί(ν): *he says;* see φημί. VIII.

φθέγγομαι, φθέγξομαι, ἐφθεγξάμην,
ἔφθεγμαι: *shout.*

φιλία, ᾱς, ἡ (φίλος): *friendship.*
XL.

φιλο-νῑκίᾱ, ᾱς, ἡ (φίλος and νίκη):
striving for victory, *rivalry.*

φίλος, η, ον: *friendly.* Subst. φίλος,
ου, ὁ: *friend.* § 48. II, VIII.

φοβερός, ά, όν (φόβος): *fearful, ter-*
rible. Comp. φοβερώτερος, sup. φοβερώτατος, § 351. *b*. XXXV.

φοβερῶς, adv. (φοβερός): *fearfully.*
Comp. φοβερώτερον, sup. φοβερώ-
τατα, § 368. XXXVII.

φοβέω (φόβος), φοβήσω, ἐφόβησα, πεφόβημαι, ἐφοβήθην: *frighten;* MID. with dep. aor. pass.: *be afraid, fear.* The mid. forms are common (φοβέομαι, φοβήσομαι, πεφόβημαι, ἐφοβήθην). LI.

φόβος, ου, ὁ: *fear.* VII.

Φρυγίᾱ, ᾱς, ἡ: *Phrygia.* LVI.

φυγάς, άδος, ὁ (φεύγω): *fugitive, exile.* XVIII.

φυγή, ῆς, ἡ (φεύγω): *flight;* φυγῇ: *in flight.* XII.

φυλακή, ῆς, ἡ (φυλάττω): *guard, garrison;* φυλακᾱς φυλάττειν: *to do guard duty* (§ 181). VI.

φύλαξ, ακος, ὁ (φυλάττω): *guard, sentinel.* XVII.

φυλάττω (theme φυλακ-, § 182, NOTE), φυλάξω, ἐφύλαξα, πεφύλαχα, πεφύλαγμαι (§ 462. 2), ἐφυλάχθην: *guard;* MID. *guard oneself, be on one's guard* (*against,* with acc.). XV, XXX.

φωνή, ῆς, ἡ (cp. φα-, φημί): *voice.* LIV.

X

χαλεπός, ή, όν: *hard, difficult, harsh, severe.* Comp. χαλεπώτερος, sup. χαλεπώτατος, § 351. *b.* XXXV.

Χάλος, ου, ὁ: *Chalus,* a river in Syria. XXVII.

χαράδρᾱ, ᾱς, ἡ: *ravine.* XLIV.

χαρίζομαι (theme χαριδ-), χαριοῦμαι (§ 543), ἐχαρισάμην, κεχάρισμαι, dep. mid.: *show a favor* to somebody (dat.), *gratify, grant* something (acc.) to somebody (dat.) *as a favor.* Cp. χάρις. XXXIV.

χάρις, ιτος, ἡ: *grace, favor, gratitude;* χάριν ἔχειν: *to feel thankful,* with dat. §§ 195, 197. XVIII.

χείρ, χειρός, ἡ: *hand.* § 336. 2. XXXIII.

Χειρίσοφος, ου, ὁ: *Cheirisophus,*

a Spartan general. See pp. 264, 265. XII.

χίλιοι, αι, α: *thousand.* XVII.

χῑλός, οῦ, ὁ: *grass,* green *fodder.* XXI.

χιών, όνος, ἡ: *snow.* XXXIV.

χράομαι, χρήσομαι, ἐχρησάμην, κέχρημαι, with pass. aor. ἐχρήσθην: *use, have the service of,* with dat. of means; cp. Lat. *ūtor* with abl. In contract forms χράομαι has η for ᾱ (§ 517). § 518. *a.* LII.

χρή (ἐστί is understood, but never expressed): *there is need, it behooves, it is necessary; one must.* Inf. χρῆναι. § 223. XX.

χρῆμα, ατος, τό (χράομαι): *a thing of use;* commonly pl., *possessions, money, wealth.* XIX.

χρήσιμος, η, ον or χρήσιμος, ον (χράομαι): *useful.* XXI.

χρόνος, ου, ὁ: *time.* XXXIX.

χρῡσίον, ου, τό: *gold.* XIV.

χρῡσοῦς, ῆ, οῦν: *golden, of gold, gold.* § 609. L.

χώρᾱ, ᾱς, ἡ: *country, place, post, land.* § 115. IX.

χωρίον, ου, τό: *place, stronghold.* IV.

χωρίς, adv.: *apart;* prep. with gen.: *apart from.* XXXVIII.

Ψ

ψῑλός, ή, όν: *bare, unprotected; light-armed.* XLVI.

Ω

ὦ, interj.: *O,* often preceding the voc. case. IV.

ὧδε, adv. (cp. ὅδε): *thus, as follows.* XXXVIII.

ᾠήθην: see οἴομαι.

ὤν, οὖσα, ὄν, pres. partic. of εἰμί: *being.* Declined in § 205.

ὥρᾱ, ᾱς, ἡ : *season, hour; fit* or *proper time; ὥρᾱ (ἐστίν)* : *it is the proper time, it is high time,* with inf. (§ 230). Lat. *hōra.* XXI.

ὥς, (1) rel. adv. (cp. **ὅς**) : introducing a comparison, *as;* with causal partic., *as, as if* (§§ 213. *a*, 401. *b*); with partic. of purpose, *as if, apparently* (§ 332); with numerals, *about;* of degree, *how, in what way* (§§ 312, 533); with sup. to express the very highest degree, cp. Lat. *quam* with sup.; thus **ὡς μακρότατος** : *as long as possible* (§ 358); **ὡς τάχιστα** : *as quickly as possible;* **ὡς μάλιστα** : *as much as possible* (§ 373). (2) Conj.: of time, *as, when;* intro-

ducing a quotation, *that* (§ 260); introducing a purpose clause, *in order that, that* (§§ 243, 208); introducing the inf. like **ὥστε**, *so as.* (3) As prep. with acc.: *to,* used only with names of persons and **βασιλεύς**, *king* of Persia. XXII, XXIV, XXVI, XXVIII, XXXV.

ὥς = οὕτως. **οὐδ᾿ ὥς** : *not even thus, i.e.* not even under these circumstances.

ὥσπερ, rel. adv.: *just as, as, as if, like.* XLI.

ὥστε, conj.: *so that, so as, therefore,* with indic. or inf. § 147. XII.

ὤφελον: *I ought,* used in wishes; see § 586.

ENGLISH INDEX

Time 9/28

Fut. M.V. { gen ἐάν + subj — fut.
              { part εἰ + opt — opt + ἄν
        L.V.   εἰ + ind — fut.
        W.   -ων   θὶ

Pres Particular   εἰ + ind   — Pr...
      General   ἐάν + subj   — Pres
                        ων   ου

Accent is on 1 of last 3.
      acute   ´ ˆ ˜
                    x x x

In vbs. if ult is short it goes to ant...
   "   "   "   long "   "   " pen...
nouns have fixed accent.

Before θ you must have X or Φ
   "   δ   "   "   "   "   γ " β
   "   τ   "   "   "   "   κ " π